THE MEANING OF PEACE

Studies in Peace and Scripture
Institute of Mennonite Studies

THE MEANING OF PEACE

Biblical Studies

Edited by
Perry B. Yoder
and Willard M. Swartley

Translated by
Walter Sawatsky

Westminster/John Knox Press
Louisville, Kentucky

Book design by Ken Taylor

First edition

Published by Westminster/John Knox Press
Louisville, Kentucky

This book is printed on acid-free paper that meets the American National Standards Institute Z39.48 standard. ∞

PRINTED IN THE UNITED STATES OF AMERICA
9 8 7 6 5 4 3 2 1

Library of Congress Cataloging-in-Publication Data

The Meaning of peace : biblical studies / edited by Perry B. Yoder and Willard M. Swartley ; translated by Walter Sawatsky. — 1st ed.
        p.   cm. — (Studies in peace and scripture)
    Essays translated from German.
    Includes bibliographical references.
    ISBN 0-664-25312-1
    1. Peace—Biblical teaching.   2. Peace—Biblical teaching—Bibliography.   I. Yoder, Perry B.   II. Swartley, Willard M., 1936–
III. Sawatsky, Walter, 1945–   .   IV. Series.
    BS680.P4M43 1992
    220.8'30366—dc20   91-39061

Contents

Series Preface

Visions of peace abound in the Bible, whose pages are also filled with the language and the reality of war. In this respect, the Bible is thoroughly at home in the modern world, whether as a literary classic or as a unique sacred text. This is, perhaps, a part of the Bible's realism: bridging the distance between its world and our own is a history filled with visions of peace accompanying the reality of war. That alone would justify study of peace and war in the Bible. However, for those communities in which the Bible is sacred scripture, the matter is more urgent. For them, it is crucial to understand what the Bible says about peace—and about war. These issues have often divided Christians from each other, and the way Christians have understood them has had terrible consequences for Jews and, indeed, for the world. A series of scholarly investigations cannot hope to resolve these issues, but it can hope, as this one does, to aid our understanding of them.

Over the past century a substantial body of literature has grown up around the topic of the Bible and war. Studies in great abundance have been devoted to historical questions about ancient Israel's conception and conduct of war and about the position of the early church on participation in the Roman Empire and its military. It is not surprising that many of these studies have been motivated by theological and ethical concerns, which may themselves be attributed to the Bible's own seemingly disjunctive preoccupation with peace and, at the same time, with war. If not within the Bible itself, then at least from Aqiba and Tertullian, the question

has been raised whether—and if so, then on what basis—God's
people may legitimately participate in war. With the Reformation, the churches divided on this question. The division was unequal, with the majority of Christendom agreeing that, however
regrettable war may be, Christians have biblical warrant for participating in it. A minority countered that, however necessary war
may appear, Christians have a biblical mandate to avoid it. Modern
historical studies have served to bolster one side of this division
or the other.

Meanwhile, it has become clear that a narrow focus on participation in war is not the only way—and likely not the best way—to
approach the Bible on the topic of peace. War and peace are not
simply two sides of the same coin; each is broader than its contrast with the other. In spite of broad agreement on this point,
the number of studies devoted to the Bible and peace is still very
small, especially in English. Consequently, answers to the most
basic questions remain to be settled. Among these questions is that
of what the Bible means in speaking of *shalom* or *eirene,* the
Hebrew and the Greek term usually translated into English as
"peace." By the same token, what the Bible has to say about peace
is not limited to its use of these two terms. Questions remain about
the relation of peace, in the Bible, to considerations of justice,
integrity, and—in the broadest sense—salvation. And of course
there still remains the question of the relation between peace and
war. In fact, what the Bible says about peace is often framed in
the language of war. The Bible very often uses martial imagery
to portray God's own action, whether it be in creation, in judgment against or in defense of Israel, or in the cross and resurrection of Jesus Christ—actions aimed at achieving peace.

This close association of peace and war, to which we have already
drawn attention, presents serious problems for the contemporary
appropriation of the Bible. Are human freedom, justice, and
liberation—and the liberation of creation—furthered or hindered
by the martial, frequently royal, and pervasively masculine terms
in which the Bible speaks of peace? These questions cannot be
answered by the rigorous and critical exegesis of the biblical texts
alone; they demand serious moral and theological reflection.
But that reflection will be substantially aided by exegetical studies of the kind included in this series—even as these studies
will be illumined by including just that kind of reflection within
them.

"Studies in Peace and Scripture" is sponsored by the Institute of Mennonite Studies, the research agency of the Associated Mennonite Biblical Seminaries. The seminaries and the tradition they represent have a particular interest in peace but, even more so, a shared interest in the Bible. We hope that this ecumenical series will contribute to a deeper understanding of both.

Ben C. Ollenburger, Old Testament Editor
Willard M. Swartley, New Testament Editor

Preface

Willard M. Swartley

Biblical scholars study and write about war in the Old Testament, says Norbert Lohfink, but when asked to preach on Sunday, they preach about peace and reconciliation.[1] While the study of war in the Old Testament is an important part of our understanding of peace,[2] this publication puts forth the call for biblical scholars to do more direct study of peace in scripture. This volume has been prepared with the hope that it will stimulate scholarly studies of peace in scripture, together with efforts to appropriate the findings to our contemporary world. The Bibliography, prepared by the editors of this volume, is intended to aid these studies to utilize the significant work already done on peace research in the scriptures.

The lack of any comprehensive biblical theology that pays sustained attention to this theme throughout the Bible is a telling indictment upon our contemporary scholarship.[3] Eugen Biser has noted this lacuna in his 1960 monograph in relation to theology generally. He says that the absence of any explicit theology of peace in the classical system is a strange fact. Writing again in 1969, he says that, except for a few essays, an explicit theology of peace is lacking.[4] Surprising as it may seem, Perry Yoder makes the same point in regard to Mennonite writings. Though pacifist in tradition and commitment, Mennonite writings, says Yoder, have not given attention to the study of peace. This deficiency is present in books on nonresistance, biblical theology, general theology, and even in studies in historical theology, including Anabaptism.[5]

Despite this lament, the extensive bibliography clearly testifies to a significant amount of work done. But the difficulty we encountered in assembling the Bibliography, specifically in locating a significant number of these sources, absent from some of the best theological libraries in the United States, indicates that the topic has been marginalized in American biblical scholarship. Beginning a Consultation on the Study of Peace in Scripture in the annual meeting of the Society of Biblical Literature (1989) and launching this series are efforts to rectify this deficiency.

The birth of this book goes back to the early 1980s, when Perry Yoder and Tom Yoder Neufeld discerned the need to have available in English a collection of German exegetical essays on shalom and *eirene*. In the mid-1980s, their concern and vision coalesced with the proposal of the Institute of Mennonite Studies to develop a series of volumes reflecting biblical exegetical study related to the understanding and appropriation of biblical perspectives on peace. As the proposal took shape, Perry Yoder and Tom Yoder Neufeld each selected about five articles that might represent complementary contributions in both Old Testament and New Testament exegesis. The Institute, with Willard Swartley as director, took up the project and hired Walter Sawatsky to translate the essays. Because graduate school responsibilities, especially his dissertation, prevented Tom Yoder Neufeld from carrying forward the extensive necessary editorial work, Willard Swartley assumed the editing responsibilities of the New Testament essays. Since Wolfhart Pannenberg's essay was selected later in the process, H. Wayne Pipkin, currently associate director of the Institute, translated the Pannenberg essay.

This volume consists of essays translated from the German, some of which were rather inaccessible. It includes six in the Old Testament section and four in the New. This particular selection was made to put the issues on the table and thus provide an exegetical context in which further research, testing, and exploration can continue. The translation and editing tasks have been most arduous at many points along the way. Finding the full citations for works in the notes and locating the English translations where such are available has been more than an ordinary challenge. As editors we have decided to keep the German citation in brackets as well, thus enabling direct access to the original and use in German-speaking circles, for even in that setting the collection is a convenient service. Because the translation of these essays was done before the appearance of the NRSV the RSV has been used for biblical quotations, with accommodation to the NRSV on occasion for the purpose of inclusive language. In a few cases the respective editor has modified the RSV to convey more clearly the sense of the citation in German, or the original in Hebrew or Greek. Our hope is that wide use will justify the labors of production.

For assistance in assessing and selecting manuscripts to be published, we express appreciation to members of the Committee on Biblical Studies and Biblical Peace Theology of the Institute of Mennonite Studies: Gerald Gerbrandt, Millard Lind, Tom Yoder Neufeld, Ben Ollenburger, Mary Schertz, George Shillington, Daniel Smith, Willard Swartley, Dorothy Jean Weaver, and Perry Yoder, and to Wayne Pipkin, the Committee's liaison to the Institute. We thank the publishers of the original German essays — in journals and books where they first appeared — for permission to translate and publish the essays in English. A special debt of gratitude goes to Erika Dinkler-von Schubert for her excellent help in the editing of Professor Dinkler's essay. We thank the translators, and Elizabeth Yoder and Jewel Gingerich Longenecker for their help in the editing process; we also express our gratitude to Wilma Cender and Kevin Miller for their many hours spent typing numerous drafts in the editing process, and to Alain Epp Weaver for preparing the textual index. Finally, we are indeed grateful to the editors of Westminster/John Knox Press for their acceptance of and helpful work in the preparation of the manuscript for publication. By publishing these essays, we are highlighting our hope and prayer that these scholarly contributions will lead not only to further careful biblical exegetical studies but also to peace-inspired living. May the God of peace bless and equip us for every good work.

Notes

1. Norbert Lohfink, "Aber wenn wir dann sonntags predigen, sprechen wir nur über den Gott des Friedens und der Versöhnung." From "Der gewalttätige Gott des Alten Testaments und die Suche nach einer gewaltfreien Gesellschaft," *Jahrbuch für biblische Theologie* 2 (1987): 106. Lohfink notes that in his 1983 bibliographic study covering twenty years, fifty articles appeared on war and only thirty on peace.

2. Millard C. Lind's *Yahweh Is a Warrior* (Scottdale, Pa.: Herald Press, 1980) contributes much to this effort.

3. The good work that has been done has either focused fairly narrowly on the theme of peace or liberation (see, e.g., Comblin and Topel in the

Bibliography) or has put the peace theme to the margin in its organization and accent (e.g., Eichrodt, von Rad, Goppelt, Ladd). The series of essays in *Horizons in Biblical Theology* 6 (1984) mark the beginning of a new effort, perhaps, to think about what place *shalom* and *eirene* should have in biblical theology as such. By accenting the theme of community, both Gerhard Lohfink's *Jesus and Community* (trans. John P. Galvin; Fortress Press, 1984) and Paul Hanson's *The People Called* (San Francisco: Harper & Row, 1986) approach this envisioned task.

4. Eugen Biser, *Der Sinn des Friedens: Ein theologischer Entwurf* (Munich: Kösel-Verlag, 1960), 34–35 n. 5, and "Der Friede Gottes," *Ist Friede Machbar?* ed. E. Biser et al. (Munich: Kösel-Verlag, 1969), 30. Wolfgang Huber makes these observations from Biser's works in his "Literaturbericht" in *Frieden — Bibel — Kirche* (ed. Liedke), 200.

5. Perry B. Yoder, "Toward a Shalom Biblical Theology," *Conrad Grebel Review* 1 (1983): 39–40. William Klassen (*Love of Enemies: The Way to Peace* [Philadelphia: Fortress Press, 1984]) has certainly made an important contribution to the need, but its focus is bifocal, sometimes directed to the theme of love of enemies together with nonretaliation and other times directed to the theme of peace. Its overall scholarly contribution is more to the former and less to the latter.

Acknowledgments

Grateful acknowledgment is made to the following for permission to translate and reprint previously published material.

Currents in Theology and Mission, Chicago, and Dr. Hans Walter Wolff for "Swords into Plowshares: Misuse of a Word of Prophecy?" from volume 12 (1985).

Forschungsstätte der Evangelischen Studiengemeinschaft, Heidelberg, for "Peace (Shalom) in the Old Testament," by Claus Westermann, translated from *Studien zur Friedensforschung* 1, edited by G. Picht and H. E. Tödt (Stuttgart: Ernst Klett Verlag, 1969), with permission of the author. Also for "The Jerusalem Conceptions of Peace and Their Development in the Prophets of Ancient Israel," by Odil Hannes Steck, translated from *Frieden — Bibel — Kirche,* edited by Gerhard Liedke (Stuttgart: Ernst Klett Verlag, 1972).

Matthias-Grünewald-Verlag GmbH, Mainz, and Dr. Hubert Frankemölle for "Peace and the Sword in the New Testament," translated from *Friede und Schwert: Frieden Schaffen nach dem Neuen Testament* (1983).

Institut für Neutestamentliche Bibelwissenschaft, University of Vienna, and Dr. Jacob Kremer for "Peace — God's Gift: Biblical-Theological Considerations," translated from *Stimmen der Zeit* 200 (1982).

Verlag Katholisches Bibelwerk GmbH, Stuttgart, and Ulrich Luz for articles translated from *Eschatologie und Friedenshandeln: Exegetische Beiträge zur Frage christlicher Friedensverantwortung* (Stuttgarter Bibelstudien 101), edited by Ulrich Luz et al. (1981): "The Significance of the Biblical Witnesses for Church Peace Action," by Ulrich Luz, and "Prophetic Speech About the Future," by Jürgen Kegler.

Wolfhart Pannenberg, for "Response to Hans Walter Wolff," translated from *Evangelische Theologie* 44 (1984).

Dr. Luise Schottroff for "The Dual Concept of Peace," translated from *Christen im Streit um den Frieden,* edited by Wolfgang Brinkel et al. (Freiburg im Breisgau: Dreisam-Verlag, 1982).

Carl Winter Universitätsverlag GmbH, Heidelberg, and Dr. Erika Dinkler-von Schubert for *"Eirene*—The Early Christian Concept of Peace," by Erich Dinkler, translated from *Eirene: Der urchristliche Friedensgedanke* (1973) (Sitzungsberichte der Heidelberger Akademie der Wissenschaften Phil. hist. Kl., Abh. 1).

Abbreviations

EKKNT	Evangelisch-katholischer Kommentar zum Neuen Testament
EKL	*Evangelisches Kirchenlexikon*
EstBib	*Estudios biblicos*
ETL	*Ephemerides theologicae lovanienses*
EvRTh	*Evangelical Review of Theology*
EvQ	*Evangelical Quarterly*
EvT	*Evangelische Theologie*
EWNT	*Exegetisches Wörterbuch zum Neuen Testament,* ed. H. Balz and G. Schneider
ExpTim	*Expository Times*
FEST	Forschungsstätte der Evangelischen Studien-gemeinschaft
FGrHistSuppl	*Fragmente der griechischen Historiker* (F. Jacoby), *Supplement*
HAT	Handbuch zum Alten Testament
HBT	*Horizons in Biblical Theology*
HNT	Handbuch zum Neuen Testament
HSM	Harvard Semitic Monographs
ICC	International Critical Commentary
IDB	*Interpreter's Dictionary of the Bible,* ed. G. A. Buttrick
IEJ	*Israel Exploration Journal*
IMSS	Institute of Mennonite Studies Series
Int	*Interpretation*
JBL	*Journal of Biblical Literature*
JJS	*Journal of Jewish Studies*
JRS	*Journal of Roman Studies*
KAT	Kommentar zum Alten Testament
KB	L. Koehler and W. Baumgartner, *Lexicon in Veteris Testamenti libros*
KD	*Kerygma und Dogma*
KT	Kaiser Tractate
NovT	*Novum Testamentum*
NRT	*La nouvelle revue théologique*
NTS	*New Testament Studies*
OTL	Old Testament Library
OTS	*Oudtestamentische Studiën*
PG	*Patrologia graeca,* J. Migne
PosLuth	*Positions luthériennes*
PrincSB	*Princeton Seminary Bulletin*
PrTh	*Praktische Theologie*
PW	Pauly-Wissowa, *Real-Encyclopädie der classischen Altertumswissenschaft*
QD	*Quaestiones Disputatae*
RAC	*Reallexikon für Antike und Christentum*

RB	*Revue biblique*
RevExp	*Review and Expositor*
SBS	Stuttgarter Bibelstudien
SEAJT	*Southeast Asian Journal of Theology*
SHAW	Sitzungsberichte der Heidelberger Akademie der Wissenschaften
SPS	Studies in Peace and Scripture
TBei	*Theologische Beiträge*
TBü	Theologische Bücherei
TDig	*Theology Digest*
TDNT	*Theological Dictionary of the New Testament,* ed. G. Kittel and G. Friedrich
THAT	*Theologisches Handwörterbuch zum Alten Testament,* ed. E. Jenni and C. Westermann
ThEv	*Theologia Evangelica*
TLZ	*Theologische Literaturzeitung*
TM.FEST	Texten und Materialien (FEST)
TRE	*Theologische Realenzyklopädie*
TRu	*Theologische Rundschau*
TTK	*Tidsskrift for Teologi og Kirke*
TWNT	*Theologisches Wörterbuch zum Neuen Testament,* ed. G. Kittel and G. Friedrich
VIKJ	Veröffentlichungen aus dem Institut Kirche und Judentum
VT	*Vetus Testamentum*
WD	*Wort und Dienst*
Wiss Prax Ki Ges	*Wissenschaft und Praxis in Kirche und Gesellschaft*
WMANT	Wissenschaftliche Monographien zum Alten und Neuen Testament
ZAH	*Zeitschrift für Althebräistik*
ZAW	*Zeitschrift für die alttestamentliche Wissenschaft*
ZEE	*Zeitschrift für evangelische Ethik*
ZNW	*Zeitschrift für die neutestamentliche Wissenschaft*
ZTK	*Zeitschrift für Theologie und Kirche*

Part I

Old Testament

1

Introductory Essay to the Old Testament Chapters: *Shalom* Revisited

Perry B. Yoder

In this introductory essay I speak to two areas. First, I survey the recent discussion concerning the meaning of the word *shalom* in the Hebrew Bible. This allows us to situate the following essays in this discussion and better appreciate their continuing significance for present and future work on the theme of peace in the Hebrew scriptures. Second, and very briefly, I say something about the selection of the material in the Old Testament section.

To take the latter first, in the process of selection we have limited ourselves, with one exception, to essays that revolve around a discussion of the word *shalom*. Not that such studies exhaust by any means what the Bible says about peace, but because such studies form the basis of research about peace in the Bible.

Further, the essays were chosen with a view to three additional criteria: (1) They are significant pieces of work that are often inaccessible to English readers. (2) They are representative of lines of research and thought that shape the state of the discussion today. (3) They fit together to form a reasonably harmonious package. This collection is offered in order to give these articles the wider readership they deserve and in the hope that they will stimulate further study of shalom and peace in the Bible.

Survey of Research[1]

We can conveniently begin our discussion with Gerhard von Rad's influential contribution to Kittel's *Theological Dictionary of the New Testament*. (His article appeared originally in 1935;

I will be citing the English translation of 1964.)[2] Von Rad begins
by noting that shalom has a wide range of meanings, since it "can
bear a common use and yet can also be filled with a concentrated
religious content far above the level of the average conception"
(*TDNT,* 2:402). This makes the investigation of its meaning
difficult, because if it "is a general expression of a very comprehensive nature, this means that there is something imprecise about
it in almost every instance" (*TDNT,* 2:402). In these two quotations we have set out the central problem in defining shalom. On
the one hand, simply stated, in the Hebrew Bible shalom is applied
to a wide range of circumstances and is used "generically," so to
speak, in stereotyped phrases and situations. An apparent fuzziness
of meaning results.[3] That is, to anticipate a bit, it is not clear in
many contexts precisely to what the term "shalom" refers. On the
other hand, because the word is theologically significant, a more
precise understanding of its meaning, especially its theological
meaning, is sought.

To solve the problem of shalom's fuzziness, von Rad, following
accepted practice, posited a basic or root meaning. In this methodology the root meaning expressed the basic, original concept
communicated by the word. This core meaning was then taken to
represent the "real" meaning of the word and was usually considered
to be at least implicit whenever the word was used. Beginning with
the basic root concept, one worked outward to understand a term's
nuances on the basic theme. (These "meanings" were linked, however, to the basic meaning which was latent, so to speak, in the
word itself.) Since the root concept allows the meaning of a word
to be recognized in spite of its various fuzzy and equivocal occurrences, discovering shalom's root conceptual meaning was the
golden grail of shalom research. Indeed, it was through this root
meaning that justice could be done to the heavy theological freight
it was thought to carry in its occurrences.[4]

For von Rad, the basic meaning of shalom was material, physical
"well-being." He finds examples of this meaning in greetings, as
in Gen. 29:6; or in the "shalom" of the wicked in Ps. 73:3, which
has in mind their unwarranted material prosperity.

Von Rad further argues that shalom most commonly refers to
a group's prosperity or well-being rather than to that of an individual (*TDNT,* 2:402). This social sense of shalom von Rad
supports by arguing that in the greater number of references shalom
denotes a relationship rather than a state. As prime evidence he
cites the linkage of covenant and shalom: shalom occurs in covenant contexts (see Josh. 9:15 and 1 Kings 5:26).[5] Indeed, we find

the phrase "covenant of shalom" in Ezek. 34:25 and 37:26, which von Rad understands as meaning a covenant that leads to a relationship of shalom.

Further, this shalom of the community is the gift of God since "the goods and values associated with shalom were always referred in Israel to Yahweh." Consequently shalom "when it is used in its full compass is a religious term" (*TDNT*, 2:403).[6] Shalom's theological significance as God's gift is thus a part of its original meaning and emerges whenever the term is used with its full value.

Von Rad ends his essay with three summary observations. First, negatively, there is "no specific text in which it denotes the specifically spiritual attitude of inward peace" (*TDNT*, 2:406). Even Lam. 3:17, he argues, refers to some form of external well-being. Second, positively, it is something palpable, material, something people can perceive. Third, shalom is a social concept; it is used more of groups than of individuals. From this summary it is clear that, for von Rad, "shalom" and "peace" as used in European languages are not at all synonyms, a point with which he begins his article.

Von Rad's understanding of shalom has tended to dominate current thinking about its meaning. It is a commonplace notion, for example, that shalom refers to material well-being or that the meaning of shalom is much broader than the English "peace." It is against this backdrop of a latent consensus about the meaning of shalom that the ensuing discussion took place.

Walter Eisenbeis in his 1966 dissertation (later published as BZAW 113) made a thorough study of the root *sh-l-m*.[7] In this work he undertook a painstaking traditiohistorical examination of the words coming from this root. He proceeds from the Pentateuchal sources through the literature of the Bible, ending with the apocalyptic material. He concluded from his study that the basic meaning of the root *sh-l-m* is "wholeness" or "intactness," a finding that appears to be compatible with von Rad's understanding. However, Eisenbeis argues that this basic idea or concept, expressed in a variety of ways or meanings, is mainly used as a theological term referring to people's relationship to God. Here he parts company with von Rad, whom he judges to have overemphasized the material aspect. Further, Eisenbeis understands shalom to refer to an event rather than a condition. Shalom is experiential and dynamic. Here again, Eisenbeis takes issue with von Rad.[8]

Eisenbeis's findings do not appear to have been widely adopted, presumably for a variety of reasons. First, since, as von Rad pointed out, shalom and its relatives can occur in a wide variety of contexts with a certain indefiniteness of meaning, it is easy to read meanings into the term. Eisenbeis's traditiohistorical theological approach seems to be especially vulnerable to this hazard. Since he focuses narrowly on specific passages rather than overall distribution or linguistic patterns, there is little barrier to finding his posited root meaning when shalom's referent is not clear in the passage itself. For example, in Gen. 28:21 Jacob vows that YHWH will be his God if he returns *beshalom.* The easy or plain sense here seems to be if he returns "okay," "safe and sound," or, perhaps, "prosperous." Eisenbeis, however, understands it to mean "If by means of salvation . . . I return, then (indeed) Yahweh is deity to me" (Ph.D. diss., pp. 167ff.). The invoking of salvation as the meaning of shalom appears to be due to Eisenbeis's assumption that salvation is part of its root concept which it carries whenever it is used.

Eisenbeis's work illustrates the problem mentioned above which has dogged the study of shalom: because of its wide range of uses and fuzziness of reference in many contexts there is a tendency to solve the problem of its theological meaning by positing a core, basic, or original value for it. This posited meaning can then usually be made to fit its context. In the absence of clear pointers in a passage one can then fall back on the abstract concept which is believed to be the basic meaning of the term latent in each of its uses.

Evidently, because his approach was theological and traditiohistorical, Eisenbeis did not develop a methodology consistent with modern work in linguistics and semantics. As suggested above, he did not attend closely enough to the patterned nature of shalom's usage in the language generally. Consequently the individual uses were not viewed as part of a wider linguistic web. Such a procedure could have provided more objective clues as to the meaning of shalom in the specific passage that he examined within the strands of tradition.[9]

E. M. Good in his article "Peace in the OT," *Interpreter's Dictionary of the Bible,*[10] defines peace as "the state of wholeness possessed by persons or groups which may be health, prosperity, security, or the spiritual completeness of covenant" (*IDB,* 3:704). In this definition he disagrees with von Rad, whom he does not mention either in the article or in the bibliography, by understanding shalom to be a state rather than a relationship, although he includes the latter along with the notion of a spiritual state. He, however, does agree with von Rad in believing that shalom is a religious term: "In the OT, peace of any kind is a wholeness determined by and given by God" (*IDB,* 3:705).

The notion that shalom designates a state rather than a relationship has been argued at length by Claus Westermann in an article published in 1969,[11] which is the first work in our collection. This article is placed first in this volume because it forms a counterpoint to von Rad's understanding of shalom and enters into dialogue with it (see its notes). Second, it forms a transition to developments in the study of the term "shalom," as we shall see below. Third, the article is basic and comprehensive — it is the best short statement on the meaning of shalom available today.

Westermann, like von Rad, begins by positing the basic meaning of shalom, which for him is "being whole or entire; intact" (Ger.: *Ganzsein*). He agrees with von Rad that shalom is usually used in reference to a community and refers to an aspect of group life. From this, Westermann concludes in opposition to von Rad, that shalom cannot properly mean peace between; this is expressed by treaty, not by shalom. Instead, according to Westermann, shalom describes a condition within a group; it refers to health or wholeness within a community context. Those references where it does speak of a relationship or a covenant of shalom — those references basic for von Rad's position — or where shalom is used as the opposite of war are an aberration or borrowing and consequently are not the proper starting point for understanding the concept referred to by shalom.[12]

Positively, Westermann begins by discussing the majority of occurrences of shalom under the title "shalom as wholeness and health in the present." Here he includes greetings, questions about someone's shalom, or statements that all is okay. Indeed, Westermann finds the English "okay" as expressing the fundamental meaning of shalom. Since shalom includes many arenas of life, such as physical, economic, and social well-being, it is not to be restricted to a single aspect of life, and it is a distortion to overemphasize one aspect. Rather, shalom expresses all the differing facets of okayness that result from good community life. As such, it does not refer to the ideal order of life but *the proper order* that can be experienced in daily life. Since Westermann understands shalom as a basic part of human existence, he deemphasizes the religious content which others have seen as a component of the basic meaning of the term. These findings are a substantial contribution to our understanding of shalom today.

Methodologically, Westermann's work raises doubt. When he declares shalom in the sense of "peace as opposed to war" to be an aberration he brings to a head a methodological question latent in previous work. Is it sensible to work with the notion of a single normative root meaning for shalom and find it everywhere or to declare those uses which seemingly do not refer to this meaning an aberration?[13] And if we do, how do we decide which is which — is it the meaning which is earliest or most frequent that is the normative meaning, while the others are aberrations? Cannot a word have more than one proper, legitimate meaning?

This problem arises in part because it is assumed that shalom has some basic referential meaning that it conveys in each usage. Thus all uses must be homogeneous in this regard. If some uses have a different referent, then they must be deviant. It seems clear, however, that we cannot operate with a monolithic idea of a root meaning that somehow is implicitly referred to in each of the word's normal uses. Nor can the meaning of shalom be discovered by seeking reference alone — that is, by asking only what the term is talking about.

In this regard, Jacob Kremer's article, "Peace — God's Gift: Biblical-Theological Considerations" (pp. 133–147 in this volume), is an antidote to this tendency. The article outlines several ways in which shalom is used, including its connection with war. We will return to this article below when we consider the relationship between shalom and war. However, here we want to recommend Kremer as a brief supplement to the Westermann article, especially as it points to the relationship that shalom may have to war.

State or relationship, secular or a gift of God? These are two of the substantive questions about the meaning of shalom that confront us from work done in the 1960s. With a turn to the 1970s, we see a tendency toward synthesis. John Durham in his study of 1970 sees three major uses of shalom which correspond to three meanings of the word.[14] First there are the uses in clichés of greeting and parting. Second, about 25 percent of the time it is used to refer to the absence of conflict; thus it can carry a relational sense. Third, about 65 percent of the time it refers to fulfillment in the sense of completeness, success, maturity, and well-being. Durham understands this well-being to be a result of God's blessing. Shalom in this view refers to both relationships and states. It is often used religiously, even in its clichéd occurrences, but room is made for nontheological usage.

Likewise Gillis Gerleman, in his article "*šlm* genug haben" in *THAT,* holds to both options.[15] Shalom, he argues, has two major senses. It can be used of relationships and thus is properly used as the opposite of war. But it also means a material state, often having the sense of prosperity, well-being, or abundance. By choosing to say that shalom is both relational and material, Gerleman holds together the tensions that separate von Rad and Westermann. These two studies just cited are helpful in recognizing the multiplicity of meaning that a word may realize in its various uses. Consequently they solve the substantive problems of the 1960s by saying "both." Shalom refers to both relationships and states; it can be used both in a religious sense and secularly. In this respect they are an advance methodologically beyond the monolithic root concept approach.

The beginning of the 1970s also saw a new direction being taken in the understanding of shalom. H. H. Schmid published his extensive work on shalom in 1971,[16] while Odil Hannes Steck's study on the conception of peace in the Jerusalem cult tradition was published in 1972.[17]

Following a discussion of the counterparts to shalom in Mesopotamia and Egypt, Schmid concludes that peace in this literature is linked to the notion of a proper order that ought to exist in nature and society. One aspect of this order in human affairs was the submission of foreign nations to the king. Here peace is to be brought about by force of arms as unruly nations are brought into line. Schmid then turns to the Bible, dividing the material into the usual literary categories and tradition streams for closer inspection. In his analysis he emphasizes the dimension of order indicated by shalom, especially pointing to its relationship with law and social justice. This seems illuminating. For example, while for von Rad the dispute among the preexilic prophets about shalom was one of political astuteness — the "true" prophets said no shalom, no material well-being, because they interpreted the political scene better than did the "false"' prophets — for Schmid it has to do with the relationship of Israelite society to the proper order of social justice which was the foundation for shalom. The "true" prophets cried out against social injustice and said no shalom; the "false" prophets proclaimed coming shalom in spite of the social injustices. For the true prophets, shalom could exist only where the proper order was being implemented.[18]

Two points are particularly significant in Schmid's work. First, in Israel, as elsewhere in the Near East, Schmid argued, the order that bears shalom was at times brought about by force and subjugation of enemies. Shalom was not the opposite of war or use of force, but quite the contrary could result from war. Here Schmid agrees with Westermann in understanding that shalom as the opposite of war was a late, deviant development.[19] Second, since shalom is understood to be linked to the idea of a correct order, to the way things should be, the notion of creation is seen by Schmid to bind the different uses of shalom together (see Schmid, *Šalom*, pp. 97–103). Biblical thought about shalom is thus embedded in the wider context of the Bible's understanding of creation and order.[20]

Odil Hannes Steck, in his study of shalom in the Jerusalem cult and related literature, also links shalom to a transcendent order.[21] He begins with a survey of the conceptions in the Jerusalem cult tradition that express the conviction that God is the ruler of the world who stabilizes and maintains the world order (Steck, *Friedensvorstellungen*, pp. 13ff.). This rule is executed through God's actions on behalf of the oppressed and needy for a just order in human society. In this context, shalom is linked to YHWH as preserver of both the natural and the social universe. Whatever blocks the well-being of YHWH's order is against shalom; whatever promotes this order works toward shalom. This understanding of shalom, Steck argues, was originally centered in Jerusalem and was expressed through the reign and military successes of the king which were an expression of YHWH's lordship over all.

But the reality of political events challenged the Jerusalem cult's view of shalom. In this new situation Isaiah acts as a reinterpreter of this tradition. The problem for Isaiah is that the present king relies on foreign treaties and tramples social justice underfoot, both contrary to the shalom ideology of the psalms. The king has thereby already destroyed YHWH's shalom. Consequently, God's judgment will fall on the breakers of shalom, even the Israelite nation itself (Steck, *Friedensvorstellungen*, pp. 53–61).

Following judgment, shalom becomes a future expectation and something that YHWH will do, as seen, for example, in Isa. 2:1ff. Shalom then will no longer be mediated through political institutions like the Davidic king but will have a universal scope. Nations will come to Jerusalem not as vassals but as religious pilgrims. The opposite of war is learning the way of YHWH, not political pacification. The recognition of the sovereignty of God becomes the way of shalom (Steck, *Friedensvorstellungen*, pp. 64–71).

Steck's work is represented in the present collection by his article "The Jerusalem Conceptions of Peace and Their Development in the Prophets of Ancient Israel."[22] While Steck's article discusses the material in the Psalms as a background to the prophets, the future and eschatological dimensions of the prophets' message concerning shalom is developed by Jürgen Kegler's contribution, "Prophetic Speeches on the Future."[23] Kegler traces the contexts and perspectives regarding shalom in the prophets Micah, Proto-Isaiah, and Deutero-Isaiah. While there is overlap in terms of the prophetic material covered by Steck and Kegler, the focus of Kegler's article is different. He sets for himself the task of determining the relationship between the prophets' proclamation of the future and their experience and action in the present. To do this he draws the connections between their future statements of judgment and salvation and their concept of peace and its reality in their own situation. His article can also serve as a bridge to the New Testament articles.

In the studies we have been considering by Westermann, Schmid, and Steck, the notion that shalom rests on a state or order instead of relationships has led to two results. First, that shalom as the opposite of war is a late development in the Old Testament material. Second, that shalom — the appropriate conditions for shalom — may result from war, subjugation, and domination. This latter point of view reaches its apex in an article by Lothar Perlitt.[24] He argues that shalom was not used during the time of the Israelite state as a positive or normative term to designate the relationship of Israel to other states. It became such a term and ideal only in the postexilic period and then merely as an element in eschatological visions as in Isaiah 2; 9; and 11. Perlitt draws the conclusion that shalom as used and understood during the monarchy has nothing positive to teach us about war and international relations. Rather, since Israel was born and maintained by the sword, we learn something from this fact concerning state relations and existence.

Gerhard Liedke, the editor of the volume in which Perlitt's article occurred, addressed himself specifically to the article and issues raised by Perlitt.[25] Also, Rainer Albertz more recently has criticized Perlitt's work for not being nuanced enough — not recognizing the changes that took place within Hebrew scriptures concerning war.[26] Albertz does this by showing how pre-state notions concerning war and Yahweh's connection with it changed during the time of the state. He also describes the prophetic critique of the state's war ideology.

More generally, two recent articles have discussed the relationship of shalom to amicable relationships between people and nations, particularly as shalom is related to covenant making. Dennis McCarthy points to both ancient Near Eastern and biblical material that relates shalom, or at least the root *sh-l-m,* to treaty making.[27] For example, *shulmam epeshu* is used in Akkadian to mean make a treaty. He also cites an Akkadian text from Ugarit in which we read *u itti shalmiya lu shalmata* ("you are the ally of my ally"). He likens this expression to Gen. 34:9–10, 16 where the

Shechemites consider themselves to be the *shelemim* of Jacob's sons — that is, his covenant allies. D. J. Wiseman, however, has taken exception to McCarthy's equation of shalom and treaty.[28] He points out that all that is demanded in the cases McCarthy cites in the biblical material is good relations, not necessarily a relationship regulated by a formal treaty. However, he most certainly agrees with and develops additional support for the notion that shalom refers to good relationships between people. He reinforces this aspect of shalom by placing these uses in the wider context of diplomacy in Israel and its Near Eastern environment. These two studies make clear, regardless of the precise connection between shalom and covenant in each case, that shalom and its relatives have to do with relationships and not just a state or order. Furthermore, shalom does seem to refer to amicable relations between peoples and is not necessarily the result of domination or subjugation. Thus Westermann, Schmid, and others seem to be mistaken in regarding the usage of shalom for friendly relations, and the opposite of war, as a late deviation.[29]

In terms, then, of the substantive issues regarding the meaning of shalom, these works demonstrate that shalom has a variety of meanings, not one of which we should regard as necessarily primary. The word may apply to a state or a relationship; it may be used in a religious or a secular sense. Shalom can be measured at least to some degree against an external standard which in the sphere of relationships is justice and conformity to the sovereignty of God. On the basis of these works it also seems clear that there is no monolithic abstract root meaning for shalom which, like a Procrustean bed, fits all uses to this meaning. Likewise, we should be cautious in looking for a religious or theological meaning under the Procrustean bed.

While past and present research has been dominated by the study of shalom within the context of literary categories and tradition streams, there are signs that a more linguistic approach may be useful and move future research forward. In such an approach the patternedness and distribution of shalom's usage would be examined. A study that points in this direction is that of W. T. W. Cloete, "*Ntn yhwh shalom*," in which he examines one particular pattern within which shalom occurs and the distribution of this pattern.[30] It is presumably in this direction that further insights regarding the meaning of shalom in the Hebrew scriptures lie.

The third- and second-last essays in the Old Testament section begin with the article by Hans Walter Wolff. It is different from the preceding ones in that it begins with two passages, Joel 4:9–12

(Eng., 3:9–12) and Isa. 2:1–5. From a study of these passages Wolff surveys the Old Testament understanding of war and peace more generally and then contextualizes the Isaiah passage within that understanding. Finally, he makes application to the debate in Germany regarding peace issues and points to the continuity of the Old Testament with the New. Following Wolff's article is a response by Wolfhart Pannenberg, who, while in some agreement with Wolff, would nuance the interpretation of Isa. 2:1–5 differently and point to the central role of justice in the notion of shalom in the Hebrew scriptures. Although these essays are not studies of the word shalom or of peace, they do provide a wider, integrative context for the studies presented above. These essays, together with the final essay of Jacob Kremer, which both summarizes the Old Testament view of shalom as a gift of God and opens up the New Testament discussion, provide a fitting conclusion to our study of shalom and peace.

Notes

1. A brief review of exegetical work on shalom can be found in Heinz-Horst Schrey, "Fünfzig Jahre Besinnung über Krieg und Frieden," *TRu* 46 (1981): 149–152; and Archibald Woodruff, "EIPHNH in the Pauline Corpus" (Ph.D. diss., Pittsburgh University, 1976), 10–19.

2. Gerhard von Rad, "Shalom in the Old Testament," *TDNT*, 2:402–406. In this article, von Rad takes up the major themes of earlier research, especially the understanding of Johannes Pedersen, *Israel: Its Life and Culture* (Copenhagen: Branner og Korch, 1926), 1:263ff., who sees shalom as designating social solidarity and the good that flows from this social unity.

3. See Jacob Kremer's recent statement (pp. 133–147 in this volume) about the manifold usage and equivocal meaning of shalom: "Der Frieden — Eine Gabe Gottes: Bibeltheologische Erwägungen," *Stimmen der Zeit* 200 (1982): 162f.

4. Linguistic and semantic criticisms of these methods as exemplified by the authors of *TDNT* have been offered at length by James Barr, *The Semantics of Biblical Language* (Oxford: Oxford University Press, 1961).

5. Here von Rad is echoing the work of Pedersen, *Israel: Its Life and Culture.*

6. For a recent statement concerning shalom as a gift of God, see also Echard von Nordheim, "Die biblische Begründung des Friedens in der Friedensdenkschrift der EKD," in *Anwalt des Menschen* (ed. Friedrich Hahn; Schmalenberg: G. Giessen, 1983), pp. 199–207. See esp. p. 201.

7. Walter Eisenbeis, "A Study of the Root Shalom in the Old Testament" (Ph.D. diss., University of Chicago, 1966), pub. as *Die Würzel* שלם *im Alten Testament* (BZAW 113; Berlin: Walter de Gruyter, 1969).

8. These findings are presented on pp. 568–573 of Eisenbeis's dissertation.

9. For a discussion of the shortcomings of Eisenbeis's work linguistically, see Fount L. Shults, "*Sh-l-m* and *t-m-m* in Biblical Hebrew: An Analysis of the Semantic Field of Wholeness" (Ph.D. diss., University of Texas at Austin, 1974), 7–21.

10. E. M. Good, "Peace in the OT," *IDB,* 3:704–706.

11. Claus Westermann, "Der Frieden (*shalom*) im Alten Testament," in *Studien zur Friedensforschung* 1 (ed. G. Picht and H. E. Tödt; Stuttgart: Ernst Klett Verlag, 1969), 144–177 (pp. 16–48 in this volume).

12. Ibid. See footnote 2, pages 148–150. His argument against shalom as designating a relationship seems to be based on two factors: first, the bulk of uses show that shalom is not a relational concept; second, the Akkadian *salimam birit* at Mari is equivalent to Hebrew *shalom ben . . . uben . . . .* Thus the Hebrew use of shalom for a relationship may be due to Akkadian influence and thus, since it is not native, is not normative for shalom's meaning in Hebrew.

13. It has been commonplace in the history of research on shalom to divide between "Canaanite" meanings of *shalom* and "Israelite" ones. This goes back at least to Wilhelm Caspari, *Vorstellung und Wort "Friede" im Alten Testament* (BFCT 14, 4; Gütersloh: C. Bertelsmann Verlag, 1910); see Woodruff's comments, "EIPHNH," 10–11. Thus a diachronic approach has been used to solve the problem of the apparent diversity of meanings that shalom seems to carry. There is little evidence that these different meanings were not functional at the same time—thus a diachronic solution is only an apparent solution.

14. John I. Durham, "Shalom and the Presence of God," in *Proclamation and Presence: Old Testament Essays in Honour of Gwynne Henton Davies* (ed. John I. Durham and J. R. Porter; Richmond: John Knox Press, 1970), 272–293.

15. Gillis Gerleman, "*šlm* genug haben," *THAT,* 2:919–935.

16. H. H. Schmid, *Šalom: "Frieden" im Alten Orient und im Alten Testament* (SBS 51; Stuttgart: Verlag Katholisches Bibelwerk, 1971).

17. Odil Hannes Steck, *Friedensvorstellungen im alten Jerusalem: Psalmen, Jesaja, Deuterojesaja* (Zurich: Theologischer Verlag, 1972).

18. For a brief statement by Schmid, see his "Frieden II: Altes Testament," *TRE,* 11:605–610.

19. Westermann, "Der Frieden (*Shalom*) im Alten Testament" (pp. 16–48 in this volume); likewise, see Kremer's article in this volume.

20. Cf. H. H. Schmid, "Creation, Righteousness, and Salvation: 'Creation Theology' as the Broad Horizon of Biblical Theology," in *Creation in the Old Testament* (ed. Bernhard W. Anderson; Philadelphia: Fortress Press, 1984), 102–117 [orig.: "Schöpfung, Gerechtigkeit und Heil," *ZTK* 70 (1973): 1–19].

21. Steck, *Friedensvorstellungen.*

22. This is the translation of "Jerusalemer Vorstellungen vom Frieden und ihre Abwandlungen in der Prophetie des alten Israel," in *Frieden — Bibel — Kirche* (ed. Liedke), 75–95.

23. Originally, "Prophetisches Reden von Zukünftigem," in *Eschatologie und Friedenshandeln,* ed. Luz, 15–60.

24. Lothar Perlitt, "Israel und die Völker," in *Frieden — Bibel — Kirche* (ed. Liedke), 17–64.

25. Gerhard Liedke, "Israel als Segen für die Völker: Bemerkungen zu Lothar Perlitt, 'Israel und die Völker,'" in *Frieden — Bibel — Kirche* (ed. Liedke), 65–74.

26. Rainer Albertz, "Schalom und Versöhnung: Alttestamentliche Kriegs- und Friedenstraditionen," *Teologia Practica* 18 (1983): 16–28. See also Paul D. Hanson, "War and Peace in the Hebrew Bible," *Int* 38 (1984): 341–362, for a survey of the historical development of the relationship between war and peace.

27. Dennis McCarthy, "*Ebla, horchia temnein, tb, slm:* Addenda to Treaty and Covenant (2 ed.)," *Bib* 60 (1979): 247–253.

28. D. J. Wiseman, "'Is It Peace?' Covenant and Diplomacy," *VT* 32 (1982): 311–326.

29. Bernard F. Batto ("The Covenant of Peace: A Neglected Ancient Near Eastern Motif," *CBQ* 49 [1987]: 187–211) traces the term "covenant of peace" back to ancient Near Eastern creation myths.

30. W. T. W. Cloete, "*Ntn yhwh shalom,*" in "Papers Read at the 24th Meeting of 'Die Ou-Testamentiese Werkgemeenskap in Suider-Afrika'" (ed. F. E. Deist and J. A. Loader), *OTS* 24 (1982): 1–10.

2

Peace (*Shalom*) in the Old Testament

Claus Westermann

That a study of the Old Testament word for "peace" should have a direct impact on the contemporary peace debate is scarcely to be expected. Nevertheless such a study can at least serve to bring clarity to the peace rhetoric within the Christian church. Official church statements on peace or on the peace issue show, sometimes in a rather shocking way, how necessary such a clarification is. Let me point out, first, the contrast in peace rhetoric between two public statements that appeared at nearly the same time, both published in the journal *Evangelische Kommentare* 4 (1968). In the statement on peace by the Württemburg Synod it is stated:

> Christians are called to be peacemakers. We live by the peace that God has brought about through Jesus Christ. We hope for the returning Lord, who will bring ultimate peace. This gives us courage and puts us under obligation to exert all our energies into working for peace in this world. (P. 220)

In Erwin Wilkens, "Peace Tasks of the Germans, for the Germany Study Project of the EKD Department for Public Responsibility":

> In this the church is well aware that it possesses no special way to peace or special solution for settling political conflicts. . . .

Translation of "Der Frieden (*Shalom*) im Alten Testament," in *Studien zur Friedensforschung* 1 (ed. G. Picht and H. E. Tödt; Stuttgart: Ernst Klett Verlag, 1969), 144–177.

The era of closed societies, that compete with each other by means of political and military instruments of power, is coming to a close. . . .

Nations today serve both as building blocks and as factors for order within a larger unity. There is no future for a nation that does not respect or foster peace and the concomitant social obligations in a supranational sphere. (Pp. 187–189)

The statement of the Württemburg Synod bases the involvement of Christians for peace on the "peace that God brought about through Jesus Christ." This assumes that one can or must base one's action on behalf of a political peace on the saving act of God in Christ, because this too can be described as "peace." Such an unclear parallel between "the peace that God has brought through Jesus Christ" and "peace in this world" cannot serve as an authentic guideline for the congregation, because the similar-sounding words serve to obscure the problem.

The language of the Memorandum "Peace Tasks of the Germans" is completely different. Here the language is secular and rational. The arguments are political and historical. It is a language suited to its subject. Yet it would still be necessary to clarify to what extent this is to be a church statement. It does not suffice to say that it is backed by theological considerations. The theological concept of peace should be clearly and tangibly distinguished from the political concept of peace.

A most pressing task is to examine the understandings of war and peace in all the statements coming from ecumenical circles, from the first to the last. See, for example, the compilation by H. J. Bargenings, "Der Frieden als Aufgabe: Die Oekumenischen Weltkonferenzen und das Problem 'Krieg und Frieden'" (*EvT* 9 [1965]: 485–512). In the subcommittee of Commission III in Stockholm it is stated:

> War as an instrument for settling international conflict through the use of physical power and involving deception and lies is incompatible with the attitude and behavior of Christ, and therefore also with the attitude and behavior of Christ's church.

The author of the article has written, "The phenomenon of war has revealed itself as that which it has always been — the meaningless and irresponsible destruction of people" (p. 486).

> Section V from Oxford (pp. 498f.) states: War includes a forced enmity, a demonic violation of the human personality and an arbitrary abuse of truth. War is a particularly impressive sign of the

power of sin and constitutes a disgrace to the justice of God as
revealed in Jesus Christ crucified. We dare not allow through any
sort of justification for war that this fact remains hidden or is
rendered harmless.

Such explanations are worthless and misleading because they
regard war as a timeless phenomenon which, as such, is supplied
complete with negative evaluation. Such generalizing, indiscriminate talk about war cannot help us further in the present situation.
When we think of peace as the opposite to war so characterized
as a timeless evil, then such an understanding of peace of necessity becomes idealized and illusionary.

Such examples show that in its talk of peace the church is caught
in what is thought to be an obvious and widely recognized contrast
of opposites, war and peace. I shall try to show in "A Comment
on War and Peace in the Old Testament" (pp. 31–33 below) that
the shalom of the Old Testament cannot be understood within this
dichotomy. The word itself was formed in a context in which its
opposite, as we conceive of it, was not present. We now find ourselves on the border of an era that has been shaped by this
dichotomy. It is the other border of this era, the period when this
dichotomy was just developing, that we encounter in the Old Testament. Hence it is important for us, in our examination of the question of peace, to become familiar with the nature of that shalom
concept and to study it carefully, noting that in the major group
of usages of the word it was neither intended as nor understood
as the opposite of war. Our study will show that the meaning of
the word "peace" (*shalom*) as used in the Old Testament does not
permit one to set up a permanent dichotomy between war and
peace.

Our research will also show how it came about that both a
political and a religious (theological) peace concept developed and
how they came to have widely divergent meanings.

The Use of Shalom in the Old Testament

Our approach to the Old Testament is to see it as one part of
the Bible. That is not to say that the conclusions drawn from the
Old Testament need say anything to us today. Indeed, it is a
conceivable possibility that the New Testament understanding of
peace should replace that of the Old Testament — in other words,
that a Christian understanding of peace can be attained only by
contrasting it to what the Old Testament says about peace. There

is, however, another conceivable possibility, namely, that one ought to expand, to add to, or even to correct the New Testament peace concept on the basis of the Old Testament understandings. Both possibilities exist, as does also a third variant, namely, that biblical speech about peace from both the Old and the New Testament has nothing to contribute to the contemporary problem of world peace. Peace in this variant remains a purely religious or inner-churchly concept.

The first task that I have set for myself here is to present the facts of the matter. If we take the biblical evidence seriously, then we must be prepared to make the assumption that when we encounter either the contemporary peace rhetoric or the peace language of the Old and New Testaments, these are not merely individually diverse understandings of the concept peace which in itself is a clear concept. Rather, we are dealing with three different concepts that happen to have the same designation because at points they came into contact with each other or overlap. They are three different concepts, whose initial definition can be attempted only out of the context in which each is used. A prerequisite for understanding the Old Testament usage is that we be prepared to learn a new and different word, a word that is not the same as our word "peace" and also not to be equated with the New Testament word *eirene*.

The Hebrew word *shalom* is formed from a verb that means to make something complete, to make something whole or holistic. Shalom is this condition of being complete, of fullness or wholeness as indicated in the verbal root.[1]

This origin of the word from the root verb helps to explain the quality that is necessarily essential to the concept: the word always means a completeness of some sort. You can only make whole something that already has inherent in it this characteristic of wholeness or completeness, as, for example, an organism, human society, a city, a group, a family, a people. In the vast majority of instances where the word appears, the wholeness of shalom is the wholeness, or completeness, or intactness of a community. We can therefore state the main meaning of the word as follows: Shalom means the wholeness, or completeness, or intactness of a community.

Given this starting point, we must first set some limitations.

1. Since shalom means the wholeness of a community, it is not really possible to speak of peace between A and B. Shalom can never represent something that exists between two entities, such as between two groups, two parties, two persons, and so forth.

In each case, the relationship between the two units could be described as an agreement, a contract, a covenant, or something similar, but shalom should not be used to describe the relationship.[2]

2. "Shalom" should also not be used when what we have in mind is inner peace or the peace of the soul. Applying the word "shalom" to the image that underlies the notion of an inner and outer sphere of existence — "outer struggle, inner peace" — is quite simply unthinkable. Rather, in such a case one ought to say that if there is an outer struggle but there is peace within or an inner peace, then this is not shalom. Shalom can only be present when the totality of existence, both inner and outer if you will, is whole or complete.[3]

3. In all those cases where "shalom" is used in its essential meaning, one can also not speak of peace with God, for this presumes that peace is something that can come about between two things. The expression "peace with God" (Rom. 5:1) does not appear in the Old Testament (for an exception, see p. 40 below).

4. Finally, shalom was originally not intended to serve as contrast to war or as the opposite of conflict. In biblical language there is, to be sure, a point of contact. The word "shalom" is used in the Old Testament occasionally to mean peace in contrast to war, but this is a secondary development which does not accord with the original usage of the word.

In its essential meaning shalom has so little of the sense of contrast to war or conflict that it is possible for both war and conflict to be part of the sphere of shalom. For example, one can ask about the shalom of a war.

Here, then, we have several delimitations that can serve to show the uniqueness, the points of difference between what is meant in the Old Testament with a word similar to our word "peace."

We encounter the word *shalom* in 210 passages of the Old Testament. It appears in virtually all books of the Old Testament and in all of the literary and preliterary layers known to us. Its main thread of meaning and usage has remained constant over a thousand years. The reemergence of the word in modern Hebrew draws directly on the Old Testament usage.

From this, one can conclude the following: Shalom is so closely linked to what it means to be human, it refers to something so elemental, that all the social, historical, and other transformations changed nothing in its fundamental meaning. To have shalom has obviously been essential for human existence throughout all the ages, through all the manner and forms of existence. It has remained the same in its essential thread of meaning in a way similar to that of "life" or "thirst" or "joy."

Shalom as Completeness
or Wholeness (Well-being) in the Present

In its most widespread and dominant use, the word means to experience well-being in a broad sense. It may mean the well-being of sufficiency and surplus. It may mean well-being in the sense of security (of having been preserved). Or it may be well-being in the sense of welfare or relief. It is used in many different connections, as applied to the individual (but who is always part of shalom only as a member of a complete entity), to a group, a people, a community, a family, or a given situation. In one case, it also applies to the human body (Ps. 38:3).[4]

We encounter this general meaning of well-being in certain quite specific and clearly designated applications.

WHOLENESS (WELL-BEING) AFFIRMED

In the Old Testament, shalom is something that belongs to living. Since human beings were created to be social beings, shalom becomes a prerequisite for societal existence. The fact that it belongs to life does not mean, however, that it is automatically present wherever there is human life. This health of society is just as susceptible to illness or injury as is the health of the body. Indeed, health in the sense of physical health and health in the sense of human society are so closely linked that in one case shalom means physical health (Ps. 38:3, "There is no health in my bones"; the parallel statement speaks of "soundness of flesh").[5]

To affirm the presence of shalom is not to state the obvious. It is always an affirmation made in the light of potential danger. The simplest affirmation of the presence of shalom is the word "shalom" used in the sentence: "She said: shalom" (2 Kings 4:23), which is translated "It will be well" (RSV), or everything is in order. This corresponds exactly to the English "okay." We find the same meaning in the expression "The signs are good for you" (see 1 Sam. 20:7, 21).

Shalom, when so employed, has no specific content. What constitutes wholeness, health, or everything being in order depends on the given situation. There is, for example, an adverbial use of the noun, where the sense is that of being safe, unharmed: "He pursues them and passes on safely" (Isa. 41:3).

An adjectival usage is also possible: Jer. 25:37, "and the peaceful folds are devastated," literally "pastures of peace" (cf. our "the peace of nature"). It can also be stated negatively in "a cry of . . . no peace" (Jer. 30:5). In this case, it is best to translate it as "peaceful" or "nonpeace." In this the Hebrew word comes close to our German (or English) usage.

A lamentation is also a form of this affirmation:

Lam. 3:17   "My soul is bereft of peace."

In this instance, shalom refers to a healthy normal life, the secular daily life of the average person.[6] Shalom refers to this life being in order, not that it consists of something special but rather this life *with its contradictions* of love and conflict, hunger and satisfaction, poverty and wealth. A person is bereft of peace, of shalom, then, when one's human dignity is denied.

The opposite situation is also possible: someone who was deathly ill is able to praise God for healing; thus, "it was for my welfare that I had great bitterness" (Isa. 38:17).[7]

This passage makes clear the degree to which shalom is specified by its opposite. In this case, the opposite of shalom is not nonpeace, nor conflict (which would accord with the contrast between war and peace in society), but rather "bitterness." Life had become sour, the person's life had been virtually destroyed through illness. Now recovered, the person rejoices in health and calls this recovered health shalom.

In the passages above, the writers have no specifically religious or moral position in mind. This shalom, this being whole and healthy, is for every person without any distinction drawn, and this is true even when it is endangered for all. It is therefore something new and special, when this shalom is stipulated for the just—Ps. 119:165, "Great peace have those who love thy law." Though necessarily linked especially to the pious and just, shalom could seldom be maintained for them. Here was where the temptation set in; real life showed a different pattern—Ps. 73:3, "I saw the prosperity of the wicked." Here a gulf appeared that was to have a widespread impact.[8]

Everyone seeks prosperity and well-being; everyone strives for success. Everyone wants his or her life to be healthy and in order. This striving for shalom is assumed, and one speaks of it only when its attainment becomes problematic in some way.

Jer. 38:4   "For this man is not seeking the welfare of this people, but their harm."

Given the statement that normally an individual is concerned for the common good of that of which the person is a part, then it is assumed that the person can do something on its behalf. That the individual is in this position is stated without hesitation. We must also keep in mind that, just as the case with our term "well-being," so also "shalom" can refer to society or to the individual.

WHOLENESS (WELL-BEING) EXPERIENCED IN AN ENCOUNTER AND PROCLAIMED

In the vast majority of instances in the Old Testament, shalom means a wholeness or completeness or a sense of well-being as it can be experienced and affirmed in an encounter between persons. This is the essential and most important sphere of shalom. Shalom is revealed in the manner in which people live together, in the way they greet each other, as they come and go, arriving and departing, and in the reception or dismissal of persons. This is the true locale for a healthy community and the well-being of people in society, rather than in a special political or social sphere, or in some particular ethical or religious sphere.

For our understanding of the word "shalom" in the Old Testament this is of fundamental importance. Shalom happens neither through a peace agreement (that happens as well, but only in an exceptional situation) nor in that God brings peace through a special action. Rather, it is grounded within the small circles of human community. Shalom is present where a small community exists; it is the well-being of this community.[9] The fact that the word "shalom" plays such an important role in the Old Testament greeting is due to the great significance of the greeting, since greeting and blessing belong together. This significance is rooted in a very early stage of human history.[10]

CHIEF FORMS OF THE GREETING

In a society where there is no war, where everything is conducted peacefully without conflict, there is still no shalom if the people are starving or if disease reigns. On the other hand, when there is nothing lacking for well-being, when all live sumptuously and joyously but the society is under a heavy yoke of some sort, then that too is not shalom. Shalom as the well-being of a community always includes all circles, all aspects of existence. The meaning of the word lies precisely in the fact that it is able to encompass all areas and spheres of life. That is most evident in the use of "shalom" in the greeting, one of the most important if not the most important group of usages. At issue in the greeting is existential wholeness in the fullest sense. At the same time, it is concerned for the welfare of life in community, since the greeting is a life function of society. I shall try to show this through two forms of the greeting.

Asking about shalom, finding out

> Gen. 43:27   "And he inquired about their welfare, and said, 'Is your father well, the old man of whom you spoke?'" (=is . . . peace?); v. 28   "Your servant our father is well."
>
> 2 Kings 4:26   "'Is it well with you? Is it well with your husband? Is it well with the child?' And she answered, 'It is well.'"
>
> 2 Kings 5:21–22   "'Is all well?' And he said, 'All is well (*shalom*).'"
>
> 2 Sam. 20:9   "Is it well with you, my brother?"
>
> Gen. 37:14   "See if it is well with your brothers, and with the flock."
>
> 2 Sam. 11:7   "David asked how Joab was doing, and how the people fared, and how the war prospered [he asked about the shalom of Joab, the people and of the war]."

Additional passages are Gen. 29:6; 2 Sam. 18:29, 32; 2 Kings 9:11, 17, 18, 19, 22, 31; Gen. 37:4; Ex. 18:7; Judg. 18:6, 15; 1 Sam. 10:4; 17:18, 22; 25:5; 30:21; 2 Sam. 8:10; 1 Chron. 18:10; Jer. 15:5 (shalom of Jerusalem); 2 Kings 10:13; Esth. 2:11. When they inquire about shalom, they are asking about a welfare that includes everything necessary to healthful living: good health, a sense of well-being, good fortune, the cohesiveness of the community, relationship to relatives and their state of being, and anything else deemed necessary for everything to be in order.

To ask about the welfare is also an expression of sympathy, although that expression is not quite adequate. With the question a point of contact is established, a link is resumed after an absence. In other words, the question about welfare does not so much seek information, even if that is implied, as that it expresses an involvement with the existence of the other person. The motive or impulse for the inquiry is not so much the interest of the individual who is asking the question as it is of the society. Behind the question as its true impulse lies the common assumption of a presumed totality to which both belong. This making contact by means of the question and answer of greeting serves as an act of integration

into the society. The belonging of both questioner and respondent to a totality that encompasses both comes to expression in
the question-and-answer exchange.[11]

The question about shalom is put to the individual person. But
the inquiry can also be about the shalom of the circle surrounding the individual such as one's relatives or herds. It can even
concern the success (shalom) of the battle.

In 2 Kings 9:14–37 this query (about shalom) serves as leitmotiv
for describing Jehu's revolution. When the watchman on the tower
in Jezreel announces the approach of Jehu, King Joram orders
that a rider be sent to meet him, to "let him say, 'Is it peace?'"
that is, to ask about shalom (v. 17). The rider meets Jehu and asks
the question, "Thus says the king, 'Is it peace?'" In Hebrew the
question is "הֲשָׁלוֹם," just the single word shalom with the inter-
rogatory particle. That could also mean "Is [everything] well?" Jehu
answers: "What have you to do with peace?" and orders him to
fall in behind him (v. 18). This exchange is repeated (v. 19). Then
the two kings ride out in their battle chariot to meet Jehu. Now
the king himself poses the question (v. 22), "Is it peace, Jehu?"
Jehu answers, "What peace can there be, so long as the harlotries
and sorceries of your mother Jezebel are so many?" At this
response, the kings flee, Jehu follows and kills both of them. Jehu
then proceeds further to Jezreel. Proud Queen Jezebel puts on
makeup, goes to the window and calls down to Jehu as he enters
the gate, "Is it peace [הֲשָׁלוֹם], you Zimri, murderer of your
master?" (Zimri refers to an earlier rebel who had killed the king
and taken over the rule).

Here the catchword "shalom" as a question, so artfully used as
to remind us of the language of the ballad, serves as motif word
for an extremely concentrated series of events. The normal daily
motif of the query of greeting becomes the bearer of deeper reflections about peace and the breaking of the peace. Jehu wants to
restore the "peace" that was destroyed through the paganism of
Jezebel. But he is able to do that only through regicide, and the
queen who coolly and supremely awaits her own death asks Jehu:
Can regicide create peace? This scene shows, on the one hand, the
great significance attached to the query of greeting and, on the
other hand, reveals the vitality and conceptual power of the word
"shalom." What is meant by the word "shalom" as the key motif
of the story is what we would likely speak of as the good of the
land. This good of the land is intimately connected with obedience
to God's will and with the faithfulness of officers to their lord.

It is connected with the (so easily damaged) responsibility that each one in his or her place bears for the totality.

Acceptance into shalom, granting shalom. Judges 19:20, "And the old man said, 'Peace be to you; I will care for all your wants.'" At evening a stranger arrives in a town and waits in the square for someone to take him in. An old man, a resident, seeing him standing there, asks him his whereabouts and then invites him into his house. Hospitably he offers him not only lodging but also food and drink and feed for the donkey. The actual acceptance and hosting logically follow from the greeting "Peace be with you." In the act of offering the peace greeting, the stranger is included within the sphere of shalom. For him that meant security, rest, shelter, and assuaging his hunger and thirst.

This hospitality to the stranger represents the acceptance of the latter into the life circle of shalom, which would normally include only the family or clan. The universal significance of "peace" comes into play in that the small, circumscribed family circle, through the possibility of accepting a strange guest into that circle of shalom, gives it an unrestricted breadth.

Additional passages are:

Gen. 43:23   "Rest assured, do not be afraid."
Judg. 6:23   "Peace be to you; do not fear, you shall not die."
1 Sam. 25:6   "Peace be to you, and peace be to your house, and peace be to all that you have."

Also the simple peace greeting as peace offering: 2 Sam. 18:28; Pss. 122:6; 125:5; 126:8; 128:6 (peace to Israel); Dan. 10:9, 19; 1 Chron. 12:18 (to the king).

That one so often encounters the actual words of greeting in the Old and New Testament stories, not merely the mention of it, is due to the importance of the greeting for human community. Both a physical and a spiritual contact occur in the greeting. To refuse a greeting signifies a breakdown of community (Gen. 37:4).[12] Without the greeting, that which is meant in the Old Testament by shalom could not exist. An essential part of the rule of peace is fulfilled in the greeting.

WHOLENESS OR WELL-BEING THAT GOES WITH YOU

Beshalom, to be safe, to be secure: One may take another person into one's peace, which means receiving that person into one's house, offering shelter and security. But the departing person may also be sent forth with peace:

1 Sam. 25:35   "Go up in peace to your house."
2 Kings 5:19   "He said to him, 'Go in peace.'"

Further passages are 1 Sam. 29:7; 2 Sam. 15:9, 27; Gen. 44:17; Ex. 4:18; Judg. 18:6; 1 Sam. 1:17; 20:42; 25:35. The same expression is often found in a report: Gen. 26:31, "They departed from him in peace," similarly in Gen. 26:29[13]; Josh. 10:21; 2 Sam. 3:21, 22, 23; 1 Sam. 19:25, 31; 1 Kings 22:17; 2 Chron. 18:16; Jer. 43:12; 2 Chron. 19:1. More conditionally, in Gen. 28:21: "so that I come again to my father's house in peace"; Judg. 8:9; 11:31; 1 Kings 22:27; 2 Chron. 18:26; and in other, mainly modal forms: Ex. 18:23; 1 Kings 22:27; 2 Chron. 18:26; Pss. 4:9; 55:19; Isa. 55:12; 2 Kings 20:13.

There is a special group of usages speaking of dying, or to "go to your ancestors" in peace:

Gen. 15:15   "You shall go to your ancestors in peace."

Additional passages are 1 Kings 2:6; 2 Kings 22:20; 2 Chron. 34:28; Jer. 34:5. In total there are 41 passages where such a usage is found. There is a going, a returning, a lying down, or a being led in peace. This also includes to die in peace. The frequency and the variety of this form of usage indicate how much it marked the word "peace." Underlying this is a certain preconception best seen through contrast. In one of the lamentations it is stated:

Lam. 3:17   "My soul is bereft of peace."

Here shalom is like a space, an area in which one can be present and from which one can be driven. This area of shalom, however, is to be found not only where the security of shelter or the peace of the house would logically provide security. Rather, it is precisely where one is released from the shelter of a house, to be under way, subject to all the possible dangers, that talk of a peace "space" occurs.

When one of the politically powerful says, "Go in peace!" it means as much as a promise of safe-conduct, for example:

Ex. 18:23   "All this people also will go to their place in peace."
2 Sam. 3:21   "So David sent Abner away; and he went in peace."

But the same expression is also used by one who has no power whatsoever. In most of the passages it is not at all clear who it is that achieves or guarantees the safekeeping on the road. Only

in a few instances is it said specifically that it is God who brings
one safely to one's destination:

> Judg. 18:6   "Go in peace. The journey on which you go is under
> the eye of the LORD."
> Ps. 4:8   "In peace I will both lie down and sleep; for thou alone,
> O LORD, makest me dwell in safety."

Important for the use of the word "peace" in all these passages
is the fact that the security implied comes from God but that it
does not need to be stated. When a person who is traveling amid
all possible dangers is conscious of being in a secure space, then
the wholeness of that person's life is especially present in that situation. Such a person need not fear and is protected from danger
because a sense of security accompanies the person, the way the
walls of a city or of a house lend it security. A sense of security
in the context of the open road with its dangers is the nature of
shalom in this situation.

The most extreme setting for this shalom is when it accompanies
one into death. When Jeremiah promises King Zedekiah on the
occasion of surrender "You will die in peace," then what is meant
is the ending of a lifetime that encompasses a complete and whole
life, just as was promised to Abraham: "You will go in peace to
your fathers." Here death is the sensible, affirmed ending to a
healthy life, and peace accompanies him unto death itself.

CONCLUSIONS

The above are the dominant usages. These show clearly that
shalom is a way of being or certainty for community or the person
living in community.

Shalom is the wellness of community or of the persons in community. It is neither a religious or theological concept nor a political
or ethical one. Even the social category does not suffice, because
the well-being intended with shalom also encompasses physical
and economic health. Shalom as wellness, as being intact, to be
in order, signifies the well-being of a human in all imaginable
aspects. It stretches from the well-being of satisfaction and con-
tentment about one's welfare, to security, to being unharmed
including keeping healthy, to getting along with each other in every
form of relationship. There is a whole series of word combinations using "well" to define shalom: doing well, faring well, being
well, keeping well. In many cases shalom is best translated as "well."

Always, however, shalom also includes the tensions within each of the spheres. To be satisfied and prosperous is shalom only for those who know hunger and want. Only that person can experience health as wholeness, as shalom, who knows what illness is. Security becomes shalom only for the one in danger. To get along with one another assumes the possibility of conflict. There is shalom when the normal way of life is in order, in all of its aspects, along with all of the tensions. Hence this word can never be used to designate an ideal condition. The word "shalom" belongs much more to people's usual, normal life together.

In accordance with this, any kind of special elevation of peace, such as an emphatic peace proclamation, a confession of peace, or something similar, is impossible and must be so. Every single overemphasis of peace in any sphere, whether it be the social or the political, is dangerous. There where they talk unceasingly of peace, or conduct peace propaganda, or turn peace into a program, it would already be destroyed or in danger, according to the Old Testament understanding. For all such overemphasis points to the loss of the self-evident and natural quality that characterizes shalom speech.

The group of usages dealt with so far have shown that the word "shalom" is centered in a small, easily encompassed community. It is spoken of where a limited circle of persons and events are in view, where the participating persons know each other. The word appears most frequently where people meet each other and inquire after their welfare, in offering peace, in departing or accompanying in peace. This is of the utmost importance. The word "shalom" has its true impact and effect where it is spoken and heard in personal interchange, in other words within a circle of people that is so small that individuals greet each other. It is therefore doubtful whether it makes any sense to speak of shalom in a situation where they no longer greet each other. In the strictest sense, shalom is impossible in a mass of people.

This can be shown even more clearly through the three main groups of usage:

1. In inquiring about well-being, we noted that the impulse for the question really begins from a whole, to which the questioner and the questioned one belong. To share in the state of the other person is an expression of belonging together or of knowing about such belongingness. The one about whose shalom I am inquiring must mean something to me. And that is possible only in a limited, relatively small community. Such sharing in the life of the other

is an occasion for exercising responsibility, which also is possible only within a limited circle.

2. In the process of refusing peace to someone, or of receiving someone into peace, that person is offered a basic trust (as is evident especially through the close tie with "Be not afraid" — e.g., Gen. 43:23). The one to whom peace is offered can rest assured that he or she need not expect anything unfriendly or evil from the other person. He or she may trust the person. That too is possible only within a small circle.

3. The one who departs in peace or is conducted in peace finds a security within the shalom space, allowing that person to travel calmly without fear. This security of being encircled by shalom can also be experienced only as a personal event within a limited circle. Responsibility, trust, and security are the life elements of shalom. They are present when one person offers another shalom, when that person entrusts himself or herself to the offered shalom, and when an individual knows himself or herself secure in shalom. Such a peace can come about only where responsibility, trust, and security are present. A public peace (in contrast to war) where these three elements are missing could not be called shalom. Nor could an inner peace be called shalom, in which the relationship to the surrounding world is unhealthy.[14]

WHOLENESS RESTRICTED TO A GIVEN SITUATION: PEACE INSTEAD OF WAR (BATTLE)

1 Sam. 7:14 "There was peace also between Israel and the Amorites."
1 Kings 5:4 "But now the LORD my God has given me peace on every side."
Eccl. 3:8 "A time for war and a time for peace."

Additional passages are Deut. 2:26; 20:10–12; Josh. 9:15; Judg. 4:17; 11:13; 21:13; 1 Sam. 16:14, 15; 1 Kings 2:13; 5:4; 20:18; 5:26; Job 15:21; Isa. 33:7; Esth. 9:30.

This is the very same usage of the word as we now know it. In these instances, shalom means the same as our "peace." That is the only translation appropriate here; none of the others, such as welfare, well-being, or health, would fit. Nevertheless one should not be deceived by the fact that in this group of usages we may render shalom with our word "peace." This is not the original usage of the Hebrew word. Our most obvious and self-evident meaning of the word "peace" represents a major shift to a specialized meaning in Hebrew. This usage became possible only following a change in meaning. How is that to be explained?

If we assume wholeness, health, well-being as the basic meaning of shalom, then the shift in meaning to peace as opposite of war points to the fact that, within this linguistic realm war had developed into an ever-increasing disturbance of this wholeness. It had not been that way from the beginning.[15] The shalom concept had been formed at a time when war did not have this impact. Only over the course of a long history did it come to mean the opposite of peace. The concept of shalom stems from a time when a battle did not destroy the shalom of a community, nor even disturb it. It was possible, for example, to inquire about the shalom of the battle. In 2 Sam. 11:7, David asked Uriah "how Joab was doing, and how the people fared, and how the war prospered." It is true that shalom is employed here in a neutral sense of "faring," but such talk is possible only where shalom does not yet signify the absolute opposite of war. War becomes this complete opposite only when it breaks into the wholeness of a community and destroys it. Several passages reveal the transition. As Samuel was arriving in Bethlehem, in order to anoint David as king, the elders of the town met him and asked him, "Do you come peaceably [=is your coming shalom]?" And Samuel answered, "Peaceably" (=shalom; 1 Sam. 16:4f., cf. 1 Kings 2:13). The passage shows that it was the potential threat to the well-being of the town rather than the phenomenon of war itself which set war as alternative to shalom.

In the other passages (see above), shalom as peace over against war has the same meaning as in our language and manner of thought. When in the case of Eccl. 3:8 war and peace are added to the list of polar opposites such as weeping and laughing, keeping silent or speaking, this paired concept carries the same general, encompassing meaning as did Tolstoy's "War and Peace" in the nineteenth century. We must keep in mind, however, that in the Hebrew this was an inappropriate and derivative use of shalom.

A COMMENT ON WAR AND PEACE IN THE OLD TESTAMENT

A conceptual alternative to war was not possible in ancient Israel, because neither war nor its alternative was understood or experienced as a state. War was understood not as a condition but always in terms of the events. It was seen as a series of battles, not as war in our use of the term. The battles were temporal and local. A condition of war only developed with the invasion of the great powers, when military measures were extended beyond the actual battles into the peace itself. Only then did a gradual rejection and negation of war as such develop. It grew out of long periods of suffering, and through it came a longing for real peace and a guaranteed peaceful condition.[16]

Today we find ourselves in a world in which war as such is rejected as a means of conflict resolution between nations, where weapons of destruction make war into an unimaginable catastrophe. In such a situation it is necessary to try to get an overview of that sweep of human history shaped by war in its totality. Living on the edge of this era, where we now find ourselves, we must try to get a view of the other edge of the era, when humanity first began to live with war.

In such a situation there is the danger that one speaks of war in very general terms without taking its history into account. This would not be in accord with the historical phenomenon of war and at the same time would distort peace as the counter concept of war so understood.[17] It is not correct to say that there have always been wars and that there will always be wars. But it is just as wrong to assume that one could attain the peace described above through the elimination of war. The Old Testament reveals at the beginning a style of life in which there were no wars in our sense of the word, because the groups of people that lived together (or wandered about together) were too small to be able to conduct war in our sense of the term. What we have here is clearly a *pre*-political form of existence, as presented in the stories of the patriarchs, in which life was lived within the family and clan and in which the nature of that life was determined by the family or clan's life setting. Here a contrast between war and peace as alternative conditions was unknown. Hence the word "peace" (*shalom*) could not be understood as a conceptual alternative to war.

In the life of the community, conflict assumed the place that war would have in our setting. Strife or conflict was the phenomenon in that smaller community that would accord with the meaning of war for us. They experienced conflict in a broad variety of ways. Conflict, like war later, had its prescribed forms and rituals. Conflict could be encountered in various aspects of life. There was the distinctive conflict of the men and that of the women.

It would be a mistake to regard these prewar stages as better or more peaceful simply because there was no war. Instead of war, there was conflict, its prototype.

For our understanding of peace, we may draw the following conclusion from this: It would be a fatal error, in seeking world peace today, to assume that the prevention or elimination of war, as it has developed in the twentieth century, would lead to some ideal condition of peace between all people with each other. Rather, one must begin with the assumption that war is an instrument for conducting conflict that belongs to a given era of human history, one that was preceded by other means of conducting conflict and that therefore could be succeeded by still other forms. We must ask, therefore, what are the forms of conflict between groups that would be appropriate in our contemporary world and its social form without leading to irrational destruction.

In our efforts on behalf of a common world peace we dare not set out with a peace concept formed as a conceptual alternative to war. In such a situation, orientation by a peace concept that was formed in an era that did not regard peace as the opposite of war, but that was bounded by the era of war, becomes highly significant.

Wholeness or Wellness in the Future
(The Promised Peace)

The dominant emphasis in the use of the word "shalom" is on the present. A community cannot exist without shalom. Wholeness or wellness is the normal state of a community. Shalom therefore does not signify some ideal of a peace, a condition to be longed for but rarely or never attained. Whenever there is talk of future peace, or the peace of the future, this always presumes a disturbance or threat to peace in the present. Whenever peace in the future was announced in a word of prophecy, it meant a restoration of what had been destroyed or a securing of the peace now threatened. It was not intended that such a peace for the future would transcend the present or become a superelevated reality.

THE CONDITIONAL PROMISE

While conditional promises receive much attention in Deuteronomy, the promise of peace nowhere occurs; in other places where conditional promises occur, the promise of peace rarely occurs. It is important to note that whereas the promised welfare of Israel is conditional on obedience, a theme developed with great variation in Deuteronomy, this promise does not include shalom as part of the rhetoric. The reason for this might well be that shalom was understood in a present sense in that linguistic context.

We encounter shalom in the context of conditional promises in only two late passages: Isa. 48:18 and Lev. 26:3–6. Neither of them is truly words of prophecy. Isaiah 48:18 occurs in the context of an admonition,[18] whereas Lev. 26:3–6 occurs in connection with a closing conditional promise of blessing, as in Deuteronomy 28.

THE SALVATION ORACLE[19]

The promise of peace is firmly anchored in the salvation oracle. Since such oracles are no longer extant, we know them only through intimations or allusions. One of the few passages in which the psalmist cites a salvation oracle in response to the people's lamentation, quoting it in abbreviation, is Psalm 85. Verse 8 states:

> Let me hear what God the LORD will speak,
>   for he will speak peace to his people."

In the same connection we encounter the word "shalom" in Ps. 85:10: "Righteousness and peace will kiss each other." Shalom seems to belong particularly to the salvation oracle for the king, as in Psalm 72:

> v. 3   "Let the mountains bear prosperity for the people, and the hills, in righteousness!"
> v. 7   "In his [the king's] days may righteousness flourish, and peace abound, till the moon be no more!"

Similarly in the royal promise of Isa. 9:1–6:

> v. 6   "Mighty God, Everlasting Father, Prince of Peace."
> v. 7   "And of peace there will be no end."

The promise of a future king grew out of the king's oracle. A part of the promise of the king is that the coming king will be a bringer of peace:

> Zech. 9:10   "He shall command peace to the nations."
> Micah 5:5   "And this [?] shall be peace."

In the wish for a king, peace is described as coming from God, this too having been determined by the king's oracle:

> 1 Kings 2:33   "But to David . . . there shall be peace from the LORD for evermore."

It is possible that the two shalom passages in the conditional promises also have their origin in the salvation oracles.

THE PROPHECY OF SALVATION[20]

A very striking collection of shalom usages as something future is evident in those passages in which the writing prophets (*Schrift-propheten*) speak about the prophets of salvation and their efforts:

Jer. 6:14 "saying, 'Peace, peace,' when there is no peace" (8:11).
14:13 "(the salvation prophets) . . . I will give you assured peace in this place."
Ezek. 13:10 "because they have misled my people, saying, 'Peace,' when there is no peace" (=13:16).
Micah 3:5 "who cry 'Peace' when they have something to eat."
Jer. 28:9 "As for the prophet who prophesies peace."

Micah, Jeremiah, and Ezekiel labeled these prophets salvation prophets. They promise salvation, but they have not been charged with such a message and hence deceive the people. In these passages, shalom — and that is true in general — can be rendered as salvation (*Heil*), but it must be kept in mind that this "salvation" means something else than in the word combinations "saving deeds" or "salvation history" in which the essential meaning is that of "having been saved from something" (*Rettung*).

If what these prophets proclaim is without exception designated as shalom, then what is intended is salvation in the sense of well-being. They therefore are to be distinguished from the judgment prophets, not only because the latter proclaim something negative whereas the former are positive, but rather because shalom does not serve as a conceptual contrast to judgment — that would be the word "salvation" (*Rettung*). What the salvation prophets proclaim is not so much an action, that is, not an act of God, but rather a condition, the state of well-being. When a prophet announces a positive event, such as the liberation of Jerusalem from the enemies threatening it, that is not a "well-being prophecy" in its essence as presented here. The subject of the proclamation of the salvation prophets is not salvation but *Heil* = well-being, that is, something essentially different in essence. Even when such salvation prophets announce an event, such as Hananiah in Jeremiah 28 announcing the return of the exiles and the collapse of Babylon, such speech is based on an understanding of salvation that refers to a state, to well-being as such. When we recognize shalom to be the actual subject of the proclamations of the opponents of the writing prophets, then the difference between the writing prophets and the salvation prophets becomes more evident.

In the statement in Jer. 4:10 (cf. 23:17), as part of the lament of the people, "Surely thou hast utterly deceived this people and Jerusalem, saying, 'It shall be well with you,'" the lamenters may have the salvation prophets in mind, or perhaps also the salvation oracles. There might be a close connection between pronouncing the oracle of salvation during worship as response to the people's lament and the work of the salvation prophets, as has been assumed by many scholars.

In a modified way, Gen. 41:16 also belongs to this group of usages. Joseph is standing before Pharaoh. Having announced his readiness to interpret the dreams, he says, "It is not in me; God will give Pharaoh a favorable answer." Joseph turns aside the suggestion that the interpretation comes from him. The interpretive word will be a word of salvation from God. This is possibly an early reference to salvation prophecy in the name of Yahweh which replaced dream interpretation. Here such salvation prophecy in the name of Yahweh is still affirmed emphatically.

SHALOM USAGE BY THE WRITING PROPHETS

It must be pointed out, first of all, that the word "shalom" does not appear in the proclamations of the writing prophets of the eighth century and that it is used only by Jeremiah of those writing in the seventh century before the exile. With the exception of Jeremiah, it first enters prophetic speech during and after the exile. Two passages in Jeremiah best explain why that is so. In Jeremiah 16 it is reported that the prophet was commanded not to start a family, or to participate in any feast of celebration, or to enter a house of mourning. The reason given is: Jer. 16:5, "for I have taken away my peace from this people." The passage shows most clearly that shalom refers to the wellness of a community. Through Yahweh's decision of judgment, which the prophet is to proclaim, the community has been cut off. With his life of singleness the prophet is to be a sign of that fact. To my knowledge, this is the first passage in which shalom is so closely linked with God that Jeremiah is able to say, "I have taken away my peace from this people." Only at this point of extreme crisis in the wellness of the people is it stated explicitly that it is the well-being established by Yahweh that has now been taken away from the people.[21]

Once the sentence has been carried out, however, it is again possible to talk of shalom. In the letter of 597 B.C. (the first conquest of Jerusalem), Jeremiah writes to the exiles admonishing them to build houses and establish families, with the following justification:

Jer. 29:11 "For I know the plans I have for you, says the LORD, plans for welfare and not for evil, to give you a future and a hope."

But in a key point the concept of welfare has changed. Up to the time of the collapse, shalom for Israel was possible only in a healthy state, where temple worship and the political kingdom provided the needed security and constancy of peace. Now shalom was to be possible within an uncertain existence in foreign places under foreign rule and without a holy place! The conceptual shift is most evident from the fact that this new shalom could be linked with the former enemies of Israel. In the same letter to the exiles Jeremiah says:

Jer. 29:7 "Seek the welfare of the city where I have sent you into exile, and pray to the LORD on its behalf, for in its welfare you will find your welfare."

When we compare the three passages in Jeremiah, we see clearly what has changed. The peace that God took away from his people is nevertheless promised, after the collapse, but to a remnant; it is no longer linked to political sovereignty. Part of this shalom now is that the remnant is to seek the peace, the welfare, of those who are keeping them in captivity (cf. Acts 27–28).[22]

All other passages in the prophets, in which we encounter the word "shalom," come from the exile or postexilic period. The most important passage is Isa. 53:5, from the fourth Song of the Servant:

Isa. 53:5 "Upon him was the chastisement that made us whole (*shalom*)."

This is to be understood in direct connection with the passages in Jeremiah. This passage too assumes the collapse of the state. Shalom is no longer what it once was. Israel has misused the peace; therefore it has been taken away (Jer. 16:5). God holds "plans of welfare" for the remnant (Jer. 29:11; Isa. 40:1ff.), and peace may be promised the remnant (Jer. 29:11; Isa. 52:7; 54:10–13). But this future peace is no longer assured through the state institutions. A completely new possibility is implied through the substitutionary atonement of an individual. Of this individual it is said, "Upon him was the chastisement that made us whole."[23] That which is merely implied here the New Testament declares about the substitutionary atoning suffering of Jesus, who "bore the sins of the world." The word "shalom" in Isa. 53:5 includes forgiveness, or presumes it, but its primary meaning is not "peace with God" but rather the wellness of the entire person, including bodily existence.

We encounter shalom also in the following passages of Deutero-Isaiah: 45:7; 52:7; 54:10, 13. Isaiah 54 and 55 expand on the promise of salvation through the promise of blessing. Verses 10 and 13 of Isaiah 54 belong in that setting:

> Isa. 54:10   "and my covenant of peace shall not be removed."
> Isa. 54:13   "Great shall be the prosperity of your children."

Formally speaking, this is the same promise of shalom as in the preexilic salvation prophets, but in substance this represents an important change. Whereas the salvation prophets promised the continuation or the return of peace, as all would like it to be, namely, a shalom based on political security and victory over the enemy, Deutero-Isaiah does indeed promise a return, but not the return of power. He does indeed promise victory over Israel's enemies, although not a victory by Israel but rather a victory by Cyrus. With these shifts the shalom promised by Deutero-Isaiah is detached from the possession of political power.

No doubt that is the reason why shalom is here linked directly with God: "My steadfast love shall not depart from you, and my covenant of peace shall not be removed." What is meant is "the peace that I give" (as in Isa. 45:7). But if shalom is now brought into a direct link with God — "my peace" — wholeness or wellness that is promised here is surely elevated as something new which can be always and everywhere. This passage appears only in this one oracle, in the context of this special salvational work of Yahweh. Here we can identify a theologizing of the concept, where shalom is closely tied to God's work of salvation for Israel.

This emphatically theological usage is also evident in Isa. 45:7:

> "I form light and create darkness, I make weal and create woe."

The dual contrast shows that this is an attempt to describe God in totality, in God's widest circumference. Here too shalom has a broader meaning. It is not merely wellness in the sense of well-being but is obviously intended to encompass everything positive, all of God's actions on behalf of humanity, including God's saving acts. Here for the first time we encounter an inclusive concept of salvation (*Heil*) as it is employed in theological language when we speak of the saving acts of God or of salvation history.

Both belong together, a theologizing of the concept ("my peace") and its extended application to all the saving acts of God.

The remaining passages are summarized briefly. Ezekiel (34:25 and 37:26) also talks about a peace covenant. The passages in

Trito-Isaiah (57:19; 60:17; 66:12) are dependent on Deutero-Isaiah, to be sure, but the usage is no longer so concise and ties in with the earlier salvation prophecy. This is true also for the promises of future peace in Haggai (2:9) and Zechariah (8:12) and in other postexilic salvation prophecies (Isa. 32:17–18; Jer. 33:6–9; 26:3, 12; 1 Chron. 22:9).

Shalom in Connection with Divine Action

We have seen that the actual theologizing of the shalom concept first takes place with Jeremiah and Deutero-Isaiah, and thereby the meaning of the concept changes. These are, however, not the only passages in which shalom is linked with divine action. More often we encounter talk of shalom being present in connection with God's acts. It remains to examine these passages and their relationship to those just discussed.

YAHWEH GIVES PEACE

Judges 6:24: Gideon recognizes the "messenger of Yahweh" and fears that he will die. The messenger of God answers: "Peace be to you; do not fear, you shall not die." Thereupon Gideon erects an altar to Yahweh and calls it "Yahweh shalom," Yahweh is peace. The passage is difficult to interpret. The most direct interpretation, drawn from the previous sentence — namely, the word of God's messenger — would suggest that the name of the altar is a statement that Yahweh is or makes peace = wellness. This passage would then constitute a very early witness to the new experience, that Yahweh, the God of the wilderness, is also the God who brings shalom.

In praise to God: That Yahweh creates or brings peace is also stated in several passages of praise to God:

Ps. 35:27 "who delights in the welfare of his servant."
Ps. 147:14 "He makes peace in your borders; he fills you with the finest of the wheat."
Job 25:2 "He makes peace in his high heaven."

In connection with blessing: The direct link between peace and divine action is especially evident in connection with blessings. The blessing also was originally not a theological concept. The Yahwist (Gen. 12:1–3) links it particularly with the work of God. Something similar occurs in the priestly language of Num. 6:22–26, where the worship blessing is celebrated as the work of Yahweh. Through this connection, peace is tied to the blessing:

Num. 6:26 "The LORD lift up his countenance upon you and give you peace."

This linkage is adopted in Ps. 29:11, "May the LORD bless his people with peace!"[24]

Two other passages also reflect priestly rhetoric. A linkage between Yahweh and a lineage of priests is established through the statement that this lineage stands in a covenant relationship with Yahweh, so that Yahweh guarantees it as shalom.

Num. 25:12 "Behold, I give to him my covenant of peace."
Mal. 2:5 "My covenant with him [Levi] was a covenant of life and peace, and I gave them to him."

In all three sets of passages the references to the peace that Yahweh gives or makes occur in the context of worship. This is also true of another group of references to shalom in the future, namely, those passages encountered in the salvation oracles. These are a smaller group, and in none of these did a consciously theological peace concept develop. Rather, these developed much more as a contrast to the talk of shalom in the contemporary situation where there was no longer true shalom.

Peace between people and God: In only a single passage of the Old Testament is there talk of peace between God and people:

Isa. 27:5 "Or let them lay hold of my protection,
          let them make peace with me,
          let them make peace with me."

Neither the text nor its meaning is completely certain. But the repeated couplet "Let them make peace with me" can only be interpreted as a peace agreement with God after surrendering their resistance to him. At the root of this expression is the meaning: shalom = peace as the opposite of war (see above). This meaning was adapted much later (*Apocalypse of Isaiah*) to the relationship between people and God. This usage, taken over into the New Testament (Rom. 5:1), is insignificant for Old Testament shalom speech. Rather, it represents a late modification of the concept, appearing once only.[25]

Summary and Conclusion

The use of the word "shalom" in the Old Testament can be divided into three areas of application. In two of them shalom is spoken of as a contemporary reality, while in the third the talk is about a future shalom. In the first, shalom means wholeness or wellness in a comprehensive sense — that is, the well-being or welfare of the person in community, including all areas of human existence, a healthy human existence in all its possibilities. Essential to this usage is the fact that special areas of existence have not yet become distinct and, above all, that shalom has primarily neither a theological nor a political tone. But it also has no specifically historical point of reference or a salvation history one. Shalom comes about neither through a peace agreement with God nor through a peace agreement between people. Shalom is present where there is a healthy community.

Characteristic for this first area of application is the greeting. Shalom is present there, where the arriving person is received into the sphere of peace by means of a personal encounter in greeting. Shalom is present when a departing person is escorted in peace. It is present where one inquires about another's shalom. Shalom is the wellness of a community and of the people in that community. Trust, responsibility, and a sense of security form an essential part, evident from the words that constitute the language of greeting.

In the second area of use and applicability we see this healthy community especially endangered through war. The threat to the community has now become so severe that shalom becomes a conceptual opposite to war. It is only in this area of application that the contrast of war to peace, as we know it, develops. Here for the first time shalom comes to mean peace in our political sense. And it is precisely here that the shalom concept becomes futurist. To the degree that war threatens to destroy the community as such, peace in this political sense becomes a future hope.

The third area of use refers to peace as something in the future. Here for the first time it attains a specifically theological character. But the broadest and most dominant area of use is the first one, in which shalom has not yet developed into a specifically theological concept. The significance of this fact can be shown by means of a comparison with the words for saving and salvation. Where the text speaks about saving or salvation, Yahweh is in almost all cases spoken of as the savior. Hence the "saving acts" are understood *eo ipso* as the saving acts of Yahweh. For the word "shalom," which in certain contexts can also be translated as salvation (*Heil*), this does not apply in the same way.

Even though the word "shalom" appears especially often and emphatically in the salvation prophecies, it is precisely there that it became uncertain whether the announced salvation was indeed the work of Yahweh. To state it more explicitly, doubt arose whether the salvation prophets were really announcing such well-being in Yahweh's name. Here it becomes evident that shalom can easily and loudly be proclaimed as God's will and action but that such proclamations can also deceive.

In contrast to this, we observe a solid, basic connection to God's action in those instances where a prophet of judgment proclaims the exact opposite of what the shalom prophets are unceasingly shouting: God takes away his shalom from the people. A process was at work that is evident through allusions to it. Already in the Jehu scenario (see above) we could detect some reflection on the fact that shalom no longer accorded with the original meaning, since it no longer encompassed all spheres of life. Jehu says shalom cannot be present where idol worship is practiced simultaneously (the judgment prophets said the same thing later!). Jezebel says that even the most zealous orthodoxy is not true shalom, if it is to be attained through regicide. In the attacks of the writing prophets on the salvation prophets, we detect the same theme of the lost totality of the shalom concept (Jer. 6:14; Ezek. 13:10; etc.).

A change in the concept has occurred by the time Jeremiah, in his words of salvation, and later also Deutero-Isaiah identify the future acts of Yahweh as shalom (salvation). Here finally shalom has become a theological concept in the strict sense. The new healing of the community that they announce is no longer simply identical with welfare. Rather, it means a wellness based on an act of judgment that preceded it; it is wellness through grace. This means that wellness need no longer rely on political power. It is this theologized meaning, a shalom tied to the saving acts of God, that is taken over into the New Testament use of the term.

On the matter of the relationship of the Old Testament shalom to the New Testament *eirene,* the following conclusions are evident. In order to understand what peace meant in the New Testament, we must take into consideration the entire range of meanings of shalom in the Old Testament and the entire history of the concept in the Old Testament. Only on this basis can the specifically New Testament meaning be clarified, which sets it off from that of the Old Testament background, on the one hand, and from the Greek background of the concept, on the other hand. This will show that the New Testament concept of *eirene* is multilayered and that alongside something specifically new, it also retains its heritage.

With regard to the question of the relationship of the biblical word "peace" to the word so widely used among us today, we will see that right through to contemporary usage one level of meaning has remained important: The Hebrew word *shalom* signifies the welfare of persons in community in the most comprehensive meaning of existence.

Notes

1. Cf. the lexica: E. M. Good, in "Peace in the OT," *IDB*, 3:705: "The root meaning of *shalom* seems to be 'completeness, wholeness' (cf. Akkadian *šalāmu*, 'to be faultless, healthy, complete')."
Literature:

> Fritz Bammel, *Die Religionen der Welt und der Friede auf Erden* (Munich: I. & S. Federmann Verlag, 1957).
>
> Wilhelm Caspari, *Vorstellung und Wort "Friede" im Alten Testament* (BFCT 14, 4; Gütersloh: C. Bertelsmann Verlag, 1910).
>
> Walther Eichrodt, *Die Hoffnung des ewigen Friedens im alten Israel* (BFCT 25, 3; Gütersloh: C. Bertelsmann Verlag, 1920).
>
> Heinrich Gross, *Die Idee des ewigen und allgemeinen Weltfriedens im Alten Orient und im Alten Testament* (Trier: Paulinus Verlag, 1956).
>
> Willem Silvester van Leeuwen, *Eirene in het Nieuwe Testament* (Wageningen: H. Veenman, 1940).
>
> E. Neumann, "Frieden als Symbol des Lebens," *Eranos* 27 (1958): 7–50.
>
> J. Nibel, *Der Friedensgedanke des Alten Testaments* (Leipzig, 1914).
>
> Johannes Pedersen, *Israel: Its Life and Culture* (4 vols.; 2nd ed.; London: Oxford University Press, 1946). Vol. 1, esp. ch. 2, pp. 263–335.
>
> Gerhard von Rad, "Shalom in the OT," *TDNT*, 2:402–406 [*TWNT*, 2:400–405].
>
> Joseph Scharbert, "SLM im Alten Testament," in *Lex tua veritas. Festschrift für H. Junker, zur Vollendung des siebzigsten Lebensjahres am 8. August 1961* (ed. Heinrich Gross and F. Mussner; Trier: Paulinus Verlag, 1961), pp. 209–229.
>
> Claus Westermann, "Shalom," *Quatember* 1966/1967, pp. 2–7.
>
> ———. "Frieden, Altes Testament," in *Theologie, VI x 12 Hauptbegriffe* (ed. Claus Westermann; Stuttgart: Kreuz Verlag, 1967), pp. 58–63.

2. Shalom can, however, be linked with *berit*—when through the covenant or agreement shalom is achieved: Josh. 9:15; 1 Kings 5:26; Obadiah 7; with Yahweh as the subject: Ezek. 34:25; 37:26; Isa. 54:10. In several passages one encounters also "peace with"; on that point, see below. But it is not possible to claim that, based on these passages, shalom is to be understood as a "relationship" (*Verhältnisbestimmung*), as does von Rad (*TDNT*, 2:402 [*TWNT*, 2:401]).

See Gerhard von Rad, *Old Testament Theology* (2 vols.; Edinburgh: Oliver & Boyd, 1962), 1:130 [*Theologie des Alten Testaments* (2 vols.; 4th ed.; Munich: Christian Kaiser Verlag, 1962), 1:144]:

A relationship guaranteed by covenant is readily described as shalom (Gen. 26:30ff.; 1 Kings 5:26; Is. 54:10; Job 5:23), for which our word peace can only be regarded as an inadequate equivalent. For shalom designates the unimpairedness, the wholeness of a relationship of communion, and so a state of harmonious equilibrium, the balancing of all claims and needs between two parties. Thus, the making of a covenant is intended to secure a state of intactness, orderliness, and rightness between two parties.

Among others, von Rad bases his claim on J. Begrich, who could say in his article "Berit . . ." (in *Gesammelte Studien zum Alten Testament* [ed. W. Zimmerli; TBü 21; Munich: Chr. Kaiser Verlag, 1964], 55–56): "Generally speaking the content of *berit* is shalom, which the guarantor promises the recipient (Josh. 9:15)," p. 56. Or p. 60: "The content of *berit* remains fundamentally the same. As earlier, it is described through the brevity of shalom (Gen. 26:30; cf. 1 Kgs. 5:26; etc.)."

Walter Zimmerli, relying on von Rad, says about Ezek. 34:25 (*Ezekiel 2* [Hermeneia; Philadelphia: Fortress Press, 1983], p. 220 [*Ezechiel* (BKAT 13/2; Neukirchen-Vluyn: Neukirchener Verlag, 1969), 845]): The word "שלם" ('peace') which is added here (as also in Isa. 54:10) indicates in the first instance the reality of which a covenant in any case consists. Covenant means the establishment of a relationship of well-being between the partners of the covenant (v. Rad, *OT Theology* I, 130). . . . When Yahweh is the covenantal partner, this well-being will extend over the whole sphere of life of the nation and will bring about peace there."

We are not calling into question that in certain passages of the Old Testament *shalom* stands in relationship to *berit;* the scholars quoted above cannot be challenged on that point. The question is, What is the significance of these passages within the overall use of the word *shalom*? There it is clearly evident that in the major groups of passages (see below) shalom is not a "relational concept" (von Rad).

Martin Noth has confirmed this fact through a study in comparative philology. See his article "Old Testament Covenant-Making in the Light of a Text from Mari," in *The Laws in the Pentateuch and Other Studies* (Edinburgh: Oliver & Boyd, 1966), 108–117 ["Das alttestamentliche Bundschliessen im Lichte eines Mari-Textes," in *Gesammelte Studien zum Alten Testament* (TBü 6; 2nd ed.; Munich: Chr. Kaiser Verlag, 1960), 142–154]. In this Mari text the word *salimum* (=reconciliation, agreement) appears in connection with making a covenant:

> There are certain uses of the word *šālôm* in the Old Testament which may very obviously be compared. The formula *salīmam birīt . . . ù . . .* is very similar to the Old Testament *šālôm bên . . . ûbhên* (Judg. 4:17; 1 Sam. 7:14; 1 Kings 5:26). Likewise the phrase *ḥayaram ša salīmim ḳatālum* reminds one immediately of the Old Testament *kārath bĕrîth šālôm* (Ezek. 34:25; 37:26). But most particularly the expression *salīmam . . . aškun* corresponds very closely to the Old Testament phrase *'āśâ šālôm;* this phrase occurs in Isa. 27:5, and especially in Josh. 9:51 where it stands in immediate association

with *kārath běrîth*. In root and meaning the Old Testament *šālôm* certainly expresses the Akkadian *šalāmu/šulmu;* it is possible that *salīmum* also entered into the make-up of the Old Testament *šālôm* at the same time, along the path of the historical relationships between the "West Semites" of Mesopotamia and the Israelite tribes. (P. 113)

If Noth's conjecture is correct, that the two different Akkadian words (coming from the same root!) influenced the usage of the Hebrew *shalom,* then that explains the diversity of meaning. In any case, Noth's research draws attention to a group of usages of *shalom* in the Old Testament that diverges from the major group of usages:

> This seems likely, in view of material found in the Old Testament, since the idiom *'āśâ šālôm* — even if perhaps not so much the use of the word in the expressions *šālôm bên . . . ûbhên,* and *běrîth šālôm* — can only be explained with difficulty and in a forced fashion on the basis of *šālôm's* original equivalence to *šalāmu* (wholeness, welfare, prosperity). Added to this we now have the formula of the Mari texts, which at least sets us the task of testing the use of *šālôm* in the Old Testament to see whether *salīmum* does not lie at the base of some uses of this word. (Pp. 113–114)

Given this evidence, it is no longer possible to treat the group of usages identified by Noth, wherein *shalom* lies close to *berit* in meaning, as the starting point for a general definition of shalom. In the passage quoted above, von Rad draws attention to this passage by Noth in a footnote but does not draw the appropriate conclusion.

3. Von Rad sees something negative in the lack of this usage: "When we consider the rich possibilities of shalom in the OT, we are struck by the negative fact that there is no specific text in which it denotes specifically a spiritual attitude of inward peace" (*TDNT,* 2:406 [*TWNT,* 2:404f.]). Here there appears to be a preconception at work that has been shaped more by the New Testament word *eirene.* To measure the use of the word by the degree to which it is material or spiritual, as von Rad frequently does (e.g., *TWNT,* 2:401, top of p.), or whether it is material or religious (e.g., *TDNT,* 2:403 [*TWNT,* 2:401, middle of p.]), also scarcely fits the Old Testament shalom. What is of decisive importance for shalom, as used in the Old Testament, is that the distinction between the material and the spiritual (religious) does not apply.

4. This all-encompassing meaning of shalom has been especially elaborated by Pedersen (*Israel: Its Life and Culture*): "Peace is the condition of all common life, or if one chooses, identical therewith" (p. 303). "Shalom designates at the same time the entirety, the fact of being whole, and he who is whole" (p. 311). "We see how comprehensive and positive is the meaning of shalom; it expresses every form of happiness and free expansion, but the kernel is the community with others." "Therefore peace comprises all that the Israelite understands by 'good'" (p. 313). "He who has shalom has everything, because it implies all the harmony and

happiness which anyone can take. Therefore peace is the first and last in life" (pp. 313f.).

5. With reference to this passage, Pedersen remarks (*Israel: Its Life and Culture*, 314): "The growth and wellbeing of the body is necessarily implied." Also Isa. 38:17.

6. H.-J. Kraus (*Klagelieder (Threni)* [BKAT 20; Neukirchen-Vluyn: Neukirchener Verlag, 1956], 56) on this passage: "a prosperous, undisturbed and complete life with its poise and assurance." Artur Weiser ("Klagelieder," in *Das Hohe Lied, Klagelieder, Das Buch Esther* [ed. Helmut Ringgren and Artur Weiser; ATD 16/2; Göttingen: Vandenhoeck & Ruprecht, 1958]) interprets *Heil* in its comprehensive sense. Such a theologization of the concept is not what is intended here.

7. B. Duhm (*Das Buch Jesaja* [5th ed.; Göttingen: Vandenhoeck & Ruprecht, 1968], 282) misunderstands the sense of shalom when he translates as follows: "zum Frieden ist bitter mir" ("peace is bitter for me") and treats it as a marginal gloss.

8. H.-J. Kraus (*Psalmen* [BKAT 15/2; Neukirchen-Vluyn: Neukirchener Verlag, 1972], 506): "It was inconceivable that God's goodness intended for the just went to the godless transgressors in the form of all-around good fortune (shalom)."

9. Pedersen (*Israel: Its Life and Culture,* 274): "Peace in the house is a common will and a common responsibility. . . . It is not something which is first created by the goodwill of men; it is given with life."

10. Pedersen has recognized the importance of the greeting in connection with blessing and peace (*Israel: Its Life and Culture,* 203ff.; esp. 202–204). On this point, see Claus Westermann, "Blessing and Greeting in the Old Testament," in *Blessing in the Bible and the Life of the Church* (Philadelphia: Fortress Press, 1978), 59–63 [*Der Segen in der Bibel und im Handeln der Kirche* (Munich: Chr. Kaiser Verlag, 1968), 61–64]; a short summary of Pedersen, pp. 24–26.

11. Pedersen (*Israel: Its Life and Culture,* 303): "It (*die Erkundigungs-frage*) is the decisive question, because peace is the condition of all common life, or, if one chooses, identical therewith."

12. The text is uncertain. A textual reconstruction of the text from the Septuagint makes it appear likely that the intended meaning is: "They were no longer able to speak shalom to him," that is, could no longer greet him. Cf. Claus Westermann, "Die Joseph-Erzählung," in *Calwer Predigthilfen* 5 (ed. H. Breit and C. Westermann; Stuttgart: Calwer Verlag, 1966), 34. H. Gunkel and von Rad in their commentaries on the passage do not even consider this possibility.

13. On these two passages, Benno Jacob, *Das erste Buch der Tora, Genesis* (Berlin: Schocken Verlag, 1934), 559. He does not quite catch the meaning when he understands peace in this case as reconciliation: "He [Jacob] is the first person, who experiences hatred, jealousy and enemies; but because he is a good son blessed of God, who has fostered

his ways, we also encounter here for the first time the word peace, reconciliation with opponents."

14. For our contemporary search for peace, this seems to me to be of special importance. Our use of the word suffers from a tendency to usurpation, either by political, social, or religious peace, in which each of these spheres makes totalitarian claims on peace. It would be in order to ask whether such a totalitarian claim makes any sense at all. Here, in any case, we encounter the word "peace" used in such a fashion that peace is acknowledged only where existence in all of its aspects was a healthy one.

15. Pedersen (*Israel: Its Life and Culture,* 311): "In the olden times peace is not in itself the opposite of war. . . . One has 'peace' in the fight when one conquers the enemy."

16. Pedersen (*Israel: Its Life and Culture,* 316–329) emphasizes this at length and then develops the idea of a transition in the understanding of peace as a result of this. He tries to identify a Canaanization of the peace concept in the sense of the influence of Canaanite notions of rulership, which resulted in a strongly negative shift in meaning of the word. I do not find the evidence very persuasive.

17. Cf. Preface, above.

18. Claus Westermann, "Jesaja 48 und die 'Bezeugung gegen Israel,'" in *Studia biblica et semitica. Festschrift für Th. C. Vriezen* (ed. M. A. Beek; Wageningen: H. Veenman, 1966), 356–366.

19. On the salvation oracles, see J. Begrich, "Das priesterliche Heilsorakel," *ZAW* (1934): 81–92 (reprinted in *Gesammelte Studien zum Alten Testament* [ed. W. Zimmerli; TBü 21; Munich: Chr. Kaiser Verlag, 1964], 217–231); idem, *Studien zu Deuterojesaja* (ed. W. Zimmerli; TBü 20; Munich: Chr. Kaiser Verlag, 1963); Claus Westermann, *Sprache und Struktur der Prophetie Deuterojesajas* (TBü 24; Munich: Chr. Kaiser Verlag, 1964, 117–120); and on this, *EvT* 7 (1964): 355–373. There is still a great lack of clarity on the salvation oracle in worship. In all likelihood, one needs to distinguish a promise of salvation, as spoken in a time of severe need, from the promise of blessing and peace.

20. On prophecies of salvation, see S. Herrmann, *Die prophetischen Heilserwartungen im Alten Testament: Ursprung und Gestaltswandel* (ed. K. H. Rengstorf and L. Rost; BWANT 85; Stuttgart: Verlag W. Kohlhammer, 1965).

21. It is good to keep in mind that this "peace of God" is not intended to distinguish between a godly and a human, worldly peace! Just as in earlier speech, here too it means wellness. It is just that in this situation of crisis it is expressly described as that which God did, which wholeness rests on God's action, because the termination of such a wholeness is to be shown as God's judgment.

22. These three passages are of particular importance in understanding shalom in the Old Testament. They show that the wellness intended is not tied to given political or religious structures. The state has broken

down, the cultus has broken down, but the potential for shalom has not yet collapsed!

23. On Isa. 53:3, see my commentary, *Isaiah 40–66: A Commentary* (OTL; London: SCM Press, 1969) [*Das Buch Jesaja: Kapitel 40–66* (ATD 19; Göttingen: Vandenhoeck & Ruprecht, 1966)].

24. The connection between shalom and blessing was already seen by F. Horst, *Segen und Segenshandlungen in der Bibel* (ed. H. S. Wolff; TBü 12; Munich: Chr. Kaiser Verlag, 1961), 188–202: "The summary word for such a content (of blessing) is shalom" (p. 194), "the concept of shalom as the essence of the most proper blessing" (p. 195). But this is too generalized, for he virtually equates the two concepts: "All of that is shalom, and all of that is Yahweh's blessing" (p. 195); both concepts are, for him, *eo ipso* theological concepts, both of which "lead to a deepening and internalization." If we are to relate *beraka* and shalom to each other, as intended in the Old Testament, then we need to start with the assumption that blessing is the basic meaning, since it has the capacity to bear fruit. Blessing is the capacity for fruitfulness (Gen. 1:28, "Be fruitful and multiply"). The power of the blessing extends on into the generations, as the capacity of passing on life entrusted from God to the next generation. This power of blessing in the vertical sexual line corresponds with shalom as the power that achieves on the horizontal line of community the health and welfare of this community (beginning with the siblings from a common father and mother, as in the Joseph story).

25. Cf. note 2 above.

3

The Jerusalem Conceptions of Peace and Their Development in the Prophets of Ancient Israel[1]

Odil Hannes Steck

In the search for Old Testament passages apparently relevant to the current discussion of the possibilities for world peace,[2] the cultic tradition from preexilic Jerusalem, whose impact continued even into the early Christian era, seems especially fruitful. This is so because there we find detailed conceptualizations of universal peace and of its prerequisites. But to discover the nature of these concepts one must work not only with the history of ideas approach but also with a more comprehensive conceptual historical method. This method must trace out the originality, the development, and the theological-historical impact of specific theological concepts.[3]

At present, however, such a study of the peace concepts of the Jerusalem cultic tradition is necessarily circumscribed by the absence of most of the preliminary specialized research. Research has barely begun even for a composite picture of the cultic tradition of preexilic Jerusalem, and it is still subject to debate.[4] In addition, little has been written on the history of tradition using the postexilic sources. Hence, a synthesizing survey of the historical impact of the Jerusalem cultic tradition still awaits us. In the light of the current state of research and the research possibilities, the essay that follows can be scarcely more than a thematic sketch of the overall phenomenon utilizing selected individual examples,

Translation of "Jerusalemer Vorstellungen vom Frieden und ihre Abwandlungen in der Prophetie des Alten Israel," in *Frieden — Bibel — Kirche* (ed. Liedke), 75–95.

knowing that these will be subject to further testing as to thoroughness and completeness in the specialized research of the future.

We must also acknowledge a more tangible barrier to a full characterization of the conceptualization undertaken here, namely, the fact that its historical-political impact in Israel is essentially unknown.[5] This lack is due not merely to the sources but must be accounted for as being inherent in the subject: the mediation of hopes and concepts through demands for real concrete political action did not emerge only today. The problem already existed in the original context of these documents.

Jerusalem Concepts of Peace

The Sources and the Idea of a Jerusalem Cultic Tradition

What is meant by the Jerusalem cultic tradition is the global, self-contained, theological conception that forms the basis for much of the psalms. The essential elements are articulated liturgically by adding to or drawing from this conception in a kind of reciprocal fashion. This is especially evident in the Psalms of Zion, the Creation Psalms, and the Yahweh-king and Royal Psalms.

That this conception was already significant for the cult in preexilic Jerusalem is evident from the dating of the psalms, or at least from the elements of tradition passed down through them. It can also be seen by hindsight through the references to it in Isaiah and in Deutero-Isaiah of the exile. Here also we find the most important sources for the preexilic form of the conception. Numerous detailed studies in the history of tradition also indicate that the major substantive elements of this conception were transmitted from the Canaanite culture, or even from ancient Near Eastern cultures via the Canaanites. This leads us to assume that we are dealing with an Israelite modification of this religious conception, stemming from the time of Jebusite Jerusalem, when Jerusalem came into the political and cultic possession of Israel.[6]

Even in the preexilic time of the kings, this Jerusalem cultic tradition was only one theological conception among others. It was the theology of the city of Jerusalem. It must be distinguished from the conceptions that governed the pre-Davidic Israelite tradition that dominated in the land of Judea and, above all, the Northern Kingdom.

A Schematic Conceptual Framework for
the Jerusalem Peace Statements

The unique character of the Jerusalem concept becomes evident only when we set aside the apparently constitutive element of the religion of ancient Israel — that Yahweh is the God of twelve tribes of Israel and that Israel is the people of Yahweh. Central to the Jerusalem conception is not the relationship of Yahweh to Israel but the connectedness of Yahweh with a certain mountain, with a certain city, Zion.

The key to the structure of the Jerusalem cultic tradition lies in the fundamental understanding that Zion is the mountain of God, the mountain of the world where the earthly and heavenly spheres intersect. This place above all others thereby relates to the world as a whole. On top of this mountain Yahweh sits enthroned as king of the world, as Lord of heaven and earth. Jerusalem, the city on this mountain, is quite simply God's city, God's residence. Correspondingly, the scope of action of this Yahweh of Zion is *eo ipso* not merely the land of Israel but the world as a whole. It applies not merely to the people of Israel, and to the neighboring nations and the individual [current] enemy nations, but to the world of nations *in toto*. The world of the cosmos, the world of the nations, and Zion-Jerusalem as residence are from the very beginning the essential arena for God. Added to this, then, is the city-kingdom of Jerusalem as the constitutive mediating point for the universal acts of Yahweh of Zion. The following comments seek to develop this briefly.

The basic action of Yahweh of Zion consists in the continuous stabilization and sustenance of the entire world as a planned, ordered totality, which Yahweh brought into being in a single act and whose existence Yahweh continues to maintain as a restraint of chaos. This world-sustaining, universal, world-creative power of Yahweh of Zion is continuously experienced in one's awareness of life and environment (*Lebensraum*). It is seen actually effective in the historical events of early Israel[7] as well as in the fate of the individual.[8]

The establishment and sustenance of the cosmic order, which in this context represents the *opus proprium* of Yahweh, making Yahweh lord of the entire earth,[9] corresponds to an appropriate action in the historical-political sphere. Here the essential relationship of Yahweh of Zion to the world of humanity, to the world of the nations as a totality, is based on the argument, on the one hand, that the earth and all life on it are the work and possession of their creator, Yahweh.[10] On the other hand, it is based on an initial act of battle analogous to the cosmic battle against chaos, in which Yahweh subdued to his lordship the world of the nations that had risen up against Yahweh in Yahweh's city. We see this in the well-known battle of the nations motif[11] which is quite definitely preexilic,[12] and very likely was already part of the pre-Israelite Jebusite strand of the conception. This world-sustaining action of Yahweh in the historical-political sphere, Yahweh's rule over all the nations,[13] serves as an all-encompassing safeguard for the realization of full justice for humanity. This notion emerges in particular in statements about Yahweh as a world judge who seeks a just order that includes the very marginalized of human society.[14]

This all-encompassing cosmic action of Yahweh of Zion relies above all, according to the conception of the Jerusalem cultic tradition, in addition to the heavenly instruments of power, on the king of Jerusalem (the royal court). According to this view, the Davidic kingdom serves as regency for Yahweh's worldly kingdom. The king both guarantees and executes the action of the Creator God whose results are blessing and fruitfulness in nature.[15] Yahweh has granted to him the lordship and power over the world of the nations;[16] he is the preserver of divine justice.[17] Hence, the Jerusalem king is no mere tribal or national king. He is quite simply the central earthly figure of the cosmos, the governor for this divine king on Zion who has brought forth this cosmos and who keeps watch over its ongoing existence.

This conception of the Jerusalem cultic tradition is an articulation of experience using those conceptual means, with fundamental Israelite modifications (Yahweh alone is God, limits on mythical thinking, and kingly office), that one finds in other monarchical cultures of the ancient Near East. The fundamental experience, as it shows through here, is the sense of living in an ordered and life-affirming world, of humans surrounded by the orderliness of the natural-cosmic sphere, to which the political-social spheres must also conform if chaos is to be prevented. In order to recognize order as necessity for life in one's own world, which is what the Jerusalem conception seeks to speak to in its universal content, the decisive issue, in contrast to our manner of asking the question, is not the problem of empirical verifications of such worldwide qualifications. What is decisive, rather, is the enduring presupposition that the world before one's eyes, in which one lives, both in its cosmic-natural as well as in its historical-political and legal-social dimensions, must remain the daily subject of attention of God on high. This attention is necessary so that it can be both formed and preserved in its entirety as a healthy (*heilvoll*), chaos-hindering bulwark for existence. Accordingly, it is doubtful that the differences, striking for us, between the universal-historical-political statements and the observed empirical reality were recognized in the self-understanding of this conception and its representatives.[18]

The fact that this conception appears in the sources without any effort to process significant experiences contradictory to it points to the early, peaceful period of the monarchy in which the positive experiences of the greater kingdom of David were still influential. This conclusion is also suggested by the intellectual and cultural consequences of the Israelization of Jerusalem. With reference to the experience of the natural-cosmic order, of the invincibility of Zion, the Jerusalemites found weighty experiential indicators for this conception in the greater Davidic kingdom. Tension apparently does not lie between claim and reality but in the reality itself. What is given in Yahweh of Zion and his acts will come to pass universally in the historical-political sphere. Or more pointedly stated: it is not a discrepancy in reality itself but rather a discrepancy in the experience of it that is allowed in statements of the Jerusalem cultic tradition.

That the elimination of such discrepancies can be done only by God is self-evident, according to the structuring of this entire conception. It is significant that the king is not called upon to eliminate such differences in the world of the nations by violent, military-expansionist means. The king's power remains tied to Yahweh and the power delegated by Yahweh. Its effectiveness is assumed or is prayed for in individual lamentations only when Zion (Psalm 46!), the king (Psalm 2), or the supplicant (individual lamentation) is threatened. Prayer is never for the total realization of universal lordship, which has already been established by Yahweh on Zion.

Let us now examine more closely the concepts of peace that are part of the Jerusalem conception.

Concepts of Peace

To see and experience the cosmic-natural world entity as a life-fostering realm established and preserved by Yahweh (characteristic of the conception of the Jerusalem cultic tradition) requires one to include a corresponding quality for the historical-political-social sphere. That this sphere also is viewed as a comprehensive life-affirming sphere established by Yahweh must be kept in mind when we examine the notion of peace contained in the Jerusalemite conception of the world. Also, the peace theme itself and the various individual notions of it stem from ancient Near Eastern cultures.[19] Here we must emphasize that the pre-Israelite transmission of this material as well as the Israelite-Jerusalem modifications of its meaning has scarcely been researched.

THE JEBUSITE-JERUSALEM BACKGROUND

According to the studies of F. Stolz, although there are only a few recognizable traces in the Old Testament,[20] there is nevertheless good reason to believe that the concept of shalom, aside from being a peace concept, was anchored firmly in the religion of pre-Israelite Jerusalem, insofar as it was linked with the god Shalem who was revered there, as is suggested by the name Jerusalem. Indicators for this, according to Stolz,[21] are that one can detect at times in the word *shalom,* as used in the Old Testament, a personified entity,[22] which is linked in striking fashion to *tsedeq,* the power behind a healthy, just world order, and which was also originally a divine figure.[23] In addition, as does *tsedeq,*[24] shalom frequently appears in firm connection with Jerusalem.[25] If in this connection we seek to discover the meaning of this shalom, for which the God of Shalem stands and which God creates, then, on the basis of the link to the universal world order power *tsedeq,* we can presume that it may refer to an all-encompassing fully intact condition of well-being, especially within the confines of the Jerusalem city-state that formed the circle of those honoring this city god.

Further, the Old Testament also seems to suggest that fruitfulness[26] and saving help in the face of threatening enemy nations[27] were integral parts of the shalom condition guaranteed and maintained by this god. In connection with Israelite acceptance of the Jebusite traditions of Jerusalem, the city deities were suppressed in part, and in part they became traits of Yahweh on Zion. That in the cultic traditions of Israelite Jerusalem the concept of shalom retreats into the background more than does the concept of *tsedeq* could have to do with the divinity of Shalem, who exhibited essential traits that could not be absorbed into the Yahweh religion (chthonic character, necromancy, and child offerings).

ELABORATIONS OF THE CONCEPT IN THE
CULTIC TRADITION OF ISRAELITE JERUSALEM

Even if the concept of shalom recedes in the Jerusalem cultic tradition for the reasons just given, its content, related to the content and associations of our word "peace," is still fully there. In qualitative terms, the Jerusalem conception of the world before one's eyes — one that appears as an ordered, life-affirming, global whole — is a world at peace. In other words, the Jerusalem cultic tradition does not begin with a world to be pacified but with one that is at peace. In terms of content, peace is seen here as that natural condition of an all-around sense of well-being[28] within the political-historical-social sphere which enables and fosters life. As the effectiveness of Yahweh of Zion and Yahweh's kings in Jerusalem demonstrate, this includes a stable world as environment (*Lebensraum*), the fruitfulness of the soil and the cattle, and the absence of a military threat, just as it includes social "justice." This justice assures the well-being of endangered social groups (widows and orphans), as it does also the well-being of individuals in all aspects. This situation is in accord with a natural-cosmic world order.[29]

At the same time, we must recognize that this does not allow us to speak here simply in terms of world peace as in common usage. In spite of their universal dimensions, these peace concepts are all centered on Zion/Jerusalem. It is the Jerusalem world which is organized for peace, and for it alone is the necessary unity of all aspects of peace regarded as a given. To the degree that the world is organized for the peace of Jerusalem, and to the degree that it fits into this peaceful order, the world as such has peace.

In such a manner the peace granted the Jerusalem world is the work of Yahweh, in terms of both its origin and its survival. It is based on the absolute sovereignty of Yahweh, God most high on Zion, the mountain of God. It is based also on the wisdom and life-fostering quality of God's ordering of the world and on God's rule over the nations. Both the presupposition and contingency of the quality peace in the world are, in equal measure, the fundamental assumption for the conception of peace and the experience of peace in Jerusalem.

When there is abundance on earth, Yahweh on Zion is giving expression to deeds of creation and sustenance. When wars are avoided on earth, specifically within the world horizons of Jerusalem, that shows that Yahweh on Zion to whom the earth and all the nations on it belong has the power to break up rebellions worldwide. It is Yahweh who "has wrought desolations in the earth. He makes wars cease to the end of the earth; he breaks the bow, and shatters the spear, he burns the chariots with fire!" (Ps. 46:8b–9). As guarantee behind Yahweh stands here, as indeed everywhere, Yahweh's nature as victor over the chaos of nations[30] that rose up against Yahweh and, in a positive sense, Yahweh's coming universal rule over all the nations.[31] This reign will show itself in a worldwide health-giving and just order. The same applies to the experience of the nation domestically and even to the lives of individuals.

Wherever peace in this comprehensive sense reigns in the world, it is the result of the order established and maintained for the world by Yahweh. That this worldwide concept of peace is linked to the God of Jerusalem is grounded in the fact that God is seen as the creator and Lord of the entire world. To use contemporary terms, this is clearly a "positive peace." One might also mention here the dynamic, associative conceptual aspect when one thinks of the peace-fostering contact of Yahweh with the world and of the implicit, factual recognition of a Yahwistic peace in the world. If, in view of this peace quality of the world, we raise the question of the *participation of the people* in it, it follows that this question can in no way be related directly to our initial question about the degree to which world peace is attainable. Since, according to the Jerusalem conception, world peace as a gift of Yahweh is already present, people can participate positively in it only when they help to preserve that peace by daily conforming to the divine order of peace which Yahweh has given the world.

Thus the king must, especially in domestic policy, enforce a justice that is life-affirming.[32] At the same time, however, through an act of ritual he also warns the nations that they not overstep their position in Yahweh's peaceful order.[33] For Yahweh's people, daily conformity to this peaceful order calls for appropriate behavior both toward Yahweh and toward the surrounding society. Concrete examples of what this means positively are found in "entrance liturgies,"[34] and the negative can be inferred from cases of violation of peace in the social sphere, which are articulated in the laments of individuals. Finally, there are statements calling the nations to join in the coronation shout for Yahweh.[35] Similarly, the supremacy of the Jerusalem king, grounded in Yahweh,[36] is articulated in statements about tribute payments by the nations[37] or a recognition of their status.

Naturally, the difference between this conception and the current realities was not hidden in the Jerusalem tradition. Such experiences of discrepancy, of the disturbances to and surrender of the world-encompassing divine peaceful order, are taken into consideration in the Jerusalem cultic tradition in a specific and characteristic way.

These differences are portrayed in the sphere of the individual and the individual's social interactions. The difference between one's personal fate in a situation of need, accident, sickness, or injustice, and how to cope with them, and the universal ordering of Yahweh in the world are the substance of countless songs of lamentation and thanksgiving by individuals. These songs point to the resolution of the difference and the returning of one's individual fate to Yahweh's world of peace. This may well include, in the case of a disturbance of the peace by a foreign factor, violent acts intended to eliminate the transgressor.

This aspect of a foreign agent also plays a role where the peace of the kingdom of Jerusalem and of its state apparatus is threatened. Here too, the kingly lamentations for a restoration of peace for the Jerusalem world are an appeal to Yahweh. And the resolution of this difference is seen either in that Yahweh grants the king victory over and destruction of the enemy[38] or (and this is the overarching aspect) that Yahweh of Zion alone masters the threat.[39]

It is striking that the phenomenon of a power in revolt, as the explanation for the difference between concept and reality, is invoked only when it is an uprising against the order of things within the state territory of Jerusalem or against the city and the person of the king. Thus Psalm 46, with reference to the return of cosmic chaos that would bring Jerusalem to collapse (vs. 3–4, 5f.) and with reference to the nations storming the city (vs. 6, 9–11), points to Yahweh's own power as sole defense, which gives to Jerusalem the quality of an invincible fortress. Similarly, Psalm 2, a cultic song for the enthroning of the king, which begins with the possibility of an uprising of the nations that have been subordinated to Yahweh and the king, proclaims Davidic rulership as administrator of Yahweh's world empire (vs. 6, 7–9) and tries to keep the world of nations from such a scheme, so that they would not fall victim to the wrath of Yahweh (vs. 10–12)![40] This indicates that disturbances to the universal peace created by Yahweh are seen as a possibility only, as a threat by the nations to the existence of the city and kingdom in Jerusalem. But in this case the powerful and quite violent preservation of peace against such an uprising is anchored solely in Yahweh. It is Yahweh who is at work in the defensive military actions of the king, should such actions be considered at all. When Jerusalem in particular is considered threatened, then such actions are absent.

Correspondingly, this applies to points of discrepancy with reference to the domain of Yahweh in the world of the nations and with reference to the world supremacy of the Jerusalem king. The full recognition that in reality he is not acknowledged through acts of subordination to him by the nations is indeed shown in the latent danger expected from the nations of the world. Yet this is not treated as an element disturbing the peace that needs to be confronted.

These statements obviously belong to a time in which they co-incided with the world of experience so closely that they can be considered realistic for the Jerusalem world, without needing to be seen as predicting the future. That Yahweh first needs to realize his and his king's sovereignty over the world is nowhere stated explicitly. The world supremacy of both Yahweh and the king, cultically proclaimed by the nations, permeates the Jerusalem world. There are no statements that would empower the Jerusalem king to make his world supremacy and that of his God felt through the use of political-military power. This emphasis is missing not merely because the Jerusalem kings, in point of fact, did not have such political-military power but essentially because, according to the Jerusalem view, the universal supremacy of Yahweh remained fully in the power of Yahweh. The king shared in that power, but he remained subordinate to Yahweh.

As a point of disagreement with H. P. Schmidt,[41] we can state that peace, as understood in the Jerusalem conception, does not serve simply to stabilize the existing Jerusalem dominance or its claims to it. Rather, it reveals a basic difference because of the persistent anchoring of peace in Yahweh as well as by binding the realization of peace to Yahweh. Yet it is an achievable order of living, and of living together meaningfully, which accords with a healthy ordering of the stars, an order to which one must conform, to which also the divinely instituted Davidic kingdom belongs. Peace is that encompassing condition established by Yahweh of Zion, and, for the sake of Yahweh's city and king, it is also defended with violence. It is the condition that makes life on earth in the political-social sphere possible. It preserves well-being in that it includes the social strata of a monarchical and city culture and the preservation of social strata that seem especially endangered.

Unfortunately, much too little has come down to us about life, experience, and faith in Jerusalem at the time of the kings to deter-mine on the basis of a concrete situation the impact of this conception on the kingdom and on the population. However, the traditions in Isaiah and later Jeremiah allow for some limited inferences.

It is possible for us to assume, however, that the Jerusalem cultic tradition with its conception of peace had an illuminating impact on the worldview and experience of the Jerusalemites as long as they were faced with a nonthreatening foreign political situation, and as long as domestically social injustices on a major scale had not yet become evident, and as long as partial differences between the experienced world of the kingdom and the life of the individual could still be contained through the institution of laments. This points to the time period from David on into the eighth century B.C.

But one detects major shifts during the eighth century in the experiences that had until then buttressed the concept. The state of Judea with its capital city, Jerusalem, came under serious threat through the expanding foreign empires around them. Finally, at the end of the period of the monarchy, at the beginning of the sixth century, it suffered the destruction and collapse of virtually all those manifestations within which the content of the conception would have made sense. We can discover the reaction of the Jerusalem cultic tradition to these *transformations* from the Jerusalem prophecies of salvation with their use of the key word "shalom,"[42] from the lamentation liturgies of the Jerusalem cultic prophecies of the late preexilic period,[43] and also, in the light of the collapse in the sixth century, from the Jerusalem popular songs of lamentation of that period.[44] In the popular songs of lamentation, what has happened is that even within the Jerusalem cultic tradition the realization of the idea of Yahweh making universal peace in the world has been separated into a phase belonging to the past and to an event in the future when peace will be restored. Here the Jerusalem cultic tradition has opened itself to a perspective that was already present long before in the prophecy of Isaiah. To this transformation of the Jerusalem peace concept in Isaiah and in the exilic and postexilic periods we now turn by means of selected illustrations.

Transformations of the Jerusalem Concept of Peace in Ancient Israelite Prophecy

Isaiah

Isaiah, who was active during the second half of the eighth century, found himself in a situation that already called into question the understandings of his hometown, Jerusalem, because of the world political events that had affected Judea and Israel. By virtue of his origins and education, Isaiah was grounded in the Jerusalem conception. Nevertheless, as Yahweh enlightened him about the current historical relations, he modified the concept at essential points.

First of all, the danger to the old royal territory of David and its Israelite population, through the expansion of Assyria, activated a sense of Greater Israel and Judea as a single people, which included some special ancient Israelite traditions (from the time of the Judges). This Greater Israel idea, somewhat alien to the Jerusalem tradition, allows us to understand Isaiah's comments about the Northern Kingdom. Also the fact that the Jerusalem universalistic conception recedes because of the threatening nations (Assyria and Egypt) is closely connected with current events. But the universal conception remains an assumption to the degree that Yahweh's sovereign behavior toward the nations on the political stage expresses Yahweh's sovereignty over the nations of the world, which the Jerusalem tradition expresses.

However, the concept of the universal pacification of the nations has been changed, at least as it applies to Jerusalem and its king, into a horrifying view of the chaos of nations being given free rein by Yahweh to storm Judea and its Jerusalem population.[45] Peace secured by violence, which, according to the Jerusalem tradition, Yahweh promises for Jerusalem, now becomes, according to the political events of the day, a violent action against Judea and its capital. A peace created by Yahweh is reversed into a war set in motion by Yahweh.

Relying on a critical application of the Jerusalem conception, Isaiah explains that the basis for such judgment is the current situation. By their own deeds the kingdom with its bureaucracy in Jerusalem, and even the population itself, calls into question Yahweh's protective power for Zion and the kingdom, which had been so praised in the Jerusalem concept.[46] Further, both the kingdom[47] with its bureaucracy[48] and the population[49] have trod underfoot the peace of domestic social justice which Yahweh had established. Here it becomes clear that although humans are unable on their own to produce the peace that Yahweh has created for the world and that Yahweh has preserved on behalf of Jerusalem, they have the capacity to hinder such a peace and destroy it. This possibility for the nations in the Jerusalem cultic tradition itself is now extended by Isaiah to the king and to the population of Jerusalem and Judea. Because of their hindrance of the divine order of peace, Yahweh now turns that peace into judgment, and indeed in a fashion that — with the exception perhaps of the final words of Isaiah — the destruction falls on those who are responsible for the peaceful order but who have been corrupted.[50]

However, the necessary divine initiation of peace itself is not surrendered. Zion/Jerusalem as the place for the realization of a wholesome justice through a civil service,[51] as the residence and city of Yahweh[52] and as a kingdom divinely established,[53] are preserved. These notions form the starting point for the Isaianic *expectation* — indeed the prophecy — of a peace that will be reestablished after Yahweh's judgment.

The view that peace is the creation and work of Yahweh conforms to the basic fact that peace does not require human action and effort. Rather, it is the expectation of a divine action, which, after removal of those elements which serve to hinder an all-encompassing sense of well-being, will restore peace. That happens through a successful defense against the nations that rise up against Jerusalem and against Yahweh.[54] It occurs through the granting of a new bureaucracy to Jerusalem as the place for a wholesome justice to be realized, which is committed to a new social justice (Isa. 1:21–26). And finally it happens also through the reestablishment of the Davidic kingdom, as promised in Isa. 11:1–5. The new David who is to come will bring about general well-being to the domestically cancerous Jerusalem-Judea society, even to those who are powerless and legally marginalized. He will bring life-giving justice and incorruptibility, which had been missing from the previous peace. What is striking, in view of the negative experiences that had resulted in judgment, is that this guarantee of domestic peace through justice, which is the thematic focus of this prophecy, draws after it an increase in the apparatus supporting the institution of kingship, as the six expressions of Yahweh's Spirit resting on the king show (11:2).

Once again, the establishment of peace, in which Isaiah tends to focus on the current situation and gives a critique of the domestic relations of the Judaic state, is entirely Yahweh's work. Hence Isaiah reveals a fundamental break with the content of the Jerusalem tradition. The peace that the Jerusalem conception of the world regarded as inherently present for the eyes of the world to see has become, in a world of unpeace and judgment, something to anticipate from a new divine creation.

The peace expectation as stated in the prophecy of Isa. 9:1–6 is somewhat different. It stems, in all likelihood, from the time of Isaiah but not from Isaiah himself. It is a prophecy of salvation that presumably comes from a time shortly after 701 B.C. when large sections of Judea were cut off by Assyria. Here is, *expressis verbis,* a shift away from the vision of a definitive, constant, and continuous salvation (v. 6). Peace as understood in its comprehensive sense forms the content, and this peace is once again based solely on the initiative power of Yahweh, who is the subject of the entire story in Isaiah 9. What is anticipated here is the restitution of the peace according to the Jerusalem concept of peace in its unlimited timelessness and universal scope.[55] This condition of peace comes about in that Yahweh successfully overthrows the invaders who prevent peace (vs. 2–4) and enthrones a Davidic king, to whom is given the universal rule as a regime of peace. Among others, he bears the title of "Lord of Peace (*Heils*)" which refers both to the external peace vis-à-vis the enemy (cf. vs. 3f.) and to the fulfillment of justice and right in his administration (cf. v. 6).

Examples from the Exilic and Postexilic Periods

Continuities with the Jerusalem peace concept that take into consideration the concrete factors and experiences before one's eyes can be identified in many and sundry ways,[56] even in the exilic and postexilic periods. Here, as we did initially, we must emphasize that research on the history of tradition and theology is still lacking to such a degree that we will need to make do with intimations based on isolated examples.

What is important to note, first of all, is that apparently in the postexilic period a restitution of the Jerusalem concept of peace in its original sense has become the standard for evaluating *contemporary* reality. But now it is the Babylonian and, especially, the Persian emperor of the world who has taken the place of the Davidic monarch in the Jerusalem concept. This can be shown through an analysis of the point of view of the *chronicler's* work and the *Daniel legend.* Nevertheless this viewpoint also falls prey to a new crisis during the confusion of the Diadoche period.[57]

On the other hand, there are continuities with the Jerusalem concept of peace in the form of expectations that serve implicitly to qualify the current conditions, since such a peace is not yet realized and thus makes them the stage on which the announced Yahwistic action will fall in the future.

In this regard we think first of all of Deutero-Isaiah. With this prophet of the exile, who is thoroughly imbued with the Jerusalem cultic tradition, we encounter the concept of shalom as [the standard of the] everlasting condition of salvation, which Yahweh is about to establish for Israel and which also includes the nations.[58] Two aspects are particularly significant in his peace expectation. In the first place, this condition of peace is preserved in the end solely by Yahweh without the use of any concrete political institutions. In this connection, the Davidic kingdom as an institution is replaced by Yahweh as the only king residing on Zion.[59] Second, with reference to the world of the nations, the establishment of a worldwide peace shows more detailed reflection. Babylon the oppressor will be overthrown by Cyrus under order of Yahweh, in an action that is temporally and materially limited.[60] But the nations of the world are to recognize through Yahweh and Yahweh's actions toward Israel that Yahweh alone is God.[61] In this, Israel functions passively as a royal witness (Isa. 43:12f.; 55:50) while this task is carried out actively by the proclamation of God's servant (42:1–4; 49:1–6) who proclaims to the nations Yahweh's all-encompassing just and life-giving order (42:1, 4!). This order consists above all in the knowledge of Yahweh as the only true God.[62]

Thus, Deutero-Isaiah states for the first time that the world peace that Yahweh is to bring not only depends on the superior power of God on high but also requires a basis of common insight and understanding on the part of the people. Accordingly, Deutero-Isaiah no longer needs to draw on the traditional theme of the war of nations to expound the inviolability of a revived Jerusalem. He does indeed refer to it but reshapes it into potential individual attacks that are doomed to failure (Isa. 54:11–17). In its stead, there now emerges the expectation of a pilgrimage of the nations to Zion, in which the preexilic promises that applied to the Davidic kingdom (Ps. 72:9–11) now apply to a Zion, embellished with royal traits, that has become the residence of Yahweh (Isa. 49:22f.; 45:14).

In this connection we may now turn to that classic text in the Old Testament, the peaceable kingdom of Isa. 2:2–4. This passage, in my judgment, can in no way be attributed to Isaiah because, quite unlike Isaiah, the writer starts with the assumption that Zion *has still to become* the mount of God. Further, it presumes the catastrophe of Jerusalem in 587 B.C. as well as Deutero-Isaiah's conception of a pilgrimage of the nations prompted by their insight that Yahweh alone is God.

We begin with a translation of the passage:

> [2]It shall come to pass in the latter days / that the mountain of the house of the LORD / shall be established on the summit of the mountain, / and shall be raised above the hills; / and all the nations shall flow to it,
>
> [3]and many peoples shall come, and say: / "Come, let us go up to the mountain of Yahweh, / to the house of the God of Jacob; / that he may teach us his ways / and that we may walk in his paths." / For

out of Zion shall go forth the instruction, / and the word of Yahweh from Jerusalem.

[4]He shall arbitrate between the nations, / and shall decide for many peoples; / and they shall beat their swords into plowshares, / and their spears into pruning hooks; / nation shall not lift up sword against nation, / neither shall they learn war any more.

Here the pacification (*Befriedung*) of the nations is no mere aspect of a comprehensive conception but consitutes the thematic center of the text. At the outset this prophecy is not directed simply toward the end of the world; rather, it presents a view of the future described as a time of well-being which is coming and will remain. In doing so, it recites a succession of events that are thoroughly founded on the Jerusalem cultic tradition but reworks them critically. The universal pacification of the world, which is not yet reality and the effect of which will be shaped by it, is once again put into effect solely by Yahweh. The entire chain of events is triggered when Zion finally becomes what it always had been and remains in the Jerusalem cultic tradition; the temple mountain will be fully anchored over the chaotic flood and will become the world mountain (cf., over against that, the present predication in Psalms 46; 48). The nations will become aware of this and as a result stream toward this world mountain. In this way, this prophecy converts the traditional notion of an attack of the nations on Zion into its positive opposite (cf. "streams," used metaphorically in v. 2).

This departure of the nations [for Zion], which leads to their pacification, is therefore dependent on an event of Yahweh, which has as its result the universal perception (cf. Deutero-Isaiah) that Zion has become the world mountain of God! The goal of the nations setting out for Zion is to receive justice and counsel from Yahweh, the one who showed himself to be the world ruler through the raising up of Zion. Here again what was a present predication in the Jerusalem cultic tradition (Pss. 48:10f.; 76:9f.) now stands as a future event. What allows the nations to stream toward Zion is not the desire for a resolution of the conflicts among themselves but rather, as v. 3 shows, something more sweeping. They are seeking the wholesome life order of Yahweh. Verse 4 applies this to the phenomenon of war where the absence of such an order of life was most noticeable.[63]

In this prophecy, therefore, war serves thematically as the highest exponential indicator for lack of peace in the world. Therefore the conditions for pacification are different from those in the Jerusalem cultic tradition. No longer is it only the superior power of Yahweh through which he protects Zion; rather, it is the universal insight effected by Yahweh that Yahweh is the God on the mountain of God. This is likewise true for the feature of the renunciation of weapons. In this way the prophecy ties in with some of the content of the Jerusalem conception. But in the place of Yahweh's demonstration of power from Zion, there is now the peace-establishing power of Yahweh and the perception of his divinity.

The expectations for this comprehensive world peace that Deutero-Isaiah and Isaiah 2 indicate is attested in the later prophets in various ways.[64] One must keep in mind, however, that the contrasting element from the Jerusalem conception, that of the enemy nations storming Jerusalem and its victorious defense by Yahweh, became part of the content of the later prophetic expectation. Here the establishment of world peace through a divine restraint of those who were hindering peace is the leading thought.[65] These prophecies, which count on Yahweh's restraining acts at the end of time, indeed Yahweh's destruction of the attacking nations, might be connected, when compared with those of Isa. 2:2–4, with changed contemporary-historical experiences. Regardless of what is accentuated as the manner of achievement, all these expectations of a future world peace conceive of peace in its full and comprehensive sense as did the Jerusalem conception with which we began. According to the leading idea of this tradition, peace cannot be achieved by humans but only by Yahweh who alone has power over the "world."

No further word is necessary to show that the peace concepts of the Jerusalem cultic tradition and their prophetic modification in approach, in experiences, in ideas, and in form and content are deeply separated from the way the problems are stated in the contemporary peace debate. Hence a direct tie-in with these statements is no longer possible. More relevant is the question whether these biblical statements *can be mediated* by the way in which the questions are posed in contemporary theological peace research. Within the scope of this historically oriented study, which seeks to provide material for such peace research, this question cannot be pursued,[66] since one should not prejudge the results of future interdisciplinary research which are indispensable here.

Notes

1. Paper presented at the sixth session of the study group "Theological-Exegetical Problems of Peace," January 15/16, 1971, in Heidelberg. The paper was expanded and refined at certain points before its original publication.
2. See the contributions by G. Picht and W. Huber, *Was heisst Friedensforschung?* (Stuttgart: Ernst Klett Verlag; Munich: Kösel-Verlag, 1971).
3. On a definition of and criteria for these history-of-tradition methods, see H. Barth and Odil Hannes Steck, *Exegese des Alten Testaments: Leitfaden der Methodik* (4th ed.; Neukirchen-Vluyn: Neukirchener Verlag, 1973), 70–80.
4. Cf. in particular Günther Wanke, *Die Zionstheologie der Korachiten in ihrem traditionsgeschichtlichen Zusammenhang* (BZAW 97; Berlin: A. Töpelmann, 1966).
5. See the study by Lothar Perlitt, "Israel und die Völker," in *Frieden — Bibel — Kirche* (ed. Liedke), 17ff., 57ff.
6. On these events, see ibid., 26ff.
7. See in particular Pss. 77:17f.; 114; Isa. 51:9f.
8. See the topic of individual songs of lament and of thanksgiving of the Psalter, and on this, see esp. Christoph F. Barth, *Die Errettung vom Tode in den individuellen Klage- und Dankliedern des Alten Testaments* (Zollikon: Evangelischer Verlag, 1947).
9. See Pss. 47:3, 8; 97:5, 9; 98:1–3; and others.
10. See, e.g., Ps. 24:1f.
11. See Pss. 46:6f.; 48:5–8; 76:2–7; and others.
12. See Isa. 7:1ff.; 8:1–8; 29:1–7; 31:1 and 3, 4–5, 8a; and also Psalm 2.
13. Pss. 46:11f.; 47:2, 4, 9f.; 96:7–10; 98:2; 99:2.
14. See Pss. 48:11f.; 76:8–10, 13; 96:13; 98:9; and others.
15. See Ps. 72:16. To be sure, this aspect recedes in Israelite Jerusalem.
16. See Pss. 2:8; 18:44ff.; 72:8–11; 89:26–28; 144:2.
17. See Pss. 45:7f.; 72:1–7, 12; 122:5.
18. Cf. now in particular H. H. Schmid, *Šalom: "Frieden" im Alten Orient und im Alten Testament* (SBS 51; Stuttgart: Verlag Katholisches Bibelwerk, 1971), 21ff.
19. Egyptian and Mesopotamian sources should be evaluated in particular. See on this, Heinrich Gross, *Die Idee des ewigen und allgemeinen Weltfriedens im Alten Orient und im Alten Testament* (2nd ed.; Trier: Paulinus-Verlag, 1967); and Schmid, *Šalom,* 13–44.
20. F. Stolz, *Strukturen und Figuren im Kult von Jerusalem* (BZAW 118; Berlin: Walter de Gruyter, 1970), 181ff., esp. 204ff., 215ff.
21. Ibid., 215ff.
22. See esp. Ps. 85:9ff.; Isa. 60:17.
23. See H. H. Schmid, *Gerechtigkeit als Weltordnung* (BHT 40; Tübingen: J. C. B. Mohr [Paul Siebeck], 1968).
24. Cf., e.g., Isa. 1:21ff.

25. Cf., e.g., Isa. 60:17.

26. See Ps. 72:3; Isa. 48:18; 66:12; and others.

27. See Stolz, *Strukturen,* 204ff., 214f.

28. On this meaning of *shalom,* see Schmid, *Šalom,* 45ff.

29. Ibid., 97ff.

30. See n. 11 above.

31. See n. 13 above.

32. See n. 17 above.

33. See Ps. 2:10–12.

34. See Pss. 15:2ff.; 24:4ff.; and on this point, K. Koch, "Tempeleinlassliturgien und Dekaloge," in *Studien zur Theologie der alttestamentlichen Überlieferungen. G. von Rad zum 60. Geburtstag* (ed. R. Rendtorff and K. Koch; Neukirchen-Vluyn: Neukirchener Verlag, 1961), 45–60; see also Schmid, *Gerechtigkeit,* 144ff.

35. See, e.g., Ps. 47:2.

36. Cf. Pss. 2; 18:44ff.; 45:18; 72:9, 11.

37. On this, see Stolz, *Strukturen,* 76ff.; and Schmid, *Šalom,* 72f. n. 101.

38. See Pss. 18:32ff.; 20 (?); 21:9ff.!; 45:4–5; 144:1.

39. Cf. the Yahweh statements in Pss. 18:32ff. (and in the context beginning already with vs. 8ff.); 20; 21:8, 14; 89:39ff.; 110:1, 5; 144:2, 5ff.

40. Ps. 2:9 does not contradict this viewpoint. When understood in its context, the verse functions to underline the sovereign prerogatives of Yahweh's power (!) over the nations, which have been turned over to the king. But it does not encompass a politically expansionist program (cf. vs. 10–12).

41. H. P. Schmidt, *Frieden* (Themen der Theologie 3; Stuttgart: Kreuz Verlag, 1969), esp. 86ff.

42. See Schmid, *Šalom,* 64ff.

43. See J. Jeremias, *Kultprophetie und Gerichtsverkündigung in der späten Königszeit Israels* (WMANT 35; Neukirchen-Vluyn: Neukirchener Verlag, 1970), 111ff.

44. See in particular Psalms 74 and 79.

45. See Isa. 8:1ff.; 29:1ff.; 31:1ff.

46. Compare (in chronological order) Isa. 7:12; 8:6; 8:11f.; 5:18; 28:14f.; 29:13f., 15f.; 30:1–5, 6–7, 15f.; 31:1; 22:11; as well as 5:12.

47. Social-critical appeals against the king have not been passed down by Isaiah; nevertheless the prophecy in 11:1–5 permits us to draw such conclusions from hindsight.

48. Cf., e.g., Isa. 1:21–26; 3:12ff.; 5:8ff.

49. Cf., e.g., Isa. 1:10–17, 18–20; 3:8f.; 5:1–7.

50. See, e.g., Isa. 7:9b, 17; 11:1 (Dynasty); 1:21–26 (Bureaucracy); similarly, the Isaianic words of judgment also apply to the population in general.

51. See Isa. 1:26.

52. See Isa. 1:26; 29:5b–7; 31:4; also 22:11b.

53. See Isa. 11:1–5.

54. See Isa. 10:5ff.; 29:6f.; 31:8a; also 22:11b.

55. V. 7 reads: "Of the increase of his government . . . there will be no end."

56. See on this point the arguments oriented toward the frequency of the use of the word *shalom* in Schmid, *Šalom,* 79ff.

57. On this, cf. the references in Odil Hannes Steck, "Das Problem theologischer Strömungen in nachexilischer Zeit," *EvT* 28 (1968): 445–458.

58. Cf. Isa. 54:10 and on that passage Claus Westermann, "Der Frieden (*Shalom*) im Alten Testament," in *Studien zur Friedensforschung* 1 (ed. G. Picht and H. E. Tödt; Stuttgart: Ernst Klett Verlag, 1969), 144–177, esp. 173 (pp. 16–48, pp. 39f. in this volume); on this and other shalom passages in Deutero-Isaiah, see Schmid, *Šalom,* 80ff.

59. See esp. Isa. 52:7ff.; also 41:21; 43:15.

60. See Isa. 48:16; also 43:14; 47.

61. Cf. Isa. 49:26; further, the judgment speeches against the nations and their gods: Isa. 41:1–5, 21–29; 43:8–13; 44:6–8.

62. On this differentiation of the tasks, see Odil Hannes Steck, "Deuterojesaja als theologischer Denker," in *KD* 15 (1969): 280–293, esp. pp. 287f., n. 12. [See also Millard C. Lind, "Monotheism, Power, Justice: A Study in Isaiah 40–55," *CBQ* 46 (1984): 432–446.—ED.]

63. Cf. Ps. 46:10, where this is based on the sovereign power of Yahweh of Zion.

64. See, e.g., Zech. 2:14f.; 8:20ff.; 9:9f.; and in part Isa. 19:23–25.

65. See, e.g., Isaiah 34; Ezekiel 38f.; Joel 4; Micah 4:11–13; Zech. 12:1–8; 14:1–5. On the difficulties these texts pose for the history of tradition, see H.-M. Lutz, *Jahwe, Jerusalem und die Völker* (WMANT 27; Neukirchen-Vluyn: Neukirchener Verlag, 1968).

66. See, however, the balanced judgment of the Old Testament scholar H. H. Schmid in the frequently cited work *Šalom,* 91–111, and also the important explanations of P. Stuhlmacher as an addendum to the New Testament discoveries in his article "Der Begriff des Friedens im Neuen Testament und seine Konsequenzen," in *Historische Beiträge zur Friedensforschung* (ed. Wolfgang Huber; Studien zur Friedensforschung 4; Stuttgart: Ernst Klett Verlag; Munich: Kösel-Verlag, 1970), 21–69, see pp. 61ff.

4

Prophetic Speech About the Future

Jürgen Kegler

Prophecy in the Old Testament is not prediction. Rather, it is speaking the word of God in a very specific situation to a real audience. In the prophet's own self-understanding, this speech is a word entrusted to him. The prophet is a messenger who is carrying out an assignment. Prophecy is thus, in the first place, *present-oriented*. To the degree that the message has the character of an announcement, pointing to something that is coming, it is at the same time *future-oriented*. As a third aspect, prophecy is *past-oriented*.

The actual speech of the prophet, usually spoken in a specific manner to a specific situation, emerges out of the prophet's knowledge of the history of God with God's people. This is evident in the way he absorbs, passes on, and works out of traditions in order for them to speak specifically to the situation. That brings us to the norms from which the prophets drew their criteria for evaluating actual events. The listener, to whom the word of prophecy is spoken, senses himself being addressed *simultaneously* about his past and about the future toward which he is now proceeding. This "where from" and "where to" mark the two polarities between which the person to whom the prophetic word is spoken moves.

An examination of the interrelationship of these three aspects (present, future, and past) is the starting point for this essay. A

Translation of "Prophetisches Reden von Zukünftigem," in *Eschatologie und Friedenshandeln* (ed. Luz et al.), 15–60.

key question will be to ask to what degree the rhetoric about the future was shaped by the practical activity of the prophet or the group within which he was working. The majority of contemporary exegetes seem to assume that the prophets were convinced of the irreversibility of the happenings they announced. That is, they did not see themselves as voices calling for repentance in order to preserve a healthy existence.[1] What this understanding meant for the praxis, the behavior, and activity of the prophet still needs to be examined. Can specific strategies for prophetic action be identified? Were there definite indicators, especially with regard to the peacemaking work of the prophets? If so, how was it realized? Can one find there a clue of an effort to influence political decisions, which went beyond verbal critique?

In the light of the vast array of biblical prophecies and their specific contexts, it is appropriate to observe some caution in making generalized statements and conclusions. Limiting the task of the exegete is likewise necessary. Observations can be made most clearly where differences are most obvious: there is a fundamental difference between the prophets of judgment before the exile and the prophets of salvation after the exile, especially with reference to the future. (For Jeremiah and Ezekiel this upheaval becomes visible in their respective biographies.) It is here that the question becomes urgent: How relevant was their prophetic speech to the actual behavior of the prophet? Proto-Isaiah and Deutero-Isaiah may serve as useful examples, since the material that has been handed down in them is differentiated and extensive enough to permit a thorough exploration of this question. In order to develop a profile for the problem presented by the prophets of judgment, we will use what are generally acknowledged to be the actual words of Micah, since Micah was a contemporary of Isaiah, facing the same social and political issues.

With the help of genre studies and form criticism, it is possible to delineate with considerable certainty those texts which are future-oriented and to categorize their form. Generally speaking these are:

—the complete judgment speech, or the judgment announcement, minus explanation, that appears as part of a judgment speech[2]
—as a complement to this, the promise of salvation
—the paradigmatic description of judgment
—again, the corresponding description of salvation
—the Qinah (Funeral Dirge)[3]

—the proclamatory sections of woe cries, visions, and symbolic actions[4]

Other forms will be generally ignored, such as disputations, admonitions, Torah or wisdom speeches, parables, or teachings to disciples. This includes also the genres influenced by the psalms, such as the prophetic liturgies and theophanic elements or oracles as well as laments of individuals or of the people, if we name only the major prophetic genres.[5]

Just this short survey of the prophetic genres shows how difficult it is to speak about "prophetic eschatology" in the sense of a doctrine. The prophets speak of the future invariably in annunciatory form, never in a dogmatic or argumentative form. They do not develop a theology of the future. Instead, they announce quite concrete divine actions with reference to a specific historical situation.

The Destruction of What Is as a Perspective for What Will Be: Micah's Radical Prophecy of Judgment

In the second half of the eighth century B.C., the foreign and domestic political situation became acute. Because of the sudden successes of Tiglath-Pileser III in invading the north of Syria and establishing Assyrian provinces in that region, an expansionist phase began that represented a direct threat to the continued existence of the states of Israel and Judah. The Syro-Ephraimitic war represents an attempt to confront this danger by means of a military coalition. The collapse of this resistance effort resulted in the conquest and splitting up of Israel and finally the siege and conquest of Samaria. These events deeply influenced the policies of the kings of Judah. Whereas Ahaz sought aid from the Assyrians in his own interest, and paid for it with vassal status, his son Hezekiah tried to regain the autonomy of Judah through loosening the feudal tie. This policy was doomed to failure, given the uneven military power relationship and the Assyrians' political and economic interests. The result was a major loss of territory.

Domestically, the situation was shaped by the deep gulf between a wealthy upper class and a poor underclass consisting of indebted peasants and small merchants, essentially disenfranchised wage laborers and indentured servants [slaves], as well as those unemployed because of sickness. The development of an economic and social order based on slavery and privilege had already been attacked sharply by Amos.[6] When Micah identifies the social dislocations concretely, he is standing in a line of tradition that is conscious of the way the shalom community has been ruptured through economic repression and social oppression.

The historical dimension of the prophetic proclamation becomes evident in two ways: the contemporary social development has a history, which the prophets always keep in mind; and the prophetic critique itself, in like fashion, has a history. This critique, most evident in the accusatory part of the judgment speeches, embraces the full reality of the contemporary life of the people: the political, the social, and the cultic-religious, that is, the relationship to God. To the degree that one of these areas is especially threatened, that is, that the ongoing existence of the society as a shalom community is threatened, this factor determines where the prophet places the emphasis. This explains why Micah centers in on social conflict, because the competition for economic power has caused the impoverishment of the lower strata to the point of hopelessness. Legal means of resistance are useless because the owner class has adapted the very institutions of justice to its own advantage. Micah states this in a most drastic and partisan manner: members of the upper class misuse their power (Micah 2:1) to seize ownership of land and houses by means of violence and deceit (2:2).[7] That they exploit and oppress the people is made vivid in the imagery of "consuming" and "cooking" the poor in the pots of the rich (3:1–3). Prophets can be bought and for a payment of money will promise salvation (3:5). Judges and priests can be bought, for corruption seems to be the order of the day (3:9–11). Merchants employ false weights and measures (6:9–11); the rich use violence and falsehood (6:12). As a general characterization Micah uses the words *pesha'* (crime) and *chatath* (falling short, sin, e.g. 1:5). These signify the complete breakdown of a healthy human society.

By referring to pre-state law and the elements of clan wisdom (*Sippenweisheit*),[8] Micah reminds the upper class of its real task: to know justice (3:1; cf. 3:9), to know good, to seek the good of society, and to hate evil.[9] These notions of wisdom have their prehistory in kinship traditions. In Micah's context, "to love the good" can only mean to stop the oppression and violent exploitation of the people, to honor old Israelite law and to practice it.[10]

Yet societal reality is characterized by constant violations of this law. At its crassest it is violated through oppression of the poor. This calls forth Yahweh's punishment (*Strafhandeln*). God's interference is justified on the basis of God's special relationship to Israel, which God manifested through helpful deeds in the history of God's people. Specifically, in the passage 6:2–5 (which is not without its problems, granted) Micah recalls the tradition of the liberation from Egyptian slavery, the appointment of Moses, Aaron, and Miriam as leaders, and the blessing of Israel through Balaam during the Moabite wars.[11] Through its own shortcomings, Israel has destroyed this relationship. Therefore the divine response can be only punishment.

Some careful distinctions are in order here. Several statements by Micah refer to the siege of Samaria already begun, or to the general Assyrian invasion which extends to the very gates of Jerusalem (1:8–9, 10–16; 5:1). Others refer to God's acts of punishment yet to come. These actions signify a complete political and military catastrophe for Judah. Yahweh destroys and lays waste not only Samaria (1:6) but also Jerusalem (3:12)! God plans judgment against the rich and propertied, those who lie on their beds and hatch new evils (2:3; here a form of *jus talionis* is used).[12] God will strike the upper strata of Judah (6:13)[13] whose efforts at carrying off and saving their possessions will be foiled by war (6:14); their land also will turn to desert (6:16). The catastrophe culminates in the outrageous announcement of the destruction of Zion, of the temple hill and of the temple itself (3:12).[14] The Holy of Holies, Yahweh's residence, will be destroyed by Yahweh! Thus the assurance of salvation (*Heilsgewissheit*), which had come to be taken for granted because of the presence of Yahweh as the guarantee for confidence and security, is dispelled as an illusion. This is the end of both states as political-military powers and the end of the dominant theology. This is the perspective of the future in Micah's prophecy.

Through the foreign political events, especially the takeover of Samaria and the deportation of the upper strata in 722/721 B.C., this perspective becomes reality. Twenty years later this holds true for Jerusalem too, even if it does not extend to the destruction of Zion. Micah's words must have been uttered in the immediacy of these events; at least for 1:6f. and 1:10–16 this seems certain to me. So the announcement of judgment cannot be regarded as eschatological. Rather, it is the announcement of immediate, direct, tangible events and developments as well as the interpretation of them from the background of a social criticism that is oriented around traditional norms. The listeners and the prophet himself experience these events as having an impact on them. The prophet interprets them as God's punishment because of demonstrable human failures and societal injustice. The future that the prophet is addressing in these announcements is the immediate future. These are events for which the political-military course has already been set. What will happen after the defeat, after the destruction of the state, is not indicated.

Alongside this specific future perspective is a second line of thought, in which the remoteness of God, God's self-hiding, and the silence of God to human cries are announced as a future catastrophe (3:4, 6, 7 and indirectly v. 12). These interrelate in complementary fashion: the remoteness of God signifies loss of aid, loss of divine attentiveness. This loss will be experienced with greater reality than a military defeat. And in pointed fashion Micah contrasts this with his personal word of trust in God and an unbroken self-confidence which grows out of that:

> But as for me, I am filled with power,[15]
>   and with justice and might,
> to declare to Jacob his transgression
>   and to Israel his sin. (3:8)

Setting this statement of trust next to the accusation, which may well be spoken in response to an attack or a challenge to his authority, emphasizes the uniqueness of the prophetic task, for it assumes trust in the experience of God's nearness and in divine support. The contrast between God's remoteness as experienced by the people and God's nearness as experienced by the prophet is indeed the condition that makes it possible to bear the coming events. It is one of the few places where the prophet as individual becomes evident. Beyond that we learn little about his own conduct. From 2:6–11 we learn that he had conducted public disputations where he had presented his accusations in drastic fashion. There is obviously a symbolic message behind 1:8; going naked symbolizes the complaints of the conquered. Obviously he is also forced to discontinue his speeches; at least he is attacked as an enemy (2:6).[16] Thus we can presume that Micah operated mainly through public appearances and courageous denunciations of abuses (3:8).

What motivated Micah to speak publicly? Was it the insight that social reality stood in disturbing contrast to old Israelite law and to a healthy relationship of people to each other and to God? That is, was it primarily contemporary criticism measured against the traditional norms of justice, right, and peace (shalom)?[17] Or was it the recognition that the coming political developments, the invasion of Assyrian troops against Damascus and Samaria, and later also against Jerusalem, represented God's punishment? That is, did the coming event motivate contemporary criticism? In the light of the double character of Micah's proclamation — the announcement of the coming military defeat, and thereby God's remoteness, which shape his wording of the collapse in which he participates — it seems to me that there is a stronger accent on the threatening future. This is understood in the sense of a synthetic conception of life (Action–Result–Connection) where something is experienced as the result of an unlawful action.

To announce and to spell out the coming event as divine punishment, that is the task of the prophet. It is a necessary and unchangeable event, because it is God's answer to human wrong. Or, to put it another way, human fault over a long period of time has produced this result.

This event sets up a discontinuity. It signifies the total break with what was: the end of the state, of the power of the ruling class, and of worship in its present form. This is the radical consequence of the unpeaceful practices of an unjust social system. "An absolute skepticism against renewal efforts goes hand in hand with a critique that no longer merely censures incidents of moral or cultic failures but calls into question fundamentally everything, including the basic legal, political, and cultic institutions."[18] It is no wonder, therefore, that there are *no aspects of peacemaking* in Micah. This may be connected with the fact that the written record of Micah's words is relatively short. It is more likely — as implied in 3:1 — that Micah affirms the possibility of peacemaking but regards it as a missed opportunity. A healthy human society would have been possible had the mighty recognized justice and loved the good. But the opposite was the case. Therefore lack of peace ends in war.

Overthrow of the Existing Order and the Possible Reign of Peace: The Proclamation of Isaiah

In comparison to Micah, the proclamation of Isaiah reveals notable differences. In the first place, there is a broader political horizon: Yahweh has power also over far distant nations and carries out judgment on them just as Yahweh does over Israel and Judah, when they violate the divine will (Isa. 10:5ff.; 18). Second, there is Isaiah's understanding of the significance of Jerusalem, of Zion, and of the traditions connected with it.[19] Since Yahweh dwells in holiness on the hill of Zion, and this is Isaiah's fundamental point of departure, then the life and behavior of the people must be determined by Yahweh's presence. Therefore Yahweh deserves intense reverence and recognition. Therefore also, those who turn away from Yahweh in spite of God's nearness commit a wrong that threatens the entire land. Finally, a unique element in Isaiah is the influence of the cult on his language and conception of God. Above all, Yahweh is the Holy One (*Qadosh*; cf. 6:3). This is not meant to describe some timeless quality; rather, it qualifies the reign of Yahweh in history, as manifesting itself in concrete deeds.[20] The holiness of Yahweh reveals itself in the experience of (cultic) uncleanness in the moment of encounter with Yahweh (6:5),[21] in the destruction of human pride and self-praise through political-military actions (2:6ff.; 5:1ff.), and in the realization of Yahweh's sovereignty over the world through the carrying out of Yahweh's counsels in history (5:19; 28:21). Even the title Yahweh Sabaoth or Qadosh Israel points to cultic roots.[22] A survey of the use of these names[23] provides a decisive insight into the special God concept of Isaiah:

—Yahweh is Lord of history; a violation of God's sovereignty by humans, be they the people of Yahweh or a strange nation (Assyria for example), brings forth a sentence of judgment (*Strafgericht*).
—Yahweh's relationship to Israel is an exclusive one. Yahweh's dealings with Israel are identifiable in the past and in the present as caring, preserving, and protecting ones.
—The cultic reverence for Yahweh requires a special language, which seeks to express the uniqueness of Yahweh in cultic terminology.
—Adequate concepts of Yahweh are those which denote Yahweh's lordship, power, majesty, esteem, and awfulness as well as those which express Yahweh's attentiveness to the people of God (e.g., Sanctifier of Israel).

The proclamation of Isaiah consists for the most part of judgment speeches and announcements of doom. For Isaiah also a military catastrophe that affects the entire population as a result of human responsibility is the center of his message. This responsibility is described with great variety and vividness but is always based on concrete, demonstrable deeds.

1. Yahweh raised up children, yet they fell away from God (Isa. 1:2). Thus the relationship between Yahweh and Judah, which was a natural one like that between a child and its parent, is broken. The children have turned away. In the explanatory section of this judgment speech, Isaiah does not present the relationship between God and people in legal categories but rather as an analogy to natural human ways of relating or to human relational models.

The verbal image of 1:3a, in which the natural creaturely relationship of animals is held up as a model for Israel, shows how self-evidently natural this relationship would be if true to its nature.[24] Perversion of the natural order signifies a flawed insight and understanding. What is meant by these concepts is not intellectual prognostications but rather a relationship in the real historical present according to the natural order, as it has been passed down from pre-state times. The element of the personal in Isaiah's God concept is striking: one senses the sorrow of the father who has been deeply hurt by the turning away of the children.

2. The desolation and destruction of Judah in 701 B.C. was a warning punishment from Yahweh, but one that is not understood as such by Judah (1:4–9). The fault of the people lies in the fact that they have become villains, children who have gone astray, much as in 1:2f. Yahweh's relationship to Judah consisted of a double action: to care for and to nurture but also to punish through political events in both recent and past history.

3. Sinning consists of refusal and resistance (1:18f.). Both the deeds and the words of the Judahites are directed against Yahweh (3:8). They are partisan and full of sins of which they are publicly proud (3:9). The nobility and the politicians oppress the landless, beat the people, and exploit the weakest of them (3:14f.). But what is striking in this accusation is that the description of Yahweh's intervention overshadows it. Yahweh appears ready to do legal battle, Yahweh rises to judge the people of God (3:13), and Yahweh comes to the judgment seat (3:14). The accusation is preoccupied not only with the content of what is said but also with the immediateness and nearness of God who is the plaintiff. Here we see an important "theological" expansion of the form of the judgment speech — the grievance is intensified by means of the presence of the accusing God. The element of theophany that undoubtedly serves as a background tradition here is interpreted as an unmediated real presence in a legal process. Whereas theophany begins with the remoteness of God, we have here a God who accuses and pronounces sentence from an inescapable and threatening nearness.[25]

4. In 3:16ff. the pride and modish vanity of the women serve to justify the announcement of judgment. The song of the vineyard (5:1–7), which is formally a love song but in content a judgment speech, contrasts an image of the laborious and hopeful deeds of Yahweh for Israel[26] with an image of complete failure. In spite of the divine effort, Israel has done nothing to justify the effort; it was a waste. Here too the God concept reveals no legalist perception.

5. The prophecy against Assyria (ch. 10) is based on the charge that, against the direct will of Yahweh, the Assyrian king did not limit himself to destroying Israel but has willfully subdued other nations as well, scornfully puffing himself up. Thus Isaiah establishes a *new understanding of history.* Yahweh utilizes the other nations to carry out God's will; they are a medium for God's action (cf. 7:18). All the same, this is not to suggest that these nations are mere marionettes; rather, human freedom is assumed. Nations are thereby able to oppose the will of Yahweh and attain their own self-realization. Isaiah perceives the theological problem of divine power and human freedom here in its full intensity: human freedom to act (the concept of freedom does not exist in Hebrew, but that is what is intended here) is retained as fundamental, but it becomes perverted at the moment where it is directed *against* Yahweh, expressing itself in self-glorification and pride and no longer reckoning with the actual presence of Yahweh. It is precisely this presence which Isaiah emphasizes with sharp polemics, not because he wants to restrict the expression of human will, the freedom of the will, but because human freedom consists solely in obedience toward the will of Yahweh. For to ignore Yahweh is to ignore the basis of human existence.

6. A specific accusation is directed toward the priests and prophets (28:7ff.) who are drunk when they prophesy and whose tables are covered with vomit. The mockers in Jerusalem are also accused because they have made a covenant with Sheol, where they hope to be protected from the presence of Yahweh. In 29:1, Isaiah attacks the practices of holidays and feast days, linking the accusation with a declaration of woe against the temple altar. The reverence of Yahweh with mouth and lips in cultic practice, speaking of the fear of Yahweh without truly experiencing and living it (29:13f.), the pro-Egyptian coalition policies of the Jerusalem politicians (30:1f.), the rejection of the seers, and the bribing of the prophets for the sake of getting positive predictions, all of these constitute the self-assured deeds of humans who no longer reckon with the aid and dynamic presence of Yahweh who is enthroned in Zion. That is, they do not expect God's participation in the reality of their lives.

A major part of the accusations is directed against human haughtiness, against self-glorification, puffing oneself up, pride and self-confidence, which had spread among the upper strata in particular. This theme gains force through the reversal poems (*Kehrversgedichte*) 2:6–17 and 9:8–21. Here we see the scope of Isaiah's perspective which is decisive for perceiving the guilt of the people in history and in the present. The all-inclusive theological reason behind the accusations is to be found in Isaiah's understanding that Yahweh alone is sublime and majestic. Yahweh has demonstrated this in divine acts in history to the people of God and to other nations. Against this, each and every sign of human hubris appears as an act of obstinacy against the holiness of God (cf. 2:9, 11, 17). Precisely because God is, for Isaiah, the holy and majestic one, he perceives that in his own time the actual threat to his people consists in the violation of the majesty of God through the self-confidence and self-righteousness of those members of his nation that he has addressed in the accusations.

This understanding of Yahweh by Isaiah is supported by a form-critical observation. In the doom announcements, the active divine "I" recedes noticeably. It is replaced by a report about God's action, establishing the facticity of the coming events without naming the initiator. For Isaiah, the knowledge of the holiness of Yahweh has resulted in a shift of emphasis in the form of judgment speech employed. An experience of the holy would be in contradiction to impartial and therefore improper speech about God, as is characteristic of Hosea, for example. Instead, for Isaiah, the form of establishing the factual becomes more central.

Only in the following Isaiah passages does Yahweh announce the execution of judgment in the "I" form:

—3:4: Yahweh will appoint babies and boys as princes. Thereby the collapse of the entire political order of the state into chaos is predicted.
—5:5–6: In the song of the vineyard a complete military destruction is announced by God. Although in the allegory the "I" of the song should not be made to refer to God, the analogous nature of the events lets the divine "I" shine through.
—28:16–19: This passage combines in a unique way a salvation speech and a judgment announcement, in which salvation is announced by the divine "I," whereas the judgment is presented in the form of stating the facts.
—29:1–5: Yahweh personally announces the siege of Zion, although to carry it out, Yahweh utilizes a foreign nation.
—29:13ff.: A wonderful action is announced. That is, it is an action which is incomprehensible to those who think they have understanding and insight, hence literally wonderful.[27]

In all other passages either God's acts are presented in the third person or the actor remains anonymous.[28] Claus Westermann has established that originally the announcement of punishment merely established the facts of the case and that the introduction of the divine "I" represented a change in form.[29] This allows us to conclude that when Isaiah utilizes the form of a simple statement of the factuality of doom — that is, to go back to the original form — he knew the tradition of the form and applied it. Theologically this means that the *inevitability* of divine judgment was a certainty for Isaiah, because it was an adequate expression of the holiness of Yahweh. In all these pronouncements the coming judgment involves a total national catastrophe from which there is no escape.[30] In those passages in which the third person is used,[31] the catastrophic is underlined and strengthened through the awful nearness of Yahweh. Isaiah says it figuratively: The Lord will shave off the hair of the proud Jerusalem women (3:17). The Lord entices a nation from afar that itches to rob and conquer Judah,[32] whistles for the Assyrians to come and make war on Israel (7:18),[33] rents a razor and cuts off the hair — a reference to prisoners of war and slavery (7:20), and lets the Euphrates spill over its banks and flood the land (as an image of the military might of the Assyrians [8:5–8]). The Lord cuts off the branches of the vine — an expression for the destruction of Ethiopia (18:1–6), casts out the palace steward Shebna like a bundle onto the open field (22:18), speaks to the drunken priests through people of a foreign tongue (28:11ff.), and appears in a theophany (28:21). Indeed, this appearance has all the attributes of a horrifying weather god (29:5c–7). Yahweh's judgment, and the future of Judah, consists of its destruction as a state, to be carried out by means of the Assyrian conquest of Judah. It is inevitable and merciless. Yahweh, as Lord of the nations, uses them as an instrument. In each case, divine punishment is a concrete event in history. Or, put another way, the political and national threat of Assyria to Judah, especially in the latter years of the eighth century B.C., is God's punishment for the continuous resistance, a resistance to God's will, holiness, and care, recognizable in ever-new concrete human deeds.

A specific form of the Isaianic concept of justice emerges from the paradigmatic descriptions of doom. Although Isaiah describes the collapse of the state, this consists primarily in the breakdown of law and order. Apparently Isaiah is picturing in this description of judgment a future that lies beyond the military destruction of the state by the Assyrians. In 3:6f. the catastrophe consists of the reversal of norms for choosing a leader. The mere presence of a cloak suffices for the election of a judge. There is no need for charisma, for a just reputation, or for the will of Yahweh. In v. 7 this perspective of the chaotic situation is sharpened further when the chosen one refuses to accept office. There is no judge; order has totally broken down. This statement can be understood only on the basis of the tradition accepted by Isaiah of the peace-making and peacekeeping function of the king and thus of the political and social order (cf. 1:21ff.; 7). The same reversal of the legal order is described in 4:1. The issue in this verse is not that the women see themselves "condemned to the deepest reproach so that in their despair they reach for any means to secure their existence and to obtain a minimum of protection for their female honor."[34] Rather, the issue is the reversal of the rules by which the women take it upon themselves to choose a man, when, in the opinion of Isaiah—in line with the understandings of his time and of his strata—that would be the right of the man. The scene describes neither despair nor a violation of moral sensibilities but rather the complete reversal of the "natural" order, which consists in the right of the man to purchase a wife. Isaiah stands in the tradition of a patriarchal society and regards its norms, especially with regard to marriage, as unconditionally binding and neces-sary. The catastrophe, as he describes it, is the perversion of this order, the destruction of the traditional legal order, and thus the elements of anarchy and chaos.[35] This chaos threatens because the relationship to God has been destroyed and because the domi-nant order has now been perverted by the rulers.

Isaiah's talk about the future is linked in a very special way with his talk about God. It is *theologically* based. Violation of the majesty of God by the people demands the action of God. For the sake of God's holiness, God punishes the breaking of the law and the violation of justice in society. The actual guarantors of the law, the protectors of the overall legal order, are above all, the king and his advisers, along with the judges, the priests, and the prophets, that is, the ruling elite. But instead of protecting the law, they have broken it (esp. 5:7). That is why a major portion of Isaiah's judgment speech is directed against them. Quite obviously Isaiah builds on the self-understanding of this upper elite, measur-ing their praxis against their self-assigned ideals. These ideals include the concepts of knowing, having insight, doing right, doing good, and practicing justice. For Isaiah these are the central norms for socially appropriate and peace-fostering behavior. These ideals were realized in the time of the Judges (1:26), but at present false self-confidence and hubris have replaced them. Thus the shalom quality of the society has been hopelessly shattered. When Isaiah then applies the old pre-state legal tradition, he does not do so only to hold up a critical mirror to the current reality of social

unrest. *As a concrete possibility for human behavior* he uses it
to serve as an impetus to change the existing reality. The way to
such change comes through the constant application of the word
of God to specific situations. At special moments or to a specific
audience it can take the form of a reproach or of an appeal. This
second line of speaking in Isaiah's speech about the future is evident
in passages such as 1:18–20, 26 and more indirectly in 8:1–4. So
also 1:19f.:

> If you are willing and obedient,
>   you shall eat the good of the land;
> But if you refuse and rebel,
>   you shall be devoured by the sword.[36]

With this word, which is part of a judgment speech in which
the impossibility of Judah to roll back its sins and wrongs is
expressed, the key condition for the possibility of transformation
is named — obedience to God's will — a possibility, however, that
the people through their behavior have constantly failed to attain.
In pointed fashion Isaiah had spelled this out in the context
of the Syro-Ephraimitic war when King Ahaz feared for his
sovereignty:

> If you will not believe,
>   surely you shall not be established. (7:9)

As a warning this means that failure to trust in God, or false trust
in one's own political options, results in the destruction of the
existence of the state. At the same time, this word contains a positive
note. Trust in God, in divine help, is the only realistic condition
for the possibility of avoiding destruction. Thus this speech is
couched in a conditional framework: unconditional trust in Yahweh
and obedience to God's will alone, as manifested in the pre-state
tradition of actualized legal norms, achieves a healthy, society-
building existence, a peaceful future. Ignoring Yahweh, and the
resultant breakdown of law, leads inevitably to catastrophe, because
God as the Holy One punishes the breaking of God's law. One
thing is decisive: Isaiah perceives Israel's future *exclusively as an
act of God.* This applies to the possibility of salvation:

> And I will restore your judges as at the first,
>   and your counselors as at the beginning.
> Afterward you shall be called the city of righteousness,
>   the faithful city. (1:26)

It also applies to the coming judgment. Isaiah expressed this theologically through the fixed expressions "act of Yahweh," "counsel of Yahweh," and the "work of Yahweh." Beyond all human planning, above all beyond human politics, which create a false sense of security (cf. 31:1–3), there stands God's plan of history, manifesting itself through specific acts of God in the coming events. This plan, which is recognizable already in God's past actions with the people of God and which still stands in this hopeless present, will flow into future acts of God toward the people of God. Thus the three aspects of past, present, and future in Isaiah's prophetic proclamations are conjoined in this concept. God reveals this plan to the prophet. The prophet thus receives a special function (8:16ff.): he is to be the announcer, the warner, and the reproacher all at the same time. The function of warning and reproaching can be seen clearly in 1:16–17:

> Wash yourselves; make yourselves clean;
>   remove the evil of your doings
>   from before my eyes;
> cease to do evil,
>   learn to do good;
> seek justice,
>   correct oppression [Ger.: restrain the violent];
> defend the fatherless,
>   plead for the widow.

These words describe the conduct that makes possible a peaceful society, a behavior that lies within the sphere of human possibility, if the people submit themselves to the majesty of God in obedience and reverence.

This problem of the dual function of the prophet as warner and reproacher on the one hand and announcer of coming judgment on the other can also be seen in the central problem of the call vision narrative, that is, the problem of impenitence. F. Hesse has conjectured that it became clear to Isaiah only in the course of his proclamation, that his words had failed to achieve any change in direction toward a more just social order. Rather, the people remained obdurate; no change of behavior resulted. The supposition of the speech about impenitence is the knowledge of the absolute power of God in history, on the one hand, and the experience of evil, the incapacity of changing sinful behavior, on the other hand, as well as an inquiry into the possibility of evil in the light of the power of God. Since evil cannot be traced back to God's self, the statement about an impenitence, which God causes, is an attempt to explain the inexplicable.[37] And it means as well that in the end the relationship between warning/reproach and announcement of judgment cannot be explained rationally.

Regardless of when Isaiah developed or expressed his beliefs about impenitence, they say something quite typical about his concept of God.

—Yahweh has a concrete plan of history for the people of God (7:11), which ends in a time of judgment.
—Holiness and a plan of history are incomprehensible to the people; the prophet therefore has a continual sense that the people close themselves to the word.
—This hardening can only be the work of Yahweh when Yahweh is, and because Yahweh is truly, the Holy One; the proclamation cannot miscarry, because it occurs under the authority of Yahweh.

So in spite of the experience of the fruitlessness of speaking, and the incomprehension of the hearers, including even their incapacity to change their current hopeless situation, reproaches and warnings as well as pointers toward the conditions for a healthy society remain part of the prophetic task. That brings us to the problem of the prophetic praxis.

Isaiah was himself a member of the upper strata. He could write (8:1; 30:8); he had access to the priests (8:2); and, above all, he had direct access to the king (7:1–9). He was married to a prophetess (8:3) and gave demonstrative symbolic names to his children (7:8). For the sake of emphasis he utilized spectacular demonstrative actions in making his proclamations. In order to announce the destruction of Egypt he walked about naked for a time (20:1–5). Such an action exposes a member of the upper elite in a special way, making him socially unpresentable. His criticism of the intensification of land speculation and the concentration of property, of the style consciousness of the women of the upper strata, and of the perversion of the legislature into an instrument for the self-aggrandizement of the rulers, and, finally, his very specific criticisms of the pro-Egyptian policies, all show that he was a sharp analyzer of the political, social, and religious conditions and that he had carefully observed and evaluated the central political events of the years 740–701 B.C. That includes even concrete statements about personnel politics at the court. The palace steward Shebna, for example, is accused of building ostentatious burial homes, and there is a word of support for Eliakim ben-Hilkiah. Isaiah, in short, was directly involved in personnel policies at the court. Whether a form of personal participation may be hinted at in 22:20–22 cannot be ascertained. What is decisive is that by means of direct conversations with the king, Isaiah offered him concrete assistance in decision making with reference to actions in the Syro-Ephraimitic war (7:1–9). A motivation for this attempt seems to have been his intense desire for the political fulfillment of his proclamation. The king is the covenant partner, with whose aid the establishment, or the reestablishment, of a shalom situation could be achieved provided that he place himself under the will of God. This proviso is theologically determinative! The challenge to the king — "Take heed, be quiet, do not fear, and do not let your heart be faint" (7:4) — stems from the holy war tradition and points to the singular effectiveness of God, in contrast to which the people may do nothing yet hope for everything. This challenge has a very pointed, concrete, dimension of peacemaking in mind. It consists of fulfilling the will of God, specifically a trust in Yahweh as the one who protects his people, even in war.

A further concretization of this peacemaking appears in 1:16–17 (see p. 83 above). Here the word "learn" (v. 17) is of decisive significance. Apparently Isaiah is making the assumption that peacemaking can be practiced, can be learned. This learning is a process. "Seek what is right (*mishpat*)" implies a procedure, not a state of being. In the Old Testament, *mishpat* is never a state or a quality of being; it is a concept that is always related to the community, containing an aspect of conciliation, of mediation between two opponents. "Correct the oppressor (or restrain him)." Since the social sphere is a dynamic one, there will also be incidents of violence. To that degree Isaiah's speech is not utopian but realistic. This correction signifies the *minimization of violence*. Misuse of power must regularly be restrained. Since peace is not a state of being but rather a constant striving, peacemaking is a dynamic process. As a final element of peacemaking, Isaiah names the support of the socially weak and the legally insecure — the orphans and widows. This speaks to the dimension of the *minimization of need*. Here too he has a process in mind. Helping and "pleading the case of" signifies a procedure that takes time. This rounds out the picture of Isaiah's proclamation. His speech about the future is influenced on the one hand by the knowledge of the sovereignty of God, who is working out God's own plan in history, even in the future. On the other hand it is shaped by God's attentiveness to the people, whose falling away is painful and for whose obedience he is appealing by challenging them to listen to the will of God and to recognize the holiness of God, which is carried out concretely through the aspects of peacemaking just mentioned. Rebellion against the holiness of God, that is, to practice social unpeace [*Unfriede*], leads to the destruction of the state through divine punishment.

Isaiah did not try to realize this as a single individual, he had about him a group of *disciples*. His marriage to a prophetess shows that even his personal relations were influenced by contact with prophetic circles. The evidence for the existence of a group of disciples is found in 8:16–20. It reveals itself above all in the recorded words of the disciples.[38] These include, among others, 7:10–16 and 9:1–6 (because of its closeness to Trito-Isaiah, 11:1–5 is most likely postexilic).

The relationship of 7:10–16 to 8:1–4 is problematic. In my judgment, 7:10ff. constitutes the report of a disciple in a form whose origin has to be explained on the grounds of the failure of the destruction of Damascus and Syria, as announced in 8:1–4, to take place. The passage 8:1–4 is in all probability to be dated to the time of the Syro-Ephraimitic war (733–731 B.C.). But the catastrophe announced there, the destruction of Syria and Damascus, took place in 722/721. Isaiah 8:4 states that this judgment will come to pass at the latest when the child can say "father" and "mother." That would be about a year after its birth (in absolute numbers this would be 730/729). But this was not the case, because the announced judgment occurred only eight or nine years later. The passage in 7:10ff. accounts for this in that the judgment is set for a time when the child is capable of distinguishing between "good" and "evil," that is, at nine or ten years of age. Thereby the precise time period between the original announcement of the prophecy (733–731 B.C.) and the destruction of the two cities (722/721) is covered. Since both prophecies share as content the announcement against Samaria and Damascus, they assume a common situation. By extending the age of the child named in the announcement in 7:10ff., the impression is created that this word was already spoken at the time of the Syro-Ephraimitic war. That suggests the conclusion that the disciples of Isaiah have corrected a prophecy of their master on the basis of the actual historical events. It is apparent that the problem of the nonfulfillment of the announced judgment preoccupied Isaiah considerably, as the lamentation 5:18–19 shows. If this view is correct, then it says something about the self-understanding of the disciples of Isaiah. They had actualized the words of their master and at the same time strengthened the tendency of his proclamation. The name "Immanuel" in 7:10–16 for the coming child (in 8:4 the boy is nameless!) shows that the group of Isaiah's disciples regarded itself as standing under an exclusive promise of assistance. Such a promise of assistance, which is usually given only to individual persons, goes well beyond that in this specific situation and applies to the entire nation that is under military threat. This belief had developed out of the experience of protection during the time of military danger.

The prediction of salvation in 9:1–6 in particular reveals the ongoing development of Isaiah's line of proclamation — the realization of peacemaking is to be expected from a *new king*. The text is written in the form of a song of thanks, but it is linked also with the tradition of the Jerusalemite ideology of kingship.[39] The factual nature of an event that Yahweh had brought to pass is declared and Yahweh is thanked for it.[40] Yahweh causes great joy,[41] provides for a great jubilation (v. 2a) which takes place in front of Yahweh, that is, it presumes a cultic situation somewhat similar to a harvest festival or a celebration over the capture of booty spoils (v. 2b). Three reasons for the joy are given (vs. 3, 4, 5): (*a*) Yahweh himself breaks the yoke of foreign oppression,[42] he had conquered the Midianites[43] in the past through a holy war;[44] (*b*) the war-making soldiers[45] are consumed in a fire — that too is a motif in a "holy war"; and (*c*) a royal son is born,[46] one who will command a peace regiment in which justice and right will always exist.

This action is linked to the zeal of Yahweh (v. 6b), thereby closing the circle that had been opened in v. 2. The following ideas are theologically significant here:

—The act of salvation is carried out exclusively by God.
—This act of salvation is to be understood as analogous to the saving deeds of Yahweh in the past (v. 4).
—This act of salvation takes place in actual history, specifically through a ruler who achieves a shalom society[47] by exercising his rule over human society in a way that is shaped by justice and right.

The mythical elements in the names of the ruler[48] draw attention to the presence of divinity in the ruler. The realization of God's act of salvation lies in the political sphere, in the concrete functioning of a ruling king. The futuristic element in these words lies in the statement that in the near political-historical future of Israel, Yahweh will bring about a reign in which foreign domination will be broken; a social order that has justice intact will be guaranteed by a king. This is carrying forward with a new accent Isaiah's speech about the future. The weight of emphasis falls on the *minimization of violence,* shown symbolically with the imagery of the burning of the boots and garments of the soldiers.

Past Forgiveness as Way to the Future: Deutero-Isaiah

The fundamental difference between the future speeches of the preexilic prophets and those of Deutero-Isaiah (ca. 587–539 B.C.) lies in the fact that Deutero-Isaiah *looks back* on the events, which the prophets before him had announced as the coming judgment acts of God. He sees the events as factual, in particular the destruction of the state and the disempowerment of the mighty. He understands this as something that God has carried to its finish and on that basis declares how a new dealing of God with the people in exile becomes possible. Through the coming to pass of what had been announced, God is revealed as the One who is sovereign over all other powers in history. At the same time, it is the self-revelation of the One whose word has been proven reliable throughout the passage of history.

> Who told this long ago?
>   Who declared it of old?
> Was it not I, the LORD? (45:21)

Judgment has come; it has become historical reality. That is one point of departure for Deutero-Isaiah.

The other is the certainty that God's history with the people did not stop there. What the new future makes possible is God's act of forgiving the people of God. What God had announced to the Israelites and what the judgment, carried out on Israel, had achieved, was

> that her warfare is ended,
>   that her iniquity is pardoned,
> that she has received from the LORD's hand
>   double for all her sins. (40:2)

That forgiveness *had already happened* is the reason that Israel has a new future. There will be further dealings of God with Israel. These new acts of God Deutero-Isaiah declares in various salvation announcements.[49] Forgiveness and the turning of destiny, proclaimed as something that has already happened, belongs to these salvation announcements precisely because they contain the conditions for the possibility of a renewed salvation.[50]

Thus we encounter in Deutero-Isaiah an entirely new dimension of speech concerning the future—the forgiveness of guilt, redemption, the washing away of sins, the forgetting of offenses. All of these divine acts make possible a new phase in the history of God with the people. They are the precondition for the possibility of a future as a health-filling (*heilvoll*) future. With due caution in the light of the New Testament influence on the concept, we can say that what we have here is a soteriologically shaped speech concerning the future. For in Deutero-Isaiah, as in the New Testament, the salvation act of God is that of a salvation produced by forgiveness. God's act of forgiveness toward Israel has provided the turning point that allows the new salvation (*Heil*) to become present reality. This finds its linguistic expression in the promises of salvation (*Heil*) for the present. Because the turn about to salvation has become fact,[51] there will also be in the future the helping hand of God to God's people. This is stated in the salvation announcements.

This future event is not utopian or transcendental—it is the return of the exiles from Babylon to their homes, a new exodus. The salvation announcements speak quite concretely about deliverance from the bondage and captivity of the people. They speak about the way home through a wilderness that will be transformed into a fruit garden for the returnees. And finally, they speak about the return home, the rebuilding of Jerusalem, and a new increase of the population. All of this reaches its peak in the announcement of a new state of shalom (*Heil*). Return to the homeland, reconstruction, and population increase—these are the key points of the coming salvation, the goals for the future. Everything remains quite strictly within the bounds of the this-worldly, within that which can be realized in history. But it is exclusively an act of God. Deutero-Isaiah emphasizes this in ever-new variations, for example:

> Fear not, you worm Jacob,
> > you men of Israel! [Do not take fright, you worm of Israel]
> I will help you, says the LORD;
> > your Redeemer is the Holy One of Israel. (41:14)[52]

> > Remember not the former things,
> > > nor consider the things of old.
> > Behold, I am doing a new thing;
> > > now it springs forth, do you not perceive it?
> > > [Ger.: you will notice it]. (43:18–19a)

> I bring near my deliverance, it is not far off,
>   and my salvation will not tarry;
> I will put salvation in Zion,
>   for Israel my glory. (46:13)

> but my salvation will be forever,
>   and my deliverance will never be ended [will not be shaken].
>   (51:6b)

In short, future events are events produced by God. Where Deutero-
Isaiah takes into account the actions of people, they are exclusively
the instruments of God. That applies in particular to Cyrus,
through whom the liberation of the exiles from their Babylonian
captivity finally became a political reality:

> I [says Yahweh] will go before you
>   and level the mountains,
> I will break in pieces the doors of bronze
>   and cut asunder the bars of iron,
> I will give you the treasures of darkness
>   and the hoards in secret places,
> that you may know that it is I, the LORD,
>   the God of Israel, who call you by your name.
> For the sake of my servant Jacob,
>   and Israel my chosen,
> I call you by your name,
>   I surname you [Ger.: give you honorary titles],
>   though you do not know me.
> I am the LORD, and there is no other,
>   besides me there is no God;
>   I gird you, though you do not know me.
>   (45:2–5)

This exclusivity in the shaping of the future corresponds to the
sovereignty of a God who alone announces *and* carries out coming
events. This gives Deutero-Isaiah the certainty that what has been
announced will indeed happen. This is analogous to the coming
to pass of the judgment announcement, whose result was the exile.
This same certainty can be sensed in the promises of salvation,
where Deutero-Isaiah proclaims the turning that has already come,
as in:

> I will strengthen you, I will help you,
>   I will uphold you with my victorious right hand. (41:10b)

Repeatedly Deutero-Isaiah speaks of the redemption of Israel through Yahweh (43:1; 44:22–23; 45:20; 52:9) whenever he wants to emphasize the new in this turning. But also the concept of election, which stems from the preexilic tradition, is given new currency (41:8ff.). The new salvation is expressed in the images of the washing away and payment for all sin (40:2; 41:25; 33:22). The jubilation peaks in the song of praise (49:13):

> For the LORD has comforted his people,
> and will have compassion on his afflicted. (cf. 51:3)

These repeated promises of salvation, which proclaim a turning in the fate of Israel as already happening, must be seen against the background of the historical situation. In view of the collapse of the state of Judah and the deportation of the upper strata, an attitude that allowed no hope for a change in the situation has obviously spread among the exiles. Alongside the lament of the people who still gathered, even in exile, for worship and who still held fast to God and in their moments of deepest despair expected something new from God, alongside this, there were voices that regarded it as impossible that God would have further dealings with and for God's people. Yahweh has been revealed as the defeated one, so this group argued, and the Babylonian gods were the stronger ones. This resigned stance strengthened the tendency toward an opportunistic adaptation and the taking on of the religious forms and cult of the ruler and conqueror.

It was these tendencies that Deutero-Isaiah struggled against so passionately. He answers those who consider God's impotence as proven. He does this in his disputations or polemics (40:12–31; 42:18–25; 45:18–19; 48:1–11a) with the argument that God is lord of history and of the nations, that God has carried out divine judgment as announced, showing that God is reliable. The destruction of Israel is not a sign of God's impotence but rather of God's power. Isaiah answered those who were assimilating themselves to the Babylonian culture with polemics about the nothingness of idols (40:19–20; 41:6–7; 42:17; 44:9–20; 45:16–17, 20b; 46:5–8). And finally it is for all those who lament, who despair, who have lost hope and become depressed, apathetic, and resigned to their despair, that he speaks the promises of salvation and the words of comfort (cf. 40:1–11).

Apathy, resignation, fatalistic surrender, hopelessness, coming to terms with the reality of the exile—these are the factors that lead to loss of perspective of the future. The consequence of such a loss is a disinterest in taking action. Rather, one conforms to the situation for the sake of optimizing the individual's position within the miserable conditions of the present, that is, to live for the moment without a longer-term dimension. Deutero-Isaiah opposes this attitude very pointedly with his proclamation of the promise of a realized salvation and future return to the homeland. Thus his speech of the future opens up anew the dimension that pours forth from the future — the old is conclusively gone, something new is beginning. The new picks up exactly those expectations which the majority of the exiled would have regarded as quite unrealistic and which were, in a hidden way, quite virulent expectations. These were the expectations that the captivity would be over, a return home was possible, and a reconstruction of the state would become a reality. This reconstruction does not signify, however, the reestablishment of preexilic Israel with a monarch but rather a new possibility to exist as a people of God *without* political power. That this is made possible through a heathen king points up a completely new type of perspective — existence as a state *without political power,* to be a *people of God* that way.

This sketches the essential function of Deutero-Isaiah's proclamation — to encourage the discouraged and to comfort the comfortless: "Comfort, comfort my people, says your God" (40:1). And, "Rouse yourself, rouse yourself, stand up, O Jerusalem" (51:17). Rousing yourself, as Deutero-Isaiah urges, does not mean activating political efforts but rather the rousing to a new hope, to a hope that God will indeed and truly create a new future for God's people, that the return home will be a lived reality, because God is the author of these events and God does what God says.

The major portion of the speeches of Deutero-Isaiah, in particular the promises and announcements of salvation but also the words of comfort and the songs of praise, are intended to awaken such a confidence in a shalom (*Heils*) future as God will create it. Their function through consolation and announcement is to *awaken a hope in the future,* because the present is experienced as hopeless and futureless. The introduction of a future dimension is his answer to a present in which the lack of a perspective dominates.

If we try to categorize this function, we can describe the role of Deutero-Isaiah by saying that he seeks simultaneously the *minimization of fear and resignation* and the maximization of trust and hope in a God who will act in the future. These are the conditions for survival for a group whose identity is threatened. That is why Deutero-Isaiah repeatedly seeks to strengthen the self-consciousness of this exiled group:

But you, Israel, my servant,
  Jacob, whom I have chosen,
  the offspring of Abraham, my friend;
you whom I took from the ends of the earth,
  and called from its farthest corners,
saying to you, "You are my servant,
  I have chosen you and not cast you off";
fear not, for I am with you,
  be not dismayed, for I am your God;
I will strengthen you, I will help you,
  I will uphold you with my victorious right hand. (41:8–10)

But now thus says the LORD,
  he who created you, O Jacob,
  he who formed you, O Israel:
"Fear not, for I have redeemed you;
  I have called you by name, you are mine.
When you pass through the waters I will be with you;
  and through the rivers, they shall not overwhelm you;
when you walk through fire you shall not be burned,
  and the flame shall not consume you.
For I am the LORD your God,
  the Holy One of Israel, your Savior." (43:1–3)

But now hear, O Jacob my servant,
  Israel whom I have chosen!
Thus says the LORD who made you,
  who formed you from the womb and will help you:
Fear not, O Jacob my servant,
  Jeshurun whom I have chosen.
For I will pour water on the thirsty land,
  and streams on the dry ground;
I will pour my Spirit upon your descendants,
  and my blessing on your offspring. (44:1–3)

Such promises, viewed sociopsychologically, are certainly meant to give a fearful and discouraged group a new feeling of security and thereby offer a new collective identity. In this, taking up and making real again the traditions that were once alive plays a vital function. By taking up the exodus tradition (43:16–21; 51:9–52:3; 52:11–12), which provides an analogy between the captivity of the Israelites in Egypt and the present situation of the exiles in Babylon, both an interpretation of and an identification with the situation becomes possible for the exiles. At the same time, the dimension of hope is historically based through a glimpse of a *onetime* real saving act of God to a group of God's people. The hope of the return is as little an illusion as the exodus of the Israelites at the beginning of the history of the people is an illusion. The remaining references by Deutero-Isaiah to tradition elements are similar:

> Look to Abraham your father
>   and to Sarah who bore you;
> for when he was but one I called him,
>   and I blessed him and made him many. (51:2)

In the same way that the blessing and increase of an entire people, originating out of the promise of blessing and increase to a single individual, was no impossibility, so is the promise of a renewed increase of the people, directed to the small group of exiles, no impossibility. Rather, it is the saving act of God, which will be worked out in history, as it already happened once before in history. The statement in 54:9 is similar: as God's oath to Noah after the Flood, so also will God's oath to Israel hold,

> that I will not be angry with you
>   and will not rebuke you.

To incorporate traditions that were alive among the exiles serves to give force and even illustrative confirmation to the newly established promises and announcements. In a sense it is a guarantee of the integrity of the divine word.

The exclusiveness with which Deutero-Isaiah proclaims God as the one who brings to pass the coming salvation corresponds to the fact that he fails to develop a concept of human action, including also peacemaking actions, even though all of his announcements are directed toward the goal of peace, of a condition of shalom. There is one exception. In 45:20–25 Deutero-Isaiah announces the gathering of all "survivors of the nations," and a saving act of Yahweh is offered to all the ends of the earth. By the "survivors" he means those persons who were able to flee from the threat of war, who were able to be saved from war. That is, these were persons with a fate similar to that of the exiles. Here we sense both the knowledge and the experience that to suffer the same or a similar fate serves to bind together people in spite of all national and religious barriers. Yahweh's invitation is for them too. Even to them Yahweh proclaims an act of salvation. That opens up a universal perspective for the coming peace: God as the creator of the world will in the future not act as savior merely for God's own people, but for all people, whose lord God is. For Israel this requires that they enlarge their vision to include the other peoples. Indeed, even in cultic practices Israel is instructed to observe that which unites rather than that which separates. The decisive point here is that peace is real only as a universal event, never as an esoteric concept or as a national effort. That such a peace begins with those persons who were the victims of war and oppression — the survivors of the nations and the exiles in Babylon — is crucial. Both of them had to bear the agony and suffering of an unpeaceful reality. Therefore they are the first to be called to experience the new peaceful acts of God. Of course, this requires that they be open to mutuality. That is indeed the practical dimension of this speech about peace.

Beyond that, there is no concrete perspective for action. Essentially everything that Deutero-Isaiah experiences as a political event, the rise of Cyrus (44:24–28; 45:1–7) or the beginning of the destruction of the Babylonian empire (46:1–3; 47), he and the exiles experience as passive observers. These are events in which they are not active participants, quite in contrast to the preexilic period, when Israel was a factor in the great power politics of the Near East. All of this — this is the unexpected climax of Deutero-Isaiah's speech — happens on behalf of Israel. It is staged by God for the people of God, in order finally to bring them back home and to lead them to a new salvation (43:14).

Because this is so, there is no need of a strategy for action. Essentially what Deutero-Isaiah advises the Israelites to do by way of concrete action is to hold fast, to hope, and to trust in God (40:29–31; etc.). In addition, at the end of his speeches, there are the calls for the exodus out of Babel: 48:20–21 and 52:11–12. Waiting on God, who sees to world events on Israel's behalf, and finally to move out of exile, those are the elements of action. Here we see mirrored the situation of a powerless group, which has absolutely no room to maneuver, and the intensity of their resignation. This sort of strong, ever-new and repetitive summons to trust, this continual encouragement to hope in God, is needed precisely where every reason to hope seems to have broken down, or at least it has broken down for the members of the group.

Concerning Deutero-Isaiah's own praxis we learn almost nothing. It is evident, based on the proximity of the words of 40:6–8 to one of the moments of call, that for him the sole guarantee of stability and certainty in this situation of living in solidarity with the suffering of the people is the reliability and effectiveness of God's word. In 42:7 the task of the called one is:

> to open the eyes that are blind,
> to bring out the prisoners from the dungeon,
> from the prison those who sit in darkness.

This is so general that it is not possible to read into it a specific function for Deutero-Isaiah.[53] The degree to which the servant of God songs can serve to interpret the person and prophetic office of Deutero-Isaiah is a matter of extensive debate. If they are related to the praxis of Deutero-Isaiah, then at the very least it is clear that he encountered some resistance to his proclamations. That would mean that he would have personally experienced the way of suffering, that he would have lived through the permanent resistance of other exiles to him personally.

It therefore makes sense to limit oneself to the words of Deutero-Isaiah. They reveal speech about a future that contains a very concrete saving act of God which will take place in the arena of history. His announcements are intended to offer courage and hope for a coming salvation as a reality to a despairing and resigned group in exile. Thus forces are mobilized that will work against the resigned apathy. The dimension of a future perspective makes it possible to survive in a situation where there seems to be no way out.

The Relationship of "Eschatology" and "Peace" on the Basis of Prophetic Proclamation

The key question in this study has been whether, and in what way, in the Old Testament record there is a discernible connection between prophetic speech about the future and the practical actions of the prophet. A study of the record of Micah, of Proto-Isaiah, and of Deutero-Isaiah has shown that this can only be answered with considerable differentiation. By differentiating, there is the danger that we lose sight of what they have in common. But there is more to it than the formal distinction between judgment and salvation speeches:

—Prophetic speeches of the future always occur in the form of announcements. In this the prophet sees himself as a messenger who is to carry out a divine task.
—The content of each of the announcements is a concrete act of God which will take place in the near future, that is, something that the addressee can expect to experience personally.
—This action takes place in history, within a foreseeable time span. Elements of transcendence are absent.

—The prophet gives reasons for God's actions:

    1. Micah and Proto-Isaiah see the coming judgment in direct connection with concrete failures of the people in the social, political, and cultic-religious spheres. It is God's answer to the humanly caused rupture of relations between God and the people on the one hand and between persons on the other hand.

    2. Deutero-Isaiah grounds the coming salvation with the forgiveness that God carries out. That opens up the possibility for a new shalom (*heilvoll*) future.

Both types of reasons are concerned with the relationship between God and the people.

—What binds together the prophets of salvation and of judgment is that both begin with the experience of the saving, helping, caring, and blessing actions of God to the people in the past, and both have seen in their own personal lives the breakdown of the relationship to God caused by the sins of the people in the political, social, economic, legal, and cultic-religious spheres of reality.

—All the announcements are *situationally based.* There is neither timelessly valid nor arbitrary repetitive talk of the future; only concrete speeches related to the political, social, and religious situation of the listeners.

—The prophetic speech of the future comes out of the background of an unpeaceful, distressing present situation. The preexilic prophets experience an external military threat and a domestic situation of injustice, exploitation, and oppression. Deutero-Isaiah experiences the situation of captivity abroad with all its characteristics of suffering and hopelessness.

—Because the prophets await the coming event as an act of God, it represents for them a discontinuity with what has been. That gives it the character of the new, of the unique.

—All the prophets know what are the conditions for a peaceful society, a shalom society, in which the relationship of people to God and of people to each other is not ruptured.

These observations provide us, in my judgment, with several important aspects for discussion of a theologically based concept of "eschatology."

a. Since prophetic speech of the future is *situationally based,* it is dynamic and open. There is no doctrine of the future, nor are there proposals that transcend the framework of history. The future actions of God always apply to the contemporaries of the

prophets, to whom the words are addressed, not to future generations. How does such situationally based speech relate to a doctrine
of "de eschatis"?

b. Speech about the future and an analysis of the present, that
is, of the political, social, and religious conditions, belong together
in the eyes of the prophet. This linkage has been seriously neglected
in the history of theology. Given this interdependence, does this
not call for a critical stance toward the independence of the criticism
of ideology, of religion, and of system or society, on the one hand,
as well as toward the abstention of theology from the analysis and
critical evaluation of politically, socially, economically, and ideologically influenced developments, on the other hand?

c. Changed situations call for diverse types of speeches of the
future. There is no timeless prophetic perspective about the future.
This is indicated by the clearly evident process of fulfillment of
the prophetic word, especially by comparing Proto-Isaiah and
Deutero-Isaiah: a new historical situation calls for completely new
talk about the future. Here too we must ask whether, in the light
of the changing social, technological, and economic conditions,
this dimension of the new has been sufficiently taken into account
by theology.

d. Behind the openness and situational basis of the prophetic
speeches about the future there lies a quite specific concept of
history. God shares a common history with God's people. The
preexilic prophets Micah and Isaiah begin from the standpoint that
they regard the past as a time where God exerted great effort for
the people of God, which was shown above all in saving and preserving actions. They see the present as the time of the complete
breakdown in relationship between God and the people, evident
in concrete failings of a political, social, and religious sort. They
see the coming future as a time of punishment in which those who
caused the breakdown in relationships will be destroyed. Deutero-
Isaiah, in contrast, understands history in such a way that he sees
in the past the punishment of the people by God, as had been
announced by his predecessors, the preexilic prophets of judgment.
But he sees the present as a time of turnabout due to the forgiveness
of God and proclaims the future as a time for the new concrete
saving and healing acts of God. This dynamic concept of history
retains an open-ended character, in that it is able to reckon with
something quite new in the future. This kind of proclamation is
in contrast to those projections of the future which are based on
the continuation from the past and from the present of trends that

have been and can be analyzed, or of those which develop a model based on the necessary consequences of inner historical developments.

In trying to describe the relationship of present and future reference in the prophets, one must begin in each case with their specific evaluation of the causes for the absence of social peace. It is a beginning assumption for Micah and Isaiah that the societal condition is one of the absence of peace, that is, a breakdown of the shalom society which includes the rupture not only of the divine-human relationship but also of the human to human. Otherwise their charges would be unthinkable. To recognize lack of peace assumes norms, or a scale of measurement, that allow current social interaction to be evaluated. Micah and Isaiah draw their criteria from traditions that reach well back into the pre-state period of Israel. Invariably these are socially relevant criteria.

Micah's concept of peace as it can be deduced from the judgment speeches consists of the respect for and the observance of *right* (*Rechts*) and of love. That means putting into practice a behavior that is healthy for the community. However, this should not be misunderstood as the formal description of an ideal situation. Rather, for Micah it assumes the quite concrete intent of putting an end to oppression and violent exploitation and beginning to practice the traditional legal norms and arbitration procedures.[54]

Isaiah's reliance on socially appropriate norms as setting the requirements for a shalom community is more varied. As is true for Micah, practicing what is right and, closely linked to that, the settling of conflicts in ways that are healthy for one's fellow humans and for the community are of decisive consequence for Isaiah. But the notably stronger theological thrust of his message corresponds to the fact that, above all, he places obedience and trust in God at the center of his peace speeches.[55]

What is distinctive in this is that this obedience must always be visibly expressed in concrete behavior toward God and toward other persons, otherwise it is not obedience. Concrete examples of this are a nonhypocritical reverence for God, good conduct toward others, and a continual effort to expose unjust conduct and to help the victim of injustice see justice done. This is where the political dimension comes in — in placing restraints on the violent and exercising solidarity with and help for the socially weak and societally disadvantaged.[56]

Isaiah attaches major importance to the application, execution, and protection of a full, unvarnished exercise of justice. This is rooted, above all, in the fact that the concept of justice, as used in the Old Testament, refers to a dynamic process that is concerned with the maintenance and restoration of a community that has been disturbed. The original function of the judge was that of arbitration (*Schlichten*). Where there is no arbitration, conflict remains or is intensified. Arbitration calls for authority.

For Isaiah, such authority can be guaranteed only through the king. That is why he considers kingship the guarantee for a shalom community. But the experience that the kings proved themselves to be incapable of carrying out this function produced in Isaiah's disciples the expectation of a *new* king as lord of peace.[57] The key point here is that Isaiah's concept of peace is dynamic, not static. Peace is an ongoing task, which is only realized in ever-new acts of right and justice, support for the weak, and the correction of the mighty. Indeed, it must be learned and practiced (1:17).

A concept of peace that focuses on the minimization of factors that inhibit peace, rather than on the [positive] description of a state, can find a serious echo in Isaiah. It should be noted, however, that in none of the prophets do we find simultaneously all three factors of the so-called zero hypothesis (*Nullhypothese*), that is, the minimization of violence, the minimization of misery, and the minimization of unfreedom. Micah tends to stress the minimization of violence. Isaiah adds to that the concern to minimize misery, for example, when he talks of aid for the societally weak.[58]

Deutero-Isaiah, in contrast, places the *minimization of fear and resignation* in the center. It is the precondition for the awakening of a new hope and the dawn of a new future. Furthermore, what is decisive for Deutero-Isaiah's concept of peace is the universal aspect: peace is peace only when it includes all the nations. That requires the perception of commonality. Deutero-Isaiah sees this in the common experience of misery. In other words, solidarity with those in misery and oppression is the precondition for a universal situation of mutual openness and mutual understanding. It should be noted, however, that in Deutero-Isaiah's eyes peace is an act of God, not an attempt of people to create it for themselves. Nevertheless it is still necessary by means of the zero hypothesis to examine critically the question of whether or not under specific circumstances the minimization of fear and resignation constitutes a peace-fostering action.

This summary of the prophets' concept of peace has ignored the question of their realizability. But when we raise the hermeneutical question of how relevant is the prophet's speech about peace for us today, then it becomes decisive. In Micah there were no indicators for a concept of peace action. As far as he was concerned, the possibilities for peace (*shalom*) to be put into practice were no longer there. It seems to me that there is a causal connection between the lack of a concept of peace action and the experience of military threat: once war is experienced physically, then the possibility for peacemaking has passed; it is too late. In view of the power relationship between Assyria and the small Palestinian states, there is only a collapse left.

We have already drawn attention to the tension between Isaiah's judgment announcements and his reproach/warning whose intention is to make possible a peace-fostering conduct.[59] For Isaiah too, the collapse is inevitable as the radical consequence of the lack of peace. Nevertheless, both he and his disciples — as seen in the words of the latter — retain a hope in a reign of peace. An obvious development is evident here: Isaiah had hoped that a king would provide the guarantee for a shalom society, but the more that Ahaz and his son showed themselves to be incompetent, the more his expectations shifted to the distant future. Now the new reign of peace is to come through a new king. This latter phase is seen in Isa. 9:2-7. This begins a long tradition extending into New Testament times — the tradition of waiting for a coming ruler of peace.[60]

With regard to Deutero-Isaiah, we note again his perspective of a universal peace. The concept is not explicit, but he does engage in a specific form of peacemaking, in that he comforts the comfortless and encourages those who lack courage. Given the situation of collective hopelessness, it is by awaking hope in a change of fate that he provides the possibility of coping with the present.

Thus the variance among the prophets on what is to be minimized is situationally conditioned. That raises the question whether it may not be necessary to establish priorities for developing a dynamic and historical concept of peace. The prophets set priorities according to the requirements of their time. Might it be that the specific developmental factors in any given country on earth force a prioritizing, or might it be that the minimization of violence, misery, unfreedom, and fear can happen simultaneously? The observations that we have drawn from but a small part of the biblical materials have shown, in any case, that the historical dynamics of a peace vision require that the emphasis be on being specific to the situation at hand.

Afterword

After the first printing of the present article, Bernhard Lang's *Habilitationsschrift* (Freiburg) appeared: "Kein Aufstand in Jerusalem: Die Politik des Propheten Ezechiel" [No uprising in Jerusalem: The politics of the prophet Ezekiel] (Stuttgart, 1978). The point of that work, among others, is to show that there is a clear political intent behind the prophet Ezekiel's efforts. With his proclamation of 587 B.C. the prophet is trying to prevent an anti-Babylonian uprising in Jerusalem. The judgment announcements are intended to prevent the announced judgment from taking place; their aim is to produce a change in the behavior of the persons addressed. The understanding, drawn from the Ezekiel text, that the prophets are trying to achieve repentance, that is, a change in the political-religious-social conduct, Lang then extends to the preexilic prophets in general: "They want to turn aside the judgment; that is the essential motive for their stepping forward" (p. 163; the supplement contains additional important citations). Although Micah is not mentioned specifically, he is included in the generalization. That would put it in tension with the article above, which developed the idea that in his situation, Micah no longer reckoned with the possibility of a reversal (*Umkehr*) as having a realistic chance.

It is not possible to develop a detailed argument here, but a few problems can be pointed out briefly. How does one relate the intention of achieving a reversal to the specific language that the prophet employs? Is such radical language, as employed by Micah in a fashion singularly drastic for the Old Testament, the appropriate medium to motivate an attitudinal change? Or is it better understood as an expression of the experience of powerlessness? I have interpreted Micah in the latter sense. To what degree do concrete assessments of political developments feed into the intentions of the prophetic proclamation? When does the prophet reach the point where he must recognize as objective fact the impossibility of a transformation/turning about? Would that be, for example, at the moment when a superpowerful army approaches? That seemed for me to be the case with Micah. The historicalness of reversal, and the possibility of reversal, demands, therefore, an especially intensive reflection.

Such questions aside, Lang's book is to be recommended, since it not only offers new, often surprisingly illuminating insights into Ezekiel's complicated imagery but also examines the problem of Ezekiel's expectation of the future and peacemaking. Since I have restricted myself to only three of the Old Testament prophets in the above article, this book offers a valuable expansion and extension, particularly with regard to the question of change in prophetic speech and conduct in the light of changed political constellations.

Notes

1. For example, R. E. Clements, *Prophecy and Tradition — Growing Points in Theology* (Atlanta: John Knox Press, 1975); G. Münderlein, *Kriterien wahrer und falscher Prophetie — Entstehung und Bedeutung im Alten Testament* (Europäische Hochschulschriften 33; Frankfurt am Main: Peter Lang; Bern: Herbert Lang, 1974); S. Herrmann, *Ursprung and Funktion der Prophetie im alten Israel* (Rheinisch-Westfälische Akademie der Wissenschaften, G 208; Opladen: Westdeutscher Verlag, 1976); H.-J. Kraus, *Prophetie und Politik* (Theologische Existenz heute, n.s. 36; Munich: Chr. Kaiser Verlag, 1952), 34ff.; G. Fohrer, "Prophetie und Magie," in *Studien zur alttestamentlichen Prophetie (1949–1965)* (BZAW 99; Berlin: A. Töpelmann, 1967), 264ff.; idem, *Geschichte der israelitischen Religion* (Berlin: Walter de Gruyter, 1969), 239ff.; and H. W. Wolff, *Joel and Amos* (Hermeneia; Philadelphia: Fortress Press, 1977), 103–104 [*Dodekapropheton 2: Joel und Amos* (BKAT 14/2; Neukirchen-Vluyn: Neukirchener Verlag, 1975), 125].

2. Claus Westermann, *Basic Forms of Prophetic Speech* (London: Lutterworth Press, 1967) [*Grundformen prophetischer Rede* (Munich: Chr. Kaiser Verlag, 1960; 2nd ed., 1978)].

3. Cf. H. Jahnow, *Das hebräische Leichenlied im Rahmen der Völkerdichtung* (BZAW 36; Giessen: A. Töpelmann, 1923).

4. On the Lamentation: C. Hardmeier, "Kritik der Formgeschichte auf texttheoretischer Basis am Beispiel der prophetischen Weheworte: Die prophetischen Klagerufe als Stilform der Redeeröffnung im Rahmen einer unheilsprophetischen Trauermetaphorik" (diss., Heidelberg, 1975) [revised and published as *Texttheorie und biblische Exegese: Zur rhetorischen Funktion der Trauermetaphorik in der Prophetie* (Beiträge zur evangelischen Theologie 79; Munich: Chr. Kaiser Verlag, 1978)]. The generic concept "Symbolische Handlungen" ("symbolic action") was influenced by G. Fohrer, "Die Gattung der Berichte über symbolische Handlungen der Propheten," in *Studien zur alttestamentlichen Prophetie*, 92–112.

5. These methodological preliminary decisions allow us to delineate the tradition complexes in the materials from Micah, Isaiah, and Deutero-Isaiah that need to be taken into consideration with reference to future speech. Arguments for the "authenticity" of the texts cited, their boundaries and chronological order, cannot be entered into here in detail.

For Micah, I am following closely the commentary of Artur Weiser, *Das Buch der zwölf kleinen Propheten* (ATD 241; 5th ed.; Göttingen: Vandenhoeck & Ruprecht, 1964); for Isaiah, H. Wildberger, *Jesaja* (BKAT 10/1; Neukirchen-Vluyn: Neukirchener Verlag, 1972) and, to the degree that he argues cautiously or conservatively with regard to authenticity, H. Barth, "Israel und das Assyrerreich in den nichtjesajanischen Texten des Protojesajabuches: Eine Untersuchung zur produktiven Neuinterpretation der Jesajaüberlieferung" (diss., Hamburg, 1974) [revised and published as *Die Jesaja-Worte in der Josiazeit: Israel und Assur als Thema einer produktiven Neuinterpretation der Jesajaüberlieferung* (WMANT 48; Neukirchen-Vluyn: Neukirchener Verlag, 1977)]; for Deutero-Isaiah, I am following Claus Westermann, *Isaiah 40-66* (OTL; London: SCM Press, 1969) [*Das Buch Jesaja, Kap. 40-66* (ATD 19, 1966)], and, so far as it is published, K. Elliger, *Jesaja II* (BKAT 11/1-5; Neukirchen-Vluyn: Neukirchener Verlag, 1971-1978).

The result is the following selections:

Micah

Complete Judgment Speech 1:2-7; 2:1-3; 3:1-4; 3:5-7; 3:9-12; 6:2-5; 6:9-16
Judgment Announcement 1:10-15
Woe Cry 2:1
Qinah 1:8-9; 1:16; 4:14
Paradigmatic Judgment Statement 2:4-5

Isaiah

Complete Judgment Speech 1:2-3; 1:18-20; 3:12-15; 3:16-17; 5:1-7; 8:5-8; 18:1-6; 22:8-11; 22:15-18; 28:7-13; 28:14-19; 29:1-5b; 29:13-14; 30:1-14
Judgment Announcement 3:1-5; 3:25-26; 5:26-29; 7:18-19; 7:20; 14:29-31; 17:1-3, 4-6; 18:1-6; 22:14; 28:1-4; 29:5c-7; 29:9-10
Lamentation 1:4; 5:8, 10, 11, 13, 19, 20, 21, 22, 23; 10:1, 4, 5; 18:1; 28:1; 29:1-7, 10-14; 32:9-14
Qinah 1:21-26; 23:1-7, 10-14; 32:9-14
Paradigmatic Judgment Statement 3:6-7; 4:1
Symbolic Action 7:1-9; 8:1-4; 20:2-4
Vision 6:1-11
Verse-poetry 2:6-17

Deutero-Isaiah

Because of the unique nature of Deutero-Isaiah's proclamation, virtually all of the texts need to be examined. Thus only a short structural survey of the more important genre:
Comfort Call 40:1-2; 40:3-5; 40:9-11
Disputation 40:12-14; 40:15-17; 40:18-24; 40:25-26; 40:27-31; 42:18-25; 45:18-19; 49:14-21

Judgment Speech 41:1–5; 41:21–28; 43:8–15; 43:22–28; 44:6–8; 45:20–25; 48:12–17; 50:1–2

Salvation Announcement 41:8–13; 41:17–20; 42:14–17; 43:16–21; 46:9–13; 49:7–12; 49:22–23; 49:24–26; 54:1–10; 55:1–5

Salvation Promise/Oracle 41:14–16; 43:1–7; 44:1–5; 44:21–22; 52:11–12

Eschatological Song of Praise 42:10–13; 44:23; 45:8; 48:20–21; 49:13; 52:7–10; 55:12–13

Song of God's Servant 42:1–3; 49:1–6; 50:4–9; 52:13–53:12

Cyrus Oracle 44:24–28; 45:1–6

Larger Compositions 47:1–15; 51:9–52:3

Mixed (genres) 45:9–13; 48:1–11; 50:10–11; 51:1–8; 54:11–13a

6. Wolff, *Joel and Amos,* 90 and frequently [*Joel und Amos,* 106 and frequently].

7. K. Koch, "Die Entstehung der sozialen Kritik bei den Propheten," in *Probleme biblischer Theologie. Gerhard von Rad zum 70. Geburtstag* (ed. H. W. Wolff; Munich: Chr. Kaiser Verlag, 1971), 246.

8. Cf. H. W. Wolff, *Amos, the Prophet: The Man and His Background* (Philadelphia: Fortress Press, 1973) [*Amos' geistige Heimat*] (WMANT 18; Neukirchen-Vluyn: Neukirchener Verlag, 1964)].

9. Stated positively from Micah 3:2.

10. Micah has given intentional priority of place to the minimization of violence.

11. Among the preexilic prophets, Micah's accentuation of this theme of salvation history is singularly unique. He is developing here a special tradition, unless one wishes to understand the entire proclamation of Micah as a deuteronomistic interpretation.

12. Use of the *jus talionis* form to express the correspondence of deeds with history can also be found in Micah 2:1–3; 3:5–7; 6:14, 15. In contrast to a magical mind-set where a bad deed has automatic consequences, the prophet develops a notable reaccentuation: the punishment is no longer the direct result; rather, it is the personal action toward another person.

13. Reading *hahillôtî* with GAØSV.

14. This word has had a great impact; a century later it was cited by spokespersons for Jeremiah (Jer. 26:18).

15. Dl. 't-rwh YHWH.

16. The word *ntf* still awaits satisfactory clarification. Most interpreters link it with "to drivel" (*geifern*), stemming from "to drip" (*träufeln*).

17. On the use of the shalom concept, cf. Wilhelm Caspari, *Vorstellung und Wort "Friede" im Alten Testament* (BCFT 14, 4; Gütersloh: C. Bertelsmann Verlag, 1910); W. Eichrodt, *Die Hoffnung des ewigen Friedens im alten Israel: Ein Beitrag zur Frage nach der israelitischen Eschatologie* (Gütersloh: C. Bertelsmann Verlag, 1920); W. Eisenbeis, *Die Wurzel* שׁלם *im Alten Testament* (BZAW 113; Berlin: Walter de Gruyter, 1969); Jacob J. Enz, *The Christian and Warfare: The Roots of Pacifism in the Old Testament* (Christian Peace Shelf Series 3; Scottdale,

Pa.: Herald Press, 1972); Heinrich Gross, *Die Idee des ewigen und all-gemeinen Weltfriedens im Alten Orient und im Alten Testament* (Trier theologische Studien 7; 2nd ed.; Trier: Paulinus Verlag, 1967); Gerhard Liedke, "Israel als Segen für die Völker: Bemerkungen zu Lothar Perlitt, 'Israel und die Völker,'" in *Frieden – Bibel – Kirche* (ed. Liedke), 65–74; Lothar Perlitt, "Israel und die Völker," in *Frieden – Bibel – Kirche* (ed. Liedke), 17–64; Leonhard Rost, "Erwägungen zum Begriff *šalom,*" in *Schalom: Studien zu Glaube und Geschichte Israels. Alfred Jepsen zum 70. Geburtstag* (Arbeiten zur Theologie, series 1, vol. 46; Stuttgart: Calwer Verlag, 1971), 41–44; Joseph Scharbert, "SLM im Alten Testament," in *Lex tua veritas. Festschrift für H. Junker zur Vollendung des siebzigsten Lebensjahres am 8. August 1961* (ed. H. Gross and F. Mussner; Trier: Paulinus Verlag, 1961), 209–229; H. H. Schmid, *Šalom: "Frieden" im Alten Orient und im Alten Testament* (SBS 51; Stuttgart: Verlag Katholisches Bibelwerk, 1971); J. J. Stamm and H. Bietenhard, *Der Weltfriede im Alten und Neuen Testament* (Zurich: Zwingli Verlag, 1959); Odil Hannes Steck, "Jerusalemer Vorstellungen vom Frieden und ihre Abwandlungen in der Prophetie des Alten Israel," in *Frieden – Bibel – Kirche* (ed. Liedke), 75–95 [see pp. 49–68 above]; idem, "Prophetische Kritik der Gesellschaft," in *Christentum und Gesellschaft* (ed. Wenzel Lohff and Bernhard Lohse; Göttingen: Vandenhoeck & Ruprecht, 1969), 46–49; and Claus Westermann, "Der Frieden (*Shalom*) im Alten Testament," in *Studien zur Friedensforschung* 1 (ed. G. Picht and H. E. Tödt; Stuttgart: Ernst Klett Verlag; Munich: Kösel-Verlag, 1969), 144–177 [see pp. 16–48 above]; see also Gillis Gerleman, "*šlm* genug haben," *THAT,* 2:919–935.

18. Koch, *Entstehung,* 238.

19. See Gerhard von Rad, *Old Testament Theology* (Edinburgh: Oliver & Boyd, 1965), 2:155ff. [*Theologie des Alten Testaments* (2nd ed.; Munich: Chr. Kaiser Verlag, 1961), 2:166ff.].

20. Wildberger, *Jesaja,* 23ff.

21. But not as an encounter with the "summum bonum" as Ludwig Köhler assumes by misunderstanding the cultic background; see his *Old Testament Theology* (trans. A. S. Todd; Philadelphia: Westminster Press, 1957), 53 [*Theologie des Alten Testaments* (4th ed.; Tübingen: J. C. B. Mohr [Paul Siebeck], 1966), 35].

22. O. Eissfeldt, "Yahweh Zebaoth," in *Kleine Schriften* (ed. R. Schellheim and F. Maass; Tübingen: J. C. B. Mohr [Paul Siebeck], 1966), 3:103–133. Westermann has helpfully drawn my attention to the fact that one must make a clear distinction between Yahweh as the Holy One in Isaiah 6 as a predicate in the cult, a commonality of Israel with its environment, for example as seen in the reverence for El as the Holy, and the new shape of the concept under Isaiah of "the Holy One of Israel," whereby the cultic-timeless holiness of Yahweh is tied to the history of God's people. The latter concept tries to indicate that the holiness of God is revealed through and in God's actions to God's people. There is

an exact parallel in P (Priestly Document), in the use of the concept *kabod Yahweh.* Cf. Claus Westermann, "Die Herrlichkeit Gottes in der Priester-schrift," in *Wort — Gebot — Glaube: Beiträge zur Theologie des Alten Testaments. Walther Eichrodt zum 80. Geburtstag* (ed. H.-J. Stoebe with J. J. Stamm and E. Jenni; ATANT 59; Zurich: Zwingli Verlag, 1970), 227–249.

23. Yahweh Sabaoth: Isa. 1:9–24; 2:12; 3:1, 15; 5:7; 6:3, 5; 8:13, 18; 9:5, 12, 18; 10:31; 14:24, 27; 17:3; 22:5, 12, 14, 15, 25; 28:22, 29; 29:6; 30:15; 31:4, 5. Holy One of Israel: 5:19; 30:11, 12; 31:1. On the origin of the concept, see H. W. Schmidt, "Wo hat die Aussage 'Jahwe der Heilige' ihren Ursprung?" *ZAW* 74 (1962): 62–66.

24. This is a pedagogical style of speech borrowed from the wisdom literature; cf. Wildberger, *Jesaja,* 14f.

25. Wildberger (*Jesaja,* p. 132) surmises a solid cultic tradition that spoke about Yahweh's appearance for judgment, but he draws no further conclusions. The fact that this coming to judgment is attached to the annunciatory section of a judgment speech implies that form (judgment speech) and content (the judicial process) are consciously being brought together in this language. At the same time, this suggests that for Isaiah the judgment speech had a mere temporal character, to be superseded by God's actual speaking in the judgment, at which time it will also be confirmed. This helps us to understand the linkage between the natural and the legal categories, both of which appear in Isaiah's judgment speeches. Analogous to the natural (childhood) relationships, the relationship of God and people is broken through the fault of the people. The efforts of Yahweh through rebukes and discipline to restore the relationship remained fruitless. All that is now left is to bring charges, to present a legal case before the court. This is an extreme consequence — what father would take his own children to court? The Old Testament concept of God includes God as both prosecutor and judge.

26. Wildberger, *Jesaja,* 164ff.

27. *'t-h'm hzh.*

28. Cf. Isa. 5:26–29; 7:18–19; 7:20; 18:5–6; 22:15–18; 28:5–13; 29:5c–7; 29:9–10.

29. Westermann, *Basic Forms of Prophetic Speech,* 108.

30. Isa. 1:18–19; 3:25–26; 17:1–5; 28:1–4; 29:9–10; 30:13–14.

31. Isa. 3:16–17; 5:26–29; 7:18–20; 8:5–8; 18:1–6; 22:15–18; 28:7–13; 28:21f.; 29:5c–7.

32. Yahweh can be assumed to be the subject of the sentence; cf. Wildberger, *Jesaja,* 226.

33. Ditto; cf. ibid., 306.

34. Ibid., 150, whereby the reach "for any means" consists of their throwing themselves open to the first man available!

35. These verses serve to confirm the impression that to some degree the prophets were a conservative element in Israelite society. They are the guardians of traditional notions of order; they are not revolutionaries.

36. The Isaianic authorship of these words is a matter of debate. See J. Schoneveld, "Jesaja I 18–20," *VT* 13 (1963): 342–344.

37. F. Hesse, *Das Verstockungsproblem im Alten Testament* (BZAW 74; Berlin: A. Töpelmann, 1955), 41ff.

38. I am following H. Barth on this point rather than Wildberger and others. Cf. Barth, "Israel und das Assyrerreich," 109–134; 44–46. With regard to my own differently nuanced understanding of 7:10–17, see the reasons given in the text.

39. Wildberger, *Jesaja,* 367.

40. To look for the person addressed in a song of thanksgiving, as does Wildberger (*Jesaja,* 371), is strange. The one addressed is Yahweh.

41. Read *haggîlah.*

42. On 'l as foreign overlordship, see Wildberger, *Jesaja,* 375.

43. Gerhard von Rad, *Der Heilige Krieg im alten Israel* (3rd ed.; Göttingen: Vandenhoeck & Ruprecht, 1958), 9.

44. See Judges 7.

45. The paired words "boot-garment" (v. 5) should be viewed as a merism; they signify the soldiers or the soldiers' gear.

46. On the enthronement formula in v. 6a and other words analogous to a royal proclamation, see Wildberger, *Jesaja,* 380.

47. On the meaning of shalom as welfare, see A. Alt, "Jesaja 8,23–9,6, Befreiungsmacht und Krönungstag," in *Kleine Schriften zur Geschichte des Volkes Israel* (ed. Martin Noth; Munich: C. H. Beck, 1959), 3:219ff.

48. Cf. G. Fohrer, *Das Buch Jesaja,* vol. 1 (Zürcher Bibelkommentar; 2nd ed.; Zurich: Zwingli Verlag, 1967).

49. Isa. 41:17–20; 42:14–17; 43:16–21; 46:9–13; 49:7–12; 49:24–26; 51:9–52:3; 54:1–10; 54:11–17; 55:1–5; 55:6–11; 55:12–13.

50. Isa. 41:8–13; 41:14–16; 43:1–7; 44:1–5; 46:3–4.

51. Westermann, *Isaiah,* 11 [*Jesaja,* 13].

52. Westermann's interpretation of the promise of salvation is as follows: "Behold, I make of you an instrument that is capable of overcoming the obstacles set up by your foes, which separate you from your homeland" (*Isaiah,* 77 [*Jesaja,* 65]).

53. See ibid., 97–101 [81–84].

54. See above pp. 72f. [22 in original, in connection with n. 10].

55. See above pp. 82f. [34f. in original].

56. See above p. 83 [36 in original].

57. See above pp. 84–89 [37–42 in original]. The notion that a remnant of the people is to be the bearer of a new future, which God is holding in readiness for them, cannot be claimed for Isaiah (cf. von Rad, *Old Testament Theology,* 2:160–161 [*Theologie,* 2:171–172]; it must be remembered that von Rad credits passages to Isaiah that the newer literature calls into question, e.g., Isa. 17:3–5; 14:32). The word "remnant" (*shear*) appears in Isa. 10:16–19 within the framework of an exilic judgment announcement of total destruction; further in exilic salvation announcements: Isa. 10:20–23; 11:11–12; 11:15–16 (these passages are close to those

of Deutero-Isaiah); 28:2–6. Further in the judgment announcements against foreign nations: Babel, 14:22–23; Moab, 16:14; Kedar, 21:16–17 and in the apparently genuine Isaianic judgment announcement against Damascus (*sic*) 17:1–3. In all these cases, "remnant" signifies the total destruction, as is true also of all other passages in which Isaiah uses the word "left over" (*ytr*).

58. The disciples of Isaiah place a stronger accent on the minimization of violence since the destruction of war materials, including the soldiers' gear, is a precondition for the coming of the ruler of peace. See pp. 87f. above [40f. in original].

59. See pp. 82–84 above [pp. 34–37 in original] (*Verstockungsproblem*).

60. A further step along this road is contained in Isa. 11:1–5.

5

Swords Into Plowshares: Misuse of a Word of Prophecy?

Hans Walter Wolff

"Swords into plowshares." Several years ago young people of the church in the German Democratic Republic chose as their motto this phrase from the Old Testament prophets. They wore it, sewn on their jackets and shirts, but this was immediately forbidden by the authorities. Yet this watchword quickly moved across the border into "West Germany," where Christians who were members of the peace movement picked it up everywhere.

This prophetic word is not only made use of — even loved — by peace advocates but it is also a matter of resolute controversy among theologians. In the face of the extreme threats to the future of the world, the lack of agreement on the meaning of this prophecy forbids us to remain silent on the matter. Rather, we ought to attempt to overcome the impasse, or lack of unity, in its interpretation. I shall attempt to make several exegetical observations which I hope will promote some unanimity in our understanding of the Christian's witness to the world.

For the sake of some methodological clarity, I begin with questions addressed to Professor Trutz Rendtorff. In an interview with Professors Rendtorff and Dorothee Soelle, reported by the magazine *Der Spiegel* (Oct. 10, 1983, vol. 37, no. 41), Professor Soelle made passing reference to the passage in Isaiah about "beating swords into plowshares." To this, Professor Rendtorff responded, "Which prophet should we listen to, Professor Soelle? Surely you

This chapter was first presented as a guest lecture at the University of Munich, January 27, 1984. From *CurTM* 12 (1985): 133–147.

know the word of the prophet Joel: 'Beat your plowshares into swords and your pruning hooks into spears' (Joel 3:10)? How do we resolve the dilemma of which biblical passage we should follow? We are not relieved of making our own individual decisions by reference to such texts." The editor of *Der Spiegel* then asked: "Who interprets the Christian teaching correctly, Professor Soelle or Professor Rendtorff?" Later, Rendtorff commented: "You can surely see that also in theology different positions can be represented. But each individual must decide for himself. For my generation, this has been a theme of life."

If I understand Trutz Rendtorff correctly in this interview, he intends to suggest in a preliminary way two things for consideration: (1) The Bible contradicts itself. Individual Bible passages do not help us to decide whether, according to Isaiah, peace will be secured through disarmament or whether, according to Joel, arming for war, at least at certain times, protects against its dangers. The Bible provides evidence for both views. (2) The criteria for our decisions in such matters are to be found outside the scripture. Therefore Christians are unable to reach unanimity on such matters. Each person must arrive at his or her own decision and also allow the decision of others to stand as valid.

Joel 3 vs. Isaiah 2?

Allow me to pose two methodological counterquestions. First, is not Rendtorff's opposing of Isaiah 2 ("swords into plowshares") and Joel 3 ("plowshares into swords") to be understood as a dramatic gesture in the discussion? Do we not agree that, for the genuine understanding of these texts, their context deserves attention?

How are we to interpret the reference in Joel 3? The context of Joel 3:9–12 (Heb.: 4:9–12) clearly indicates that the prophet proclaims Yahweh's judgment on the nations. Because nations of the world have severely mistreated Israel, the people of God (cf. Joel 3:1–3), they are all to bestir themselves and be gathered together before their judge (Joel 3:12). With biting sarcasm this gathering for punishment is characterized as an all-inclusive mobilization for war:

> Proclaim this among the nations:
> Prepare for a holy war!
> Arouse the warriors!

> Let all the men of war draw near,
> let them come up! (Joel 3:9)

And then the entire war is turned into irony by the reversal of the passage in Isaiah:

> Beat your plowshares into swords
>   and your pruning hooks into lances!
> Let the weak say: "I am a warrior." (Joel 3:10)
> Come, all you nations round about.

(But for what purpose? For a great war and victory? No!):

> So that Yahweh may shatter your heroes. (V. 11)
> For there I (God, the Lord) will sit to judge
>   all the nations round about. (V. 12).[1]

Here we find it blatantly stated that all military preparation — even when peaceful farming and vinedressing implements are turned into weapons, even when all the men are summoned, including the weaklings, untutored in war — is completely in vain. Thus, in principle, Joel 3 by no means stands in contradiction to Isaiah 2. Joel emphasizes with sarcasm that all military preparation must come before the judgment seat of God and be annihilated. The phrase "plowshares into swords" makes a blunt mockery of the world powers, who think that by completely arming themselves with much effort they will have power and superiority over the people of God. Joel 3:16b then adds:

> But for his (weaponless) people Yahweh is a refuge,
> and a stronghold for the people of Israel.

Once the context of the passage is correctly understood, we find not an opposition between Joel 3 and Isaiah 2 but instead in both texts the declaration of an end to the wars of the nations. It seems to me that, on the basis of these observations about the context, there can be agreement among us.

Second, how are we to evaluate Trutz Rendtorff's statement which emphasizes that each individual must make his or her own decisions? Is a person — including each Christian — really free to make up his or her own mind regarding military armaments, since our modern weaponry brings humankind closer to total self-destruction than ever before? The slogan from Joel, "plowshares into swords," by no means has the sense of a divine command to make military preparation; rather, it is a divine judgment upon massive armaments. Surely, as always, we may not arbitrarily isolate a given passage from its context. But, as Christians, where else should we seek help for making decisions in these matters, if not in the entire kerygmatic intention of the Old and New Testaments? In view of military threats capable of annihilating the human race, where else should we Christians find an orientation for our yes or no than in the foundational concepts of the canon of our faith? The Sixth Assembly of the World Council of Churches has challenged the church "to increase its efforts, in a common witness to a divided world, to oppose with renewed energy the threats to peace." So we want the endeavors of our biblical exegesis to arrive at a common understanding and decision about peace in our world. Of this I am certain: if we will listen to the biblical witness, there need not be a permanent split on matters of war and peace also in the church.

War and Peace

Before we investigate more closely the disputed meaning of the prophetic words "swords into plowshares," and before we make at least a preliminary comparison of related themes in the New Testament, let us discuss the main themes connected with war in the Old Testament.

Ancient Israel was well acquainted with the "war cry." In 1916 Hermann Gunkel described Israel's "warlike spirit" under the title "Israelitisches Heldentum und Kriegsfrömmigkeit im Alten Testament" (Israelite heroism and martial piety in the Old Testament). The nature and disposition of the ancient Israelites can hardly be distinguished from that of the neighboring peoples, and, unfortunately, an even smaller distinction exists between the broadest streams of Christianity and the world, even in the twentieth century. Nevertheless we have been made more and more aware of a series of voices that indicate that in the "flesh" of the Old Testament we encounter the "spirit" of Israel's God. In several highly significant streams of tradition, even in the midst of the old words, we hear a new word, pointing toward the future, giving us hope and directing our path.

To begin with, I call attention to the narratives that attest to the so-called holy war, in which Israel, without any weapons, stands before its heavily armed enemies and then in a wondrous manner experiences the truth that Moses calls out to them in Ex. 14:14:

> Yahweh will fight for you, and you
> have only to be still and astonished.

This is the way Israel experienced the exodus, and so Israel's faith was founded and ever and again renewed.[2] Later narratives attest to the same faith, as we find, for example, in the taking of Jericho (Joshua 6: Jericho's walls collapsed without the use of any weapons, as the priests marched around the city with the ark, trumpets, and shouting); or when Midian was defeated (Judges 7: Israel's army, having been repeatedly reduced, used no weapons, but smashed jars, torches, and trumpets to put holy terror into the enemy, a terror that caused them to destroy themselves); or, when David fought Goliath (1 Samuel 17: the giant Goliath, his sword, lance, and spear notwithstanding, was defeated by the shepherd boy, who marched forth in the name of Yahweh of Hosts). Seen from a historical point of view, these may have been quite insignificant experiences of deliverance from some difficulty, but Israel's faith had shaped them into a grand narrative in order to awaken new faith. In this way, prophetic expectation about the future could look backward into Israel's history.

Isaiah condemned the attempts of his contemporaries to find security through military power:

> Woe to those who go down to Egypt for help
>   who rely on horses.
> They trust in chariots because they are many,
> but they do not look to the Holy One of Israel
>   or consult Yahweh. (Isa. 31:1–3)
> In returning and rest
>   you shall be saved. (Isa. 30:15)

Israel's continued existence is never guaranteed by the usual deterrence of the enemy through fearsome armaments. Thus we find the prophet Hosea making an absolute contrast between military security and trust in Yahweh:

> Assyria shall not save us,
>   we will not ride upon horses,
> Nor will we any longer say "our God"
>   to the work of our hands. (Hos. 14:3)

The notion that "Yahweh destroys weapons" becomes one of the great themes of the Old Testament.[3] Psalm 46, a Song of Zion, puts it this way:

> The nations rage, the kingdoms totter,
>   . . . Yahweh of Hosts is with us.

> Come, behold the works of Yahweh,
> ... He makes wars cease to the end of the earth:
> He breaks the bow, shatters the spear,
>   and burns the chariots of fire. (Ps. 46:6–9)

One cannot miss hearing in the Old Testament a decisive "No" to every trust in any kind of weapons. Biblical faith decisively rejects all that has to do with war, not only in the outside world but also in Israel! Entirely unambiguous is the new tone sounded in the midst of the Old Testament: faith in the God of Israel and security through military power are not compatible.

Alongside this "No" to military weapons stands an equally clear "Yes" to peace.[4] Here I shall refer to a series of prophetic texts that we think of as messianic prophecies. Too little attention has been paid to the fact that all of these texts proclaim peace as well as a coming Messiah. We shall examine the most important prophecies, which strengthen the expectation that something new is coming into the world, which will nullify the old rules of war, whereby one group or nation was pitted against another.

In Isaiah 9, God is given praise first of all because he — once again — has overcome military oppression (Isa. 9:4) and destroyed the last traces of the soldiers' equipment (v. 5) in preparation for handing over sovereign authority to the Messiah. The Messiah himself, however, is given the lordly titles of "Wonderful Counselor, Mighty God, Everlasting Father, Prince of Peace" (v. 6). The primary accent apparently rests on the last title, for the coming ruler is enthroned only so that "peace without end" can be established. The pedestal upon which his throne rests is called "justice and righteousness."

The promise in Isaiah 11 goes into more detail about the instruments the Messiah will use to bring about and maintain peace:

> He will smite the violent with the rod of his mouth
> and with the breath of his lips he will slay the wicked. (Isa. 11:4)

Thus it is exclusively "word" and "spirit" which are used by the Messiah to stop those who commit deeds of violence. The power of his words and the authority of his spirit do away with injustice, the source of discord. The churches of the third world in their meeting at Vancouver placed special emphasis on the connection between righteousness and peace (cf. Isa. 32:17: "The fruit of righteousness will be peace"). The Messiah offers care and concern especially for those who are weak and have few legal rights.

In addition to this peace which society will enjoy, Isa. 11:6–8 speaks of an unprecedented ecological peace:

> The infant shall play over the hole of the cobra. . . .
> The wolf shall live with the sheep,
>   and the leopard shall live with the kid.

This messianic ecology amazes us. The narrow confines within which we usually envision the development of a future peace are widened through fables and leave quickly behind the sphere of what is humanly possible. In Isa. 11:10 the messianic age is also described in terms of world peace:

> The root of Jesse shall stand
>   as an ensign for the peoples.
> Him shall the nations seek.

The Messiah is the last refuge to whom the peoples can turn with their problems. In Micah 5:5a it can even be said of the Messiah: "He shall be the peace" (or: "He will bring about peace" [?])[5] and, indeed, even "unto the ends of the earth" (Micah 5:4b). He will be the son of the small town of Bethlehem, which never mustered a significant number of troops for the Israelite army ("little among the thousands of Judah," 5:2). He will conduct his office as a shepherd (5:4: "he will feed his flock in the strength of Yahweh"). There is no mention of any kind of military weaponry.

Zechariah 9:9–10 is very clear on this point and goes further by adding three ideas. (1) Although the Messiah himself is proclaimed also as a king ("Behold, your king comes to you!"), the traditional picture of a king is completely changed. Lacking power of any kind, he is even described as "poor and needy." He does not ride upon a charge (an animal of war), but upon an ass, indeed the weak foal of an ass (the animal of the common people). (2) This king, himself weaponless, will disarm his own people:

> He will cut off the chariot from Ephraim
> and the war horse from Jerusalem,
>   and he will break the battle bow. (Zech. 9:10)

Those who are most closely connected with this king (Ephraim, Jerusalem), his own people, are the first to be disarmed. (3) Finally, he will "command peace to the nations"; indeed, this peace will encompass the world ("from sea to sea, from the River to the ends of the earth").[6]

Now let us summarize: The expectation of a Messiah belongs inseparably with the hope for an end to war, the destruction of weapons, and the establishment of peace between nations, including social justice. When the disciples of Jesus called their master the Christ, that is, the Messiah, they hardly could have been unaware of these motifs from messianic prophecy. Does not the passage in Eph. 2:14, "He is our peace," recall Micah 5:5a and Isa. 9:6-7? Is it not true that the hymnic praise of the inaugurator of peace is at the heart and center of messianic thinking?

But what is the relationship of the one whom Jesus' disciples saw as "their peace" and peace for the nations? At this point we must turn our attention, unhurriedly and with exegetical precision, to the prophetic text from which the catchphrase "Swords into plowshares" is taken.

An Interpretation of Isaiah 2 and Micah 4

Our passage is the most significant promise for Jerusalem on the theme of world peace that is known in the Old Testament. In this particular text are combined the most important elements of tradition concerning the theme "war and peace." This prophecy comes down to us in two similar, almost verbally identical traditions, in Isa. 2:2-4 and Micah 4:1-3. In their present literary compositions, both passages are attached immediately to older prophecies that threaten Zion with devastating blows of destruction, a destruction that surely had already taken place by the time of this prophetic word of promise. This promise is to be regarded as "eschatological" in the strict sense of the term. It reckons with a great change in the world. Mount Zion and the temple of Yahweh, which had become an expanse of ruins, will in the end range above all mountaintops of the world. The nations of the world, until then in conflict, will stream to Zion for universal instruction through the word of Yahweh. And thus the prevailing world politics will be put to an unequivocal and final end.

> Nations shall not lift up sword against nation
> neither shall they learn war anymore. (Isa. 2:4)

The introductory formula "It shall come to pass in the latter days" (RSV) is meant to be understood in an eschatological sense. The Septuagint correctly rendered the eschatological expression, as did the Vulgate (*in novissimo dierum*). I translate "But in days to come, at the passing of this age," because the text refers less to the "last days" (Luther) or the "end" (thus the German Einheitsübersetzung) of the present age than it does to the age that is presently still hidden, a time that is entirely new. In the postexilic literature we find the expression "in the latter days" more frequently used to characterize a change of fortune, especially for hostile nations (Jer. 48:47; 49:39) and, indeed, for all peoples (Ezek. 38:16). Evidence for an early postexilic date of the prophetic promise in Isaiah 2/ Micah 4 is also found in the word statistics and the new thematic connection of older traditions.[7]

We turn now to the structure of the basic text as it has been handed down similarly in the books of Isaiah and Micah. We may distinguish between three strophes.

The first strophe consists of Isa. 2:2 and Micah 4:1, including in each instance the first three words of the following verse. In three double triplets (3+3), the first strophe announces the vision of the surpassing height of the temple mount in Jerusalem and streaming of the nations to it:[8]

> But in the days to come, at the passing of this age,
> the mountain of Yahweh's house
>   shall be established as the highest of mountains.
> It shall be raised up above the hills.
> To it will flow (all) peoples (nations),
>   and the multitude of the nations (peoples) will come.

The second strophe consists of the continuation of the third verse of Isaiah 2 and the second of Micah 4. It offers a report of unnamed nations summoning one another to make the pilgrimage to Zion:

> They say: "Come, let us go to the mountain of Yahweh,
> to the house of the God of Jacob."

They expect that Yahweh's voice will provide them with instruction; this is made emphatic by a brief verse formulated as a double doublet (2+2):

> That he may teach us his ways,
>   and that we may walk in his paths.

Then another double triplet (3+3) speaks of the fulfillment of this expectation that the word of Yahweh will come forth out of Zion:

> For out of Zion shall go forth instruction,
>   the word of Yahweh from Jerusalem.

The third strophe (v. 4 in Isaiah 2; v. 3 in Micah 4) contains the specific promise of the word of Yahweh, which is the particular scope of this great prophetic text. Indeed, we read for the first time a conciliatory statement about justice from Yahweh:

He will make conciliation between (Micah: many) peoples (nations), give justice for numerous nations (peoples) (Micah: afar off).

Two further double triplets express the effects of peace among the peoples, namely, the transforming of weapons into peaceful implements and the end both of war and of the study of war:

> Then they shall beat their swords into plowshares,
>   and their spears into pruning hooks.
> No longer shall nation lift up sword against nation
>   nor shall they learn war anymore.

The Hebrew texts in Isaiah and Micah exhibit small variants when compared with one another. Such variations suggest that there was a lively oral tradition that handed on this great prophetic promise. (An early example of the modern popularity of this pericope!) A most significant addition occurs in Micah 4:4. Whereas the basic text in Micah—almost identical with that in Isaiah—speaks of overcoming the conflict among the nations, this later addition in v. 4 draws the consequences for the peaceful individual life which is to be hoped for. The idyllic sketch presented in this verse departs from the context and, with its lines of four stresses each, is also rhythmically different:

> They shall sit every man under his vine
>   and under his fig tree—
>   and no one shall be afraid.
> For the mouth of Yahweh of Hosts has spoken.

In postexilic times such words were also used to portray the golden age of peace during Solomon's reign (1 Kings 5:5; cf. 2 Kings 18:31) as a time of security, free from the dangers of war; as a life of joy (cf. 1 Kings 4:20 with 5:5) and neighborly friendship (Zech. 3:10, "In that day every one of you will invite his neighbor under his vine and under his fig tree"). No terror disturbs a sociable, serene community life. By the addition of v. 4, the universal promise of this prophetic text is reinterpreted in terms derived from the sphere of intimate peasant life.

A different sort of addition to the unconditional promise of peace just noted in Micah 4:4 are those expansions which are not a part of the promise but instead draw conclusions that are for the purpose of offering helpful orientation for a present crisis. The additions occur in Isaiah (2:5) as well as in Micah (4:5), but each differs considerably from the other. This, once again, may indicate a lively oral tradition through the recitation of these words in the worship service.

Let us begin with the shorter, more prosaic text in Isaiah. To the grand, three-strophied promise an admonition has been attached which is meant to address the then present audience:

> O house of Jacob!
> Come and let us walk in the light of Yahweh. (Isa. 2:5)

One cannot fail to recognize the connection of the wording with the previous verses. The address "house of Jacob" recalls Isa. 2:3, according to which the peoples are to go up to the "house of the God of Jacob." Similarly, the exhortation "Come and let us walk in the light of Yahweh." It also takes up the wording of the expectation that is expressed in 2:3a: "that we may walk in his paths." Other early postexilic texts about Jerusalem also speak about walking "in the light of Yahweh"; indeed, these texts speak not only of the "peoples" (Isa. 60:3) but also of Israel (Isa. 60:1–3, 19; cf. Micah 7:8; Pss. 56:14; 89:16; 27:1).

It is to be noted that the grand promise (Isa. 2:2–4; also Micah 4:1–3) spoke not of Israel but of the peoples inclusively and of their relationship to the house and the word of Yahweh. On the other hand, now the leader in liturgical worship summons in Isa. 2:5 only the worshipers in Jerusalem, as "house of Jacob," to walk in Yahweh's light. What else can this mean than that the Israelite hearers already now should follow the instructions of Yahweh, which at a future time will lead all peoples to peace with one another (Isa. 2:3–4)? Thus the eschatological promise for the peoples has become a word to help give direction for Israel for the present.

That such a summons belongs to a crisis in the orientation of the life of the people of God is made even more clear when we examine the corresponding passage in Micah 4:5. For in this verse the difference at that time between the world of the nations, on the one hand, and Israel, on the other, is made explicit. At the same time, the nonfulfillment of the promise of peace among nations stands in contrast with Israel's accomplishment of obedience to God:

> All the peoples walk
>   each in the name of its god.
> But we will walk
>   in the name of Yahweh,
> Our God for ever and ever.

The connection between v. 5 and vs. 1–4 in Micah 4 has until now been given too little attention. The difficulty is related to the meaning of the conjunction that connects v. 5 with vs. 1–4. Usually the particle is translated in the causal sense as "for." It is thus translated in the Septuagint and the Vulgate as well as in the older Luther translation, the Zürcher Bibel (1954), the Jerusalem Bible (1968), and unfortunately also now in the Unified Translation (Einheitsübersetzung, 1980). Such a translation of the particle makes the significance of the connection of v. 5 with vs. 1–4 completely unclear, for the declaration in v. 5 can just as little serve as a motivation for vs. 1–4 as does the exhortation in Isa. 2:5 for vs. 2–4. It is probably for this reason that the revised Luther translation of 1964 leaves the conjunction untranslated—an unsatisfactory solution offered out of embarrassment.

But the connection between v. 5 and the preceding context becomes quite clear if we understand the conjunction to have a concessive meaning ("although," "even if," "notwithstanding"), as Th. C. Vriezen[9] has convincingly demonstrated (cf., e.g., Isa. 54:10, "Although the mountains depart and the hills be removed, my steadfast love shall never depart from you"; cf. also Isa. 51:6; Prov. 6:35). Thus the connection of v. 5 with the preceding word of promise becomes clear. It may be paraphrased:

> Even though all peoples go (their own way)
>   each in the name of its god,
> we ourselves go (even now our own way)
>   in the name of Yahweh, our God, for ever and ever.

Thus we have here a confessional statement, which the worshiping community speaks in the first person plural and which is solemnly concluded with a liturgical expression ("for ever and ever," as in Pss. 45:18; 145:21; etc.). This confession, in relation to the preceding words of promise, precisely corresponds in substance to the exhortation in Isa. 2:5. But it points out clearly to the spiritual crisis for Israel in order to lead it away from this to an unequivocal action of the worshiping community. The universal promise, according to which all nations will be at peace by walking in the ways of Yahweh, is at that time completely unfulfilled. The nations of the world do not yet think about directing their lives in accordance with the word of Yahweh. But the community of Yahweh even now should (Isa. 2:5) and will (Micah 4:5) obey his instructions and his word; even now it is to make its swords into plowshares and not learn war anymore. So the worshipers of Yahweh even now are to walk on the path which is promised for all peoples for the days that are to come. Even now! — although the nations still follow their gods of war. The way of Yahweh is the only lasting way, the path that leads to what is ultimate and final, the path that also all people must tread in the future.

In the fifth of these considerations, several questions arise that I would like to put to Wolfhart Pannenberg and his article "Swords Into Plowshares —The Meaning and Misuse of a Prophetic Word."[10]

1. Pannenberg correctly states that the prophecy about "Beating your swords into plowshares" is not found in the context of a direct political challenge; rather, it belongs to an eschatological vision. Nevertheless, did not our exegetical observations convince us that this form-critical analysis of the context is yet incomplete? The present literary context of the promise makes it apply to the contemporary times of a new audience, with the exhortation to the house of Jacob that it should even now walk and act in the light of Yahweh (Isa. 2:5). Our analysis further showed that in Micah 4:5 there is a corresponding clarification of the divine will that, unlike the nations, the house of Jacob is to act even now according to Yahweh's will for peace. Does this not fully justify the use of this passage by the Protestant youth in the German church? Indeed, does it not unambiguously require it for the worshiping community which hears these words?

2. Pannenberg refers in his article to Isa. 2:5 and suggests that the prophetic vision, with its reference to law (Isa. 2:3), could become a certain signpost in our own historical situation. However, does not this restriction of focus on the concept of law in the passage arbitrarily diminish the contemporary significance of the text's content and meaning? Pannenberg's admonition to work on international law is of course useful. But does it in fact correspond to the content of the text? The expectation voiced in the text points ahead not to the law as such but to the fact that Yahweh judges the nations: that Yahweh's word and instruction will lead to peace. In this passage those who hear the word of God have a question put to them for the present as well as for the future. And what about the consequences that the text draws? Those who hear these words are to transform their weapons into implements of peace; they are to stop learning about and declaring war. As a consequence of Yahweh's mediating and judging of nations, it is apparent that the decision to beat swords into plowshares cannot be evaded. The direction things are to take is unambiguous. Any alternative to this, especially in the direction of building modern weapons capable of annihilating humankind, is surely not to be found here or among the many related Old or New Testament texts. Surely it is most

urgent that we work toward an international legal agreement on disarmament, but such acts of conciliation ought not to take the place of what is proclaimed here as the consequences that Yahweh's word wants to call forth. As people who listen to the God of the biblical witnesses, must we not take upon ourselves the rigorous requirements of a special and proleptic, one-sided life of peace, as this text and many of the words of Jesus and the apostles teach us in the New Testament?

3. I hope that I have been able to convince Professor Pannenberg that the confession in Micah 4:5 has great significance for the broader understanding of this prophetic text and for the problem of its misuse. In this passage the conduct of the nations in those days and the community of Yahweh is clearly distinguished. This clarity of distinction is completely absent in Pannenberg's article. In Micah 4:5 the people of God clearly perceive that the nations for the time being are a long way from hearing God's word, which can help them achieve peace. But this cannot and should not hinder the worshipers in Zion from following already the ways of their God, in the certainty that the ways of God are the ultimate and final path which, sooner or later, the nations must also tread. But how does this expected action of God's people relate to Pannenberg's idea that "we must hold fast to the principle of mutuality, to the conception of mutual obligations, even when it has to do with questions of disarmament"? The community spoken about in Micah 4:5, in the midst of a world crisis, confesses its faith that it must already work unilaterally for that peace which the nations in general did not yet practice. Pannenberg thinks that even during a time of nuclear armament "peace can be attained and guaranteed only on the basis of mutual give-and-take, and thus on the basis of political agreement." Is this conception of mutuality representative of biblical thought if, as we read elsewhere, "to give is more blessed than to receive"? In any case, it is not compatible with Micah 4:5.

In my opinion, the fear of a misunderstanding and a misapplication of this prophecy is justified only when the watchword "Swords into plowshares" is banned from the historical present of the worshiping community and its members and their public actions and is relegated to an indefinite, far-off future for the nations (or else applied to a spiritual inwardness). One can ask, in the light of present-day Christianity, whether the negotiations of the major powers would not be more successful for achieving world peace if the politicians who want to be Christians would allow a more unequivocal impact of this prophetic word upon their work. In any case, there remains the question about what it is that specifically distinguishes Christian actions in this matter.

4. We have examined a prophetic text that occurs twice in Israel's literary tradition and that exhibits several variations and interpretations in its oral transmission. This prophecy not only takes up those strands of tradition which allowed a new theme to break forth in the midst of the war cry in ancient Israel (we noted above the experience of faith in narratives about the war of Yahweh; the theme "Yahweh destroys weapons" in Zion psalms; the prophetic condemnation of self-security through the politics of military power; and the connection of messianic expectation with a hope for peace); it also stands in a relationship to New Testament texts, which we must now seek to determine. In conclusion, let us ask whether the New Testament, in the light of the life and activity of the followers of Jesus, at some point reflects the meaning and the spirit of our prophetic text and whether the New Testament does not disclose even more the ultimate basis for the text.

Some New Testament Parallels

According to Romans 12, with the appearance of Jesus Christ the eschaton of the mercy of God has entered into our history. Accordingly, the community of Jesus' followers is not to be conformed to this world; rather, in its reasonable worship, the community should repay no one evil for evil (cf. Rom. 12:17–21!). This means: "If possible, so far as it depends on you, live peaceably with all" (v. 18). "Do not be overcome by evil, but overcome evil with good" (v. 21). The First Letter of Peter reckons with the fact that the Christian community, like its Lord, will experience suffering. The letter reminds the community that its conduct should conform to the example of Christ, who "when he was reviled, he did not revile in return; when he suffered, he did not threaten; but he trusted to him who judges justly" (1 Peter 2:21–24). Jesus' disciples, according to Luke 9:51–54, were inclined to let "fire from heaven" fall upon their enemies (Luke 9:54). "But Jesus rebuked them and said, 'Do you not know what manner of spirit you are of?'" Do not all of these passages from different areas within the New Testament point in the direction of our prophetic text? Do they not make clear the meaning, the spirit, and the essential foundation of our deeds and actions?

Now, it can be said that, considered sociologically and also in the light of their political problems, the New Testament followers of Jesus are comparable neither to ancient Israel, nor to our national churches, large denominations, nor to the ecumenical movement of the twentieth century. But concerning this, let me ask two questions:

1. In the midst of our human and political problems, must not the church today—if it is to be, remain, or become the church of Jesus Christ—hold fast to the apostolic exhortation, as did early Christianity: "Let your manner of life be worthy of the gospel of Christ" (Phil. 1:27; cf. Col. 1:10)?

2. Does not the church of today in many respects stand closer sociopolitically to the problems of Old Testament Israel than it does to the New Testament community?

Thus we may draw the conclusion that a prophetic text such as Isaiah 2/Micah 4 elucidates and makes concrete for us our responsibilities, though the final basis for our actions is laid in the New Testament.

It is said that everyone wants peace. What is disputed among us is the way to achieve peace: occasional threats with weapons that annihilate humanity or immediate disarmament. Is there a clearer help for Christians in their decision making than the prophetic passage about "turning swords into plowshares," supported by other theological traditions proclaimed in the Old Testament, and by further motivations found in the New Testament? It would be an immeasurable gain if the churches of the world would become more and more unified on this point. There are certainly no significant words of the prophets, of the apostles, or of Jesus that point in any other direction than the prophetic text, "Beat your swords into plowshares." I ask you: if we listen to God's word of reconciliation and if we look to the way of Jesus' cross, must there still be a parting of our ways? No! Nor should this be the case when our encounter with this prophetic word is similar to what Mark Twain once wrote: "It is the Bible passages which I understand that give me a stomach ache, not those that I don't understand." "Beat your swords into plowshares"—that is easy to understand.

Notes

1. This and the following renderings are those of the author, here translated from the German. On the text, cf. H. W. Wolff, *Joel and Amos* (Hermeneia; Philadelphia: Fortress Press, 1977), Joel 3:9-12.

2. Cf. Gerhard von Rad, *Der Heilige Krieg im alten Israel* (3rd ed.; Göttingen: Vandenhoeck & Ruprecht, 1958). [ET: *Holy War in Ancient Israel,* trans. and ed. Dawn Marra and J. H. Yoder (Grand Rapids: Wm. B. Eerdmans Publishing Co., 1991).]

3. Cf. R. Bach, "Der Bogen zerbricht, Spiesse zerschlägt und Wagen mit Feuer verbrennt," in *Probleme biblischer Theologie. Gerhard von Rad zum 70. Geburtstag* (ed. H. W. Wolff; Munich: Chr. Kaiser Verlag, 1971), 13–26.

4. Cf. J. J. Stamm and H. Bietenhard, *Der Weltfriede im Alten und Neuen Testament* (Zurich: Zwingli Verlag, 1959).

5. Cf. H. W. Wolff, *Dodekapropheton 4: Micha* (BKAT 14/4; Neukirchen-Vluyn: Neukirchener Verlag, 1982), Micah 5:5a.

6. W. Rudolph, *Micha–Nahum–Habakuk–Zephanja* (KAT 13/3; Gütersloh: Gütersloher Verlagshaus Gerd Mohn, 1975): "with words he will establish peace for the nations."

7. For further support of this date for the passage, cf. Wolff, *Micha,* 88f.

8. The following translation is based on the text in Micah. The variants in Isaiah are placed in parentheses. Later additions to the Micah text will be noted as such.

9. Th. C. Vriezen, "Einige Notizen zur Übersetzung des Bindewortes *ki*," in *Von Ugarit nach Qumran* (ed. O. Eissfeldt and others; BZAW 77; Berlin: A. Töpelmann, 1961), 266–273; KB (2nd ed.), 433 no. 20.

10. Wolfhart Pannenberg, "Schwerter zu Pflugscharen — Bedeutung und Missbrauch eines Prophetenwortes," *Briefdienst 3/83 des Arbeitskreises* "Sicherung des Friedens," Bad Boll.

6

Response to Hans Walter Wolff

Wolfhart Pannenberg

The epigram taken from Isaiah, "Swords into plowshares," has in our day become a symbol of the church's peace movement in the German Democratic Republic, the symbol of a peace movement that is oppressed, since it directs its demand for disarmament not only to the outside but also to its own state system. In this regard it is easy to sympathize in our country with the demand for disarmament in the East. Nevertheless it would be unjust to appeal to the Christian peace movement in the German Democratic Republic and to its biblical motto if one only applauds the courageous demand for disarmament on the eastern side while drawing back from corresponding demands for disarmament in our own western state system.

To be sure, the word we encounter with the prophets Isaiah (2:4) and Micah (4:3) on the turning of swords into plowshares does not have directly to do with the character of a political demand. It is a constituent part of an eschatological vision of a future time of salvation which, in contrast to the threat of war at that time, will no longer know war and armaments. It is a different picture from the historical present which is distinguished by war and preparation for war.

The prophets Isaiah and Micah are not calling for unilateral

Translation of "Diskussionsbeitrag," *EvT* 44 (1984): 293–297. This article grew out of Wolfhart Pannenberg's comment made in the discussion that followed Hans Walter Wolff's guest lecture at Munich, which is given in the preceding article. — Ed.

disarmament, nor for remaining inactive over against the continuing threats of war, but they are speaking of a time in which there will be no longer any warlike threatening of one people by another: "No nation will again lift up the sword against another and they will not learn war any longer" (Isa. 2:4). Armaments will fall away when they are no longer necessary because threats of war are no longer being made. In this passage the qualitative opposition of the future time of salvation to the de facto historical situation becomes clear. Thus, as now, the present was characterized by the opposing threats of people and nations influenced by the conflicting power claims and governmental systems.

Israelite prophecy cannot rest with the mere establishment of the contrast of the future time of salvation, which will not know war or the threat of war, as over against the life situation of the historical present. The point of the prophetic vision is not yet in view with this. The point consists of an answer to the question, By what means can such a situation of peace be made possible wherein there will be no longer fear of war? The answer to this question stands in the middle of the text in which the word occurs concerning the changing of swords into plowshares. It consists of a prophetic vision of a pilgrimage of people to Zion where the God of Israel lives: the people of all nations will seek instruction from this God concerning justice. This is how the prophet sees it. And that justice which is founded on the authority of the God of Israel will make possible that circumstance of peace which will set aside all threat of war and render superfluous all armaments.

The prophets are very well aware that peace will not be won through the renouncing of armaments. Rather, it will come about by the creation of conditions wherein war and armaments become superfluous. These conditions, however, are contained in the concept of the condition of justice: where justice and righteousness are realized in relations between people and nations, then peace in human relationships is the result. Now, certainly, the content of justice is debatable in the face of the conflicting claims of righteousness which people and nations make against one another. Truly, the content of impartial justice is just as infrequently understood as in its realization.

The prophets were also conscious of this fact in their vision of the pilgrimage of the peoples to Zion. The image of this pilgrimage contains within it the idea that the nations subject their own opposing conceptions of justice and claims to justice under the judgment of the God of Israel, since before all others this God is a God of justice. They seek instruction from him about the content of true justice, and thereby peace is established between them, a peace of such lasting quality that people can come to the place where they forget how to carry out war. Peace, justice, and religion thus belong inseparably together: assured peace stands there where justice is observed. Regard for justice, however, presupposes agreement concerning its content as an expression of true righteousness and such an agreement requires finally a religious foundation in a common faith.

For all of that, the discussion about the actual problems of peace and disarmament at first glance does not become easier, but more difficult. The more clearly one understands the conditions contained in the prophetic vision of a future kingdom of peace in which people can forget the conduct of war, the clearer becomes the distance from that state of affairs and conditions in our own historical situation. In the present world situation, there are few indications that the peoples of the God of Israel, who also is the Father of Jesus Christ, seek instruction concerning the content of justice. Nowhere in our own society does one encounter agreement over the religious bases and criteria of our conception of justice.

In the face of this lack of unity in the consciousness of justice and in the light of the prophetic vision of the conditions for the kingdom of peace in a future time of salvation, it must be considered amazing that the condition of peace between people and nations can still be somewhat realized. Indeed, this external state of peace is always subject to ever-recurring visible regional breakdowns. With this vision, however, a beginning point is already reached so that in spite of the gap between the world political realities of the present and the conditions of the prophetic vision of a future kingdom of peace, this vision can nevertheless become a guide for behavior in our historical present. The prophet Isaiah also does not rest with this opposition of that future kingdom of peace to the politics of his age characterized by war and armaments. He concludes, rather, in his vision of the future kingdom of peace transmitted to us, with a call to the house of Jacob: "Up, let us walk in the light of the LORD" (Isa. 2:5; see also Micah 4:5).

What does it mean, however, to walk in the light of the Lord in this connection? It can only mean to seek justice as it corresponds to the just will of God. For that is the basis of peace. Therefore, peace can be maintained only insofar as one succeeds in preserving the enduring minimum, an agreement in justice consciousness, and where possible to enlarge upon it. That happens inside a state by the reform of legislation or the constitution. In relations between states, however, it happens in the form of a treaty. Negotiations and the observance of treaties create and protect the basis of peace in the relationships between nations.

In comparison with that, questions of armaments are of secondary importance. Neither armament nor disarmament is in itself a dependable enough way for the preservation of lasting peace. Unilateral disarmament and one-sided refusal to arm may be taken as an expression of peaceful intentions; however, they can also tempt opposing states to the misuse of resultant existing military superiority as, among others, the prehistory of World War II teaches. On the other hand, one-sided rearmament can cause the other side certainly to be cautious and to abstain from military adventurism, but it also creates anxiety which can lead to a preventive war. Usually, however, it leads to a process of competitive rearmament. Mobilization can also serve to heighten the risk of breaking apart an existing condition of peace, and it also creates new dangers and can never alone assure for itself a lasting peace.

Peace can only take place by agreement over a reciprocally acceptable and observable condition of justice in the common life of nations. Therefore it was indeed realistic that the prophecy of Old Israel had always warned against an improper trust in armaments and military alliances. Excessive trust in armament and military strength can lead directly into destruction, since it turns aside from the question of justice and from the demand for a timely agreement for a condition of justice supportable for all participants.

Thus the prophet Joel represented the call to forge plowshares into swords and pruning forks into spears as an expression of the delusion that drives nations into their mutual destruction (Joel 4:10). With that, Joel reversed the peace vision of Isaiah and Micah in a self-conscious ironic play on words: if there the change of the weapons of war into instruments of peaceful cultivation of the earth was an expression of the condition of peace which was made possible by justice, then in the prophecy of Joel the transformation of the instruments of peaceful life into a preparation for war conjures up the appropriate destruction of that condition.

Such a prophetic critique of the trust in armaments and military strength may certainly not be misunderstood as a call to unilateral disarmament. The criticism has much more to do with pride and the delusion of power. The right for collective self-defense is not thereby called into question; it is, rather, presupposed as self-evident.

The same Isaiah who with biting sharpness could turn against the trust of armaments and military alliances in the year 701 B.C. encouraged King Hezekiah in Jerusalem which was besieged by the Assyrians to stand his ground in an apparently hopeless situation against the overwhelming military superiority of the Assyrian world power: he moved the king to reject the demand for capitulation by the besiegers. Also in that situation the viewpoint of the justice of God appeared to be decisive again. Conviction of the inviolability of Zion was grounded for Isaiah in the divine election of Jerusalem and its dynasty.

Before I deal with Hans Walter Wolff's questions, I must first say that in my opinion he has oversimplified the exegetical matter all too much when he wants to limit the "warring spirit" of the earlier traditions of Israel to only among "the flesh of the Old Israel," as if "the spirit of his God" had nothing to do with that. After all, according to Ex. 17:14, it is Yahweh himself who informed Moses that he wanted "to remove the memory of Amalek completely from under the heavens" (cf. Ex. 17:16). The extermination command which can be seen exactly in accordance with the religious-cultic viewpoint of Deuteronomy (Deut. 20:17f.; cf. 7:16), and the corresponding application of the ban in the Book of Joshua to the whole population of a city, cannot make the hearts of modern friends of peace beat any faster. Nor are they compatible with present-day views of humanity that have been influenced by Christianity. Especially the tradition of peace ideas bound up with Jerusalem is part of a very complex general picture in the Old Testament. This tradition does not unconditionally contradict different warlike strains in the traditions of Israel, since the order of peace is threatened from outside by the "rage of the nations," so that the king had to "break . . . with a rod of iron" (Ps. 2:9) the revolt of the nations against the sovereignty of the peace of Yahweh which he represents. The image of the pilgrimage of the people to Zion in Isaiah 2 and Micah 4 reverses the idea of the rage of the nations into an expectation of a future universal and final peace, as the classical prophet formed it in distinction to the peacelessness of his own time [Odil Hannes Steck, *Friedensvorstellungen im alten Jerusalem* (1972), 70]. That this expectation, according to Isa. 2:5 (as also according to Micah 4:5), should already determine the behavior of the people of God in the present (Wolff's first question) was also emphasized by me. The question is only how this happened. At this point our understandings depart from one another.

Important for my argument is the observation that in Isa. 2:2-4 a significant shift occurs on the turning of the people to the instruction (Isa. 2:2f.) going out from Zion and their reception of the word of the justice of Yahweh (v. 4a), with the result that no armaments are any longer necessary, since no war will take place (v. 4b). This shift cannot be disregarded. Whoever thinks that one can ignore opposing ideas of justice and the demands of the nations, as well as their connections with religions and ideologies, and begins instead with disarmament, cannot call upon Isaiah 2 and Micah 4. Both texts teach that peace is the result of the understanding and realization of justice. Now, Wolff says (in his second observation) that the expectation of the text does "not point to justice as such but to the word of Yahweh and to instruction toward peace." Certainly both belong together. However, I see no justification in the text for the assumption that the *content* of the justice instruction by Yahweh would concern in particular the obligation of peace (or indeed disarmament). Wolff would be entitled to his exposition of Isa. 2:5 (or Micah 4:5) only where "walking in the light of the LORD" has reference to obedience in the face of such instruction. The idea that God speaks justice "between" the nations (v. 4a) concerns, quite generally, the mediation of opposing claims of justice. In addition, the "ways" of Yahweh over which the nations seek instruction, according to 2:3, is to be understood in general in terms of the proclamation within Israel of the justice of God. Where this is heard and followed, the peace obligation is no longer needed as an additional demand. The text portrays peace and disarmament as the natural result of the agreement over disputed claims of justice on the basis of the justice of God and as a consequence of the mediation of justice by God.

Therefore the call to Israel to "walk in the light of the LORD" (Isa. 2:5) is nothing other than to hold firm to the divine justice of Yahweh in distinction to the rest of the nations (Micah 4:5). In my opinion, Wolff can only miss the point of the difference between Israel and the nations (third concern), since he ignores my argument for the priority of the theme of justice and, to be sure, with respect to the fundamental significance of God for the content and obligation of justice. Only from God do the relationships of justice between people come into view here; true justice is dependent upon the foundation of religion, which, to be sure, is "still completely unfulfilled" in the present world. Therefore, in the relationships between people and nations in this world, determined by the power of sin, only a more or less fragile and external condition of peace occurs. Therefore Christians must speak for the enablement and preservation of peace. Even external peace is not possible without a minimum of agreement on justice. This relates to my comments on treaty and mutuality, which are neglected by Wolff. Finally, there is the anthropological root of all ideas of justice, as it comes to expression in the formulation of the golden rule.

7

Peace—God's Gift: Biblical-Theological Considerations

Jacob Kremer

The song of the angels in the Christmas Evangel celebrates and interprets the birth of Jesus in the hymnic form that one finds in apocalyptic writings as well as in the Revelation of John. "Glory to God in the highest" (Luke 2:14) are the well-known words. In the Latin Vulgate it continues: *Et in terra pax hominibus bonae voluntatis* ("And on earth peace to persons of good will"). From this the conclusion was drawn that "peace" was dependent in the first place on the goodwill of people. Martin Luther, in translating the Greek textual version available to him—a later correction of old manuscripts—rendered it: "And peace on earth and a satisfaction for the people." Exegetes are in agreement today that neither the Vulgate, as usually interpreted, nor the Luther Bible represents the original text exactly. The original text would more correctly be translated: "And peace for the people with whom he is pleased" (as in the revised Luther translation of 1975), or else "of his grace" (as in the ecumenical translation, 1981). Some authors would argue that this is also the correct sense of the Vulgate, for the phrase *bonae voluntatis* does not signify the goodwill of the people but rather the *voluntatis Dei* toward the people. That is, even in this old Catholic translation, peace was proclaimed as God's gracious gift.

But what kind of peace is that? What is meant by "peace" here and in the many other Bible passages to which reference is made

Translation of "Der Frieden—Eine Gabe Gottes: Bibeltheologische Erwägungen," *Stimmen der Zeit* 200 (1982): 161–173.

so often in the discussions of peace? Within the framework of this presentation, only a few aspects relevant to the current theme can be developed from the perspective of a New Testament scholar.

Peace/Shalom in the Old Testament

In our daily usage, the word "peace" reflects to a large extent the content of the Latin *pax*. It signifies a reciprocal legal relationship, the elimination of a state of war by means of a pact. In the Bible, including in the New Testament, "peace" has been substantially shaped by the Hebraic *shalom.* The etymological root is drawn from *shalam,* a verb meaning "to have enough, to equalize" (in *Piel:* to pay, to requite). The substantive *shalom,* as frequently used in daily life, usually had an iridescent meaning. Surveying the varieties of usage, one can consider "wholeness," "intactness," "well-being" as the fundamental meaning. (In many passages, that is the sense of "peace" in translation.) But in individual instances, the word can mean quite a variety of things, from "prosperity" to "retaliation" and "punishment" (as in Isa. 53:5). Only seldom and rather late does it occur with the meaning of an alternative to war. Three groupings from the great variety of occurrences in the Old Testament are listed here in brief:

1. The use of shalom as greeting is widespread and ancient. In this case, whether in Israel or in the ancient Near East in general, shalom meant the sense of the good, of faring well, which now was missing and which therefore through the spoken greeting was promised to come. Closely linked to the greeting is the use of shalom in the blessing, as in "The LORD lift up his countenance upon you, and give you peace [wellness]" (Num. 6:26; cf. Pss. 125:5; 128:6). Here it is the opposite of a curse, namely, a God-given order of affairs that makes prosperity possible. A state of peace can also be included as one element alongside others, for example, at the conclusion of the laws on holiness: "And I will give peace in the land, and you shall lie down, and none shall make you afraid; and I will remove evil beasts from the land, and the sword shall not go through your land" (Lev. 26:6).

2. As a clear contrast to war, shalom functions in a contrasting word pair: "a time for war, and a time for peace" (Eccl. 3:8). Nevertheless, "peace" when used in these passages as a contrast to war should not be understood in its contemporary sense. An illustration

for that is Deut. 20:10f.: "When you draw near to a city to fight against it, offer terms of peace to it. And if its answer to you is peace . . . , then all the people who are found in it shall do forced labor for you and shall serve you." Here "peace" means to surrender, to subordinate oneself, to accept service obligations. This unrefined understanding that Israel had of peace was hardly different from that of other nations of the Orient.

The same applies to the use of "peace" in the conflict with the false prophets during the years that preceded the exile. These prophets talked, so it says, to please the king and the people. They proclaimed peace and kept silence about the calamity threatening the people because of their sins (cf. 1 Kings 22:13–28). "They have healed the wound of my people lightly, saying, 'Peace, peace,' when there is no peace" (Jer. 6:14). In this case, "peace," following ancient Oriental understandings, is the order established by the king in the name of God, which preserves the well-being and safety of the people. Over against their rivals, the prophets of Yahweh emphasized that shalom is substantially linked to the just behavior of the kings and of the people. This tying of shalom to a faithful observance of the Torah becomes very clear in the later flashback to the destruction of Jerusalem and going into exile: "O that you had hearkened to my commandments! Then your peace would have been like a river, and your righteousness like the waves of the sea" (Isa. 48:18).

The expectation that the king, on behalf of and in the power of God, can grant peace is also echoed in the passages about a future ideal king, to which the hope for a messianic prince of peace was tied (Ps. 72:2–10; Isa. 6:1–9; 11; Micah 5:1–5). This peace, although painted in part in paradisiacal colors, as in the statement about beating swords into plowshares (Isa. 2:4; Micah 4:3) or the wolf lying down with the lamb (Isa. 11:6–9), is nevertheless the peace of Israel gained by the violent subjection of the other nations. Micah 5:4f. [5f. Eng.] demonstrates this especially well (following on from the announcement of a leader from Bethlehem and Ephrata [cf. Matt. 2:6]):

> And this shall be peace. . . . They shall rule the land of Assyria with the sword, and the land of Nimrod with the drawn sword; and they shall deliver us from the Assyrian when he comes into our land and treads within our border.

This even holds for the expectation of a king of peace in the post-exilic image of one who is poor and just, riding on an ass (Zech.

9:9f.). The context relativizes this ideal image; it concerns the destruction of the opponent in war ("I will brandish your sons, O Zion, over your sons, O Greece, and wield you like a warrior's sword . . . and they shall devour and tread down the slingers" [Zech. 9:13–15]). Later, the saying about beating swords into plowshares is inverted (only as irony?): "Beat your plowshares into swords" (Joel 3:10).

3. For Judaism and for the New Testament, it was, above all, the peace statements in the prophets' words of comfort, after the great catastrophe of exile, that became a guide. To a people that acknowledges its sin and suffers under it, the prophet can now proclaim the shalom of God: "For I know the plans I have for you, says the LORD, plans for welfare (*shalom*) and not for evil [suffering], to give you a future and a hope" (Jer. 29:11). Only God, the Creator, in a kind of new creation can bring about this peace: "I am the LORD, and there is no other. I form light and create darkness, I make weal (*shalom*) and create woe. I am the LORD, who do all these things" (Isa. 45:6f.). In this case, shalom is the "weal" created by Yahweh, the contrast to evil (woe). The same well-being is what is meant in another passage:

> Because of their wicked covetousness I was angry; I struck them, I hid and was angry; but they kept turning back to their own ways. I have seen their ways, but I will heal them; I will lead them and repay them with comfort, creating for their mourners the fruit of the lips. Peace, peace, to the far and the near, says the Lord; and I will heal them. . . . There is no peace, says my God, for the wicked. (Isa. 57:17–21)

The announcement of this peace which God establishes and which consists of fellowship with God is a joyous message: "How beautiful upon the mountains are the feet of the messenger who announces peace, who brings good news, who announces salvation, who says to Zion, 'Your God reigns'" (Isa. 52:7). No matter how these and other promises can be interpreted individually, they did manage to create high expectations among the Jews, whether in the form of an eschatological hope for a Messiah-king from the lineage of David, who would establish a reign of peace, or in the form of apocalyptic, with the expectation of a new Zion descending from heaven to earth, the expectation of a new heaven and a new earth. It is to these hopes that the New Testament books above all, aside from the Jewish writings, bear witness.

"Peace" in the New Testament

1. In the words of Jesus which higher criticism has established as his actual sayings (*ipsissima vox*), little space is given to the word "peace." Yet the central theme, "The time is fulfilled, and the kingdom of God is at hand" (Mark 1:15), builds on these expectations of a new order of life brought about by God. The reign of God as proclaimed by Jesus is that shalom which was promised in the later Old Testament writings as a gift of God (cf. the words of Isa. 52:7, cited above, concerning the good tidings: "Your God reigns.")

When Jesus said to the woman with the hemorrhage, "Go in peace" (Mark 5:34), he was utilizing an old Jewish formula for dismissal. But in his mouth it becomes a promise of salvation for this woman who was suffering and now is healed. Her relationship to God is now in order and she need fear no further sickness as divine punishment; her life is no longer meaningless. This promise of peace and well-being interlaces the entire work of Jesus. Through his healing of the sick he reveals himself as the one who is able to offer troubled people forgiveness of sin and God's salvation, and who does so now already.

When he sent out his disciples, Jesus gave them the authority to mediate "peace," that is, God's salvation: "Whatever town or village you enter, find out who in it is worthy, and stay there until you leave. As you enter the house, greet it. If the house is worthy, let your peace come upon it; but if it is not worthy, let your peace return to you" (Matt. 10:11–13). By means of their words and actions (cf. Matt. 10:7f.) his disciples can and should proclaim and mediate peace as the salvation of God. This proclamation of salvation confronts those being addressed with the decision to open themselves up to this peace through their conversion and faith (Matt. 10:13–35) and to show themselves to be "sons of peace" (Luke 10:6).

It has often been pointed out, quite rightly, that Jesus gave no advice for political action, and this in a time when his people lived in greatest need, and more than a few—and not always the worst ones either—were choosing violent resistance. In the face of a brutal act of violence by the authorities, in which rebels were slaughtered during a ritual offering, Jesus did not call to resistance but to repentance: "Do you think that these Galileans were worse sinners than all the other Galileans, because they suffered thus? I tell you, No; but unless you repent you will all likewise perish" (Luke 13:2f.). Why did Jesus conduct himself so nonpolitically? Because for him, in the end, the peace that he was proclaiming was more than peace on earth and a merely this-worldly salvation, regardless of how much the reign of God already affects the present! Only under this aspect was Jesus able to give his premature death a positive meaning, since for the devout Jew this represented a thwarting of all hope in the attainment of the peace promised in the Old Testament as understood in purely this-worldly terms. Jesus' words and actions show that, for him, the Old Testament promises of shalom as God's gift (peace and salvation) were not understood literally but were to be interpreted in a new transformed meaning.

These statements need to be expanded through the following. Jesus challenged the disciples to maintain peace among themselves: "Have salt in yourselves, and be at peace with one another" (Mark 9:50c). This old saying is tied to the saying about salt: "Salt is good; but if the salt has lost its saltiness, how will you season it?" (Mark 9:50a, b; cf. Luke 14:34f.; Matt. 15:13). In this context he implies that his disciples can be salt only when they maintain peace among themselves. From this we must also understand the Beatitudes as being addressed to the disciples: "Blessed are the peacemakers, for they will be called children of God" (Matt. 5:9). If someone wants to make peace, he conducts himself as does God and can therefore be called God's son since he, as a son, is like the father. The demands of the Sermon on the Mount, to forgo retaliation and to love peace, are themselves a guide to show in what manner the disciples are to make peace within their fellowship (Matt. 5:38–47; cf. Luke 6:27–34).

Jesus, however, takes into account that it is impossible to be at peace with all persons. That is the teaching in particular of the well-known saying about the sword: "Do not think that I have come to bring peace on earth; I have not come to bring peace, but a sword" (Matt. 10:34). The next sentence indicates how this is to be understood: "For I have come to set a man against his father, and a daughter against her mother, and a daughter-in-law against her mother-in-law; and one's foes will be members of one's own household" (Matt. 10:35f.). This quotation, drawn from Micah 7:6, implies that Jesus was picking up on the well-known apocalyptic motif of the separating of households in the end time. Both here and in related texts there is no indication that Jesus favored revolution or did not refuse the sword, an orientation that the church might later have suppressed. With this imagery Jesus is saying, rather, that his commissioning will call forth resistance in many persons. The predictions of persecution for the disciples (Mark 13:9–13) are also in line with these words. With his penetrating admonition to peace, to make peace and to maintain it, Jesus did not promise any peace paradise on earth. Whoever confesses loyalty to Jesus must reckon with resistance.

2. The oldest statements on the meaning of Jesus' preaching, life, and death are found in the writings of the apostle Paul. They include important declarations about the "peace" mediated by Christ, which rely on the earliest Christian sermons and are developed further by Paul as well as by his disciples in later writings.

a. Reflecting back on the justification by faith in the crucified One, as spelled out in Romans 1, Paul writes: "Therefore, since we are justified by faith, we have peace with God through our Lord Jesus Christ. Through him we have obtained access to this grace in which we stand" (Rom. 5:1f.). The apostle says this because he regards sinful humanity as those people living in enmity (Rom. 5:10, "while we were enemies"). Through Jesus' act of reconciliation, which achieved the atonement, justification, and sanctification of the sinner (cf. Rom. 3:25f.), this enmity has been eradicated. People no longer stand before God as sinners, as the unjust and as enemies, but rather as the reconciled and just, as those whom God through his Spirit has given a share in his love (Rom. 5:5) and as those who may be called his "children" (Rom. 8:15; cf. Gal. 4:6). This "peace" was achieved in that God through the death and resurrection of Jesus created new people out of those believing on Christ: "Therefore, if any one is in Christ, he is a new creation; the old has passed away, behold, the new has come. All this is from God, who through Christ reconciled us to himself" (2 Cor. 5:17f.). This passage makes clear that the new situation is possible only on the basis of a substantive prerequisite of peace with God or the elimination of the disunion between God and the people caused by sin.

Based on this situation achieved through Christ, the apostle is able to affirm "Grace and Peace" to his readers in the epistolary salutations. Thereby the Old Testament greeting of peace receives a new content. It is the peace and blessing given by God through Christ. "Grace to you and peace from God the Father and our Lord Jesus Christ, who gave himself for our sins to deliver us from the present evil age, according to the will of our God and Father" (Gal. 1:3f.). This same Christian content is repeated in the blessing of peace repeated at the end of the letter: "The God of peace be with you all" (Rom. 15:33; cf. Phil. 4:9). According to Rom. 15:13 — here alone it is stated specifically (but cf. Rom. 14:17) — this "peace" means the peace of the heart, that is, a confidence full of joy and peace that "the God of hope fill you with all joy and peace in believing, so that by the power of the Holy Spirit you may abound in hope."

In formulating his bestowal of peace at the end of 1 Thessalonians, Paul states that the peace mediated by Christ involves all of human existence and enables the Christian, at the Parousia, to stand before the Lord: "May the God of peace himself sanctify you wholly; and may your spirit and soul and body be kept sound and blameless at the coming of our Lord Jesus Christ" (1 Thess. 5:23). Among other things, this suggests something that is often present in the letters of the apostle, namely, that the salvation attained through baptism will come to completion only in the redemption at the time of the Parousia (cf. Rom. 5:9–11). The sufferings that a Christian encounters, according to the example of Christ and in fellowship with the crucified One, are not in contradiction, for the "God of peace" stands beside and protects (cf. esp. Rom. 8:18–39).

Thanks to the Spirit mediated through Christ, the person who is baptized participates in the life of God, which represents "peace/salvation" and enables that person to work peace (Rom. 8:6; cf. Gal. 5:22 on "peace" as "fruit of the Spirit"). This gift challenges Christians to give attention to peace among themselves: "Let us then pursue what makes for peace and for mutual upbuilding" (Rom. 14:19). That is why it is so important to be considerate of the weak (Rom. 14:1ff.), not to repay evil with evil, but in keeping with the Sermon on the Mount to forgo the attaining of one's rights (Rom. 12:17–21). Paul also recognizes, however, that it is not always possible to be at peace with everyone: "If possible, so far as it depends upon you, live peaceably with all" (Rom. 12:18).

b. In the Letter to the Colossians, which many exegetes do not consider to be by Paul's own writing, the theme of peace produced by Christ is formulated in a manner that reminds us of the concepts that were widespread among later Gnostics. Jesus brings peace between God and the person in that he was victorious over the powers. These ethereal powers were able to enforce their claims on people in that by violating God's directives, humanity had at the same time put itself in debt to them. In that Jesus nailed the debenture note to the cross, figuratively speaking, he liberated humanity from its obligations and disarmed the ethereal powers (Col. 2:14).

Ephesians presents this view in somewhat modified, more developed form. On account of the law of the old covenant, which really helped to make sin effective, a tension arose between the Jews, on the one hand, who had the law and could appeal to it, and the Gentiles, on the other hand, who, without the law, seemed to be given over to ruin. By repealing the law through the death of Jesus, the wall of partition between Jew and Gentile was essentially removed. Humanity, separated by sin and by the law of Moses, was once more joined into one. In a loose adaptation of Micah 5:4 ("he will be peace" [as in the German Bible, RSV has it as 5:5, "This shall be peace"]), Christ can be called "our peace," that is, peacebringer (Eph. 2:14). The passage from Isa. 57:19 can be applied to his coming: "He came and preached peace to you who were far off [i.e., those born as Gentiles] and peace to those who were near [those born as Jews]" (Eph. 2:17). This peacemaking between two groups of people, Jews and Gentiles, is a result of and also an image for the peace between God and the people, which Christ brought. Ephesians utilizes an old Jewish notion of a cosmic-spatial wall of partition between God and the people (cf. *Ethiopian Enoch* 14:9) and applies it to the national-historical separation between Jew and Gentile. That is, the pacification of the cosmos with God is applied to the peace of humans among themselves. At the conclusion of the letter, in a play on Isa. 52:7 the reader is challenged with "having shod your feet with the equipment of the gospel of peace" (Eph. 6:15). Just as Jesus before Easter and the disciples after Christ's resurrection, the reader is called upon to spread the good news of the peace brought through God.

3. The way in which Jesus' message is reported in the Gospels and the way in which his actions are described allow us to detect in numerous ways the impact of a post-Easter point of view. For the sake of brevity, only a few examples from Luke and John must suffice.

a. Already in the Benedictus of Zechariah, Luke points to the fact that the sending of the Baptist is intended to open up "the way of peace" (Luke 1:79). In the Christmas story quoted at the outset, the Hellenistically trained writer of this Gospel sets the gift of "peace," inherent in Jesus' birth, over against the forcefully induced Pax Romana of Augustus. (It is not Caesar, under whose tax decree Mary and Joseph had to suffer, who deserves honor, but God.) Perhaps the evangelist thereby is combining Jewish peace hopes with aspects of Hellenistic expectations, envisioning for the Christians a time of peace, that is, a time free of persecution (e.g., Acts 9:31; cf. Acts 28:31). For him it is of the essence that this "peace" is a gift of God and is bigger than this world. It is offered to the people, initially to the people of Israel. But at the end of his ministry, Jesus, who enters Jerusalem as the prince of peace, weeps over the city and laments: "Would that even today you knew the things that make for peace!" (Luke 19:42). According to the Gloria that was pronounced together with the acclaim for Jesus on entering Jerusalem, this peace is already reality in heaven: "Blessed is the King who comes in the name of the Lord! Peace in heaven and glory in the highest!" (Luke 19:38). Not without cause has this strange-sounding call been linked with the visions of John's Apocalypse — for there the descriptions of persecution on earth are repeatedly interrupted with announcements about the victory celebration and everlasting salvation in heaven (cf. Rev. 12:10f.; 19:1).

b. In John's Gospel the word "peace" is found in passages that indicate some reflection on the meaning of the peace that Jesus brought. At the end of the first part of Jesus' parting speech we read, "Peace I leave with you; my peace I give to you; not as the world gives do I give to you" (John 14:27). Here one can see a Johannine interpretation of the shalom as used in the Jewish farewell. What Jesus wishes for his disciples and affirms as a blessing is more than the Jewish peace farewell. It is also more than the "peace" that the world, as in the form of the Pax Romana, is able to give. The peace that Jesus left behind for his own is a peace made possible by his victory over death, which again gives people a share in the Spirit (*pneuma*) of God (cf. John 20:22f. with Gen. 2:7). It is thus no accident that, in the Johannine version, the risen One repeats this peace greeting on Easter eve: "Jesus said to them again, 'Peace be with you'" (John 20:21; cf. 20:19, 26). Because Jesus gives this peace, the disciples have no need to fear the distress in the world. The Lord says this explicitly at the end of the second section of his parting speech: "I have said this to you, that in me you may have peace. In the world you have tribulation; but be of good cheer, I have overcome the world" (John 16:33).

Summary and Conclusions

This fragmentary survey of New Testament peace statements produces the following:

1. The term "peace" (*shalom*) as used in the Bible has a more comprehensive meaning than is true for the normal use of the term, which has been shaped by the Latin *pax*. With his appearing, Jesus proclaimed the peace that the prophets anticipated as "peace" (salvation) from God as the result of his creative power. The prophets had hoped for this peace to come initially for their country, and later for all people; they saw it as surpassing normal life and

relationships. Bringing this peace, Jesus affirmed the "reign of God" to the people, both in word and through signs, as being already present. In the light of this he finally took death upon himself, thereby ever giving up hope in the full realization of this salvation.

2. After Jesus' death and resurrection, the early church proclaimed that God, both in and through Jesus Christ, had fulfilled the expectations of the old covenant. But this fulfillment did not come in the manner in which many Jews had imagined it (in the form of an earthly reign of Israel and as a restoration of paradise), but rather in a new fashion — as salvation for all people, salvation from the power of sin and death, and participation in the "life" and "Spirit" of God. To be sure, this must come through a new creation of God, which only after many afflictions would reach its completion at the time of the Parousia. This new interpretation of shalom by the church follows the same line as that already evident in the later Israelite writings and in the work and teaching of Jesus.

3. Jesus required of his disciples that they be concerned to maintain peace with each other, in that way to be able to mediate his "peace" through participating in the reign of God in word and deed. According to the view of the early church, those who have been baptized have been empowered and are obliged through their fellowship with the risen One, and in the power of the Holy Spirit, to realize this peace among themselves within the church.

In view of current "peace" expectations, three conclusions can be drawn:

1. The "peace" talked about in the peace movement and in peace discussions is only a partial aspect of that which the Bible designates as "peace." That applies as well to the newer definitions of peace, for example, the statement in *Populorum progressio* (Paul VI) that "development has become the new name for peace," or the concept of peace in peace research as a "process of the minimization of need, violence, and oppression." Biblical peace statements can therefore not be applied without qualification to the problems raised in contemporary peace efforts and discussions. If a political peace is also only a partial aspect of that which the Bible calls "peace," it is still closely linked to it and is in essence therefore also a gift of God.

In this connection the contemporary discussion about peace follows the secularizing process characteristic of modernity: Events in the world are interpreted from a purely this-worldly perspective, without any reference to God. But according to the Bible, every war and every conflict is ultimately a result of the disturbed relationship between God and the people. Unrest is a result of sin. As long as the world, in spite of the Easter victory of Jesus, remains under the power of sin, in whatever form, we must reckon with disunity, conflict, and war as a result. The kingdom of God in the form of a continuing general peace cannot be accomplished before the Parousia of the Lord; that is the conclusion to be drawn from the biblical references. Yet there will be, thus we may hope, times of peace, which, like the miracles of Jesus, will be "signs" of an eternal peace and salvation.

The human contribution to the possibility of such times of peace, according to the biblical perspective, is to become conscious of one's own sin and, through faith in Jesus Christ, receive as a gift redemption for this guilt. For peace with God is the prerequisite of peace among the people.

2. "Peace" among the people was not in itself the central concern, either in the Old Testament or with Jesus. This insight relativizes every threat to political peace, including even the threat of an atomic war that would follow from it. This assertion is not intended to minimize the terrible nature of the threat hovering over this world. But this danger is not of a sort that it can destroy all hope. For a believing Bible reader there is a still greater danger — the loss of true living, that is, vital fellowship with God. The biblical word still applies, even if in the past it was often falsely interpreted and misused for hellfire sermons: "And do not fear those who kill the body but cannot kill the soul; rather fear him who can destroy both soul and body in hell" (Matt. 10:28; cf. Luke 12:4f.; cf. "For what does it profit a man, to gain the whole world [or, so we could interpret it today, to preserve the world in its present existence] and forfeit his life [the true life]?" [Mark 8:36]). Therefore the nuclear war that threatens this world points all Christians to a still worse danger of loss of fellowship with God and spurs us on to become completely involved in the proclamation of God's peace. The preaching of the church, when it is filled with a genuine concern for the true life of all people, is, according to the New Testament, borne up by confidence and not by fear. For salvation has been promised us through Christ. Indeed, it has already been given us in an initial way. Here is the ground of Christian hope.

Therefore the church may, and indeed must, proclaim this peace of God as a joyful message, even in times of greatest threat to world peace: "Be of good cheer, I have overcome the world" (John 16:33). The believer who knows that God loves her or him, and already shares in Christ's life, has no need to worry fearfully (cf. Matt. 6:25–34; Rom. 8:31–39, especially the words "Who shall separate us from the love of Christ? Shall tribulation, or distress . . . , or peril, or sword? . . . Neither death, nor life, . . . will be able to separate us from the love of God in Christ Jesus our Lord"). Christians must distinguish themselves through hope and confidence from those for whom an earthly peace and an earthly existence represent the only good and who think they can or should secure this with their own strength. The fear, which in the past year [1981] was often named as characteristic of our day, is a symptom, from the biblical perspective, either of unbelief or of a faith that is too small.

3. Even though true peace is a gift of God and surpasses our earthly existence, it still remains the task of Christians to work for peace here on earth. God's gift does not render unnecessary human freedom and action. The eschatological salvation is not creation from nothing, but rather a new creation of this world. In the same way that the earthly person who will be awakened from the dead will live eternally in a new way, so also for the entire world. Therefore, Christians may not leave the world unto itself because of their hopes for the other world, simply accepting fatalistically the coming fate of an atomic war. As "God's co-workers" (1 Cor. 3:9) we are called upon, in our own way, to co-work with God for the completion of the creation. That includes making possible, restoring, and securing peace.

We Christians have received this task because the struggle for peace among ourselves and in the world is the way shown by Jesus to lead people to faith in the gospel (cf. John 17:22). The entire church, indeed each individual congregation, has been put under obligation by Jesus and has been empowered by his Spirit to be a place of harmony and peace. Only in this way can the church witness to the world in signs, that God is giving it the true peace, through Jesus Christ. Only in this way is the church able to take away the fear of people in this world of death—and nuclear death is only one form of a death that threatens us all—thus protecting people from resignation and encouraging them to cooperation.

The directive of the Sermon on the Mount and other passages to make peace without asserting one's own rights is a challenge to show oneself to be a follower of Jesus and to break the bonds of the evil one. Nevertheless these admonitions of the Sermon on the Mount, which were directed to the disciples and stated in rhetorical style, cannot be interpreted simply as a law for political action (e.g., as forbidding every form of violence, even when it would be required for self-defense or love of neighbor; nor as a directive to take the first step in disarmament unilaterally without guarantee of a corresponding response). Radical pacifists can base their claims on isolated texts but not on the biblical message (as a whole). The Bible offers no ready recipes for politics. But Christian politicians should orient themselves toward the Bible and try to recognize, on the basis of their fundamental understandings, what is the will of God, what "is good and acceptable and perfect" (Rom. 12:2). From this comprehensive perspective decisions must be made in individual cases. Thus Christian politicians may never support a defense policy whose means violate the will of God (a weapon, e.g., that cannot be controlled and destroys entire countries or parts of the earth). In such cases they are called upon to surrender their nation, for whose powerful protection they are responsible (cf. Rom. 13:3f.), to an enemy aggressor without any resistance. In biblical language, they implore the nation to bear great suffering as sharing in the passion of Christ or as judgment of God (in the knowledge of human guilt).

The most important contribution to peace in this world is that each individual tries to live as a Christian, whether in the private sphere or in the political one. In that way such a person can contribute so that humanity withdraws from the power of evil and opens itself up in faith to the gift of peace. The conviction, anchored in the Bible, "The world is moved by every single heart" (R. Schneider), has been demonstrated in the lives of many saints. Even today it is not so alien to reality as it seems at first. The poet Elias Canetti in his paper "The Poet's Calling" (Münchener Rede 1976) reflects back on the statement of an anonymous poet of August 23, 1939 (one week before the outbreak of World War II): "It is all over. Were I truly a poet, I should have been able to prevent the war." Initially, Canetti dismisses this as silly but then describes it as "an acknowledgment of a responsibility." Speaking from a biblical perspective, every individual shares responsibility for what happens in the world.

Like Jesus and the apostles, every Christian will experience, whether privately or in the churchly or political sphere, that in spite of all personal effort he or she can neither preserve peace nor make peace. If "the world" is not prepared to listen to the admonition to turn back, to repentance and to peace, Christians should not be surprised. On this point the followers of Christ are not above their master. But because the issue concerns not merely an earthly peace, the Christian may be certain that his or her efforts are not in vain, even when they remain without tangible results. The "peace" promised in the Christmas story will not become ours ultimately in any other way than through the way of the cross.

That is why our "carrying in the body the death of Jesus" (2 Cor. 4:10) is able to mediate peace as the gift of God. What Paul said at the conclusion of his explanations on the resurrection from the dead, which is the achievement of the new creation and thereby the attaining of the peace longed for in the old covenant, applies also to every effort for peace: "Therefore, my beloved brethren, be steadfast, immovable, always abounding in the work of the Lord, knowing that in the Lord your labor is not in vain" (1 Cor. 15:58).

(Out of the vast literature on the topic, I draw attention to the following: Peter Stuhlmacher, "Der Begriff des Friedens im Neuen Testament und seine Konsequenzen," in *Historische Beiträge zur Friedensforschung* [ed. Wolfgang Huber; Studien zur Friedensforschung 4; Stuttgart: Ernst Klett Verlag; Munich: Kösel-Verlag, 1970], 21–69; H. H. Schmid, *Šalom: Frieden im Alten Orient und im Alten Testament* [SBS 51; Stuttgart: Verlag Katholisches Bibelwerk, 1971]; Gillis Gerleman, "*šlm* genug haben," in *THAT,* 2:919–935; V. Hasler, "*eirene,*" in *EWNT* 1 [1980]: 958–964; Ulrich Luz, in *Eschatologie und Friedenshandeln* [ed. Luz et al.; SBS 101, Stuttgart: Verlag Katholisches Bibelwerk, 1981].)

Part II

New Testament

8

Introducing the New Testament Essays on *Eirene*

Willard M. Swartley

Of the numerous essays in German on *eirene* the following four
have been chosen because they represent complementary types of
contributions.

Luise Schottroff's brief essay and Erich Dinkler's study represent divergent methods and emphases. The difference in position
is sharpest in their treatment of Jesus' own contribution to the
topic of peace. Dinkler's study is distinctive in its thorough and
helpful study of *eirene* in the Greek world; Schottroff's essay
helpfully focuses the sociopolitical significance of Jesus' and the
Gospels' teachings in the context of their social world, especially
the Pax Romana. Hubert Frankemölle's article shows distinctive
views at several places, for example, the ambiguity of Luke's *eirene*
contribution. It also points us to his fuller study of "Peace and
Sword in the New Testament," the most complete to date. Ulrich
Luz's concluding essay represents the most careful work to date
that puts at the center the hermeneutical concern whether and in
what way scripture addresses the contemporary issues of poverty,
oppression, and violence.

The setting of the world political agenda as a backdrop for these
essays is important. Dinkler's, written in 1973, appeared during
the time of mounting protests worldwide against the Vietnam War.
Peace movements were strong in Germany, and the Bible and Jesus
were often used to endorse specific political action. Dinkler's article
undertakes an extensive study of New Testament thought to show
that its peace teaching is part of a larger vision, God's salvific action
in Jesus Christ. Peace action at the horizontal level cannot be

unhooked from the reconciliation of the gospel that unites humans with God. The primary focus of the New Testament peace teaching concerns the divine-human relationship which in turn unites peoples in the salvation reality of Jesus Christ. Thus peace in its biblical meaning cannot be reduced to a political agenda. It is embedded in the gospel's message of salvation and reconciliation.

Schottroff's article, coming a decade later, appeared also when the European churches and larger society were again waging a strong peace movement in reaction to President Ronald Reagan's new militarist initiatives, especially pouring more missiles into Europe. Employing social world analysis in her method, she works by hermeneutical analogy. Jesus' own ministry is portrayed as politically consequential; his nonviolent teaching in resistance and confrontation of evil was a revolutionary force within first-century Jewish religio-politics. Her essay thus contributes a different effect from Dinkler's. The scripture, though not employed as proof text to demand political resistance to violence and spiraling militarism, is utilized as a source of empowerment for peace action, in that the repressive politics of the Pax Romana is analogical to contemporary first world oppression of small developing countries.

Frankemölle's essay, written around the same time as Schottroff's in the early 1980s and excerpted from his larger extensive study, seeks to understand the scriptural teaching within the coherence of specific biblical narratives placed within purported sociopolitical settings. His overall conclusions support a Jesus and an early Christian gospel committed to peace and nonviolence; but the matter is not ironclad, since Luke makes accommodation to those who joined the revolt, according to his interpretive reconstruction.

Luz's essay represents reflection that spans the entire time period of the other essays, extending through to the early 1980s. It casts a wider thematic net than the others, represents an extensive group effort, and pays special attention to hermeneutical issues: how scripture addresses contemporary issues of poverty, oppression, and violence. This study project extended through the Vietnam period and into the beginning of the Reagan years. Its conclusions speak clearly to the church, calling for its reformation and an alternative value structure. By reflecting the biblical moral priorities of justice and peace, the church in its life and work can become a significant force for peace and justice in the larger world society. Clearly the vision and witness of the church are for the sake of the renewal of humanity in the light of God's reign and the gospel's peace praxis.

We now summarize further these four contributions.

Dinkler's extensive study consists of probes in four directions:

a review of the scholarly work done on *shalom* in the Hebrew scripture, a very detailed and insightful investigation of the meaning and function of *eirene* in the Greek world, a survey of the use and meaning of *eirene* in the various layers of the New Testament literary traditions, and a brief analysis of the use and meaning of *eirene* in several early extracanonical writings, especially *1 Clement* and Gregory of Nazianzus. His view of the data argues for three significant positions: the New Testament use and meaning of *eirene* are largely coherent with the Hebrew scripture's use and meaning of *shalom;* early extracanonical writings show the convergence of a sociopolitical *harmonia* with *eirene,* thus introducing a specifically political dimension into *eirene* not present in the New Testament use and meaning — thus aligning peace with order at the outset of the postbiblical Christian tradition; and the New Testament meaning centers on the exclusive claim that Christ's cross makes peace. Hence the New Testament peace teachings should not be restricted in meaning to nor coopted directly into contemporary political peace causes; rather, the peace experienced between God and humans and among humans in communities of faith by means of Jesus Christ must be valued as a unique achievement that in turn provides a distinctive offer of peace and reconciliation to the world.

In much briefer scope Schottroff considers some of the same general terrain that Dinkler investigated in greater detail. Unlike Dinkler, she highlights the oppressive effects of the Pax Romana upon subjugated peoples. This sets up a contrast between the Pax Romana and the Pax Christi, which she anchors in the direct contribution of Jesus' own teaching on peace and love for enemy. She describes the early Christian communities of faith as a small minority living amidst a colossal system of brutality. Hence, although they were in no position to practice nonviolent resistance, they aided the poor and oppressed and thus gave hope, identity, and a new communal solidarity that empowered the oppressed.

Frankemölle's essay highlights, first, the early Christians' reality of experiencing persecution and the brutality of the "sword." Hence Jesus' and early Christian teaching against the use of sword is not to be understood in terms of an ideal or a vision but against the bloody origin of Christian existence (Jesus' own death and numerous early Christian martyrs). Second then, the early Christian confession that "Jesus is Lord" is a confession of political significance: for Jesus, not Caesar, is Lord. Third, Frankemölle regards Luke's special attention to *eirene* as two-sided. While, overall, Luke presents the gospel of Jesus as a call to peace that refuses use of the sword, the enigmatic command in the passion narrative to "Go, and buy swords" is an accommodation to those Christians who stayed in Jerusalem, rather than fleeing to Pella, and fought in the A.D. 66–70 war against Rome. In Luke's narrative strategy this falls into the "Satan time" part of the Gospel (here Frankemölle uses Hans Conzelmann's view that in Luke we have a Satan-free time between the temptation and the passion).[1] Thus Luke's theology of peace and sword recognizes the ambiguities of history—that the time of evil prevents a totally swordless existence even on the part of Christian believers. Fourth, congruent with this emphasis, Frankemölle then discusses the reality of God, a reality that embraces judgment and wrath as well as love and peace. Then, fifth, Frankemölle notes that while Jesus' own peace actions comprised the physical (healings) and social (overcoming class and race barriers) spheres, Paul's peace teaching was directed to the principalities and powers dimensions of life, even the ecological in Romans 8. Thus Pauline theology viewed peace comprehensively and even structurally. Nonetheless, the primary focus of peace injunctions, whether in Paul or elsewhere, was to communities of faith. This is the locus of the peace of Jesus Christ.

Luz's contribution is a summation of the biblical component of an ambitious interdisciplinary FEST study project in Heidelberg (see Luz's own introduction to his essay). The focus of this study was the bearing of scripture on the minimization of poverty, oppression, and violence. Luz's summary emphasizes five main conclusions:

1. God is actor in history in a real sense. The work for justice and peace is first of all God's work; it is not simply a goal of human aspiration. Scripture shows other considerations besides those identified as the study's focus, namely, that the giving of identity and comfort to the oppressed and the inner personal experiences of shalom are significant emphases. Peacemaking occurs within an eschatological orientation, which enables a certain indifference to the cultural hegemony of the Pax Romana. The individual person is called to conversion within this sociopolitical context and here finds new identity and values for life.

2. Canonical diversity appears in the orientation of apocalyptic, and thus its effect upon the Christian communities' task of reshaping the world differs as well. Generally, the more world-affirming strands, such as Luke, show a greater social ethic and call to responsibility and transformation through small steps; Revelation with its strong apocalyptic outlook, however, is simply a call to endure and be faithful.

3. While eschatology itself provides no concrete norm for ethical action, the degree to which eschatology is christologically oriented

determines in turn its import for ethical conduct. Jesus' proclamation of the dawning kingdom of God is a primary example of this: "It is Christology that makes the traditional Jewish apocalyptic eschatology relevant for peace."

4. Jesus is the center of the biblical witness linking eschatology to peace witness. Providing this link, Jesus stands against alienating forces that produce poverty, oppression, and violence. In contrast, Jesus calls to new life which gives identity and empowerment to oppose alienating forces.

5. The christologically determined mode of biblical peace action accents love and freedom in the new community. Any situation today that suppresses one's own freedom or hinders new proposals for peace is to be rejected. In establishing criteria for evaluating contemporary initiatives, we must bear in mind the diversity in biblical thought, the appeal to the individual, and the appeal to the church as a corporate body. In Luz's conclusion to his own study of the Pauline corpus (not translated here), Luz accents the calling of the church to a self-critical reflection upon its own nature, its commission, and its own reformation, both as a whole body and individually as members. By repenting and learning "to bear in its body the death of Christ" and thus live by God's power, the church may make its most important contribution to peace in the world.[2]

Taken together, these four essays map out the scope and type of concerns that bear upon the aims of this new series of studies. Readers of this volume may sometimes question the handling of the biblical evidence by these authors or perhaps believe different interpretations or conclusions from those proposed to be more viable and correct. This volume is intended to stimulate study in this area and, specifically, to assist American scholarship to participate more fully in and carry forward the discussions of this topic that have been in progress on the Continent now for some time.

Notes

1. Susan Garrett's recent study (*The Demise of the Devil;* Minneapolis: Fortress Press, 1989) argues convincingly against this position. In my judgment she is correct and Conzelmann is wrong. This jeopardizes Frankemölle's ingenuous interpretation of the "sword" saying considerably.

2. Ulrich Luz, *Eschatologie und Friedenshandeln* (ed. Luz et al.), 193, 213.

9

The Dual Concept of Peace

Luise Schottroff

Caesar Augustus thought of his rule over the Roman Empire as a time of peace: Pax Augusta/Pax Romana. "Peace" was indeed the key religious-political concept of the Roman caesars. In Rome, altars were erected for peace, for harmony, and for the well-being of the Romans (10 B.C.; 11 B.C., Ara Pacis Augustae on Mars Hill). Coins imprinted with "peace" and "security" proclaimed the blessings of the government.

After the destruction of the temple in Jerusalem in A.D. 70, Vespasian in A.D. 75 built a temple of peace in Rome. Here they celebrated the bloody triumph over the Jews. Until the present, the Jewish people have not forgotten this deadly peace that Vespasian celebrated. We need only to be reminded of the significance of the Wailing Wall in the temple section of Jerusalem today. Even now this victory of Vespasian and the Romans over the Jews is often more vivid in Jewish consciousness than is the still more ghastly destruction of the Jews by Hitler and the German nation.

Pax Romana was defined by the rulers of the Roman Empire without any sentimental or humanistic façade. Peace and security meant the subjugation of and victory over other nations. It meant the suppression of even the mere hint of resistance. In such cases, crucifixion was the normal manner of imposing death. In this sense the cross served as guarantee of the Roman peace, as a deadly instrument for subjugation.

Translation of "Der doppelte Begriff vom Frieden," in *Christen im Streit um den Frieden* (ed. Brinkel et al.), 135–140. Originally published in *EPD Documentation* Nr. 11/1981, 1 Folge.

The Roman peace was guaranteed by military might at a high price. At the time of Augustus, 28 legions, each with 6,000 professional soldiers, stood under arms. After the defeat in the Teutoburger Wald and the loss of three legions, there remained only 25 legions with about 150,000 soldiers. It has been estimated that this meant that about 3 percent of the population was in the army. Added to that were 6,000 to 12,000 guard soldiers in Rome, the fleet and the auxiliary troops, the military contingents of so-called allies, that is, subjugated nations, who were not Roman citizens. This massive professional army was formed both by pressure and through volunteers. Unemployment and increasing landlessness forced many people to accept the relatively well paid but hard life of military service. The Roman forces were a decisive political force; domestically they provided the infrastructure of power for the Roman caesars.

During Jesus' lifetime Herod and his sons were allies of the Roman caesar in order to guarantee the Roman peace in Palestine. The land was ruled above all by military means through a large number of Herodian fortresses (such as the Herodium or Masada). Starting in A.D. 9, part of the country was administered by a Roman procurator located in Caesarea, who relied on Roman auxiliary troops based in Jerusalem.

"Peace" and "security" were the political-religious words with which this situation was normally summarized. In the middle of the first century, in his first letter to the Thessalonians, Paul offered a very terse summary of the feelings that Jews or Christians had toward this political and military situation: "The day of the Lord will come like a thief in the night. When people say, 'There is peace and security,' then sudden destruction will come upon them as travail comes upon a woman with child, and there will be no escape" (1 Thess. 5:2f.). The day of the Lord, the day of God's judgment over the world, seemed near to him. He was filled with dismay and feared the worst when he heard the slogans "peace and security," as if they signaled the end. This was a sentiment shared by the prophet Jeremiah long before him: "'They have healed the wound of my people lightly, saying, "Peace, peace," when there is no peace. Were they ashamed when they committed abomination? No, they were not at all ashamed; they did not know how to blush. Therefore they shall fall among those who fall; at the time that I punish them, they shall be overthrown,' says the LORD" (Jer. 6:14). Paul read Holy Scripture and from it learned how to discern the present. Peace slogans are the beginning of the end; the prophets already knew that. This consciousness that the present is a prewar period is evident in many texts from the Jesus tradition as well as from Paul. They turned out to be right.

Jesus and his followers traveled as prophets throughout the country. They used the word "peace" in a quite different sense. They were Jews living out of the religious tradition of Israel. Shalom/peace—that meant for them something like life, life in its comprehensive sense. It included eating, health, fellowship, and hope. It included being whole or complete. The word had such an all-embracing connotation that many Jewish rabbis would say: shalom is a name for God.

Jesus and his followers announced the onset of the kingdom of God. Where they received a hearing, the lives of the people changed. "Whatever house you enter," Jesus had instructed them, "first say, 'Peace/shalom be to this house!'" It was like a password, not a careless greeting, for the text continues: "And if anyone is there who shares in peace, your peace will rest upon him; but if not, it will return to you" (Luke 10:5f.). This peace greeting of Jesus' messengers immediately clarified relationships. The scene is almost magic: *Peace*—that meant "the kingdom of God is near." A "child of peace" would be such a person who would accept this message with all its consequences. Those who rejected the message showed themselves to be persons who had taken God's judgment upon themselves. "I have not come to bring peace, but a sword" refers to this separation.

This announcement of the beginning of the kingdom of God produced division in Israel, as in a legal judgment, between the children of peace and those who, in the anger of God, would pass under the sword if they did not repent. This eschatological peace greeting was no unconditional spreading of hope for salvation, a salvation that cost nothing. It had immediate practical consequences. For example, such a child of peace would take in the messengers of Jesus and feed them. In a small town or village, and even in Jerusalem, this was a public act of solidarity. Thereby the child of peace became a participant in the work of the kingdom of God. Given the economic conditions in Palestine at this time, this also meant sharing a limited fare. The population in general survived as poorly paid landless day laborers or had plots of land far too small for farming. If a guest was received into such a situation, then that was a literal application of what John the Baptist had said: "He who has two coats, let him share with him who has none; and he who has food, let him do likewise."

Soon they found themselves in the market square gathering in the wretched of the village, the sick and the poor. Most were poor.

They told themselves that one did not need to wait any longer for the Messiah. Jesus is the Messiah. God has acted, and now we can act. We will wait no longer until those up there help us; we will help ourselves. We can do it because God is on our side. One Gospel passage shows in a few short sentences how following Jesus in this way changed one's life: John the Baptist, already in prison because his message seemed dangerous to the Herodian-Roman rulers, sends a rather skeptical-sounding question to Jesus: "Are you the Messiah, or should we wait for another?" And Jesus does not merely reply with the simple assertion: I am the Messiah. Rather, he directs John the Baptist toward the visible practical results. "Go and tell John what you hear and see: the blind receive their sight and the lame walk . . . and the poor have good news preached to them."

I would like to restate these events in our terms. The Jesus movement formed a community of solidarity with the poor in an oppressed country, in which people helped each other, by sharing their limited food, and made the sick well through love. Even we can understand that kind of miracle as a messianic miracle, the beginning of the kingdom of God: "Blessed (*Makarioi*) are the poor, for theirs is the kingdom of God."

In this sense, therefore, Jesus and his followers carried peace about in the land, the peace of the kingdom of God, which one could already see and touch when a cripple stood up and walked. The conflicts that these messengers of Jesus encountered were tough. Upon the instigation of Jewish leaders, Jesus was executed by the Romans in the interests of Rome. His death was no isolated event. Other Jews and many of Jesus' followers in later years were killed in similar fashion. The followers of Jesus said they were living in the land of the prophet killers. And they said they did not wish to withdraw into a small circle of the pious, who wanted to have nothing to do with those out there. Jesus' word, "Love your enemies," fits this situation. The enemy is those who murdered the prophets, the persecutors of Jesus and his followers. "Love your enemies and pray for those who persecute you, so that you may be children of your Father who is in heaven; for he makes his sun rise on the evil and on the good, and sends rain on the just and on the unjust."

"Bless those who curse you." God is God, and he is God of the whole nation, of all people, of the entire creation. When the messengers of Jesus saw the goodness of the sun, or felt the rain, and saw that this divine goodness was also bestowed upon the persecutors, then they knew they dare not give up. Blessing and prayer — these signified that ever and again they must confront with the message of the nearness of the kingdom of God even those who were rejecting them. Greet them again: Shalom. Tell it again: *Makarioi*/blessed are the poor; the kingdom of God is near.

Enemy love was not a striving to feel sympathy for the opponent, nor was it some grand lofty idea. Rather, it had to do with praxis. It was the consequence of God's love for a disobedient people. God loves all. That includes even those who cast stones in the street and those who allowed the messengers to be tortured by Roman soldiers. These too must be confronted with the truth over and over again. It takes great courage to enter consciously into such a situation of conflict, to look the tormentors in the eye and to say that they are prophet killers. This courage was understood by them as imitation of God, *imitatio Dei*. That is how one became a child of God, God's imitator, by trying to bring people to the truth, even those people who were resisting the truth. The avoiding stance of those people, who did not want to see the true situation of need in their country, made them like those who refused to know anything at the time of the Flood: "As were the days of Noah, so will be the coming of the Son of man. For as in those days before the flood they were eating and drinking, marrying and giving in marriage, until the day when Noah entered the ark, and they did not know until the flood came and swept them all away."

"Blessed are the peacemakers, for they shall be called children of God." This beatitude from the Sermon on the Mount articulates this content once more. The children of God do not give up when the prospects seem hopeless; they continue to struggle against the rejection and refusal to know. The children of God behold creation, and from it they grasp God's love for all people.

I envy Jesus' followers of that day; they knew the world of their time to be a corruption of creation. But they still saw the will of God working unbroken in the world of nature. The fact that the trees grew, and that rain fell on the entire town, was a visible sign of the acts of God. The corrupted world of humanity must again become fruitful like the earth: a new heaven and a new earth, a reconstructed creation. Nature is for me no longer a point of consolation, because we have incorporated even it into the world of human corruption. The fact that rain falls on the entire city is only sometimes still a reminder of an undisturbed creation. Often rain makes me afraid of the acid that it spreads over the whole city.

The children of God do not give up. Blessed are the peacemakers means, at least, blessed are those that engage in the struggle for an all-encompassing living creation, that try to bring people to the point that they will again participate in the reconstruction of corrupted creation.

The word "nonviolence" is often linked with the command to love the enemy or with the Beatitudes. That is correct, as long as one understands nonviolence in the sense of a nonviolent strategy, that is, as an active movement of struggle. But it would be false, if with "nonviolence" one meant a passivity that tolerates everything, that even advises the oppressed to accept their suffering as their fate.

In repeating "Love your enemies" and "Blessed are the peacemakers," one indeed needs to examine the issue of violence. Among the Jews in the first century A.D. there were frequent resistance struggles, both against the lords in their own land and against the Romans. At times this led to armed resistance. When the Romans invaded in A.D. 66, even the respectable Josephus, who came from an aristocratic priestly family, was leader of a militarily armed and fortified resistance in Galilee. The resistance was not able to withstand the totally superior forces of the Romans. The dexterous Josephus changed sides, even supporting the Romans ideologically, insultingly declaring the remnant in the resistance to be tyrants, while labeling himself and his compatriots as the "peace party." The Jewish upper class was oriented toward cooperation with the Romans for political and economic reasons; hence they were the "peace party." Most of the resistance efforts during the first century originated from below, from the exploited Jewish people. They already had a long tradition of resistance to the point of martyrdom.

Repeatedly there were actions that relied on collective suicide as a means, as happened in A.D. 40 when Caligula demanded that a portrait of Caesar be hung in the temple in Jerusalem, thereby hoping to seal the subjugation of the Jewish nation. At a time when they should have been preparing their fields, thousands of Jews left their homes and moved to the coastal flatlands near Jaffa. They told the Roman governor that they opposed the putting up of the portrait. "Don't you know that that means war?" He asked: "Do you really intend to carry on a war with Caesar, without considering his forces and your own weakness?"

They answered: "We have no interest in making war. We would rather die than break our laws." They refused to return to their houses. Failure to prepare their fields would mean their death. But this was also their best weapon. The Roman governor would not have been able to export many goods for tribute and Rome would then dismiss him. So he found himself in an impossible situation and was forced to appeal to Caesar to forgo the erection of his official portrait.

Here is an example from a long history of nonviolent resistance. They were not nonviolent for religious reasons (there was no such discussion then as now in our midst) but rather because the people were so poor and oppressed that they were unable to buy weapons. Early Christianity fits into the history of this Jewish nonviolent resistance movement. In any case, the Romans took great care to make sure the oppressed peoples would have no weapons. The military superiority of the Roman Empire was far out of proportion. So in such a situation the issue for Jews like Jesus or his followers was not one of military resistance; rather, it was one of strengthening and encouraging the hungry and discouraged people, who were being exploited so easily.

The reason that the Romans persecuted Jesus and similar prophets, often killing them, was that the organizing of solidarity seemed to them to be at least as dangerous as armed resistance. This was precisely what they saw as dangerous in the Jesus movement. It led to persons forming unions, to living together in justice, equality, and love with an intensity quite unique in normal society. It led to the formation of congregations that were stronger than the large families, which, thanks to the policy of the Romans, were becoming increasingly fragmented and insignificant.

Currently the Sermon on the Mount is often viewed as a program for Christian nonviolence. In some of the newer Bible translations, such as Ulrich Wilckens', the third beatitude reads, "Blessed are the nonviolent . . ." (Luther has "the meek" [*Sanftmütigen*]). In the writings of a military bishop I read that "the Magna Charta of Christian pacifism" is in the Sermon on the Mount and that Jesus preached "the principle of nonviolence" to his followers. These statements would need some historical differentiation, as is evident from what was said above. Nevertheless, the decisive issue is, What do we do about it? What conclusions do we draw from the blessing of the peacemakers?

There are many theological traditions that allow one to push aside the Christian identity that is at issue here. This happens, for example, when one says that one must distinguish between the praxis of a small troop of Christians "who take their Christianity seriously" and the "law of the state." One can recommend pacifism to a group of nuns and at the same time recommend for the state a policy of "peace and security," which is to be secured with weapons of an order that was not even imaginable in those terrible apocalyptic nightmares of early Christianity.

Christians may not participate in the preparation for war, in the production of atomic weapons, nor in the maintenance of a system of deterrence which includes ever-more dangerous weapons. The resolutions along this line as approved by the Synod of the church province of Saxony, which the Synod of the Evangelical Church in Hesse and Nassau accepted in November [1981], must be widely discussed in our churches and adopted. Christian faith is nothing less than discipleship (*Nachfolge Jesu*). Either you practice it or you reject it.

The messianic peace and the Pax Romana are incompatible. There is only one Jesus praxis. The Sermon on the Mount (as indeed the entire Bible) is unmistakable and clear when we read it not as a mere collection of isolated sentences but as statements linked to the praxis of the people who stood behind them, namely, the followers of Jesus.

10

Eirene—The Early Christian Concept of Peace

Erich Dinkler

(In memoriam amici Stefan Weinstock—Oxford †)

In current usage, the word "peace" has become increasingly iridescent. In the political sphere, where the word has primarily claimed citizenship for a long time, the Roman polarity of *pax* ("peace") and *bellum* ("war") is assumed, but "peace" is spoken of also then when conflicts can only be contained or limited. In the psychological and sociological spheres, peace and aggression are spoken of both as polarities and as correlatives. In the theological context one hears, on the one hand, references in liturgy to the peace that is not of this world, which comes as a gift, and yet, on the other hand, one hears in ecclesiastical and ecumenical statements a rather indiscriminate use of both an organized world peace and the gift of Christ's peace. Also at times contemporary peace efforts have precipitated violence.

These indications of the complexity and ambiguity of both the word and its substance are not restricted to the English "peace" [or the German *Friede*] but can be observed in all languages of East and West, North and South. Arabs and Israelis greet each other with a word derived from the same root, *slm*. Indeed, Islam, the name of the religion of Arabs, is a derivative of *slm,* yet how different are the meanings and the implications.[1] Persons who are knowledgeable about ancient Rome will recall that there was a connection between *Pax* and *Janus,* and they will not be able to avoid

Translation of *Eirene: Der urchristliche Friedensgedanke.* Sitzungs-berichte der Heidelberger Akademie der Wissenschaften Phil. hist. Kl., Abh. 1 (Heidelberg: C. Winter Verlag, 1973).

the observation that, whether in past or current history, "peace" is, as a rule, determined by the contrasting concept of "war."[2]

It is beyond the capacity of a scholarly examination such as this to change present-day habits of speech. But it can draw attention to the fact that there is a specifically Christian understanding of peace, which by means of the Greek word *eirene* provided the basis in early Christianity for a new direction in thought and language. Our interest here, therefore, is in the concept of *eirene* and in the understanding of peace in early Christian literature, that is, the writings of the New Testament and of the Apostolic Fathers which were fixed in written form between about A.D. 50 and 150. It will not be possible to identify every individual nuance or to present the entire scope of usage of the word "peace." My concern is primarily with the notion of peace that is linked with the person of Jesus of Nazareth, with Jesus Christ. Even if this theological concept of peace should turn out to be strangely apolitical, it could still provide some enrichment for our reflections on the nature of the *polis*.

The thesis for this study is the following: the concept of *eirene* in early Christianity is essentially shaped by the adoption of the Hebraic concept of *shalom*. Citations from the Old Testament in which *shalom* is rendered as *eirene* are utilized in early Christian writings to explain the soteriological meaning of the crucifixion of Jesus of Nazareth. Beyond that, the Old Testament concept of a messianic king who will inaugurate the messianic peace with his reign is applied to Jesus of Nazareth. By using the word *eirene* to interpret the crucifixion of Christ the specifically Christian notion of peace is established. Only toward the end of the first century of the Christian era does the secular Greek understanding of *eirene*, one often linked in antiquity with *homonoia* ("concord"), enter early Christian literature, specifically through Clement of Rome.

After that, the notions of peace as salvation and/or peace as innerworldly concord and, politically, absence of war become intermixed. Both are labeled *eirene*, although in liturgy and in commentary on scripture during worship, differences in accent are noticeable. It is clear that, when viewed against the entire Western development of the concept of peace, the translation of *shalom* and *eirene* as *pax* resulted in a politicalization of the concept and that, through Augustine's *De civitate Dei* [*City of God*], *ordo* ("order") became the complement to *pax*, with *bellum* ("war") its opposite.

Our study is organized around the quest for a specifically Christian concept of peace, as attested in early Christian literature. First, we will discuss the presuppositions, that is, *shalom* in the Old Testament, then *eirene* in common Greek usage. Finally and most centrally, the early Christian concept of peace will be developed.

Shalom in the Old Testament

In an article published in 1935, Gerhard von Rad discerned, "Seldom do we find in the OT a word which to the same degree as שָׁלוֹם can bear a common use and yet can also be filled with a concentrated religious content far above the average conception."[3] In point of fact, the 236 instances[4] of the use of the noun form alone range in meaning from the formulaic greeting, a sepulchral engraving, to a wish for good health and material well-being, and to God's gift of salvation now and at the end of time. Indeed, the oldest occurrence of *shalom* in the vow of Jacob at Bethel (Gen. 28:21) already refers to peace as protection, for which God is to be thanked. It can be translated as follows: "If I return to my father's house in peace, בְּשָׁלוֹם (*beshalom*), then the Lord will be my God"; or also: "If I return whole (uninjured, in good condition) . . . ." From the beginning one is confronted with whether to translate *shalom* as "peace" or "salvation" (*Heil*), on the one hand, or as "uninjured" and "well-being," on the other. There is another passage from the Deuteronomistic History (Judg. 6:23f.) where an ancient tradition tells of Gideon, who, seized with fear because he has seen the angel of the Lord face-to-face, hears the Lord say to him, שָׁלוֹם לְךָ (*shalom lecha*): "May it be well with you, be not afraid, you will not die." In response, Gideon builds an altar and calls it *Yahweh shalom,* which exegetical scholars agree should be translated as a nominal sentence: "God is [or: grants] salvation." The context of the text is revealing: first, Gideon's fear; then the promise of the Lord: "May it be well with you, fear not, you will not die"; and finally, the naming of the place of the event with a statement of thanksgiving and praise: "God grants salvation." And since an altar as such is respected as a place of encounter with God,[5] such an encounter is now also identified as *shalom.*

Both of these initially quoted occurrences of *shalom* show us the breadth of meaning with which contemporary Old Testament scholarship is preoccupied. On the one hand, there is the greeting, "May it be well with you," which, the context shows, is returned to the greeter and giver of salvation with thanksgiving, expressed in the naming of the altar. Here *shalom* is linked with God as the giver. On the other hand, *shalom* is used to refer to being uninjured, healthy, whole. Here the word could be employed without reference to God's action, although that reference should not be discounted in principle. It is possible to trace the foundational meaning back to two etymological Akkadian roots that are not fully related to each other,[6] but it does not really solve the problem. More helpful is the hint provided by Martin Noth,[7] that in the Mari texts the word *salimum* in the sense of reconciliation and agreement appears in connection with a discussion about forming a covenant, thus giving the multiple meanings of the Hebraic *shalom* a new basis.

It would be wrong to claim merely on the basis of statistics a semantic prevalence for the one group of meanings over against the other group. The interconnection between the two fundamental meanings is never to be disclaimed.

In the greeting formula, we can presume that to be healthy and without injury is the primary thought, as in "Shalom be with you" (Judg. 6:24; 19:20; 1 Sam. 25:6; 2 Sam. 18:28; Pss. 122:6; 125:5; 127:5; 128:6; etc.) and similarly in the question form of the greeting: Does your old father have shalom? (Gen. 43:27) — as well as in the answer, "He has shalom." Nevertheless the nuance of meaning is dependent on the situation at the moment of encounter. There is always the possibility that the relationship of those greeting each other could lead to thoughts about God as the giver of shalom, or the greeting could remain a mere formality. From the Old Testament text we cannot determine whether the shalom greeting was also offered to non-Israelites.[8] This question should be kept in mind, for it could be that shalom is the gift of Yahweh only within the boundaries to which the Decalogue applies.[9]

The fundamental sense of "well-being" or "wholeness" is inherent even when the word "peace" is used in connection with war. It is true[10] that to speak in Hebrew of peace in contrast to war involves a subordinate thread of thought, a special meaning for the word. To what extent this special use of the word can be attributed to influences from the Greek environment still needs to be studied. When 1 Sam. 7:14 states, "There was peace also between Israel and the Amorites," this refers to the prevention of war by treaty with that generic ethnic group, the semitic West. Second Samuel 11:7 in particular shows the level of complexity of such speech when David asks the Hittite Uriah, "How is the shalom with Joab and the people, and how is the shalom of the war?"[11] What was really meant by these contrasts? Comparing this with similar passages,[12] one must conclude that shalom in this case can only mean whether everything was in order, well organized, and properly implemented, with reference to the life of Joab and of the people as well as to the course of the war.[13] But again, that is not to say that shalom is completely cut off in meaning from the concept of "God's salvation," since order as well-being might well be thought of as a victory anchored in the hand of God, even if there is no explicit reference to that effect. "Well-being" (Judg. 19:20), good fortune (Ps. 73:3), health (Isa. 57:18) — in each case rendered as *shalom* in Hebrew — need not be understood only in an innerworldly sense. There are, rather, numerous indicators that the word shalom as such usually carried, for the Israelite, an additional sense, that of gift from Yahweh. In this sense it is possible to ask about the well-being of the people who are in a state of war, without thereby blessing the war. However, no matter how strong the singular connotation might be, it is not possible to claim that "peace" in a political sense as "absence of war" has a root meaning of its own.[14]

Nor does peace appear in the social sphere. In Amos, where the social theme has priority, there is no linkage to the shalom theme. This is all the more striking, because peace for the community of the people is specifically prayed for and hoped for: "May the LORD bless his people with peace!" (Ps. 29:11), and more acutely, "Great peace have those who love thy law; nothing can make them stumble" (Ps. 119:165).

How seldom the use of the word can be restricted to a single thread of meaning is seen in the use of בְּשָׁלֹום (*beshalom,* "in peace") in connection with dying and death. In Gen. 15:15 in connection with establishing the covenant with Abraham, it is said, "You shall go to your fathers in peace; you shall be buried in a good old age." This reference to dying in peace could be taken as dying under God's protection. But it is used differently in 2 Kings 22:20, where God promises shalom to Josiah, the king of Judah, as reward for his humility: "I will gather you to your fathers, and you shall be gathered to your grave in peace." [Josiah's death, in the battle of Megiddo (609 B.C.), was a great shock to the hope of God's protection of the righteous king.—ED.] In Isa. 57:2 (according to the LXX) it is said of the just: "Peace will be over your grave." That can scarcely mean they will be safe from grave robbers — there are enough specific curses for that[15] — nor does it imply completeness, in the sense of the uninjured state of the dead.[16] It must mean "divine protection," that is, a well-being provided by God. The shalom wish[17] in Jewish sepulchral inscriptions and graffiti on ossuaries (see Fig. 1 and 2), a widespread phenomenon since 100 B.C., can only be explained if the word has an implicit theological meaning.

This theological component is explicit in the second basic meaning of the word. Since the time of the exile (597–586 B.C.), the theological concept of shalom had attained such weightiness that it cannot have failed to influence those uses of the word, as described above, for which a reference to the divine was not inherently necessary. Let us consider, in the first place, Isa. 54:10: "For the mountains may depart and the hills be removed, but my steadfast love shall not depart from you, and my covenant of shalom shall not be removed, says the LORD, who has compassion on you." In this case, an entire chain of salvation words (*Heilsworte*) are linked together: grace, covenant, shalom, compassion — all timeless divine promises from the Lord. Thus, given the background of the Babylonian exile, it seems that only a single dominant meaning presents itself. This can be argued all the more since at this time there was an ongoing debate about when to use *shalom,* so that the word was used with great care. In five passages Jeremiah and Ezekiel warn against false, premature hopes for shalom: "The prophets . . . saw visions of peace for her, when there was no peace": אֵין שָׁלוֹם. The Septuagint translates this: εἰρήνη οὐκ ἔστιν (Ezek. 13:16). In the final analysis this is a warning against a false religious security.

Yet Jeremiah, apparently having a concrete situation in mind, turns this around in stating that Yahweh has "plans for welfare and not for evil, to give you a future and a hope" (Jer. 29:11; LXX: 36:11). In this case, *shalom* does not mean a spiritual or eschatological salvation but refers to the exiles' return to their homeland, regarding their release from captivity as a gift from Yahweh. Or in Isa. 45:6c–7: "I am the LORD, and there is no other. I form light and create darkness, I make weal (*shalom*) and create woe." Also along this line we can point to the words of Jeremiah where the prophet is bidden to go to a house of mourning, "for I have taken away my peace from this people" (Jer. 16:5). And finally, there is the blessing of Aaron: "The LORD lift up his countenance upon you, and give you shalom" (Num. 6:26). Two things are common to all of these citations: The giver of well-being is God; and the shalom that is given produces something innerworldly, namely, God's protection in time and history.

The fact that shalom is linked with God and his covenant seems to form the basis for the strictly theological use of the word. At the same time, it should not be overlooked that the linkage of the word to justice (Isa. 32:16; 48:18; Pss. 72:3–7; and 85:10: "Righteousness and peace will kiss each other")[18] points to the fact that shalom does not assume an independent character but retains its healing power only in relationship to the giver.

The new style of speaking about a peace related to God which is promised, that is, is not yet present, leads to something new which is not really fully developed but remains at the level of prophetic intimations. There is talk about a coming king, in whose reign well-being (*shalom*) will be in full bloom — "till the moon be no more" (Ps. 72:7). Or in Isa. 9:6f.: "Mighty God, Everlasting Father, Prince of Peace. . . . Of peace there will be no end, upon the throne of David." Here the shalom hope takes on a new shape, recognizable particularly in Deutero-Isaiah, where "my covenant of peace" (Isa. 54:10) is seen together with Yahweh's proclamation of an "everlasting covenant" (Isa. 55:3); it becomes even more precisely messianic with the phrase "my steadfast, sure love for David." Splendor, well-being, and glory are the distinguishing characteristics of the awaited end time (Isa. 62:1–2). Even when the accent on the future increases, and peace is promised to the "remnant" (Jer. 29:11; Isa. 52:7; 54:10–13), it attains cosmic dimensions only in the imagery of a peaceable animal kingdom (Isa. 11:6–9; cf. Lev. 26:6).[19] Above all, the speech about a king humbly riding on a donkey, a king who through his victory will achieve peace for the nations sounds an eschatological note (Zech. 9:9–10). But that brings us, presumably, to the end of the Old Testament period (ca. 150 B.C.), at which time the expectations for the future were expressed primarily in apocalyptic imagery. Now peace is expanded beyond Israel to include a dominion "from sea to sea, and from the River [Euphrates] to the ends of the earth" (v. 10), as a consequence of the victory.

Von Rad is right when he states that it is the *theological* concept of shalom that was not only most operative historically but that is also dominant in the Old Testament. It becomes clear that the gift of shalom effectively concretizes "salvation" as well as "peace," and that it is not some notion of peace, as living peacefully together, which creates the precondition for the possibility of salvation. Defining the temporal boundaries of shalom is of no great significance, because the future reality of shalom as promise is already there proleptically. Exegetical scholars of the Old and the New Testament agree that it is this theological meaning of shalom which Christian theology and language took over, even though this does not eliminate the possibility of nontheological usages.

Early Christian literature cannot be directly connected to the scriptures, known to us as the Old Testament and composed in Hebrew. Between them lies the Greek translation of the Old Testament, produced in the third and second centuries B.C. in Alexandria. On the basis of the legend reported in the *Letter of Aristeas,* we now refer to it as the Septuagint. It is probably sufficient to point out that *shalom* was translated as *eirene* in almost every case, but not always. In addition, in the concept of *eirene* in the Septuagint also a few other Hebrew words have been included. But for the purposes of our approach, this does not constitute a substantially new factor.[20]

Eirene in Secular Greek Usage

As to Greeks living in the eastern part of the Roman Empire during the first century A.D., it is difficult to ascertain what precise connotations and nuances of meaning they heard when the word *eirene* appeared in a biblical context. On the one hand we can ascertain its meaning in the Septuagint texts relatively well, but, on the other hand, the range of meanings linked with *eirene* in Greek poetry and philosophy, as well as in some religious texts, though determinable in these literary documents, still does not allow us to presuppose them in the New Testament writings. The classical writings, including the Homerian Epic,[21] presume a higher level of education and represent the perspective of a different cultural history. They undoubtedly influenced the Koine Greek, but to what precise degree can be established only in rare instances. It would be wrong to evaluate the early Christian authors, whether in or outside the New Testament, only by the presence of citations from classical Greek authors and to ignore the creative power of their new language, mistaking it as lack of education. Besides, it would be superficial to overlook the fact that one encounters in the writings of the New Testament not only folk wisdom but also *citations from Greek authors* which can be checked.

The most obvious example is the Gospel writer and Hellenistically trained historian Luke. Nearly thirty years ago Martin Dibelius produced a careful compilation of the literary references in the Acts of the Apostles.[22] It is quite certain that Acts 17:28b is a quotation from Aratus's *Phaenomena* and quite possibly 26:14 is taken from Euripides' *Bacchae.*[23] It is also possible that Acts 14:15–17 rests on a turn of phrase in Thucydides,[24] and that reflected in the Aeropagus speech in 17:28a is an idea from Posidonius's *Timaios Commentary.*[25] The citation from Menander by Paul in 1 Cor. 15:33

has long been recognized, and one can detect tones of Antisthenes in 1 Cor. 9:24–27.[26] Very early it was recognized[27] that a citation from Epimenides' *Theogony* was woven into the second-century Letter to Titus (1:12).

This listing of citations from classical Greek literature is not intended to serve as a means to measure the educational level of the early Christian writers. Rather, it serves to point out that when we rank their writings among the "Minor Writings"[28] this does not mean that we use merely ostraca with their mundane jottings for the purposes of studying the language of the New Testament.[29] When we turn then to the "higher" literature of secular Greek, we discover first of all that it provided no quotations for the New Testament on peace themes. Indeed, generally speaking, *eirene* appears relatively late in secular literature to refer to a condition or even to designate a divinity. For example, when Homer speaks in the *Iliad* 22.156 "ἐπ᾽ εἰρήνης," about a time of peace, this may mean the political condition of nonwar, but it might also mean the period when Eirene ruled as divinity.[30] In any case, what is clear is the contrast to war. A passage in the *Odyssey* is more difficult to understand in its context: Odysseus has come and has destroyed his enemies[31] in order "to begin his everlasting kingdom."[32] What follows is a time of blessing:

> All shall love each other as always,
> wealth shall increase and peace shall overflow.[33]

Here *peace* is the time after a victory, when weapons are laid to rest, a time bringing peace and concomitant wealth. This perspective is reflected especially by Hesiod in *Erga kai Hemerai:* A city of the just is established: no one is hungry anymore and there is joyous work, interrupted with feast days; the earth is fruitful and trees bear fruit, bees gather honey, and one's progeny is extensive and expansive.[34] This positive picture of peace is all the more notable because in Greek and Roman antiquity, war was usually affirmed as a positive instrument of politics, without the sense of the self-destructive, mechanized murder that war has come to mean through the experiences of our century. War was not inhuman or evil. Nor was it a mere option of the *polis*. Rather, it was ethically justified and striven for politically in an often idealistic and heroic fashion.

This makes the more important all those voices which disregard the odium attached to criticism of war as a weakening element endangering Paideia [i.e., classical education aiming at physical as well as moral and intellectual perfection.—ED.]. It is the philosophers who, in trying to think through the problem of justice, talk of peace in terms of a theory of state, thereby reflecting a thread spun by the poet Pindar:[35]

> Sweet is war to the novice,
>   but the man of experience fears its coming in his heart.

In this connection the poet speaks of peace as ἀπόλεμος (*apolemos,* nonwar). That is also how we encounter the concept in Plato[36] and Aristotle.[37] At best, that simply points to the fact that *eirene* was still understood as the time of nonwar.[38] More important, Plato recommends striving for a "life oriented around peace," because war produces more damage than benefit. Yet he also worries about the possibility that a victory and the resultant peace could become burdensome as a source of idleness and hubris.[39] In short, there are critiques both of war and of peace that can be traced topically through to the panegyrics of the Neronic era.[40]

Aristotle's debate with the Sophists on the degree to which slaveholding and the purchase of slaves through war is just or arbitrary[41] leads in the middle period of the Stoics, especially in Panaetius but also in his disciple Posidonius, to the issue of justice, in which both peace and war are discussed. Here too the perceived problem under discussion is doubt about the justice of separating humans into the free and the slaves, and the justification of war by the free. Panaetius calls for mutual human concern, for the humaneness of the victor, who determines the nature of the peace.[42] Whether in this case Panaetius shares with the other Stoics the argument that the principle of equal human rights includes freedom, or whether Cicero's well-known passage in *De republica* 3.36 concerning the Carneades Disputation of 155 B.C. represents the views of Panaetius remains a point of debate among scholars.[43] If we take Cicero's exposition as an echo of Panaetius, this would mean that the conquered, as the weaker ones, are "justly" condemned to a status of nonfreedom (*Unfreiheit*) in the service of the free. That may well stand in the tradition of Platonic-Aristotelian teaching, but it is in contrast to that of the Stoics.[44] The assumption that Cicero is accurately reflecting Panaetius's view cannot be proven, since no fragment of his teaching that speaks to his political ideas is extant. Thus one cannot make a claim to justify the Roman peace ideology by appeal to the Stoics.[45] It is legitimate to draw on Panaetius as a preparatory Greek philosophical source for the Roman *humanitas,* but not to make him responsible for

the justification of the lordship of the "more worthy" victor over
the "less worthy" loser.

In the histories of Herodotus (1.87) and Thucydides (2.61.1),
peace is presented as something desirable for society on humani-
tarian grounds. Political, not ethical, considerations are dominant.
The ethical perspective appears more often in poetry. Between 429
and 425 B.C. Euripides in *Cresphonte's Song of Peace*[46] warns
Thebes and Athens that "spear-raging" Hellas, δοριμανὴς Ἑλλάς,
would destroy herself. One should turn to Eirene and be open to
her blessings. Here Eirene is quite clearly personified as a goddess
acting in history.

Aristophanes seems to have known of this song. In any case,
he develops some of those thoughts further in his comedy *Eirene*,[47]
presumably in 421 with the Peloponnesian War as background.
In it, the Attican winegrower Trygaios rides a giant dung-beetle
to heaven, in order to confront Zeus. Yet all the gods, except Hermes
and Polemos, are not to be found, since they are angry about the
fraternal wars of the Hellenes. Finally, a chorus of peasants and
petty townspeople manage to free Eirene from the cave where
Polemos had imprisoned her. Woven into the story is a prayer to
Eirene for an innerworldly political peace: "O most holy Queen,
Goddess, Lady Eirene, Lady of the Choral Dance, Lady of the
Wedding, accept our offering."[48]

That brings us to the threshold of religious conceptions of peace
that appear relatively late in the Eirene cult. In his *Antidosis,*
Isocrates provides older evidence of an Eirene altar and thereby
for such a cult.[49] The peace treaty between Sparta and Athens,
presumably the peace of 375/374, according to Philochorus of
Athens,[50] resulted in establishing an annual offering. All this means
that Eirene was publicly proclaimed as a goddess. The fact that
a statue of Eirene was put up on the Agora in Athens in 375 B.C.
corresponds to this deification. Literary evidence[51] for this is a
work attributed to Cephisodotus: Eirene holding the boy Pluto
on her arm. The "Leukothea" in the Munich collection of antiquities is widely recognized to be a copy of this work by Cephisodotus.[52] A second extant statue of the goddess of peace, now
latinized, stems from the middle period of the Roman emperors.[53]

The symbolism on coins is important for the spread of the concept of Eirene. Around 350–330 B.C., silver coins from Locri
appeared picturing Eirene, sitting on an altar embellished with
bukranion, in her right hand holding a staff with a snake coiled
around it, the caduceus [*kerykeion*].[54] Nevertheless, in the world

of the Greeks, the peace goddess remained a rarity, never numbered among the great and highly respected deities. That must be taken as a significant point in the history of ideas. In spite of the way she is classified by Hesiod[55] she is not considered a regular part of the Horai[56] and had scarcely any political significance. The remark of H. Fuchs about Eirene is fitting: "Although she is peace, she is not the one that brings peace."[57]

The following short excursus into the Latin West is noted not simply for purposes of balance but mainly because Rome with its bilingual culture dominated the East during the transition period around the beginning of the Christian era in both political and religious policy. It is no doubt a historically remarkable coincidence that, in the decades before the birth of Jesus of Nazareth, Caesar had already committed himself to what was implemented only under Augustus, namely, introducing the Pax cult in the Roman Empire.[58] Beside the Concordia cult, Pax also now appeared, both of them borrowing from Greek developments. Pax was directed toward foreign policy, whereas Concordia was oriented toward internal policy.[59] They were dependent on each other and therefore named in Sallust's first "Epistula ad Caesarem senem" as the primary task: *pacem et concordiam stabilivisse* [i.e., to stabilize peace and concord].[60] Caesar possibly designated himself as *pacificator* or *pacificus,* with reference to the foreign nations.[61] Increasingly, the pax ideal became popular, most fully under Augustus. The republican Pax Romana became the Pax Augusta and Pax Augusti, indeed a *pax perpetua.*[62] The Ara Pacis Augustae standing on the Campus Martius in Rome, which was dedicated on the birthday of Livia on January 1, 9 B.C., reveals the programmatic elements of the new direction.[63]

The Pax Augusta as a cultural idea of the Roman imperial period with its vision of a golden age subsequently influenced the early Christian and medieval church, and even that of the Romantic period.[64] The first thematic discussion of peace was already written before the beginning of the Christian era by Varro in the no longer extant *Logistoricus "Pius aut De pace"* (after 40 B.C.). It seems to have been less a philosophical, more an antiquarian work about *ius fetiale.*[65] On the other hand, Cicero's *Philippica* reveals a sudden preference for this religious-political term.[66] With Virgil's *Georgica* and with Tibullus, Roman literature increasingly celebrates this peace concept.[67] But we should not overlook that even in Virgil's 4th *Eclogue* (v. 17) the paean to peace is linked with a paean to the virtue of the ancestors, which has victory as a prerequisite:

pacatumque reget patriis virtutibus orbem . . .
And he will govern the earth that has been pacified
by the manly virtues of the fathers.
                                —following H. Hommel's translation

Did this conscious shift in Roman thought toward the ideal of
peace, which occurred in the period immediately before the entry
of the Christian church onto the stage of history and the beginning of the early Christian writings, have impact upon the Greek,
Asia Minor, and Palestinian provinces to such a degree that the
word *eirene* would cause the listener to take notice? Had Pax
become a political slogan? One should not overestimate the
immediate impact of the spread of this religious-political idea, so
carefully developed by Caesar and put into effect under Augustus,
particularly in the eastern provinces where there was frequent
unrest. The concept of Pax Romana, as tied to the certainty of
victory, did not change. The Flavian coins of Vespasian and Titus,
struck after the fall of Jerusalem in A.D. 70, with their "*capta
Judaea*" caption and her personification sitting under a Roman
tropaeum,[68] bear witness to the prevalence of this concept of peace.
That is, it was still the notion of peace through victory.

Does this mean that early Christian terminology remained un-
influenced by the history of the peace cult and the peace ideas of
the pre- and non-Christian Greek- and Latin-speaking world? A
simple affirmation to this question is impossible, given that the
Greek word *eirene* contained a breadth of meaning, that it was
capable of numerous emphases and nuances, and, in contrast to
shalom, could occur in a completely untheological context.[69] We
will need to pay careful attention to the context of the utterance
in each case before we draw any conclusions.

Christian vocabulary was full of words from the Hebrew and
Greek Old Testament, as well as words from both secular Greek
and Latin which were not always clear in their meaning. The
iridescence that is often present in the use of *eirene* appears to have
a pre-Christian origin.[70]

The Early Christian Concept of Peace

Let us turn now, after this brief survey, to our actual subject,
the peace concept in early Christian literature, as it has come down
to us in the Koine Greek of Attica. Were we to present all the semantic possibilities for the use of *eirene,* we would reach the same
conclusion as the one about *shalom* in the Old Testament as cited

from von Rad above.[71] In early Christian usage, peace can be a "virtue"; as such, it is a "fruit of the Spirit."[72] Peace connected with "security" can endanger apocalyptic watchfulness, that eschatological "keeping watch, staying sober."[73] Peace can be set in contrast to "disorder";[74] in another case, it is a saving element in the kingdom of God.[75] This variety of meanings does not result from selections taken from the various authors of epistles and books; rather, they all stem from letters clearly written by the apostle Paul between A.D. 50 and 55. This reference to Paul's word choice should suffice to indicate that numerous influences flow together in early Christian usage. Hence it will hardly be possible to develop a uniform, exact definition of the concept of peace.

The historical and theological aspects are interlinked in our quest, as was already seen in our examination of the classics and the Old Testament. Perhaps we could even say that problems in the history of tradition are interlinked with linguistic-semantic and hermeneutical ones. Thus we begin with the question: Where, and in what context, did the early Christian writings utilize peace quotations from the Old Testament? Might this internal joining have brought about an influence of shalom on the New Testament concept of *eirene*? Further, our intent is to determine the specific early Christian share of influence in a possible translation of the Hebraic peace concept into a Greek Christian one.

The Letter to the Ephesians was obviously not the first chronologically, since it was written between A.D. 60 and 70, most likely composed by a disciple of Paul.[76] Like the Letter to the Colossians, it must be attributed to the Deutero-Pauline writings. The author addresses himself to heathen Christians, reminding them of the past and contrasting it with the present—a favorite form of theological *paraklesis:* they had no citizenship rights in the house of Israel, no covenant and promise, no hope; indeed, they were ἄθεοι ἐν τῷ κόσμῳ ("without God in the world").[77] Then follows, for our purposes, a most decisive passage (Eph. 2:13–18):

νυνὶ δὲ ἐν Χριστῷ ᾿Ιησοῦ ὑμεῖς οἵ ποτε ὄντες μακρὰν ἐγενήθητε ἐγγὺς ἐν τῷ αἵματι τοῦ Χριστοῦ. Αὐτὸς γάρ ἐστιν ἡ εἰρήνη ἡμῶν, ὁ ποιήσας τὰ ἀμφότερα ἕν καὶ τὸ μεσότοιχον τοῦ φραγμοῦ λύσας, τὴν ἔχθραν, ἐν τῇ σαρκὶ αὐτοῦ, τὸν νόμον τῶν ἐντολῶν ἐν δόγμασιν καταργήσας, ἵνα τοὺς δύο κτίσῃ ἐν αὐτῷ εἰς ἕνα καινὸν ἄνθρωπον ποιῶν εἰρήνην, καὶ ἀποκαταλλάξῃ τοὺς ἀμφοτέρους ἐν ἑνὶ σώματι τῷ θεῷ διὰ τοῦ σταυροῦ, ἀποκτείνας τὴν ἔχθραν ἐν αὐτῷ· καὶ ἐλθὼν εὐηγγελίσατο εἰρήνην ὑμῖν τοῖς

μακρὰν καὶ εἰρήνην τοῖς ἐγγύς· ὅτι δι᾽ αὐτοῦ ἔχομεν τὴν προσαγωγὴν οἱ ἀμφότεροι ἐν ἑνὶ πνεύματι πρὸς τὸν πατέρα.

But now in Christ Jesus you who once were far off have been brought
near in the blood of Christ. For he is our peace, who has made us
both one, and has broken down the dividing wall of hostility, by
abolishing in his flesh the law of commandments and ordinances,
that he might create in himself one new humanity in place of the
two, so making peace, and might reconcile us both to God in one
body through the cross, thereby bringing the hostility to an end. And
he came and preached peace to you who were far off and peace to
those who were near; for through him we both have access in one
Spirit to the Father.

At issue is the justification for the fact that now, in the time of
faith in Jesus Christ, the position of these heathen Christians has
changed both before God and with reference to the world of Israel
and its promises. In this carefully composed text the writer draws
on two Isaiah passages (Trito-Isa. 57:18f. and Deutero-Isaiah 52:7)[78]
in order to relate them to Christ. More than forty-five years ago
Martin Dibelius had already described this passage as an excursus intended to spell out the relationship of Trito-Isaiah 57:18f.
to Christ, and to indicate to *what degree Christ is our peace.*[79]
Since then, thanks to the study of the impact of Gnostic concepts
of salvation on the imagery of certain New Testament writings,[80]
the opinion has emerged that precisely in this passage the author
of the canonical letter took what was originally a Gnostic early
Christian image of salvation with some cosmic overlay, revised it,
and historicalized it theologically.[81] We agree with this opinion
to a great extent but do not intend to pursue that question here,
preferring to take the text as it is — that is, we leave aside a study
of tradition and redaction at this point. This approach is justified
by the stylistic and thematic completeness of these verses, including
also the way the verses are bracketed into the preceding and succeeding context.

In a predicate sentence at the beginning, a decisive statement
is made concerning Christ: αὐτὸς γάρ ἐστιν ἡ εἰρήνη ἡμῶν ("for
he himself is our peace"). This sentence provides the basis for the
earlier statement: You heathen Christians, who were once godless,
have now been brought near through the blood of Christ. These
statements draw on Trito-Isaiah 57:19, resulting in an epexegetical
gloss: that the peace spoken of there is our *eirene,* and it was given
to us historically in Jesus Christ. Furthermore, those *far off,* which

historically for Trito-Isaiah meant the people of Israel in exile, are interpreted as far from God—as the heathen—whereas those who are near are the citizens of the πολιτεία τοῦ ᾿Ισραήλ ("the commonwealth of Israel").[82] These exegetical liberties of the author result in a reinterpretation, in that the near and the far off of v. 13 serve to determine the relationship to God, and the obvious intention is to proclaim that the division of people into Israelites and ἄθεοι ("those without God" = ἔθνη), into Jews and Gentiles, has been done away with in Jesus Christ, our *eirene*.[83] The Trito-Isaiah text does indeed endeavor to express peace as the oneness of the near and the far-off of the people of Israel, but he explicitly excludes the godless from this salvation. This contradiction in content between the Old Testament text and its interpretation in Ephesians no longer holds when we recognize that the author addresses himself to heathen Christians only with reference to their past and that these now (νυνὶ δὲ ἐν Χριστῷ ᾿Ιησοῦ) have come near through "the blood of Christ," that is, through his death on the cross.

Peace is thus clearly featured in the proclamation to all people, nations, and races as *part of the offer* through Christ, but it is not specifically the "pacification of the κόσμος,"[84] nor is "peace with God and the peace of humanity"[85] given a universal application. The text in Eph. 2:14 does speak of τὰ ἀμφότερα ("both," neuter), and then in Eph. 2:18 of οἱ ἀμφότεροι ("both," masculine), in order to explain that the "becoming one" is the tearing down of the wall of partition, and to interpret "making peace" as creating a new person in Christ.[86] But linked to this imagery is the sense of enmity, understood here as also in Rom. 8:7 and James 4:4, as human disobedience through disregard, and thus an objective enmity toward God.

This enmity has nothing to do with war,[87] even though peace is set in contrast to enmity in a fashion similar to Paul's "being reconciled" in Rom. 5:10. Abstract statements become interwoven with imagery. The theological word needs the picturesque analogy: "tearing down the wall" shows the meaning of "abolishing the enmity."[88] But then the enmity is defined by the additional phrase "the law of commandments and ordinances,"[89] and abolishing this law "through his [Jesus'] flesh" becomes the basis for making peace or, better still, "establishing peace." That can only mean that the law as means and occasion of sin signifies the enmity as the disregard of God.[90] In our opinion, the reference to Christ's flesh refers to the historical death on the cross, not to the incarnation.[91] The cross event ("on the cross"), to which there is a further reference in v. 16, specifies how the bringing of peace through Christ can be documented on the basis of a historical event, that is, by his death on the cross. Negatively, this event is the "abolishing of the enmity" (Eph. 2:16). This idea, that "abolishing the enmity" leads to reconciliation and that the "blood of Christ" is the basis for peace, can only be understood in the context of the Jewish concept of sacrifice. It is an expression of the early Christian struggle to understand the death of Jesus Christ as salvation and peace for those who believe it.[92]

There is a point of difficulty in understanding the dual orientation of enmity and peace. They refer to the relationship of the person to God and to the relationship of those near to those afar off, namely, the relationship of the Jews to the Gentiles.[93] The concluding v. 18 declares, "For through him we both have access in one Spirit to the Father."[94] Here is an idea which appears again in different form in Eph. 3:12 and above all in Rom. 5:1f. in connection with the statement about "peace with God," to which we turn later.

The passage just discussed, which posits enmity and peace to be antithetical, marks the crucifixion of Christ as a turning point. It declares Christ to be the bringer of peace, the one providing access to God as well as creating a new unity for those once separated in this world and living as enemies, objectively speaking. The *dual element* of the passage is:

> 1. Peace and reconciliation are tied to Jesus Christ in such a way that the cause for peace is anchored in the blood of Christ, in his crucifixion. Peace is constituted through the cross, and at the same time the crucifixion with its offensive character as *skandalon*[95] is interpreted as peace.
>
> 2. Peace as the abolition of enmity carries two dimensions of meaning, though with no clear separation between them: the reconciliation affects the *God-human* relationship, giving the reconciled person free access to God; and it leads to the *unity in the church* of those separated, thus tearing down the walls of enmity. This joining together of peace as gift of God in Jesus Christ to the believers, which grants them access to God, with peace as humanity's unity of racially separated peoples in the body of Christ, is constitutive, that is, foundational to the understanding of *eirene*.[96]

Thus far we have ignored a statement resulting from the use of the Old Testament text, Isa. 52:7. In Eph. 2:17, it does not say, "And so he came and became the peace,"[97] but rather, "and proclaimed peace." There is the following progression of statements:

v. 14: Christ is our peace.
v. 15: Christ brings peace.
v. 16: Christ reconciles the enemies in one body with God.
v. 17: Christ proclaims peace.

With this last verse, the borrowed inner structure of the shalom sayings in Deutero-Isaiah becomes quite evident. Jesus Christ, who is the peace, now proclaims himself and the cross event as peace.[98]

Isaiah 52:7 is taken up again at the end of the epistle, in Eph. 6:15, where the verb turns into a substantive, the "gospel of peace." Outfitted with the "breastplate of righteousness" and "the shield of faith," and "having our feet shod with the preparation of the joyful gospel of peace," thus we shall proclaim.[99] That the content of the good news is now described with "peace" is understandable: as to content, by Eph. 2:14ff.; as to form alone, from the Isaiah text. This concept of peace as used in Ephesians, with its accent falling heavily on the reconciling action of God in Christ as crystallized in the cross event, has been a formative influence on the history of the word "peace" in theology and liturgy.

The foundational text in Ephesians examined above appears to represent a hymnic elaboration and, by means of the citation from Isaiah, a further development of the ideas contained in Col. 1:19f. Let us examine this passage, even if no explicit use of the Old Testament is evident:

ὅτι ἐν αὐτῷ εὐδόκησεν πᾶν τὸ πλήρωμα κατοικῆσαι καὶ δι' αὐτοῦ ἀποκαταλλάξαι τὰ πάντα εἰς αὐτόν, εἰρηνοποιήσας διὰ τοῦ αἵματος τοῦ σταυροῦ αὐτοῦ, δι' αὐτοῦ εἴτε τὰ ἐπὶ τῆς γῆς εἴτε τὰ ἐν τοῖς οὐρανοῖς.

For in him all the fulness of God was pleased to dwell, and through him to reconcile to himself all things, whether on earth or in heaven, making peace by the blood of his cross.

Here too, we have a hymn extending through the passage of Col. 1:15–20,[100] which Ernst Käsemann attributes to an early Christian baptismal liturgy[101] and which also assimilated some Gnostic motives. The saving work of Christ is introduced through the incarnation and conceived in an almost cosmic dimension of reconciliation, interpreted and at the same time founded on the parenthetical statement: "making peace by the blood of his cross." Once again "peace" and "reconciliation" are linked and serve as an expression of that which happened "by the blood of his cross." But here the subject of the action and of the peacemaking is God, not Christ as in Ephesians. Peace and reconciliation have cosmic dimensions, bringing together heaven and earth, that is, people and God.[102] But here nothing is said about the results of peace as a gift of shalom that affects inter-human relations. The more central thought is apparently "salvation in Christ" rather than "peace." At the same time, the succeeding passage, with its schematic "then-now"[103] contrast and paraenetic function, recalls the former enmity of thought and attitude, as well as reconciliation "in his body of flesh by his death" (Col. 1:21f.). Once again we find bound together as foundational peace and reconciliation through the cross event; hereby the concept of peace, here clearly cosmic in dimension, is completely anchored in history.[104]

Since we are speaking here about peace and reconciliation of the cosmos, we cannot avoid the question of whether this peace as salvation in Christ is universal in its cosmic meaning and thereby unlimited. This question can be answered fully—in keeping with the intentions of the writers of Ephesians and Colossians—by turning to 2 Cor. 5:19ff., where it says that "God was in Christ reconciling the world to himself."[105] In Paul's usage, "world" means the world of humanity. That is, the reconciliation event was set by God for everyone. Now God is "entrusting to us the message of reconciliation" because peace, as well as salvation, anticipates that those hearing the message will "be reconciled to God," that is, will be completely captured by it. One can say already here that in the early Christian literature there is no human peace outside of God and Christ, no nontheological, hence *religiously neutral,* peace. The Christian concept of *eirene* has a striking exclusivity about it because of the prerequisite for, and the achievement of, a relationship to God through the death of Christ, which is alien to the cosmos as such.[106]

An important passage in Romans, though debated by textual critics,[107] clearly shows the degree to which the train of thought developed in the two deutero-Pauline epistles rests on the basis of Paul's theology. The passages are Rom. 5:1–2 and 9–10 [here we follow Dinkler's reading: ἔχωμεν]:

Rom. 5:1–2   Δικαιωθέντες οὖν ἐκ πίστεως εἰρήνην ἔχωμεν πρὸς τὸν θεὸν διὰ τοῦ κυρίου ἡμῶν Ἰησοῦ Χριστοῦ, δι᾽ οὗ καὶ τὴν προσαγωγὴν ἐσχήκαμεν [τῇ πίστει] εἰς τὴν χάριν ταύτην ἐν ᾗ ἐστήκαμεν, καὶ καυχώμεθα ἐπ᾽ ἐλπίδι τῆς δόξης τοῦ θεοῦ. . . .

Therefore, since we are justified by faith, let us have peace with God through our Lord Jesus Christ. Through him we have obtained access to this grace in which we stand, and let us rejoice in our hope of sharing the glory of God. . . .

Rom. 5:9–10 πολλῷ οὖν μᾶλλον δικαιωθέντες νῦν ἐν τῷ αἵματι αὐτοῦ σωθησόμεθα δι᾽ αὐτοῦ ἀπὸ τῆς ὀργῆς. εἰ γὰρ ἐχθροὶ ὄντες κατηλλάγημεν τῷ θεῷ διὰ τοῦ θανάτου τοῦ υἱοῦ αὐτοῦ, πολλῷ μᾶλλον καταλλαγέντες σωθησόμεθα ἐν τῇ ζωῇ αὐτοῦ.

Since, therefore, we are now justified by his blood, much more shall we be saved by him from the wrath of God. For if while we were enemies we were reconciled to God by the death of his Son, much more, now that we are reconciled, shall we be saved by his life.

The textual tradition for Rom. 5:1 is weak in support of "we have peace." The great majority of textual witnesses and all the old manuscripts have the subjunctive or hortative; a minority have the indicative.[108] Although it is correct that no distinction was made in vocalizing the long and the short o, in my judgment the *lectio difficilior* as methodological priority calls for the use of the hortative reading,[109] as we have done in our translation above.

The line of thought in Rom. 5:1–10 can then be summarized as follows: We are justified by faith; we should not give up the peace with God which we received as a gift; we, as former enemies, are reconciled to God through the death of the Son of God; as the reconciled, we will be saved. That is the effort to declare and witness to the perennial experience of salvation through ever-new expressions. If then in this train of thought Paul inserts the exhortation to keep the peace, this can be attributed to his linking of the indicative and the imperative, as evidenced in many places. It could also be a formulation relying on Ps. 34:14, "Seek peace, and pursue it."[110] Three things are of the essence here. First, one cannot say that Paul was forced, by means of a quotation from the Old Testament, to write about peace in this fashion and in no other. Second, the apostle speaks of salvation in the sense of shalom; proleptically this can already be present for him, even though it still lies in the future. Finally, in Rom. 5:9–10 the words "justified" and "reconciled" are used interchangeably as synonyms. From this it follows that 5:1 could also be interpretively read: "since we are reconciled by faith, [and continuing with 2 Cor. 5:20] be reconciled to God."[111]

The Letter to the Hebrews brings us more firmly into the sphere of Old Testament influence and its concept of shalom. The foundational idea is taken from Psalm 110; Jesus is the eternal high

priest, Melchizedek. The theme appears frequently: Heb. 5:5ff.;
6:20; 7:10ff.; but it is spelled out only in Heb. 7:1–3 by citing Gen.
14:17–20:

> Οὗτος γὰρ ὁ Μελχισέδεκ, βασιλεὺς Σαλήμ, ἱερεὺς τοῦ θεοῦ τοῦ
> ὑψίστου, ὁ συναντήσας ᾿Αβραὰμ ὑποστρέφοντι ἀπὸ τῆς κοπῆς
> τῶν βασιλέων καὶ εὐλογήσας αὐτόν, ᾧ καὶ δεκάτην ἀπὸ πάντων
> ἐμέρισεν ᾿Αβραάμ, πρῶτον μὲν ἑρμηνευόμενος βασιλεὺς
> δικαιοσύνης, ἔπειτα δὲ καὶ βασιλεὺς Σαλήμ, ὅ ἐστιν βασιλεὺς
> εἰρήνης,—ἀπάτωρ, ἀμήτωρ, ἀγενεαλόγητος, μήτε ἀρχὴν ἡμε-
> ρῶν μήτε ζωῆς τέλος ἔχων, ἀφωμοιωμένος δὲ τῷ υἱῷ τοῦ θεοῦ,
> μένει ἱερεὺς εἰς τὸ διηνεκές.

> For this Melchizedek, king of Salem, priest of the Most High God,
> met Abraham returning from the slaughter of the kings and blessed
> him; and to him Abraham apportioned a tenth part of everything.
> He is first, by translation of his name, king of righteousness, and
> then he is also king of Salem, that is, king of peace. He is without
> father or mother or genealogy, and has neither beginning of days
> nor end of life, but resembling the Son of God he continues a priest
> for ever.

Given the context of the epistle, the thrust of the Melchizedek
reference—not an essential figure in the author's salvation
history—is to emphasize not the Aaronic type but the Levitical
priesthood and to show, by means of typology, Christ as Son of
God and king of peace and justice, through a christological interpretation of Ps. 110:4: "Thou art a priest for ever, after the order
of Melchizedek."[112] By connecting two Old Testament texts, the
intention is to prove on the ground of the Old Testament, through
a person of the Abraham story, that Jesus is the Son of God, the
high priest and mediator between God and humanity. In the view
of Hebrews 7, since Jesus is "king of justice, king of peace" and
"without genealogy," the message of Psalm 110 is clearly pointing
to him.

This passage is to be understood in connection with Isa. 9:6:
"For to us a child is born, to us a son is given; and the government
will be upon his shoulder, and his name will be called 'Wonderful
Counselor, Mighty God, Everlasting Father, Prince of Peace.'" This
phrase "Prince of Peace," together with Heb. 7:2 and Eph. 2:14,
has decisively confirmed the linkage between Christ and *eirene*,
a link of historical bearing by its manifestation in the liturgy.[113]

Aside from these christological statements which utilize the
shalom concept as it was translated into Greek, it is necessary to

examine the originally nonchristological, Jewish greeting, "Peace be with you."[114] Because of its incorporation into Jesus' commissioning speech to the disciples (Matt. 10:12; Luke 10:5), "Whatever house you enter, first say, 'Peace be to this house!'" the greeting developed a sense of authorization, even though the shalom greeting of the Old Testament is to be found in it genetically. Clearly this greeting quickly gains a special quality, when at the end of John's Gospel the risen One three times greets those he meets with "Peace be with you," thereby granting peace.

There is a parallel development for the literary greeting *"Eirene"* in the formulae of the early Christian epistles. Almost without exception there appears in the preface after the forms of address the salutation containing the words, "Grace be with you and peace, from God our Father and the Lord Jesus Christ."[115] These epistolary formulae with reference to the peace greeting also represent the adoption of shalom as Yahweh's gift. We have evidence of the shalom greeting in Hebraic ostraca going back to the sixth century B.C. This literary evidence continues into the letters of the Bar Kochba period in the world surrounding the early Christians.[116] Nevertheless, it is not merely through the concept of grace and its linkage to peace, but above all through the reference to "God the Father" and to "Jesus Christ our Lord," that a Christianizing was achieved, when compared with the Hebraic tradition. The greeting does not express merely the wish for wholeness, wellness, and health, in such an encounter, but rather the gift of the grace of God and of peace in Christ.

The essential point in the passages from the New Testament examined thus far is the linking of the concept of peace with Jesus Christ, most explicitly with his death on the cross as the basis of peace. In Paul this is for the first time developed also to mean the reconciliation of God with the people. This is then carried forward theologically in Ephesians by saying that Jesus Christ is peace, that he *brings* peace and that in his message he *proclaims* the gospel of peace.

Thus far we have oriented ourselves toward that New Testament understanding of peace for which quotations from the Old Testament constitute evidence of influence. This involved early Christian writings after A.D. 50. Now we must ask, Does this early Christian concept which relates peace to Christ and his work have any historical background? Where are possible roots? Israel and the Jews, of course, had linked shalom to the messianic hope in a Messiah, and had even envisioned a peace of the nations after a victory.[117] We have already drawn attention to the passage in

Isa. 9:5f. that links the throne of David with an everlasting reign. No less clear is Micah when he prophesies in Micah 5:4f.: "And he shall stand and feed his flock in the strength of the LORD, in the majesty of the name of the LORD his God. And they shall dwell secure, for now he shall be great to the ends of the earth. And this shall be peace."[118] Pointing in the same direction are Zech. 9:9f., the *Sibylline Oracles,* and the *Testament of Levi.* Functioning as a topos, the image has had striking influence upon literature and iconography reflecting the apocalyptic peaceable kingdom of Isa. 11:1–10. Some of these Old Testament statements are also alluded to in the Gospels, although not under the rubric of "peace," but merely under "empire" and "king."[119]

We are concerned here not simply with the continuation of a Jewish motif but with early Christian evidence from the scripture for the person of Jesus, especially the kingship of the crucified One. We must take into account that the messianic expectation was very much alive but was directed toward a political Messiah and a political peace. In that moment when the crucified Jesus of Nazareth became identified with the title of king[120] and Christ,[121] these concepts had to be transferred from the world of *political* understanding to an *eschatological* one. The titles "King" and "Messiah" (= Christ) were *depoliticized,* as were "Empire" and "Peace," and by relating them to the crucified and risen One, they were Christianized. Thus the early Christian peace concept received a powerful eschatological emphasis.

Even though we can trace a line from the Old Testament concept of a messianic reign of peace to early Christianity's use of *eirene,* it is too general — indeed, too vague — to locate here the real point of contact. One cannot identify in the texts the process of transformation from the Jewish apocalyptic peace to the Christian eschatological peace. Rather, the result appears suddenly with faith in Jesus as the Christ. One must therefore ask whether Jesus himself may have interpreted his activities on the ground of a peace concept or whether we are dealing with a postresurrection linkage and interpretation.

With reference to the concept of peace, the Synoptic Gospels in the Markan tradition are of little help. We can point to only two passages: in Mark 5:34 the farewell salutation is "Go in peace" and in 9:50, "Have salt in yourselves, and be at peace with one another."[122] The story of the healing of the blind man with the use of the title "Son of David" (Mark 10:46–52), the messianic entry into Jerusalem (Mark 11:1–11), and the miracle stories as such are, in my opinion, not part of the peace motif complex.[123] On the other hand, more frequent references appear in the Sayings Source (Q), which offers a more careful collection of the sayings and speeches of Jesus, and also in the sources peculiar to Matthew and Luke. For the longer historical impact, the passage in the Sermon on the Mount, "Blessed are the peacemakers, for they shall be called children of God" (Matt. 5:9), carried special weight. The verse sounds somewhat alien because of the use of the rare noun εἰρηνο-ποιός, a *hapax legomenon* of the New Testament and the Septuagint as well. We will need to assume that here the Hebraic statement, "It is God who makes peace,"[124] ὁ ποιῶν εἰρήνην, led to this equivalent translation. The name "children of God" also indicates this origin. A political peace, one made by appointed negotiators, is not what is meant; rather, it is the bringing of God's "peace" in the sense of shalom.

Alongside this we must immediately consider the only apparently contradictory saying, recorded in Matt. 10:34: "Do not think that I have come to bring peace on earth; I have not come to bring peace, but a sword." The parallel passage in Luke 12:51f. replaces the sword with "division," thereby bringing the concept of peace close to that of "concord."[125] In all likelihood, however, this is not an actual saying of Jesus but a prophecy drawn from Micah 7:6, that the Parousia must be preceded by a time of terror and persecution. As in Mark 13:12, the apocalyptic disorders are brought together as if predicted by Jesus, thus explaining the absence of peace.[126] The present is the time of decision, and precisely thereby also the time of salvation; but the present does not possess *eirene,* in the sense of contrast to discord and war.

If our historical-critical method is reliable, then the historical Jesus made little use of the Old Testament concept of peace, even though in all likelihood he too practiced the shalom greeting. It is striking that in the Synoptic tradition the concept of peace is never linked to the proclamation of the coming of the kingdom of God.[127] This happens only after Easter, specifically in Paul's letter to the Romans (14:17).[128]

Thus the specific Christian concept of peace cannot be traced back to the proclamation of the historical Jesus. Rather, its historical roots lie in the postresurrection period when the congregation that believed in the crucified and risen One connected the messianic title and the hope for "peace," "life," and "resurrection from the dead" with Jesus as the Christ and Son of God. The interpretations of the cross event as that which makes peace and enables reconciliation belong to these crucial first decades of the church. The formulations of Luke's Gospel, which appear at the end of the Christmas story (Luke 2:14) and which have had significant historical impact, must be seen as having developed at a later period toward the end of the first century. The heavenly host that suddenly appears with the angel of the Lord sings the song of praise that we know from its use in the liturgy in its Latin form as the "great Gloria": *Gloria in excelsis Deo et in terra pax hominibus bonae voluntatis.* [129] As far as the Gloria (δόξα) is concerned, this song of the angels is addressed to God, but the promise of peace is for the people who receive mercy. This in all likelihood is the meaning of the last phrase, according to von Rad. [130] Even though the context is not entirely free of Hellenistic expressions, [131] it seems that we should understand *eirene* as the well-being offered to the people, that is, shalom. The apparent restriction of this salvation to those persons who receive mercy is not intended as predestination. Rather, it is the apocalyptic style and expression for peace as the gift of grace. It is not the idea of *aurum saeculum* that is intended here, even if Luke were acquainted with the theme of Virgil's 4th *Eclogue.* [132] The angels' song of praise is to be understood as an exposition of the epiphany of the Son of God with a view to its universal significance. For God this epiphany is the glorification of his own divine being; for humans encountered by the mercy of this epiphany event, it is salvation.

A final set of New Testament texts to be examined concerns the Johannine concept of peace. In the farewell speeches, whose final form came from the evangelist, [133] Jesus Christ says to his own whom he leaves behind in the world:

> Εἰρήνην ἀφίημι ὑμῖν, εἰρήνην τὴν ἐμὴν δίδωμι ὑμῖν· οὐ καθὼς ὁ κόσμος δίδωσιν ἐγὼ δίδωμι ὑμῖν. μὴ ταρασσέσθω ὑμῶν ἡ καρδία μηδὲ δειλιάτω.

> Peace I leave with you; my peace I give to you; not as the world gives do I give to you. Let not your hearts be troubled, neither let them be afraid. (John 14:27)

> ταῦτα λελάληκα ὑμῖν ἵνα ἐν ἐμοὶ εἰρήνην ἔχητε. ἐν τῷ κόσμῳ θλῖψιν ἔχετε· ἀλλὰ θαρσεῖτε, ἐγὼ νενίκηκα τὸν κόσμον.

> I have said this to you, that in me you may have peace. In the world you have tribulation; but be of good cheer, I have overcome the world. (John 16:33)

Both passages present the reader with a vision of an eschatological salvation to be found in Christ, an *eirene* that is to be received as a gift. Unmistakable here is the fact that the gift[134] of an eschatological peace is raised above every worldly gift. *Eirene* and the eschatological χαρά ("joy") belong together (cf. John 15:11 and 17:13) and are given to his own by the departing Lord; *eirene* here means "salvation in the full content of meaning of the Semitic *shalom*."[135] Only now it applies to peace in Christ which is able to liberate from the bonds of worldly entanglements so that fear — or despair — disappear, and at the same time a freedom from the world is possible. In John 16:33 this eschatological peace is tied even more precisely to the person of Christ, or rather, to faith in Jesus Christ. For in the promise of peace the emphasis falls on *"in me* you may have peace." That is, peace does not become the possession of the world or even of the believer; rather, it remains anchored outside human self-discretion.[136] In the act of faith in Christ a person receives peace, a grace that takes away the sense of abandonment. The peace of God is now the peace of Christ.[137] To be sure, the gift cannot be separated from the Giver; it is a gift only as long as the "remaining in" faith continues.[138]

Even though, similar to the Old Testament, a variety of references to peace can be recognized, and alongside the Semitic there are also Hellenistic influences, what shows through as something special and new in the New Testament is: *Peace makes itself present in the encounter with Christ or with his word.* This element of encounter is also present in the shalom of the Old Testament, but now in the New Testament the encounter with Christ takes on a historical dimension and serves as a *determinant of the relationship* between God and the human being as well as between fellow human beings. Here peace breaks in and remains only as long as the encounter is an actual reality.

Early Extracanonical Christian Writing

The above comments have reference primarily to Paul and John. Yet in the same decades in which the evangelist John, as well as Luke, was writing, that is, at the turn of the first century, the presbyter Clement in Rome wrote a letter of admonition to the church in Corinth. In spite of its Greek form, that letter breathes a Latin spirit.[139] The Roman congregation which had serious conflict in its own ranks admonishes the congregation in Corinth to peace. The purpose and goal of the letter are evidently unity and concord. Discord is to be eliminated through strengthening faith. The difference from the Johannine concept of peace appears in the fact that in Clement *eirene* and *homonoia* ("concord") appear

side by side seven times, as hendiadys.[140] That is as much a
Hellenistic inheritance as it is Roman, as proven by evidence from
coins — in the West especially since 44 B.C. when a temple for
Concordia Nova was decreed.[141] This ancient pagan pairing is now
adopted at the end of the early Christian period, thereby transforming the early Christian concept of peace into a subchapter
on ethics. Even though peace citations from the Old Testament
frequently appear,[142] the context shows that now the Christocentric
and eschatological concept of peace is less determinative than is
the ethical one. Also connected to this concept is the concept of
order, without a tangible point of reference to Jesus Christ. The
climax of this influence of the ancient pagan concept of peace
which began with the Apostolic Fathers is to be found in Augustine's *City of God* 19.13 in which scarcely any traces of a peace
concept shaped by Christ can be detected.[143] No doubt other
sections of his work correct this one-sidedness, in which the
eschatological *eirene* is strikingly identified as one with the celestial
city.[144]

Gregory of Nazianzus, one of the three great Cappadocians,[145]
who later became known as "the theologian" and friend of the
brothers Basil and Gregory of Nyssa, left behind three "orations"
on peace addressed partly to his congregation and partly to the
conflicting bishops.[146] To some extent, similar to that of the Roman
presbyter Clement, the references to the examples from the Old
Covenant are extensive. But to some extent the speech also switches
back and forth between *eirene* and *homonoia*. Occasionally,
Gregory even turns to the Letter to the Ephesians in order to preach
the essential Christian concept of peace to his fellow bishops who
were in disagreement about a christological definition. Preserved
in the University Library of Basel, Manuscript Department,[147] is
a commentary on Gregory's sermons, written 1120/1130 by Elias,
Metropolitan of Crete.[148] The manuscript is embellished with
sixteen miniatures from the time around 1200, one of which (see
Fig. 5) was placed with Gregory's second *eirene* sermon. The top
half of this picture is a reference to the content of Gregory's
admonition. It shows an architectural drawing of two long
buildings joined by a single wall, in the middle of which, crowned
with a cupola, is a clipeus. It surrounds a female half-figure with
crown and halo, and the inscription H EIPHNH.[149] The halo with
a cross leaves no doubt that the reference is to Christ as peace,
as *eirenopoios*.[150] The representation of the two buildings joined
in Christ as *eirene* reminds one of Eph. 2:14, the wall of partition
broken down by Christ and the joining of the two parts of

Christianity that had been separated until then, a text that was also cited in Gregory's sermon. In the lower half of the picture Gregory stands behind a pulpit, pointing to Eirene-Christ. Before him on the right two parties are in discussion, obviously not yet unified by this peace. This miniature naturally does not precisely explicate the peace theology of Gregory of Nazianzus but reflects a much later period. Whether this work was preceded by earlier ones is, to my knowledge, unknown. But it conforms to the thrust of Ephesians, that peace between two Christian parties is preached as the peace of Christ.

We cannot bring this to a conclusion without addressing a point of view that has been left out of consideration thus far. Although the early Christian literature presents to the world no purely ethical or socio-ethical peace postulate, it would be wrong to minimize the value and the political urgency of *secular peace work,* arguing that it lacks the theological and specifically early Christian dimension. My presentation was intended as a reminder in the light of a far too common and seemingly self-evident restriction of "peace" to the political sphere that as far as the original Christian concept of peace is concerned, even the best-organized nonwar situation remains something different from peace and reconciliation in Christ. If in antiquity it was said: *Eirene* is peace, but she does not bring it, then in early Christian literature, if we reduce it to a short formula, it is said: Jesus Christ is peace; he grants peace and issues the challenge to offer to the world this reconciling act of God in Christ as a gift of peace.

Yet even this antithetical formulation still leaves unclear what is the actual place of peace. As seen in Greek and Roman culture, an externally oriented *eirene* followed upon victory over the foreign political enemy, whereas the internally oriented political peace was called *homonoia* or *concordia.* Both were so interconnected that for the sake of *eirene* the classes (or estates) were striving for *homonoia.* In early Christian thought, *eirene,* following the Old Testament *shalom,* was tied to the inner sphere of the people of God: brotherly love and faith in Jesus Christ, faith in Christ's crucifixion as victory for us, are the prerequisites for and the result of peace. Upon this foundation of peace as the gift of God to those justified and reconciled, peace as forgiveness and reconciliation in Christ is offered to the world. Thus the original Christian concept of peace cannot be separated and neutralized from the Christ event. That is why it can be witnessed to outside the church only in connection with the message of Christ.

Addendum

Attention needs to be drawn to a work that appeared after this study was already submitted for publication: Lothar Perlitt, "Israel und die Völker," in *Frieden — Bibel — Kirche* (ed. Liedke [1972], 17–64). It is a further elaboration, starting from different questions, of the section above (pp. 166–171) concerning the Old Testament concept of peace. The author examines the issue of "war and peace" during the four hundred years of Israel's independence as a state — that is, from David to the exile. Methodologically complementary to our study, the author also avoids a comparison of the use of the words *milchamah* ("war") and *shalom,* in favor of an analysis of the historical situation of the relations between Israel and the nations. One should keep in mind that in this case by focusing on "war," peace becomes "nonwar." The result shows that under Saul and David, Israel pursued wars of conquest, expansion, and defense and that precisely during this period Jerusalem became the "city of David." Through war the kings had become monarchs, pursuing power politics. The Yahwist interprets the victories achieved by David as fulfillment of the promise to Abraham (Gen. 12:2). Perlitt shows how the Israelite understanding of history is shaped by following the theme: "Yahweh wins the victory, not Israel." That is, "Yahweh battles, Israel watches" (see above) is the ideal structure for the war of Yahweh. It is also within this context that Exod. 15:3, "Yahweh is a warrior," is to be understood. The song of praise for the salvation of Israel by passing through the Red Sea and the destruction of the Egyptians sounds forth unto Yahweh, who appears anthropomorphically as a warrior. When the author comes to the conclusion (Perlitt, p. 57) that there were no "official theological formulations in Israel for a peaceful regulation of relations . . . to the nations," one must put alongside this, as reported in 1 Kings 4:20–5:8, that peace as prosperity, calm, and order for Israel because of the subordination of the nations paying tribute, is received with joy. "For the theme 'Israel and the Nations' the Hebraic word *shalom* carried no key force" (Perlitt, p. 58); it is not a significant category in foreign policy.

All of this points to the nonpolitical and theological usage of the concept of shalom. "The prophets of judgment called for a decision and for peace with Yahweh. Peace among the nations as an achievement of the nations, as reward for human effort, was not a point of theorizing for them" (Perlitt, p. 63).

The article has its special merits in that it gives greater priority to the historical situation, showing the political power activities of ancient Israel through examples; it also helpfully puts the concept of Yahweh as God of peace alongside that of Yahweh as warrior. We would be restricting the picture of Old Testament shalom, were we not also to acknowledge this possible line of thought.

Notes

1. Walter Eisenbeis (*Die Wurzel* שׁלם *im Alten Testament* [BZAW 113; Berlin: Walter de Gruyter, 1969], in Part 1, pp. 10ff.) examines the root *šlm* in the nonbiblical Semitic languages, briefly in the Arabic and more thoroughly in the Akkadian (pp. 35–43). This monograph, which seeks to combine linguistic and hermeneutical concerns, is fundamental to our section on the Old Testament. In addition, for the Old Testament, see the following: Wilhelm Caspari, *Vorstellung und Wort "Friede" im Alten Testament* (BFCT 14, 4; Gütersloh: C. Bertelsmann Verlag, 1910); Gerhard von Rad, "שׁלום in the Old Testament," *TDNT,* 2:402–406 [*TWNT,* 2:400–405]; Claus Westermann, "Der Frieden (*Shalom*) im Alten Testament," in *Studien zur Friedensforschung* 1 (ed. G. Picht and H. E. Tödt; Stuttgart: Ernst Klett Verlag, 1969), 144–177; Erich Dinkler and Erika Dinkler-von Schubert, "Frieden," in *RAC* 8 (1972): 434–505; H. H. Schmid, *Šalom: "Frieden" im Alten Orient und im Alten Testament* (SBS 51; Stuttgart: Verlag Katholisches Bibelwerk, 1971); and Leonhard Rost, "Erwägungen zum Begriff *šalom*," in *Schalom: Studien zu Glaube und Geschichte Israels* (ed. Karl-Heinz Bernhardt; Festschrift Alfred Jepsen zum 70. Geburtstag; Stuttgart: Calwer Verlag, 1971), 41–44.

2. Harald Fuchs, *Augustin und der antike Friedensgedanke* (2nd ed.; Berlin: Weidmannsche Verlagsbuchhandlung, 1965), passim.

3. Von Rad, *TDNT,* 2:402. Two other views are Jacob Levy, *Neuhebräisches und Chaldäisches Wörterbuch* (1876–1889), 4:564; concerning *shalom:* "A word, which because of its ambiguity, can scarcely be translated into another language"; and Ludwig Köhler, *Old Testament Theology* (trans. A. S. Todd; Philadelphia: Westminster Press, 1957), 240: "To translate שׁלום 'peace' is a makeshift; prosperity would be better" [*Theologie des Alten Testaments* (Tübingen: J. C. B. Mohr [Paul Siebeck], 1936), 232].

4. Eisenbeis's statistics (*Wurzel,* pp. 58ff.) show the frequency of the root *šlm* in the Old Testament: as noun, 236 times; as adjective, 28 times; as verb, 119 times; plus many derivatives.

5. Kurt Galling, *Biblisches Reallexikon* (HAT 1; Tübingen: J. C. B. Mohr [Paul Siebeck], 1937), 13f.

6. Westermann ("Der Frieden," 148f., n. 2) rejects much of von Rad's article, because he traces back the line of thought too much from the New Testament concept *eirene* and does not pay enough attention to the

nontheological meanings. As far as I see, Westermann, for the sake of
the independence of the Old Testament, treats the theologically shaped
concept of *shalom* much too marginally. The article on Akkadian roots
(Westermann, "Der Frieden," n. 2) requires more differentiation in the
light of Eisenbeis. Egon Brandenburger, "Grundlinien des Friedensverständnisses im NT," *WD* 11 (1971): 21–72, esp. p. 24, relying on H.
H. Schmid (see n. 1 above) dismisses von Rad's work too readily.

7. Martin Noth, "Das alttestamentliche Bundschliessen im Lichte eines
Mari-Textes," in *Gesammelte Studien zum Alten Testament* (TBü 6; 2nd
ed.; Munich: Chr. Kaiser Verlag, 1960), 142–154. Cf. my short reference
in *RAC* 8, pp. 436f.

8. The sole exception to my knowledge is Jer. 29:7 in which peace also
for the Babylonians — naturally in the interests of the exiles — is to be
prayed for. But may one draw conclusions from this passage? Cf. Westermann ("Der Frieden," p. 170), who would answer in the affirmative. The
text in Jeremiah reads: "But seek the welfare of the city where I have
sent you into exile, and pray to the LORD on its behalf, for in its welfare
you will find your welfare." See also p. 170 below, concerning Zech. 9:9–10.

9. Hartmut Gese, "Der Dekalog als Ganzheit betrachtet," *ZTK* 64
(1967): 124ff. The Decalogue specifies the boundaries of *shalom* as the
sphere of welfare, in which Israel can live.

10. Westermann, "Der Frieden," 162f.

11. The LXX translates: καὶ ἐπηρώτησεν Δαυίδ εἰς εἰρήνην Ἰωαβ
καὶ εἰς εἰρήνην τοῦ λαοῦ καὶ εἰς εἰρήνην τοῦ πολέμου.

12. 2 Sam. 20:9 and 1 Sam. 17:18; 20:7.

13. Similarly 2 Kings 4:26.

14. Westermann ("Der Frieden," 162f.) is right.

15. Cf. F. Cumont, "Les ossuaries juifs et le Διάταγμα Καίσαρος,"
Syria 14 (1933): 223f.; and Johannes Irmscher, "Zum Διάταγμα
Καίσαρος von Nazareth," *ZNW* 42 (1949): 172ff.

16. For the sake of expiation for breaking the law, the Israelite and
the Jew wished for a rapid decomposition of the "flesh"; the "bones"
which were buried in the ossuary were without sin.

17. The oldest evidence: Jason grave with Aramaic *shalom* graffiti from
the beginning of the first century B.C.: *IEJ* 17 (1967): 101ff., Fig. 1; and
two graffiti on ossuaries with *shalom* from Jerusalem: *IEJ* 20 (1970): 36f.
On the adoption of the sepulchral peace wish on Greek grave inscriptions in Jewish catacombs, see Figs. 3 and 4. The sepulchral peace
inscriptions have their origin in Judaism and first appear in Christianity
in the third century: Erich Dinkler, "SHALOM-EIRENE-PAX: Jüdische
Sepulkralinschriften und ihr Verhältnis zum frühen Christentum," in
Rivista di Archeologia Cristiana 50 (1974): 121–144.

18. On the iconography of this psalm: Utrecht Psalter, fol. 49ᵛ; Canter-
bury Psalter, fol. 150ᵛ; Cod. Vat. Graec. 1927, fol. 156ʳ; Stuttgarter
Psalter, fol. 100ᵛ; cf. Herbert von Einem, *Das Stützengeschoss der
Pisaner Domkanzel* (Cologne: Westdeutscher Verlag, 1962), 5–8.

19. *Lexikon der christlichen Ikonographie* (Rome: Herder, 1972),

4:317–320, s.v. "Tierfriede" (Erika Dinkler-von Schubert).

20. On this problem, see Willem Silvester van Leeuwen, *Eirene in het Nieuwe Testament* (Wageningen: H. Veenman, 1940), 13–117; Dinkler, *RAC* 8, p. 454; Schmid, p. 45.

21. On Homer and the problem of folklore and oral tradition, see Albrecht Dihle, *Homer-Probleme* (Opladen: Westdeutscher Verlag, 1970), 45ff.; and F. Dirlmeier, "Das serbokroatische Heldenlied und Homer," *SHAW* (1971), passim.

22. Martin Dibelius, *Studies in the Acts of the Apostles* (trans. of 1951 ed. Mary Ling and Paul Schubert; New York: Charles Scribner's Sons, 1956), 186ff. [*Aufsätze zur Apostelgeschichte* (3rd ed.; Göttingen: Vandenhoeck & Ruprecht, 1957), 159ff.]; also Werner Georg Kümmel, *TRu* 22 (1954): 205.

23. Hildebrecht Hommel, "Neue Forschungen zur Areopagrede Acta 17," *ZNW* 46 (1955): 155ff.; cf. Ernst Haenchen and Hans Conzelmann, in their commentaries on Acts 17.

24. Ibid., 156.

25. Hildebrecht Hommel, "Platonisches bei Lukas," *ZNW* 48 (1957): 193ff.

26. Hermann Funke, "Antisthenes und Paulus," *Hermes* 98 (1970): 459ff. For earlier commentary on this passage, Arnold Ehrhardt, "An unknown Orphic writing in the Demosthenes scholia and St. Paul," *ZNW* 48 (1957): 107ff.

27. Already Clement of Alexandria, *Strom.* 1.59. Cf. Max Pohlenz, "Paulus und die Stoa," *ZNW* 42 (1949): 101ff.; and Martin Dibelius and Hans Conzelmann, *The Pastoral Epistles* (trans. Philip Buttolph and Adela Yarbro; ed. Helmut Koester; Philadelphia: Fortress Press, 1972), 136 [*Die Pastoralbriefe erklärt* (HNT 13; 4th ed.; Tübingen: J. C. B. Mohr [Paul Siebeck], 1966), 102].

28. Martin Dibelius, *A Fresh Approach to the New Testament and Early Christian Literature* (London: Ivor Nicholson & Watson, 1937; repr. Westport, Conn.: Greenwood Press, 1979), 17–18 [*Geschichte der urchristlichen Literatur* (Berlin: Walter de Gruyter, 1926), 1:7].

29. Adolf Deissmann, *Light from the Ancient East* (trans. Lionel R. M. Strachan; London: Hodder & Stoughton, 1910), 55 [*Licht vom Osten* (4th ed.; Tübingen: J. C. B. Mohr [Paul Siebeck], 1923), 48], wrote that there was agreement that "the starting-point for the philological investigation of the New Testament must be the language of the non-literary papyri, ostraca and inscriptions." Given the history of the study and discovery of the Koine, that is an understandable one-sidedness.

30. Fuchs, *Augustin,* 168f.

31. *Odyssey* 24.480 and 482.

32. *Odyssey* 483: ὁ μὲν βασιλευέτω ἀεί.

33. *Odyssey* 485f.: τοὶ δ᾽ ἀλλήλους φιλεόντων / ὡς τὸ πάρος, πλοῦτος δὲ καὶ εἰρήνη ἅλις ἔστω. On this passage, see Fuchs, *Augustin,* 175; and Hildebrecht Hommel, "Aigisthos und die Freier," *Studium Generale* 8 (1955): 244f.

34. Hesiod, *Erga,* esp. pp. 228f.: εἰρήνη δ᾽ ἀνὰ γῆν κουροτρόφος οὐδέ ποτ᾽ αὐτοῖς ἀργαλέον πόλεμον τεκμαίρεται εὐρύοπα Ζεύς. Ulrich von Wilamowitz-Moellendorff, *Der Glaube der Hellenen* (Berlin: Weidmannsche Buchhandlung, 1928), 21.68.

35. Pindar, frag. 110 (2, 98 Snell).

36. Plato, *Leges* 1.628 C/E.

37. Aristotle, *Politica* 7.14.1333a; and *Ethica Nicomachea* 10.7. 1177b.5–12.

38. Plato, *Resp.* 465 B; and *Leges* 863 DE: τὸν κατ᾽ εἰρήνην βίον.

39. Plato, *Leges* 641 C. Cf. Harald Fuchs, "Der Friede als Gefahr," *Harvard Studies in Classical Philology* 63 (1958): 363–385.

40. W. Schmid, in *Bonner Jahrbuch* (Cologne: Rheinland Verlag, 1953), 63–96; and Fuchs, "Der Friede als Gefahr."

41. Aristotle, *Politica* 1.3.1253b.20f.: δίκαιον or βίαιον.

42. Wilhelm Capelle, "Griechische Ethik und römischer Imperialismus," *Klio* 25 (1932): 90ff., who relies on August Schmekel, *Die Philosophie der mittleren Stoa in ihrem geschichtlichen Zusammenhange* (Berlin: Weidmannsche Buchhandlung, 1892), 61ff., and R. Reitzenstein, in *Nachrichten der Gesellschaft der Wissenschaften in Göttingen* (Berlin: Dieterich, 1914), 254ff. See also Max Pohlenz, *Die Stoa* (Göttingen: Vandenhoeck & Ruprecht, 1948), 1:206; 2:102; and again more recently Heinz Haffter, *Römische Politik und römische Politiker* (Heidelberg: C. Winter Verlag, 1967), 43f., and Stefan Weinstock, *Divus Iulius* (Oxford: Clarendon Press, 1971), 267 n. 6.

43. Hermann Strasburger, in "Poseidonios on Problems of the Roman Empire," *JRS* 55 (1965): 45; note 50 provides a summary of the discussion and of the justified doubts about Cicero, *De republica* 3.36, as influenced by Panaetius.

44. For the old Stoic idea of human equality in the world, Strasburger cites Zeno, frag. 262 in Plutarch, *De Al. fort.* 1.6; Chrysippus, frag. 334–366; Eratosthenes in Strabo 1.66f.; Seneca, *Ep.* 47; Epictetus, *Diatr.* 1.13.3f. ("Poseidonios," 45 n. 50).

45. Ulrich von Wilamowitz-Moellendorff, *Reden und Vorträge* (5th ed.; Berlin: Weidmannsche Buchhandlung, 1967), 2:211; and Strasburger, "Poseidonios," as well as "Der 'Scipionenkreis,'" *Hermes* 94 (1966): 63. It is curious that Karl Hans Abel ("Die kulturelle Mission des Panaitios," *Antike und Abendland* 17 [1971]: 141) returns to the old theses.

46. Euripides, frag. 53N.

47. Cf. Friedrich Wilhelm Hamdorf, *Griechische Kultpersonifikationen der vorhellenistischen Zeit* (Mainz: Verlag Philipp von Zabern, 1964), 53–55; and Victor Ehrenberg, *The People of Aristophanes: A Sociology of Old Attic Comedy* (3rd rev. ed.; New York: Schocken Books, 1962) [*Aristophanes und das Volk von Athen* (Zurich: Artemis Verlag, 1968), 299–321].

48. Aristophanes, *Eirene (Pax)* 974/7.

49. Isocrates, *Oratio* 15.109f.1. With reference to Isocrates, *De Pace,*

see Klaus Bringmann, "Studien zu den politischen Ideen des Isokrates," in *Hypomnemata, Untersuchungen zur Antike und ihrem Nachleben* 14 (Göttingen: Vandenhoeck & Ruprecht, 1965), 58; and Daniel Gillis, "The Structure of Arguments in Isocrates' De Pace," *Philologus* 114 (1970): 195ff.

50. Felix Jacoby, *Die Fragmente der griechischen Historiker* (Leiden: E. J. Brill, 1954), 328, F 151 (in vol. 2, 419–422): ὅτε καὶ τὸν τῆς Εἰρήνης βωμὸν ἱδρύσαντο. On that, see *Suppl.* 1, pp. 522f. and 2, p. 419 Nr. 2–4; and Dinkler, *RAC* 8, pp. 438f. On conjectures about a cult as early as the fifth century, see Friedrich Matz, *Die Naturpersonifikationen in der griechischen Kunst* (Göttingen: Dieterichsche Univers.-Buchdruckerei W. F. Kaestner, 1913), 21; and Fuchs, *Augustin,* 170 n. 3; in contrast, critically Hamdorf, *Kultpersonifikationen,* 53ff., 110.

51. Pausanias 1.8.2; 9.16.2. Other Eirene images are named in *CIG* 1.150.47: Ἐν ἑτέρῳ κιβωτίῳ Εἰρήνη ἐλεφαντίνη κατάχρυσος. See Pausanias 1.18.3.

52. Heinrich Brunn, *Kleine Schriften* (Leipzig: B. G. Teubner, 1898), 1:328; and Georg Lippold, *Die griechische Plastik* (Munich: C. H. Beck'sche Verlagsbuchhandlung, 1950), 224. Doubts about the identity were stated by Andreas Rumpf, *Archäologie,* vol. 2: *Die Archäologensprache: Die antiken Reproduktionen* (Berlin: Walter de Gruyter, 1956), 88ff.; Stefan Weinstock, "Pax and the 'Ara Pacis,'" *JRS* 50 (1960): 44. As Mr. R. Hampe has kindly informed me, the latest research does not support these doubts.

53. From Thysdrus, Africa Proconsularis, now in the Rijksmuseum von Oudheiden in Leiden: J. P. J. Brants, *Description of the Classical Collection of the Museum of Archaeology (Leiden)* (The Hague: Gov't Print. Off., 1927), 2 and pl. 2, 4; Weinstock, "Pax," 46 and pl. IX.2; and Dinkler, *RAC* 8, pp. 494f.

54. Cf. Peter Robert Franke and Max Hirmer, *Die griechische Münze* (Munich: Hirmer Verlag, 1964), pl. 101; and Weinstock, "Pax," 44.

55. Hesiod, *Theogonia* 902.

56. *FGrHist Suppl* 2, 421, nr. 28.

57. Fuchs, *Augustin,* 171, 1.

58. Weinstock, "Pax," 46; and idem, *Divus Iulius,* 267ff.

59. Weinstock, *Divus Iulius,* 260ff. Cf. on Cicero: Hermann Strasburger, *Concordia Ordinum: Eine Untersuchung zur Politik Ciceros* (diss., Frankfurt, 1931; pub. Borna-Leipzig: Robert Naske, 1931).

60. Sallust, *Ep. ad Caes.* 1.5.3; 1.6.5; cited according to Eiliv Skard, "Zwei religiös-politische Begriffe *Euergetes-Concordia*" (Oslo: I kommisjon hos Jacob Bylwad, 1932), 99.

61. Cf. Weinstock, "Pax," 46, who refers in turn to Dio Cassius 44.49.2. ["Anthony praised Caesar in his funeral oration as peace-maker, εἰρηνηποιός (Dio 44.49.2), and we have good reason to believe that the epithet, probably *pacificator* or *pacificus,* was Caesar's own choice" (46).—ED.]

62. Cf. O. Brendel, "Die Friedensgöttin," in *Numen und Allegorie,* ed. Corolla L. Curtius (Stuttgart: H. Kohlhammer, 1937), 212–216; Carl Koch, "s.v. pax," PW 18, 4 (1949): 2432–2434.

63. Weinstock, *Divus Iulius,* 269. Concerning the Ara Pacis, see his article, "Pax," 44–58. For a counter position: Jocelyn M. C. Toynbee, "The 'Ara Pacis Augustae,'" *JRS* 51 (1961): 153ff.; and Erika Simon, *Ara Pacis Augustae* (Tübingen: Ernst Wasmuth Verlagsbuchhandlung, 1967).

64. Hans J. Mähl, *Die Idee des goldenen Zeitalters im Werk des Novalis* (Heidelberg: C. Winter Verlag, 1965), passim.

65. Substantiated by Hallfried Dahlmann (and Reinhard Heisterhagen), *Varronische Studien* 1 (Mainz: Abh. der Akademie der Wissenschaften und der Literatur, in Kommission bei F. Steiner, 1957), 167ff.

66. Weinstock, "Pax," 46.

67. Virgil, *Georgica* 2.425; idem, *Aeneid* 8.185ff.; and Tibullus 1.10.69: *at nobis, Pax alma, veni spicamque teneto.*

68. Jocelyn M. C. Toynbee, *The Hadrianic School* (Cambridge: Cambridge University Press, 1934), pl. 17, 1–14; and Adolf Reifenberg, *Israel's History in Coins from the Maccabees to the Roman Conquest* (London: East and West Library, 1953), nos. 27–35.

69. The sevenfold occurrence of combining "peace and concord" in the *First Letter of Clement* alone provides evidence for a direct influence at the end of the first century A.D.

70. For reasons of time and space it was not possible, within the limits of this essay, to include Philo and Josephus, necessary sources for Grecian Jewry. Cf. references in Dinkler, *RAC* 8, pp. 455–457.

71. See p. 166 above and n. 3.

72. Gal. 5:22.

73. 1 Thess. 5:3. In this case it is the unbelievers who are talking about εἰρήνη καὶ ἀσφάλεια and whose blind sense of security is punished. One is reminded of the εἰρήνη οὐκ ἔστιν in Jeremiah and Ezekiel (see p. 169 above).

74. 1 Cor. 14:33: "For God is not a God of confusion (ἀκαταστασία) but of peace."

75. Rom. 14:17: "For the kingdom of God does not mean food and drink but righteousness and peace and joy in the Holy Spirit." Aside from the secular point of comparison in Luke 14:31f., nowhere in the New Testament is "peace" set in contrast to "war." Rather, it is in contrast to "enmity," whether it be with reference to God or to fellow humans.

76. That both Ephesians and Colossians were written by a Pauline disciple, presumably in the seventh decade A.D., is now certain, in my opinion; similarly in E. Käsemann, *RGG*³, 2:517ff.; Günther Bornkamm, *Paul* (trans. D. M. G. Stalker; New York: Harper & Row, 1971), 241f. [*Paulus* (Stuttgart: Verlag W. Kohlhammer, 1969), 245f.]. The question of authenticity is irrelevant for our purposes in tracing the line of thought. The Heidelberg dissertation of Walter Bujard (*Stilanalytische Untersuchungen zum Kolosserbrief als Beitrag zur Methodik von*

Sprachvergleichen [Göttingen: Vandenhoeck & Ruprecht, 1973]) provided convincing evidence for the non-authenticity of Colossians.

77. The expression ἄθεοι, which appears only here in the New Testament, means substantially the same thing as οὐκ εἰδότες θεόν in Gal. 4:8. For the coherence of our argument it is vital that in this case the Hebrew expression of Trito-Isa. 57:20f. רשׁע is taken over here, whereas in the LXX it was translated as ἄδικοι or as ἀσεβεῖς. See the next note.

78. The relevant texts according to the LXX are:

Trito-Isa. 57:18b–21   καὶ ἔδωκα αὐτῷ παράκλησιν ἀληθινήν, εἰρήνην ἐπ᾽ εἰρήνην τοῖς μακρὰν καὶ τοῖς ἐγγὺς οὖσιν· καὶ εἶπεν κύριος Ἰάσομαι αὐτούς· οἱ δὲ ἄδικοι οὕτως κλυδωνισθήσονται καὶ ἀναπαύσασθαι οὐ δυνήσονται. οὐκ ἔστιν χαίρειν τοῖς ἀσεβέσιν, εἶπεν κύριος ὁ θεός.

Deutero-Isa. 52:7   ὡς ὥρα ἐπὶ τῶν ὀρέων, ὡς πόδες εὐαγγελλιζομένου ἀκοὴν εἰρήνης, ὡς εὐαγγελιζόμενος ἀγαθά, ὅτι ἀκουστὴν ποιήσω τὴν σωτηρίαν σου λέγων Σιων Βασιλεύσει σου ὁ θεός.

The rabbinic literature regards this last passage as referring to the Messiah: H. L. Strack and Paul Billerbeck, *Kommentar zum Neuen Testament aus Talmud und Midrasch* (Munich: C. H. Beck, 1922–1961), 3:587. Cf. also Micah 5:3f.:   διότι νῦν μεγαλυνθήσεται ἕως ἄκρων τῆς γῆς. καὶ ἔσται αὕτη εἰρήνη.

79. Martin Dibelius, in *An die Kolosser, Epheser und Philemon* (HNT; ed. Heinrich Greeven; 3rd ed.; Tübingen: J. C. B. Mohr [Paul Siebeck], 1953), 69f.

80. Heinrich Schlier, *Christus und die Kirche im Epheserbrief* (Tübingen: J. C. B. Mohr [Paul Siebeck], 1930); Rudolf Bultmann, *Theology of the New Testament* (2 vols.; trans. Kendrick Grobel; London: SCM Press, 1952, 1955), 166ff. [*Theologie des Neuen Testaments* (Tübingen: J. C. B. Mohr [Paul Siebeck], 1965)]; and Kurt Rudolph, "Gnosis und Gnostizismus, ein Forschungsbericht," *TRu* 37 (1972): 295ff.

81. Following Schlier's theses in *Christus:* Gottfried Schille, *Frühchristliche Hymnen* (Berlin: Evangelische Verlagsanstalt, 1965), 24ff.; Joachim Gnilka, "Christus unser Friede—ein Friedens-Erlöserlied in Eph. 2:14–17," in *Die Zeit Jesu. Festschrift für Heinrich Schlier* (ed. Günther Bornkamm and Karl Rahner; Freiburg: Herder, 1970), 190–207; and idem, *Der Epheserbrief* (Freiburg: Herder, 1971), 147ff. Against a literary copy from Gnostic circles: R. Deichgräber, *Gotteshymnus und Christushymnus in der frühen Christenheit* (Göttingen: Vandenhoeck & Ruprecht, 1967), 165ff.; the most recent treatment of this passage by Helmut Merklein, "Zur Tradition und Komposition von Eph 2:14–18," *BZ* 17 (1973): 79–102; [also Peter Stuhlmacher, "'He Is Our Peace' (Eph. 2:14): On the Exegesis and Significance of Eph. 2:14–18," in *Reconciliation, Law and Righteousness: Essays in Biblical Theology,* by Stuhlmacher (Philadelphia: Fortress Press, 1986), 180–200.—Ed.].

82. The context makes it clear that *eirene* in this case means well-being, wholeness, the elimination of the split in the fellowship, but not the end

of a war. The word stands in a semantic line back to *shalom*.

83. Dibelius (*Epheser,* p. 69) draws attention to the fact that "near" and "far" or "strangers" were Jewish labels for Israelites and heathen. Cf. Billerbeck, 3:585–587.

84. A somewhat awkward rendering by Gnilka, "Christus," 206; the following Christocentric interpretation of this Ephesians passage rightly eliminates that formulation.

85. Werner Foerster, *TDNT,* 2:415–416 [*TWNT,* 2:414].

86. The statements, ὁ ποιήσας τὰ ἀμφότερα ἕν (v. 14) and κτίσῃ ἐν αὐτῷ εἰς ἕνα καινὸν ἄνθρωπον ποιῶν εἰρήνην (v. 15): ("the one who has made the both one" and "he created in himself one new humanity, making peace"), interpret each other and clarify that in this case the Hebraic shalom concept is being elaborated on and related to Christ.

87. The first time in Christian literature, aside from a debatable passage in Clement of Rome, where εἰρήνη and πόλεμος ("war") are set opposite each other is in Ignatius, *Eph.* 13:2: οὐδέν ἐστιν ἄμεινον εἰρήνης, ἐν ᾗ πᾶς πόλεμος καταργεῖται ἐπουρανίων καὶ ἐπιγείων ("nothing is better than peace when all war in heaven and earth is brought to an end"), in which case, however, the words express a mythological viewpoint on δύναμις τοῦ σατανᾶ ("the power of Satan") against which the congregation is urged to have frequent gatherings εἰς εὐχαριστίαν θεοῦ καὶ εἰς δόξαν ("unto the thanksgiving and glory of God"). See also Luke 14:31f. On the concept "enmity," see Foerster, *TDNT,* 2:811ff.: the linguistic usage in both the Old and the New Testament confirms what was said about peace.

88. That with the opening or tearing down of the "wall" Gnostic imagery was incorporated into Ephesians has been demonstrated by Schlier, *Christus,* 18ff. The neuter form of ἀμφότερα ("both") in 2:14 might also be attributed to a traditional Gnostic phrase.

89. Another version of the Greek genitive connective: "The law of the commandments with their directives" (Gnilka, "Christus," 206).

90. Another possibility might be that the law is the means or expression of the split between Jews and Gentiles. F. Mussner (*Christus, das All und die Kirche* [2nd ed.; Trier: Paulinus Verlag, 1968], 82ff.) points to the *Epistle of Aristeas,* par. 139, as evidence for this interpretation. But the primary enmity is that of Gentile humanity against God.

91. With reference to the incarnation of Jesus, referring to John 1:14 and the hymns in Col. 1:15–20 and Phil. 2:5–11 that are free of redactional addenda, see Gnilka, "Christus," 199f.

92. To this subject in Paul, Bultmann, *Theology,* 289ff. [*Theologie,* 289ff.].

93. Gnilka ("Christus," 196ff.) seeks to make the side-by-side presentation of "cosmic space" considerations with "ethnic-historical" considerations as a criterion for a literary division between source and redaction. It seems to me that the paradoxical intermeshing of the cosmic and the historical dimensions, of the theological-existential with the

theological-ethnological idea, is what is specifically Christian in this passage and cannot be separated on literary-historical grounds.

94. Gnilka ("Christus," 206) would like to end the "hymn" with Eph. 2:17, seeing 2:18 as a reworking.

95. Repeatedly in the beginnings of Christian theology the concern is to take away from the death of Christ on the cross its element of offense and to see it as salvation. That is the intent of Ephesians 2; Col. 1:20; 1 Cor. 1:18ff.; 2 Cor. 5:14ff.; and Rom. 5:1–11. The theme is the cross, whereas *peace* is an interpretation of the cross of Christ.

96. Dibelius (*Epheser,* 69) sees here an elaboration of the theme of the cosmic reconciliation of the universe in Col. 1:20.

97. Dibelius, *Epheser,* 94: actually ἐγενήθη εἰρήνη would be appropriate here.

98. There is a similar line of thought in 2 Cor. 5:18–21, there with reference to the καταλλαγή and the λόγος τῆς καταλλαγῆς; see Erich Dinkler, "Die Verkündigung als eschatologisch-sakramentales Geschehen," in *Die Zeit Jesu,* ed. G. Bornkamm and K. Rahner (Freiburg: Herder, 1970), 169–189; cf. also Acts 10:36.

99. In connection with the πανοπλία τοῦ θεοῦ (Eph. 6:11) this concerns ἑτοιμασία, a concept taken from the LXX, which, following on Ps. 9:38 [10:17 in RSV; trans. "strengthen" —Ed.], expresses the readiness for the gospel of peace, i.e., of Jesus Christ as shalom. Here too the entire vocabulary should be viewed through the Old Testament, not merely the image of the armor, which appears again in Rom. 13:12 and in Qumran in a developed form. Heinrich Schlier (*Der Brief an die Epheser* [6th ed.; Düsseldorf: Patmos Verlag, 1968], 296) has it right: The emphasis in 6:15 is on εἰρήνη, not on εὐαγγέλιον.

100. On the form of the hymn: Rudolf Bultmann, in *Exegetica: Aufsätze zur Erforschung des Neuen Testaments* (Tübingen: J. C. B. Mohr [Paul Siebeck], 1967), 290.

101. Ernst Käsemann, "Eine urchristliche Taufliturgie," in *Festschrift Rudolf Bultmann* (Stuttgart: Verlag W. Kohlhammer, 1949), 133–148; also idem, in *Exegetische Versuche und Besinnungen* (Göttingen: Vandenhoeck & Ruprecht, 1960), 1:34ff.

102. On the text in the context of the letter: Eduard Lohse, *Colossians and Philemon* (Hermeneia; trans. William R. Poehlmann and Robert J. Karris; ed. Helmut Koester; Philadelphia: Fortress Press, 1971), 41ff. [*Die Briefe an die Kolosser und an Philemon* (Göttingen: Vandenhoeck & Ruprecht, 1968), 77ff.].

103. The theme of conversion, ποτέ . . . νυνί, preceded the hymn in Ephesians.

104. The possible pre-Christian Gnostic hymn, as delineated by Käsemann, will not be discussed here, since we are concerned solely with the canonical text of the redaction.

105. The passage reads: ὡς ὅτι θεὸς ἦν ἐν Χριστῷ κόσμον καταλλάσσων ἑαυτῷ which Luther in accordance with the Vulgate translated:

"God was in Christ and reconciled the world with Himself." Philologically this is not impossible, but it would postulate Paul's thought only in this passage, that God is in Christ. On the translation as presented, see Hans Lietzmann, *An die Korinther* (5th ed.; Tübingen: J. C. B. Mohr [Paul Siebeck], 1969), 126; and Dinkler, "Verkündigung," 177f.

106. It follows that the New Testament peace sayings cannot be separated from the cross event and ideologized, in order to obtain in the political realm a "contribution from the church" or of Christian theology. On the christological thrust of the Pauline and Johannine peace concepts in particular, see Peter Stuhlmacher, "Der Begriff des Friedens im Neuen Testament und seine Konsequenzen," in Wolfgang Huber, *Historische Beiträge zur Friedensforschung* (Stuttgart: Ernst Klett Verlag; Munich: Kösel-Verlag, 1970), 21–69.

107. As a rule, Protestant exegetes of this passage read the present indicative tense, whereas Catholic exegetes read it as subjunctive or hortative. *On the one hand:* Hans Lietzmann (HNT 8 [4th ed.; 1933], 58) explains the ω (omega) instead of the o (omicron) as a possible hearing mistake when Paul was dictating: "Perhaps he said *echomen,* and meant ἔχομεν, but Tertius (Rom 16:22) wrote ἔχωμεν. Even that could be accepted without difficulty, were it possible to trace the ω back to the original letter. But the sense of the passage must triumph here over the letter: ἔχομεν is the only genuine Pauline meaning." *On the other hand:* O. Kuss (*Der Römerbrief* [2nd ed.; Regensburg: Verlag Friedrich Pustet, 1963], 201), pointing to the consistency of the manuscripts as handed down, continues: "Above all one has to keep in mind the fact that the cohortative in this passage of Pauline thought is indeed not impossible in any way." Similarly for the subjunctive tense: W. Sanday and A. C. Headlam, *Romans* (ICC; New York: Charles Scribner's Sons, 1902), 120, and C. H. Dodd, *Romans* (Moffatt New Testament Commentary; New York: Ray Long and R. Smith, 1932), 72f.

108. The manuscript evidence, in the absence of papyri (the text of P46 only begins with 5:17), as collated by the Institut für neutestamentliche Forschung (K. Aland), Münster, as well as the witness of the Fathers in the Vetus Latina Institute in Beuron (Bonifatius Fischer), shows the following:

ἔχωμεν: ℵ* A B* C D K L 049. 056. 1142. 0151. 7. 33. 61cor.. 81.
Augustine, Pelagius, Paulinus of Nola, Cassiodorus.

ἔχομεν: ℵ1 B3 G P Ψ 0220vid.. 51. 57. 61*. 88. *pm al*
Ambrosiaster, Leo, Prosper, Beda.

(Complete listing of majuscules; selections from the minuscules, etc.) It is pretty difficult to imagine that a copyist of the Sinaiticus (i.e., ℵ1) would have undertaken to correct ω with o. On the basis of external textual criticism, there can be no doubt of the priority of the subjunctive reading.

109. In favor of an indicative tense, and for the translation: "after we

have now been justified by faith we have peace with God," it should be noted that the development of the New Testament text base is generally "from indicative to subjunctive and not the reverse," so rightly K. Aland in a letter; finally, that the content of the argument as developed in Romans would require in 5:1 a résumé stating what is the significance of faith for justification. On this latter reason: Bultmann, *Theology*, 274 n. [*Theologie*, 275 n. 1]; Bultmann also in *Exegetica*, 202f., cf. 424ff. My decision against these expositions that are based on a substantive critique [*Sachkritik*] of Paul's thought is based on the weighty and unanimous external evidence of the handwritten sources, the manuscripts for this passage. The *lectio difficilior* of the subjunctive form is within the sphere of theologically possible thought for the apostle; it is not decisive for the New Testament peace concept as discussed here, but it does bring in a new nuance.

110. Ps. 34:13–17 is cited in 1 Peter 3:10–12 where it also says: ζητησάτω εἰρήνην καὶ διωξάτω αὐτήν. Cf. also Isa. 27:5 according to the LXX: ποιήσωμεν εἰρήνην αὐτῷ, ποιήσωμεν εἰρήνην. Romans 14:19 could be compared with the imperative of Rom. 5:1: ἄρα οὖν τὰ τῆς εἰρήνης διώκωμεν καὶ τὰ τῆς οἰκοδομῆς τῆς εἰς ἀλλήλους. Of course two features here count against the use of subjunctive in Rom. 5:1: this does not refer to the gift of εἰρήνη πρὸς τὸν θεόν, and also here the hortatory reading occurs with an indicative variant. Evidence from the manuscripts (majuscules complete; minuscules and Fathers selected):

διωκομεν: ℵ A B F G L P 048. 0150. 0209. 88. 326. *al.*
διωκωμεν: C D Ψ 049. 056. 0142. 0151. 33. 81. *pm al.*
Ambrosiaster, Augustine, Sedulius. Cassiodorus, Gregory of Tours, furthermore the Aethiopic and Armenian mss. (kind information from K. Aland)

On the basis of the breadth and weight of the manuscript evidence, here too the hortative subjunctive reading has preference. There is a gap at this point in the textual tradition of P⁴⁶.

111. This is a similar line of thought as in Gal. 5:25: εἰ ζῶμεν πνεύματι, πνεύματι καὶ στοιχῶμεν. On the question of indicative-imperative: Bultmann, *Theology*, 332f. [*Theologie*, 334f.]. On διώκειν εἰρήνην: 2 Tim. 2:22; Heb. 12:14. The option presented here for ἔχωμεν as the original reading in Rom. 5:1 is motivated by method alone, and the decision in favor of it was taken in conscious disagreement with Lietzmann, Bultmann, and many others. On the matter of the synonymous nature of justification and reconciliation in Pauline thought, see Stuhlmacher, "Begriff," 35.

112. On the debatable passage: Hans Windisch, *Der Hebräerbrief* (HNT 14; 2nd ed.; Tübingen: J. C. B. Mohr [Paul Siebeck], 1931), 61; Ernst Käsemann, *The Wandering People of God* (trans. Roy A. Harrisville and Irving L. Sandberg; Minneapolis: Augsburg Publishing House, 1984), 172–173 [*Das wandernde Gottesvolk* (Göttingen: Vandenhoeck & Ruprecht, 1939), 134]; Bultmann, *Exegetica*, 377; and Otto

Michel, *Der Brief an die Hebräer* (12th ed.; Göttingen: Vandenhoeck & Ruprecht, 1966), 255ff. For evidence from the Qumran sources: Yigael Yadin, "A Note on Melchizedek and Qumran," *IEJ* 15 (1965): 152–154.

113. Luke 1:32–33 is suggestive of this passage. The German text is oriented toward the Hebrew original. LXX translates Isa. 9:5–6a as follows:

ὅτι παιδίον ἐγεννήθη ἡμῖν, υἱὸς καὶ ἐδόθη ἡμῖν, οὗ ἡ ἀρχὴ ἐγενήθη ἐπὶ τοῦ ὤμου αὐτοῦ, καὶ καλεῖται τὸ ὄνομα αὐτοῦ Μεγάλης βουλῆς ἄγγελος· ἐγὼ γὰρ ἄξω εἰρήνην ἐπὶ τοὺς ἄρχοντας, εἰρήνην καὶ ὑγίειαν αὐτῷ. μεγάλη ἡ ἀρχὴ αὐτοῦ, καὶ τῆς εἰρήνης αὐτοῦ οὐκ ἔστιν ὅριον ἐπὶ τὸν θρόνον Δαυιδ. . . .

114. The greeting εἰρήνη ὑμῖν is a direct translation of שלום לכם: Luke 24:36 (textus receptus) and in the expanded εἰρήνη τῷ οἴκῳ τούτῳ of Luke 10:5; Matt. 10:12f.

115. The salutation is a curious combination of the Greek epistolary greeting with χαίρειν and the Hebrew greeting with *shalom*-εἰρήνη, in which the substantive χάρις involves a theologizing of what is said with the verb. With minor variations, this formula is found in Rom. 1:7; 1 Cor. 1:3; 2 Cor. 1:2; Gal. 1:3; Eph. 1:2; Phil. 1:2; Col. 1:2; 1 Thess. 1:1; 2 Thess. 1:2; Titus 1:4; Philemon 3. Cf. Rev. 1:4 and 2 Peter 1:2. As an expanded triadic formula χάρις, ἔλεος, εἰρήνη ἀπὸ θεοῦ πατρὸς καὶ Χριστοῦ Ἰησοῦ . . . : 1 Tim. 1:2; 2 Tim. 1:2; 2 John 3.

116. The ostracon from Arad (ca. 60 km south of Jerusalem; 598 or 587 B.C.):

אל אדני אלי   To my Lord Elia-
שב יהוה יש   shib. May Yahweh to you
אל לשלמך   give peace . . . (Y. Aharoni, *IEJ* 16 [1966]: 5f.)

The Lachish-Ostraca (also from the first decade of the sixth century B.C.):
Letter II, 1, 2:

אל אדני יאוש ישמע   To my Lord Ya'osh. May Yahweh
יהוה את אדני שנמ[ע]ת שלם   allow my Lord to hear news of peace.

(David Diringer, in Olga Tufnell, *Lachish III: The Iron Age, Text* [London: Oxford University Press, 1953], 332; and similarly Letter III, 2). On the epistolary forms of the Bar Kochba era, with *shalom* greeting from Murabba'at: R. de Vaux, "Quelques textes hébreux de Murabba'at," *RB* 60 (1953): 270 and 277 [the latter in J. T. Milik, "Une lettre de Siméon Bar Kokheba"]; from the so-called letter cave: Yigael Yadin, *Bar Kochba* (Hamburg: Hoffmann & Campe Verlag, 1971), 134, 137f. English: *Bar-Kokhba* (London and Jerusalem: Weidenfeld & Nicholson; New York: Random House, 1971).

117. Wilhelm Bousset, *Die Religion des Judentums im späthelle-nistischen Zeitalter* (3rd ed., by Hugo Gressmann; Tübingen: J. C. B. Mohr [Paul Siebeck], 1926), 260f. A recent thematic treatment: Brandenburger (see n. 6 above).

118. LXX: Micah 5:3b–4: διότι, νῦν μεγαλυνθήσεται ἕως ἄκρων τῆς γῆς· καὶ ἔσται αὕτη εἰρήνη; v. 4a: וְהָיָה זֶה שָׁלוֹם.

119. Isa. 9:6=Luke 1:31–33; Zech. 9:9=Matt. 21:5; John 12:15. An exception is Luke 19:38 where the peace announcement of Zech. 9:9–10 must have exerted an influence: Eisenbeis, *Wurzel,* 251f.

120. In my judgment the text of the titulus, the inscription above the crucified, as given in Mark 15:26, Ὁ ΒΑΣΙΛΕΥΣ ΤΩΝ ΙΟΥΔΑΙΩΝ, can be regarded as historical. Christian apologetics would have chosen the formulation: ὁ Βασιλεὺς Ἰσραήλ.

121. Mark 8:29, 33 indicates, in my opinion, that the historical Jesus rejected the political Messiah-Christ title; cf. Erich Dinkler, "Petrusbekenntnis und Satanswort," in *Signum Crucis, Gesammelte Aufsätze zum Neuen Testament und zur christliche Archäologie* (Tübingen: J. C. B. Mohr [Paul Siebeck], 1967), 289ff.

122. Salt as a valuable possession (cf. Matt. 5:13; Luke 14:34f.). The admonition εἰρηνεύετε ἐν ἀλλήλοις appears also in Paul in 1 Thess. 5:13. It shows that the Hellenistic ὁμόνοια idea missing in the Old Testament is able to insert itself into early Christian Greek.

123. Brandenburger's work (see n. 6 above) is the first to show the connection between Jewish-apocalyptic ideology of kingship and the peace motif, on the one hand, and the Christian peace motif and peace concepts in the New Testament, on the other. His starting point is early Christian apocalyptic, and then via the Synoptics he moves on to John and Paul. This work complements mine as presented; but, in my opinion, it is in part an over-interpretation of the evidence in the New Testament, in that peace connotations are presumed in places where I am unable to affirm them. An example: the miracles of Jesus should not be seen as mere θεῖος ἀνήρ concepts, but belong within the framework of the Jewish notion of a Messiah as a healing miracle worker and thus serve as examples of the messianic peace brought by Jesus (Brandenburger, 47ff.). Also his system of coordinates as applied to New Testament peace statements: apocalyptic or wisdom theology (with a process of dualization) is too schematic, in my opinion. Brandenburger is clearly right in that he draws out the relationship of Christ to peace in the New Testament. In line with his somewhat different intent, he does not go into the world of secular Greek and relies for the Old Testament mainly on H. H. Schmid (see n. 1 above).

124. Isa. 45:7: ἐγὼ ὁ κατασκευάσας φῶς . . . , ὁ ποιῶν εἰρήνην: עֹשֶׂה שָׁלוֹם; cf. Job 25:2; Judges 18:6; Ps. 4:9; and esp. Num. 6:26.

125. Luke 12:51 speaks of διαμερισμός. For a discussion of Matt. 10:34 compared with 5:9, cf. also Fuchs, *Augustin,* p. iii, n. 1.

126. On this passage, Rudolf Bultmann, *The History of the Synoptic Tradition* (trans. John Marsh; 2nd ed.; Oxford: Basil Blackwell, 1963), 154–155. [*Geschichte der synoptischen Tradition* (7th ed.; Göttingen: Vandenhoeck & Ruprecht, 1967), 166].

127. It is therefore very noteworthy that in the *Ethiopian Enoch* 71:14–17

peace and justice are linked to the "son of man" and appear as apocalyptic gift.

128. See n. 75 above. Otto Michel (*Der Brief an die Römer* [4th ed.; Göttingen: Vandenhoeck & Ruprecht, 1966], 346 n. 3) views Rom. 5:1f. as a parallel, except that there the order is justification, peace, and hope (= χαρά)(?).

129. The Vulgate reads: *Gloria in altissimis Deo* . . . ; at the end of the two-part praise the Greek text reads: εἰρήνη ἐν ἀνθρώποις εὐδοκίας. The Latin text stems from the seventh century, from Antiphonal of Bangor: Josef Andreas Jungmann, *The Mass of the Roman Rite* (trans. Francis A. Brunner; New York: Benziger Bros., 1951), 1:346ff. [*Missarum Sollemnia* I (3rd ed.; Vienna: Herder, 1953), 446ff.].

130. Gerhard von Rad, "Noch einmal Lc 2:14 ἄνθρωποι εὐδοκίας," *ZNW* 29 (1930): 111–115; on a possible Aramaic text base, cf. Matthew Black, *An Aramaic Approach to the Gospels and Acts* (3rd ed.; Oxford: Clarendon Press, 1967), 281.

131. Bultmann (*Synoptic Tradition*, 325) draws special attention to εὐαγγελίζεσθαι (v. 10) and σωτήρ (v. 11). Further, one must keep in mind that σωτήρ is attested to be Χριστὸς κύριος ἐν πόλει Δαυίδ, and that *shalom* belongs to David's throne (Isa. 9:5f.) and kingdom.

132. Ernst Haenchen has kindly drawn my attention to the fact that for this early period we are unable to assume any knowledge of Virgil in the world of educated Greeks.

133. The speeches in John's Gospel are compositions of the evangelist, not the words of Jesus as handed down. The "departure sayings" in John 13–17 are intended to assure the eschatological community of the presence of the resurrected One and to that degree lead into the postresurrection period already before the passion story (18:1–19:41).

134. Corresponding to ἀφίημι, δίδωμι signifies: to give.

135. Rudolf Bultmann, *Das Evangelium des Johannes* (7th ed.; Göttingen: Vandenhoeck & Ruprecht, 1959), 485.

136. Ibid., 457.

137. This phrase εἰρήνη τοῦ Χριστοῦ appears, to my knowledge, only in Col. 3:15, but the content is present in John's Gospel as well as in Paul and in Eph. 2:14. Cf. in Rom. 8:9–11 the switch from πνεῦμα θεοῦ to πνεῦμα Χριστοῦ.

138. A pointed expression for that is John 15:4: μείνατε ἐν ἐμοί, κἀγὼ ἐν ὑμῖν. On the usage of μένειν ἐν in the Fourth Gospel, see Bultmann, *Evangelium*, 200 n. 5 and 411 n. 3.

139. Adolf von Harnack, *Einführung in die alte Kirchengeschichte (1. Clemensbrief)* (Leipzig: J. C. Hinrich, 1929), 97. In the recent discussion about peace in Clement's letter between W. C. van Unnik, "'Tiefer Friede' (1. Klemens 2,2)," *VC* 24 (1970): 261–279, 426ff., and Karlmann Beyschlag, "Zur EIPHNH BAΘEIA (1 Clem 2,2)," *VC* 26 (1972): 18ff., and van Unnik, "Noch einmal 'Tiefer Friede,'" *VC* 26 (1972): 24ff., I clearly support van Unnik's point of view.

140. *Clem. Rom.* 20:10, 11; 60:4; 61:1; 62:2; 63:2; 65:1. Compare also the combining of ὁμόνοια and ἀγάπη: 49:5; 50:5 and others. The conflict between Peter and Simon Magus, as described in the Pseudo Clementines, about the true concept of peace (cf. *Recogn.* II, 26f.) sets εἰρήνη equal to ὁμόνοια. As far as I know, this is the first explicit debate about εἰρήνη and *pax* in the Christian writings, first half of the third century.

141. Cf. Weinstock, *Divus Iulius,* 260ff. and pl. 20.

142. In *Clem. Rom.* 20:4: Ps. 34:11ff.; in 60:3 the Aaronite blessing of Num. 6:26 and elsewhere.

143. The idea presented impressively by Fuchs (*Augustin,* 93–95), that Augustine relied for his pax tablet on Varro's *Logistoricus "Pius aut De pace"* (composed ca. 40 B.C. but unfortunately lost), the first thematic discussion on peace to our knowledge but "not a philosophical or semi-philosophical essay . . . but of an antiquarian character" (Weinstock, *Divus Iulius,* 268f.), can no longer be supported, according to Dahlmann, *Varronische Studien* (cf. n. 65 above).

144. On this topic, cf. Fuchs, *Augustin,* passim; and Dinkler and Dinkler-von Schubert, "Frieden," *RAC* 8 (1972): 477–480.

145. On Gregory's personality and historical-theological significance, see Hans von Campenhausen, *The Fathers of the Greek Church* (trans. Stanley Goodman; New York: Pantheon Books, 1959), 95ff. [*Die griechischen Kirchenväter* (Stuttgart: W. Kohlhammer, 1955), 101ff.].

146. Gregory of Nazianzus, *Orationes* 6.22.23 (Migne *PG* 35:721/51; 1132/52; 1152/68).

147. Konrad Escher, *Die Miniaturen in den Basler Bibliotheken, Museen und Archiven* (Basel: Kober C. F. Spittlers Nachfolger, 1917), 23 and pl. 3 (=our Fig. 5).

148. Concerning Elias of Crete: H. G. Beck, *Kirche und theologische Literatur im byzantinischen Reich* (Munich: C. H. Beck, 1959), 524, 588, 615, 655, 793. Elias, Metropolitan of Crete ca. 1120/1130, ranks as the most learned commentator on Gregory of Nazianzus. Escher dated the miniature to the beginning of the fourteenth century. A more recent and more accurate dating by A. Xyggopoulos, in *Arch. Ephem.* 81/83 (1942/4): 26f., is around 1200 (reference thanks to K. Weitzmann).

149. The medallion carries the inscription H EIPHNH. In the lower half of the picture: (ὁ ἅγιος) Γρηγόριος ὁ θεόλογος, then to the right of Gregory's head and nimbus: εἰρηνεύων τοὺς ἐν Κωνσταντινουπόλει μαχομένους ἐπισκόπους ἄρχεται δὲ οὕτως· Εἰρήνη φίλη τὸ γλυκὺ καὶ πράγμα καὶ ὄνομα. The latter words represent the opening of Gregory's *Oratio* 22.

150. The reference to Christ as peace in the sense of Eph. 2:14 results from the citation of this passage (as well as Phil. 4:7 and 2 Cor. 13:11) in *Oratio* 22 and in *Oratio* 6, 8.

Remarks on the Figures

Figures 1 and 2. These figures give Aramaic inscriptions on paired ossuaries, which were found *in situ* in 1968 in the same necropolis, Giv'at ha-Mivtar, a site northeast of Jerusalem. The report of the discovery was published by J. Naveh in *IEJ* 20 (1970): 36f. While Figure 1 presents no problems — on the reverse side, *shalom* appears twice and is repeated once on the lid — the inscription of Figure 2 seems enigmatic. The text, according to the publisher, reads:

חלת שלום ברת שאול
די שברת שלום ברתה

Ossuary of Salome, daughter of Saul,
who could not give birth — Peace, Daughter

The Hebrew word form שלום instead of the Aramaic שלם occurs in the context of Aramaic grave inscriptions. The anthropological investigation proved that a woman with a fetus was buried in the ossuary. Figures 1 and 2 show the oldest known Jewish ossuaries with *slm* inscriptions.

We thank the generosity of the Israel Department of Antiquities and Museums for the submission of these figures: Negative Nos. 54313 and 53826.

Fig. 1. Front side of an ossuary with a threefold
shalom inscription, from Giv'at ha-Mivtar,
northeast of Jerusalem. First half of first
century A.D.

Fig. 2. Narrow side of an ossuary with inscription for
the daughter Salome (first line); with *shalom*
wish (second line). From Giv'at ha-Mivtar.
First century A.D.

Remarks on the Figures

Figure 3. A marble plate from the Monteverde Catacomb, Rome. Compare N. Müller-N. A. Bees, *Die Inschriften der jüd. Katakombe am Monteverde zu Rom* (1919), 67f., No. 66. Today in the Inscription Department of the Museo Pio Cristiano, Vatican; formerly Lateran, Jewish Inscr. No. 108, cf. CIJ 1,374, with the text:

ενταδε κιτε Μαρια γυνη Σαλουτιου οστις καλως
εζησεν μετα του ανδρος αυτης εν ιρηνη η κοιμησις αυ[τ]ης

Here lies Mary, wife of Salutios, who
lived with her husband in perfect harmony.
May she rest in peace.

Under the inscription: menorah, lulav [bundles of tree branches], ethrog [a citrus fruit], and shofar [a ram's horn].
   Figure submission: Archivio Fotogr. Gall. Musei Vaticani, Negative No. XXVIII.35.268.

Figure 4. A marble plate from the Monteverde Catacomb, Rome. Compare N. Müller-N. A. Bees, 169f., No. 183. Today in the Inscription Department of the Museo Pio Cristiano, Vatican; formerly Lateran, Jewish Inscr. No. 15, cf. CIJ 1,385, with the text:

ενθαδε κειτε πριμειτιβα μετα του εγγονου
αυτης Ευφρενοντος εν ειρηνη κοιμησις αυτων

Here lies Primitiva with her
grandson Euphrenon. May they rest in peace.

On either side of the inscription: menorah, lulav, ethrog, and oil vessel.
   Figure submission: Archivio Fotogr. Gall. Musei Vaticani, Negative No. XXVIII.35.230.

Figure 5. Cf. notes 147–150. Figure according to K. Escher.

ENTAΔE·KITEMAPIAΓY
NHCAΛOYTIOYOCTIC
KAΛωCEZHCENME
TATOYANΔPOCAYTHC
ENIPHNHHKOMMHCICAYHC

Fig. 3. Plate of a loculus [niche for burial in a
catacomb] from the Jewish Catacomb of
Monteverde, Rome. Vatican, Museo Pio
Cristiano. Fourth century A.D.

ENΘAΔE
KEITE
ΠPIMEITI
BAMETA
TOYEΓΓO
NOYATHEEY
ΦPENONTOC
ENEIPHNHKOI
MHCICAYTωN

Fig. 4. Plate of a loculus from the Jewish Catacombs
of Monteverde, Rome. Vatican, Museo Pio
Cristiano. Fourth century A.D.

Fig. 5. Scholia [marginal annotations] of Elias of Crete to the sermons of Gregory of Nazianzus. Basel, University Library A. N. I. 8. Figure at lower left: Gregory preaching to the quarreling bishops (*Oratio* 22). Ca. A.D. 1200.

11

Peace and the Sword in the New Testament

Hubert Frankemölle

The focus of this article will be on the fundamental problem emerging out of the contrasting concepts of "peace" and "sword." In opposition to the one-sided tendency to talk of God as the friend of humanity and of Jesus as peacemaker (also evident in religious education and in sermons), it is worth recognizing that the New Testament, in contrast to Marcion, also speaks of the judgment and wrath of God. One should note also the prophetic and provocative conduct of Jesus, "which on the surface functioned as a restraint on peace."[1] Examples are the statements about leaving family, marriage, and home and forgoing the burial of the dead; actions such as the cleansing of the temple; and, above all, Jesus' criticism of the Sadducees and the Jerusalem Pharisees, which entailed risk and threat upon his own life.[2]

Before turning, however, to what might be called "biblical sobriety," that is, claiming to have experienced peace in the face of experiencing the opposite, we must draw attention to the connectedness of all New Testament congregations to their social and political environment. In actual fact this meant experience of the following situations: political oppression of the Jewish people and of the early Christian congregations by occupying Roman forces; economic and social deprivation because of the tax system, slavery, and crop failures; and, finally, violence at the hands of, among

Translation of chapter 2 of *Friede und Schwert: Frieden Schaffen nach dem Neuen Testament,* by Hubert Frankemölle (Mainz, 1983).

others, Herod, procurators, and the resistance groups, as well as fighting among religiopolitical groups.

When we examine the New Testament from a historical-critical perspective, it is sobering to note how little, if any, reaction exists on the part of Christians to this "peace-less" reality. From the perspective of the contemporary Christian sense of responsibility for all humanity and for the entire global reality, the New Testament is deficient. That must be asserted here as a clearly stated thesis. This has far-reaching consequences for the understanding of peace on the part of New Testament theologians. However, to be forced to recognize deficiency out of one's own perspective does not allow a negative evaluation of the historically given reality of early Christian congregations. That would be quite unhistorical.

What indeed do we see when we look more closely at the life situation of early Christian congregations?

The Experience of the "Sword" in the New Testament

1. We begin with a preliminary remark, but one that is hermeneutically decisive for a correct understanding of the conception of peace in the New Testament. Like the Old Testament, the New Testament is a library of writings that emerged from most diverse linguistic contexts. Since every text demands to be understood as an element of its historical reality and within its quite specific linguistic context (this is the intent of historical-critical exegesis), there can be no suprahistorical, harmonized New Testament concept of peace but only conceptions of peace characteristic of individual writings. God becoming human in the flesh (*sarx*) of the world (John 1:14) conforms to a truly historical, and thus also a sociopolitical, dimension of the New Testament writings. Their own authentic historicity is premised christologically on the incarnation, while literarily they share the dependency that all texts have on their own world, of which they constitute one element.

2. In order to describe more concretely the nature of the world of early Christians within which the biblical texts are meant, in the broadest sense, to offer assistance for coping with life (by means of faith in Yahweh's working through Jesus of Nazareth and the history of the Jesus movement), a few general comments can validly serve for all New Testament congregations.

The social and political history of Palestine under Roman rule[3] was not that of a "healthy world." Rather, it was characterized by change and revolution, in which the old order repeatedly collapsed. Serious social and political upheaval with its concomitant religious

unrest represented the life situation of Jesus and the first generations of Christians. No generation was spared hunger and famine;
none was spared the conflicts between the religious political groups
(Sadducees, Pharisees, Zealots, Sicarii). Indeed, there is evidence
even of violent disputes between various types of Pharisees (*Shab.*
3c, 34ff.). No generation was spared the uprisings and war resistance
movements against Roman power or the bloody countermeasures
of the Romans, especially in the large uprisings of A.D. 66–74 and
A.D. 132–135.

Persistent inflation and exploitation were common, as were
forcible foreclosures of small and middle level farmers. In addition, increases in state taxes and interest of necessity led to social
tensions and crises between the various classes. Slaves, wage
earners, and tenant classes were at the mercy of the owners, who
in turn were tenants of the state. Conflicts, even violent ones, were
common between classes. Thus, for example, the parable in Mark
12:1–12 "is a realistic description of the revolutionary attitude of
the Galilean peasants towards the foreign landlords" as is Luke
16:1–8 in speaking about a "steward who saw imminent disaster
threatening him with ruin" but who managed by falsifying documents, specifically by reducing the size of outstanding loans, to
secure for himself a chance of survival.[4] "The radical democratic
traditionalism of the Galilean population was likely the political
milieu which Jesus presupposed. . . . The parables of the Gospels . . . present a world divided into two classes: the rich and the
poor, the world of the estate owner and that of the small indebted
peasant."[5]

The past establishment, often forcibly, of new Hellenistic cities
had ongoing consequences that led to conflicts rooted in the higher
social status of these inhabitants and separation from the Aramaic-
speaking Jews because of their Greek language. The Latin-speaking
soldiers of the Roman occupation also created new tensions.

It was not only these specific aspects as named but "wherever
we look we find deep-rooted tensions, tensions between the pro-
ductive groups and those who enjoy the profit, between city and
country, between alien and native structures of government,
between Hellenistic and Jewish culture," which led to a crisis of
orientation for the society, "to which the Jesus movement sought
to give an answer,"[6] by proclaiming a message of liberation and
joy (i.e., evangel) and by attempting to make peace a reality. It
sought to provide an answer to the oppression and exploitation,
to the bloody and violent encounters, to isolation and fears, to
the world of the sword. This was the world of Jesus and the New
Testament theologians, whose theological action represented a

reaction to the concrete and inhuman circumstances, both private and social.

Taking this context into account aids our understanding of the New Testament texts that proclaim a loving and peacemaking God. Consideration of the sociohistorical dimensions is helpful for finding a concrete, practical-theological understanding of these texts and of peace. "The sociohistorical approach is not merely a way of making our picture of the past more colorful. Its real purpose is a theological one. Following Jesus was a way of life that brought together human beings who were living lives of affliction. The affliction, then as now, was produced by repression, hatred, violence, and exploitation. Anyone who reduces the following of Jesus to an enterprise of the heart, the head, and private interpersonal relations restricts the following of Jesus and trivializes Jesus himself."[7]

The world of Jesus and the New Testament theologians was no romantic "world of wholeness." "The good old times" then, as for the majority of the world's population today, was an inhuman world without peace, a bit of hell, similar to H. Glaser's description of the Middle Ages. "European culture was largely a fiction, sustained by poets and artists. In reality Europe was much like an ideological sewage-field, 'Golgotha' (field of skulls), a place of massacres."[8] It is to such life experiences that theology must provide an answer, today as in the New Testament, if it is to contribute to peace.

3. When we narrow our focus on the churchly aspects of the Jesus movement, then the ideal image in Acts (2:43–47; 4:32–35) in which the fellowship of believers was of one heart and one soul, having all things in common (really a literary fiction), must be countered with the sober historical facts: tensions, partisanship, conflicts (cf. Acts 6:1; 1 Cor. 1:12), disruption of missionary successes (cf. Galatians), theological disputes resulting in break-away movements (beginning already with the splitting away of the Jesus movement from the Jewish mother congregation), the bloody persecution of Christians (beginning in Acts 8; cf. the murder of Stephen and the killing of James; cf. also the commissioning reports in the Gospels, as in Matt. 10:17–25), and so forth. Since, as Matt. 10:25 says, "it is enough for the disciple to be like his teacher," the Christian who is a disciple of Jesus is reminded that this is, repeatedly, a discipleship of the cross (cf. esp. Mark 8:31–38 as a rebuttal to the apocalyptic "Messiah of glory" as envisioned by Peter in 8:27–30).

We must point out not only that the Old Testament represents one of the bloodiest books in world literature but that in the New Testament also the central event is a monstrous bloody deed, the killing of Jesus.[9] That is the case even if theologians in particular with their penchant for deeper interpretations are scarcely able anymore to visualize the brutality of this most cruel of all forms of death of that time.[10] Sword and cross as symbols of political power were not limited to Paul (as Roman citizen) or Jesus (as Jewish criminal and seditionist). They were symbols much more for the fact that the politically proclaimed "pacification" by Rome, the *Pax Romana,* rested on countless dead bodies. For Roman power policy, crucifixion was an instrument of war and securing the peace in order to wear down rebellious cities under siege, to humiliate defeated powers, to bring to reason mutinous troops or restive provinces. That it was employed in excess in order to "pacify" rebellious provinces is evident from Josephus's many examples from Judea (on mass crucifixions, cf. *War* 2.75; 2.241; 5.449–451; *Ant.* 17.295; etc.).[11]

The metaphor of the night comes not only at the end of Jesus' life when "there was darkness over the whole land" (Mark 15:33) and when Judas' hour had come (John 13:30), but, according to Luke 2:8, night and darkness also marked the situation on the fields of Bethlehem with the newborn child in a feeding trough. The survival of this child, according to Matt. 2:16–18, leads to the killing of many small children. This too we should not forget when reading the Christmas story. According to Luke 2:35, aged Simeon prophesies to Mary that a sword will pass through her soul. The verses immediately preceding state the reason: "Behold, this child is set for the fall and rising of many in Israel, and for a sign that is spoken against" (Luke 2:34).

Even if what we have here is a subsequent Lukan interpretation[12] of the entire fate of Jesus from the perspective of hindsight (a *vaticinium ex eventu*), its intention accords, nevertheless, with the oldest sayings of the Jesus tradition. Jesus understood his commission to Israel as occasion for conflicts in the family and with sacrosanct traditions. "Do not think that I have come to bring peace on earth; I have not come to bring peace, but a sword. For I have come to set a man against his father, and a daughter against her mother, and a daughter-in-law against her mother-in-law; and a man's foes will be those of his own household. He who loves father or mother more than me is not worthy of me" (Matt. 10:34–37). For Jesus, the eschatological time for decision has come, but the sword, as evident from the context, does not imply a call to arms — like that of the Zealots — against Rome. Rather, this imagery depicts the radical nature of Jesus' demands, on the basis of which even families will break up, if the members do not all choose to follow Jesus.

Peace on earth? Which peace is meant? How are we to describe the peace perspectives of the oldest Synoptic tradition, of the evangelists, and of other New Testament theologians in relation to the political peace theme?

The Peace Perspective of
the Early Christian Fellowships

The Davidic temptation to power did not exist for any of the theologians of the New Testament, since Christians did not have access to power. They were powerless. The oldest Jesus movement was not marked by a "downward tendency" ("*Zug nach unten*," E. Bloch); it was already at the bottom politically and economically. Since we need to assume a specific interplay of world experience with theological meaning (and vice versa), this also applies to the peaceful and nonpeaceful experiences of the Christians. Specifically, Israel since A.D. 6 was a subordinate state under an imperial procurator. This did not raise the problem for either Jews or Christians of how to handle the political task on the basis of a biblical ethic. (The question of whether one, as a Christian, can rely on the Sermon on the Mount for engaging in politics today would, in that direct form, not be proper to Matthew's Gospel.)

At a subordinate level to political issues of state, the problems for Christians emerge at the point where one acknowledges the power of the state (the "sword" image, Rom. 13:4) and the "authority of the state" (cf. the famous passage in Rom. 13:1–7: "Let every person be subject to the governing authorities. For there is no authority except from God"). Herein, however, the critical test lines (*Grenze*) of "ordered by God" in v. 2 and "conscience" in v. 5 are given (cf. also 1 Peter 2:13f.). The church is to pray for the heathen authorities, according to 1 Tim. 2:1f., more precisely "for kings and all who are in high positions, that we may lead a quiet and peaceable life, godly and respectful in every way." The sayings of Jesus in the Synoptic Gospels also assume complete loyalty to state authority (cf. Luke 23:4, 13–16, 22; Mark 12:13–17). In an unreflective and unproblematic fashion, kings, rulers, and large estate owners appear in the parables of Jesus. One cannot find any fundamental discussion in the Gospels of the existence of the Roman state as such, or even a questioning of its right to exist (which is different in the apocalyptic literature[13] or indirectly so in Luke 2:1–20).

Clearly in points of conflict, God stands above Caesar, because of the monotheistic nature of the faith. In the oft-cited passage, "Render to Caesar the things that are Caesar's, and to God the things that are God's," the concern is not to achieve an even balance. It would be more appropriate to translate the "and" with the adversative "but." Monotheism will not tolerate any equating of divine power and worldly power.[14]

The problem of peace for the early Christians lay beyond the issues of state policy. The Jesus traditions were concerned about renewal, a reformation of Israel. That was the most genuine concern of the oldest Jesus movement, and this was connected with the hope that this "world" will be a passing one and will soon, or in any case suddenly, end. Even toward the end of the first century this is given clear expression, as in Phil. 3:20: "Our commonwealth is in heaven," or Heb. 13:14: "For here we have no lasting city, but we seek the city which is to come." The evangelist John in 18:36 has Jesus saying, "My kingship is not of this world." The background for this saying may be a conventicle type of separation from this world, over against a Christian citizenship that has settled into the world.

Any application of the New Testament peace perspective to state politics is noticeably restricted (this too is an indicator of historicity). Since the Christians do not bear political power, the New Testament theologians have no reason to offer a general theological reflection on power. The peace problems are at a different level, as is shown in the extraordinarily sharp debate of Jesus and the Gospel writers with Jewish believers, or also the appeals to inner church peace in the epistolary admonitions. That does not change the fact that these peace concepts can also have social-political relevance (even if not in the sense of power politics). Even then, when the internal congregational and the Christian-Jewish dimensions were primary, Christians were not living outside the world. Rather, as is so evident from the early history of mission, it was precisely their peace praxis that was so attractive to religiously oriented persons of the time.[15] Not without reason did both Caesars Licinius and Constantine seize on the Christian peace praxis as a factor for social stability. What becomes evident in the post-New Testament historical developments is that in a relatively short time the New Testament model of peace praxis attains state importance. This can be explained on the basis of the societally oriented reflections in the New Testament, even if they were not oriented toward state politics.

Indeed, the earliest New Testament proposals for living peacefully as Christians were oriented toward the internal congregational dimension. Yet because these congregations were always an element of this world, they also set loose powerful external, that is, societal and in the widest sense political, impulses. This was true even if this was not intended by the first congregations and theologians. One can observe clearly how this primarily internal churchly peace perspective has implications for external problems from the way in which Luke in his Gospel works with the peace proposal of the Sayings Source.

Peace and the Sword in Luke

What Luke formulated in programmatic fashion in 2:1–20, especially in "peace on earth" (2:14), he makes concrete in his Gospel through stories about the peace praxis of both Jesus and his disciples. [The peace practices of rich Christians in the Lukan writings are discussed in section 7 of Frankemölle's book, not translated here. In section 1 he begins with the peace motif of Luke 2:14 and devotes section 6 to Luke 2:1–20 to examine whether this peace narrative conforms to the Pax Romana or Pax Christi.— ED.] The general view of the literature holds that Luke received peace concepts from Mark, from the sayings of the Q source, and from the Lukan special source. This means that his Gospel and the Acts of the Apostles as a unit must be understood as a compromise. Nowhere is this as clear as on the theme of peace.

It is with the work of Jesus that the time of peace, that is, the messianic time of salvation, begins. It is to be interpreted personally, for it is tied to the person of Jesus. From the time of the temptations of Jesus onward (4:13), and continuing wherever Jesus is at work, up to the beginning of his passion, evil and Satan no longer have any effective power. Only at the point before the Lord's Supper when Satan takes possession of Judas (22:3) does the ambivalence, the dual character of reality, appear again with effect. The passion and the cross are not part of the "Satanless" period: "But this is your hour, and the power of darkness" (22:53). Nevertheless, just as in Bethlehem's night there is the "glory of the Lord" (2:9) in the angels' song of peace, so Luke does not (as do the other evangelists) separate the cross from the resurrection. This unity of death and resurrection is assured not only through the threefold announcement of suffering and resurrection (cf. 9:22; 9:43b–45;

18:31–34), nor by the narrative progression from ch. 23 to ch. 24; it is also achieved in that, even in the deepest hour of humiliation at the death of Jesus, whether by signs (for the heathen centurion and the affected viewers) or by the imagery of natural phenomena (eclipse of the sun, tearing of the temple curtain), a deeper dimension of reality becomes visible (cf. Luke 23:44–49; Mark 15:38f.; Matt. 27:51–54). Here arises the fundamental confession of the Christian faith, that God brings salvation and peace to the people through the most shameful of deaths, death on the cross. The ambiguity of all reality is nowhere so clear as here. Peace, in the Christian perspective of the New Testament (all the theologians agree on this with Luke) comes only in this apparently nonpeaceful reality. Thus peace is not a future concept or a utopia but rather a possibility, provided through the ambiguity of reality.

In the final chapter of his Gospel, Luke has demonstrated in dramatic story form that this Christian peace is tied to the cross. While the disciples are thinking they are hearing a spirit greeting them with "Peace be with you," Luke emphasizes the vitality of the crucified One, who is urging the disciples to touch him and to give him a fish to eat (24:37). So peace is not tied to the resurrected Lord as much as it remains tied to the risen crucified One.

This genuinely Christian concept of peace, which for Luke is part of his Christology, is confirmed in his outline of an ethical peace praxis for the disciples. It is presented with brevity, so that it is helpful to compare the peace actions of the Lukan congregation (around A.D. 80–90) with that of the group from the oldest Jesus movement, who were the carriers of the Sayings Source (in the years before the Jewish-Roman war). Both the Christians of the Lukan congregation and the Christians of the Sayings Source saw themselves as Jesus' disciples.

But the times had changed. According to the Sayings Source (Luke 9:2f.; cf. also 10:4), Jesus had sent out his disciples as poor, wandering charismatics,[16] with a radical faith that God would look after their daily needs, without making any normal human preparations: "Take nothing for your journey, no staff, nor bag, nor bread, nor money; and do not have two tunics" (9:3). "Whatever house you enter, first say, 'Peace to this house!' And if any is there who shares in peace, your peace will rest upon that person. . . . Heal the sick . . . and say to them, 'The kingdom of God has come near to you'" (10:5f., 9). A radical trust in God characterized Jesus and the prophets of the Sayings Source (cf. Luke 12:22–31, 33f.). They overcame violence with good (Luke 6:29f.) and loved their enemies (Luke 6:27f.). Not only for tactical reasons did these followers of

Jesus forgo resistance to the enemy as the actual persecutor (Matt. 5:44) but also from inner conviction, as the reference to praying for the enemy shows (Matt. 5:44; Luke 6:28). Anyone who prays for his or her persecutor or murderer, as did Jesus (Luke 23:34), has conquered hate emotionally and existentially.[17] Then the Christian (in the meaning of Matt. 5:45) is a "child of God."

Jesus and the prophets of the Sayings Source stood at the bottom of the social scale. Their life-style was not an alternative to that of the rich but rather to that of the little people who were living with the constant fear about day-to-day survival.[18] They practiced a radical poverty and criticized the rich, calling on them to give up all their possessions. Out of his own social situation Jesus, as well as the Jesus movement, was able to link the peace longings of his time with rationality, in that he guided the peace visions of the zealots and the apocalyptic utopians back to that measure of humanity which allowed people in their encounter with Jesus to experience peace with themselves, with their surrounding world and with God.

For Luke the situation had changed in all aspects. The Christians he describes are settled urban Christians, some of them quite well-to-do (cf. Luke 8:1–3; etc.). Luke's social program for the congregations was that following Christ must prove itself "through a fellowship of solidarity between the rich and respected Christians and the needy and despised Christians."[19]

Luke makes a similar compromise on the question of violence and the attitude to war. Among the disciples there was, with the beginning of the new time of Satan (22:3), no less than "a dispute . . . among them [about] which of them was to be regarded as the greatest" (22:24). Also peace, which in 2:11–14 is celebrated as a peace on earth, becomes restricted to heaven during the triumphal entry into Jerusalem (Luke has made this pericope a parallel to the birth story). Jesus, who rides into Jerusalem as a nonpolitical Messiah, as a special type of prince of peace seated on an ass (Luke 19:28ff.; Matt. 21:4 quotes directly from Isa. 62:11 and Zech. 9:9), is received with the cry, "Blessed is the King who comes in the name of the Lord! Peace in heaven and glory in the highest!" (Luke 19:38).

This reserve is characteristic for that current time of pressure. The reader may think at first of the passion of Jesus, but the context makes it clear that Luke has the situation of his own congregation in view. As an argument to show why the peace is no longer on earth (cf. 2:11), but in heaven (19:38), Luke points to the destruction of Jerusalem. The statement about Jerusalem reads: "Would that even today you knew the things that make for peace! But now they are hid from your eyes. For the days shall come upon you, when your enemies will cast up a bank about you and surround you, and hem you in on every side, and dash you to the ground, you and your children within you, and they will not leave one stone upon another in you; because you did not know the time of your visitation" (Luke 19:42–44). With the death of Jesus, for which the representatives of the Jews took responsibility, the offer of a peace for Jerusalem is at an end. The punishment for rejecting this offer becomes concrete in the Jewish-Roman war, above all in the destruction of Jerusalem (A.D. 70). Luke interprets these not as historical coincidence but as the fulfillment of scripture: "But when you see Jerusalem surrounded by armies, then know that its desolation has come near. Then let those who are in Judea flee to the mountains, and let those who are inside the city depart, and let not those who are out in the country enter it; for these are days of vengeance [Deut. 32:35], to fulfil all that is written. Alas for those who are with child and for those who give suck in those days! For great distress shall be upon the earth and wrath upon this people; they will fall by the edge of the sword, and be led captive among all nations; and Jerusalem will be trodden down by the Gentiles [Zech. 12:3], until the times of the Gentiles are fulfilled" (21:20–24).

Again in 22:35–38 Luke takes up a saying of Jesus from the tradition, which no longer reflects the situation of the messengers of the Sayings Source but rather reflects the new situation of the Christians: "'When I sent you out with no purse or bag or sandals, did you lack anything?' They said, 'Nothing.' He said to them, 'But now, let him who has a purse take it, and likewise a bag. And let him who has no sword sell his mantle and buy one. For I tell you that this scripture must be fulfilled in me, "And he was reckoned with transgressors"; for what is written about me has its fulfilment.' And they said, 'Look, Lord, here are two swords.' And he said to them, 'It is enough.'"

The allegorical interpretation common in the early Middle Ages of a temporal sword and a spiritual sword in the sense of the "two swords theory" [see untranslated section 2 in book.—ED.] is quite unacceptable because of the Lukan context. The historicizing tendency of Luke in the sending out of the early messengers of Jesus (cf. 9:2f.; 10:4) also disallows a selective recourse to a metaphorical and symbolic interpretation (with such an interpretation there would be here a mere reference to the tough Christian struggle against temptation, especially during persecution). Because of the parallelism to the literally understood ethical praxis in the commissioning speech, we must retain the concrete sense of 22:35ff.—even if the content is contradictory, although it is relativized in the context of ch. 22.

In the pre-Lukan tradition, which shows through in general vocabulary uncharacteristic of Luke, either these verses take up the preconceptions of a Christian-zealot group, who, in the context of Jesus' promises about the end, were reckoning with a messianic last struggle,[20] or the verses are appealing for understanding for those Christians in Jerusalem who were unable to flee and were forced to participate in the battle. In like manner to how Jesus (Luke 22:37) was falsely reckoned with the criminals and the lawless (as fulfillment of Isa. 53:12: "and was numbered with the transgressors"), the way in which Jesus, even according to Luke, promises salvation to the one on the cross who was lawless in the political sense (Luke changes the term *lestes* as terminus technicus for the Zealots, as found in Mark 15:27, to *kakourgos*=criminal, lawless) yet without an extenuation of his conduct, so Luke pleads on behalf of those Christians who took part in the armed struggle against Rome. "Christianity is not called upon to judge those engaged in deeds of violence such as the Zealots or those poor Jewish Christians drawn into the uprising."[21]

The Lukan manner of composition shows that Luke is not seeking to justify the use of force in itself but rather shows understanding for those who used force to defend themselves in an emergency. To the question posed by his associates at the time of his arrest: "Lord, shall we strike with the sword?" and the actual using of the sword before awaiting a reply, Jesus clearly answers with "No more of this!" (22:51). Since Luke alone immediately reports that Jesus healed the ear of the slave, which one of the disciples had struck off, it is made clear that Jesus expected no salvation by the sword, nor from the freedom struggle of the Zealots, and that peace cannot be achieved through the sword. Only the peace praxis of Jesus who "went about doing good and healing all that were oppressed" (as the summary note in Acts 10:38 puts it) can guarantee the real peace of God. On this point Luke leaves no doubt, even if he fails to condemn the use of the sword in principle (cf. below about the soldiers).

Luke also recognizes that force produces a counterforce, as one of those crucified with Jesus observes explicitly in 23:41: "And we indeed justly, for we are receiving the due reward of our deeds; but this man has done nothing wrong." The evangelist Matthew, in factual agreement with Luke, articulated even more precisely this recognition that the devilish spiral of violence cannot be broken by the sword when he wrote: "For all who take the sword will perish by the sword" (Matt. 26:52). Luke makes the same point thematically with the example of the person crucified with Jesus, but in his rendering of Jesus' reaction in 23:43 ("And he said to him, 'Truly, I say to you, today you will be with me in Paradise'") he makes it clear that he is concerned with something more than mere revenge.

Luke's writing thus reflects the twofold response of early Christians to the historical situation: the major part of the Jerusalem congregation had belonged to the peace party or peace movement[22] which, on the basis of the prophetic warnings as handed down in Eusebius the church father (*Hist. Eccl.* 3.5.3), had moved out of Jerusalem before the war that was threatening and had settled in Pella on the other side of the Jordan in the neutral region of the Decapolis; the other part of the Jerusalem congregation had participated in the uprising against Rome. In view of this situation the Lukan thesis must be understood as an appeal for understanding for the latter group, yet without glorifying their conduct. Because of his own experience, Luke is neither a utopian nor a fanatic advocating a sword-free reality, nor does he sweeten the reality of the sword. He is a realistic theologian.

This realistic attitude to the power of the sword is also evident in his interest in the members of the armed forces[23] (cf. Luke 7:1–10: the centurion in Capernaum; 23:47: the centurion under the cross; Acts 10: centurion Cornelius in Caesarea). It is Luke who, in a section from his special source, has soldiers asking John the Baptist: "'And we, what shall we do?' And he said to them, 'Rob no one by violence or by false accusation, and be content with your wages'" (Luke 3:14).

Christianity also did not demand of soldiers that they immediately leave the forces, as accords with Paul's remark: "Every one should remain in the state in which he was called" (1 Cor. 7:20). There was an attempt, nevertheless, even in the unchangeable reality of the sword, that is, in war, to observe the love command. The fact that Diocletian initiated the persecution of Christians within the armed forces (Eusebius, *Hist. Eccl.* 8.3f.) is an indicator that Christian soldiers had already become a quantitative political reality.

The soldiers who figure in the Lukan writings, as well as Luke's formula for personal nonresistance in 3:14, seem to have been a *modus vivendi* of his era, serving to even out the challenge of Christianity with the reality of the state with its soldiers. In the subsequent period the radical nature of Jesus' challenge to forgo all use of force and to overcome force with paradoxical activity (Luke 6:29f., 32f.) was retained only by a minority and through the freeing of clergy and monks from induction. Yet precisely this step had major repercussions. The just exercise of violence was no longer constantly being relativized and corrected by nonviolence. Precisely this arrangement sacrificed once again the dialectic of the Christian life in the world, that is, to fully bear this world and yet not to give up the example of Christ in it.[24]

Luke in particular retains a grasp of the ambivalent reality. This is most evident in a unique passage: "Being asked by the Pharisees when the kingdom of God was coming, he answered them, 'The kingdom of God is not coming with signs to be observed; nor will they say, "Lo, here it is!" or "There!" for behold, the kingdom of God is in the midst of you'" (17:20f.). Where else but in the ambiguous reality are people to gain peace experience? Luke is no supporter of a utopia of universal, everlasting peace, no supporter of the slogan "Swords Into Plowshares" or "Peacemaking Without Weapons." Luke reflects in a more realistic and sober fashion on the possibilities for peace in this world. Even for some Christians today, being forced to recognize this realism of Luke could be a sobering thought.

One element of this realistic interpretation of reality throughout the entire New Testament is the image of God as it is implied in the individual outlines for Christian peace action. This will be discussed briefly in the following section.

The Biblical Witness to the Reality of God

There is widespread agreement in the field of biblical studies that Jesus' witness to the reality of God is grounded in a genuine faith in Yahweh and that it was his message of the nearness of God's reign articulated through his deeds and his person that was the decisive novelty [Frankemölle expands this in the next untranslated section.—ED.]. Jesus expected the person living in a world characterized by calamity, forced to experience disastrous debts and all other sorts of evils, to be able to draw sustenance from the assurance and promise of divine salvation, in the face of the existing conditions. The divine will to save is already at work in this eon, showing itself as the saving power of those who place their trust in the message of salvation.[25]

As accurate as this characterization may be, and as appropriate as the talk of God's friendliness to humanity as expressed anew in Jesus' message may be, this does not change the fact that the wrath of God and the idea of divine judgment is an essential and inescapable theme in the biblical, including the New Testament, imagery of God.[26] The letters of Paul in particular emphasize God's wrath alongside God's love, whereas in the Gospels, God's wrath is noticeably less evident, and instead the idea of God's judgment plays an important role.

The manner of speech about God's wrath may seem alien to us, but we should take into account that the biblical statements about the wrath of God are in no way more anthropomorphic than are those about God's fatherly love. Second, in the biblical understanding God is the answer of believing Jews and Christians to the totality of reality which humans experience in ambiguous terms. No theologian in the Bible has managed to formulate faith in the one God as consistently as did Deutero-Isaiah in the sixth century B.C. in 45:6f.: "I am the LORD, and there is no other. I form light and create darkness, I make weal and create woe, I am the LORD, who do all these things" (cf. Amos 3:6). Regardless of how one may seek to explain theologically the existence of evil in the world, for Jews and Christians this is done within the framework of monotheism, because the God question comprehends the totality of existence and because to confess God is to confess to the meaningfulness of one's own life, of history, of society, and of the world — this in spite of deeply experienced meaninglessness.[27] A Christian approach to the world and Christian peace activity relies on a faith in the meaningfulness of being. Yet even the Christian experiences this being in its ambiguity. Such specific and fundamental experiences of world reality shaped the image of God given in the Bible. They do the same today.

The reality of God cannot be resolved one way or the other, since according to Ex. 20:4 humans are forbidden to make for themselves an image of God. That included neither an anthropological nor a spatial nor a temporal image. As a consequence, both for the believing Jew and for the believing Christian, the entire Bible offers a God who remains enigmatic, because reality is enigmatic and ambiguous. Accordingly, the "God of peace" (cf. Rom. 15:33; 16:20; 2 Cor. 13:11) is at the same time always also the "God of wrath" (cf. Rom. 3:5f.; 5:9; 1 Thess. 1:9f.). It is impossible to devise a logical, noncontradictory theological system, for reality is itself contradictory. This is true even if all the New Testament theologians remain convinced that faith in the meaningfulness of being and in the certainty of salvation (evident in Jesus' praxis both in his death and in his resurrection) will endure: "that is, God was in Christ reconciling the world to himself, not counting their trespasses against them" (2 Cor. 5:19). As much as Paul was convinced that "we have peace with God through our Lord Jesus Christ" (Rom. 5:1), this statement applies only to those who have found this peace through faith. Other than that, all people encounter both wrath and salvation in the very same gospel (cf. Rom. 1:17–18). To the same degree that Paul stresses that salvation is offered unconditionally, so it is he in particular who stresses that each individual must find the way through to a fundamental decision about reality, to decide for a peace praxis and for a "faith working through love" (Gal. 5:6).[28] The biblical witness to the reality of God as well as to the reality of humanity is optimistic, but not illusory. That can be seen also in other peace aspects of various New Testament theologians, which will be sketched here in a summary conclusion.

Peace Dimensions in the New Testament

A few short references may suffice to indicate how various New Testament theologians speak of peace (in God and in Jesus) and about peace action. In those passages, above all, where there is no fundamental theological reflection about peace, it is quite evident that peace is a dynamic concept and that peace activity is seen in a comparative fashion, consisting of small steps on the road to ever more peace. It is, above all, the reality of the cross of Jesus and the unpeaceful experiences of individual New Testament theologians (conflicts, persecution, etc.) which determine the New Testament peace concept.

In the oldest layers of the Synoptic Gospels, the peace that Jesus brings reveals itself in the healing of the sick and the casting out of demons. At issue here is the wellness and well-being of persons in physical and socioreligious terms, since the healed leper, for example, is also re-socialized. Prominent here is the peace of the individual. In the later miracle stories shaped by Hellenist influence (calming the storm, etc.), cosmic aspects also come into view. Through the peace brought by Jesus, the cosmic powers of evil, including death, are conquered by means of raising the dead. This cosmic peace reaches its apogee in Colossians: God desired through Jesus Christ "to reconcile to himself all things, whether on earth or in heaven, making peace by the blood of his cross" (Col. 1:20); the principalities and powers were disarmed (Col. 2:15).

The social aspects of peace appear in the Synoptic literature in Jesus' praxis (eating with Pharisees and with tax collectors and sinners, and, above all, in the circle of the Twelve as a reconciled community in which Zealot and tax collector lived together).[29] Luke's social utopia (the solidarity of the rich and the poor in one congregation) as well as Paul's lifting of social barriers in the house churches of Galatia are concrete examples of Jesus' praxis (cf. Gal. 3:28: "There is neither Jew nor Greek, there is neither slave nor free, there is neither male nor female"). The writer of the Letter to the Ephesians is able to observe with thankfulness the ecumenical peace in his congregation between Jews and Gentiles through faith in Jesus, a peace that Jesus Christ brought: "For he is our peace, who has made us both one, and has broken down the dividing wall of hostility . . . so making peace" (Eph. 2:14f.).[30] Quite in contrast to this experience, Paul's entire life's work consisted of trying to maintain unity between Jews and Gentiles (cf. Romans), although we must acknowledge as historical fact that neither Paul nor Matthew nor John was successful in this. Matthew and John devote more space to a theological consideration of the situation following the excommunication of the church from the synagogue. Peace between Jew and Gentile was a local experience, a notable exception to the rule. This is still true today (also with reference to the other separated churches).

The New Testament has nothing to say about an ecological peace already present (cf. the groaning and longing of creation which, according to Rom. 8:19–21, is described by the travail of birth). The new creation, according to 2 Cor. 5:17; Gal. 6:15; Eph. 2:10, 15; 4:24; Col. 3:10; 2 Peter 3:13; Rev. 21:1, is a constant element in the hope structure of faith, as is true in Jewish apocalyptic (cf. *Ethiopian Enoch* 72:1; *Jub.* 4:26; 1QS 4:25) and in prophetic eschatology (Isa. 43:2, 15, 19, etc.). But the fundamental enabling for this has been provided by the Christ event (cf. Gal. 6:14f.; 2 Cor. 5:17), even if its fulfillment has not yet come (1 Cor. 15:22f.; Rom. 8:19–30; etc.). Peace is a dynamic concept, pointing to the future, but traces of it are already experienced in all dimensions of existence.

Not least but, rather, the primary element in the Christian peace dimension of the New Testament is ecclesial peace, peace among the Christians (Mark 9:50: "Be at peace with one another"; similarly in Rom. 12:18; 2 Cor. 13:11; 1 Thess. 5:13). As did Jesus, so also should the Christians after the death of Jesus form a fellowship (*koinonia*) of peace within their own social sphere. It is to these groups of Christians, the local church as sphere for peacemaking, that most of the admonitions in the epistles are directed, as are also the incessant admonitions in the Gospels.[31] This is an indicator that these admonitions about the practical conduct of Christians were urgently needed.

A fundamental conviction of all New Testament theologians is that peace in any form whatsoever cannot be achieved by people, yet they must do all in their power to pursue peace (cf. Rom. 14:19; Heb. 12:14), to make peace (Matt. 5:9), and to be involved in maintaining peace (Eph. 4:3–6; 6:10–20; Col. 3:8–15). It is through Jesus Christ and in him that the "God of peace" (Rom. 15:33; 16:20; 1 Cor. 14:33; Phil. 1:2; Col. 1:20) has made peace, so that even Jesus Christ himself in this function can be called "our peace" (Eph. 2:14). It is through him that people find peace — peace with themselves, their fellow humans, and the environment, that is, holistically with God as the comprehensive fundamental reality of all being — in spite of all contrary, nonpeaceful experiences with themselves, their fellow humans, and the world. This "in spite of," this risk, this wager (Blaise Pascal, *Pensées,* no. 233) is the root structure of Jewish and Christian hope for peace and of a belief in the peace that is now already experienced in every possible dimension.

No New Testament theologian talks of a fundamental resolution of this ambiguous experience of reality. Each in his or her way emphasizes the already and the not yet, the eschatological proviso. For now, the Christian retains the hope that the fundamental dimension of all reality is truly peaceful; he or she also retains the momentary experience of such a reality, which one gains in the peacemaking of others and which one can introduce to others through one's own peace actions. No other New Testament theologian has described this fundamental structure of Christian peace action more fittingly than Paul. "For now we see in a mirror dimly, but then face to face. Now I know in part; then I shall understand fully, even as I have been fully understood. So faith, hope, love abide, these three; but the greatest of these is love" (1 Cor. 13:12–13).

Notes

1. Ulrich Luz, "Die Bedeutung der biblischen Zeugnisse für kirchliches Friedenshandeln," in *Eschatologie und Friedenshandeln* (ed. Luz et al.), 195–214; see p. 200; cf. pp. 9f., 198f. on the four dimensions of nonpeace (want, violence, oppression, and fear).

2. Cf. the fundamental treatment of Heinz Schürmann, "Wie hat Jesus

seinen Tod bestanden und verstanden?" in his *Jesu ureignener Tod* (Freiburg: Herder, 1974), 16–65, esp. 16–46.

3. Cf. the recent presentation of Jewish origins by S. Safrai in *A History of the Jewish People* (ed. Haim Hillel Ben-Sasson; Cambridge: Harvard University Press, 1976), 305–342 [*Geschichte des jüdischen Volkes* (Munich: C. H. Beck, 1978), 1:295–340].

4. Joachim Jeremias, *The Parables of Jesus* (trans. S. H. Hooke; rev. ed.; New York: Charles Scribner's Sons, 1963), 74 (relying on C. H. Dodd) and 182 [*Die Gleichnisse Jesu*[8] (Göttingen: Vandenhoeck & Ruprecht, 1970), 72, 181]. Cf. on the general economic situation, *Jerusalem in the Time of Jesus* (trans. F. H. and C. H. Cave; Philadelphia: Fortress Press, 1969).

5. H. G. Kippenberg, *Religion und Klassenbildung im antiken Judäa: Eine religionssoziologische Studie zum Verhältnis von Tradition und gesellschaftlicher Entwicklung* (Göttingen: Vandenhoeck & Ruprecht, 1978), 130; see pp. 106–172 for a well-documented presentation of the crisis in Judea.

6. Gerd Theissen, *Sociology of Early Palestinian Christianity* (trans. John Bowden; Philadelphia: Fortress Press, 1978), 94–95 [*Soziologie der Jesusbewegung* (Munich: Chr. Kaiser Verlag, 1977), 89f.].

7. Luise Schottroff and Wolfgang Stegemann, *Jesus and the Hope of the Poor* (trans. Matthew J. O'Connell; Maryknoll, N.Y.: Orbis Books, 1986), 5–6 [*Jesus von Nazareth — Hoffnung der Armen* (Stuttgart: Verlag W. Kohlhammer, 1978), 14].

8. So the fitting résumé of H. Glaser on the work by Léon Poliakov, *The History of Anti-Semitism* (trans. Richard Howard [from the French]; New York: Vanguard Press, 1965); the review appeared in *Zeit,* May 29, 1979.

9. Norbert Lohfink and Rudolf Pesch, *Weltgestaltung und Gewaltlosigkeit* (Düsseldorf: Patmos Verlag, 1978), 13.

10. Martin Hengel, "Mors turpissima crucis. Die Kreuzigung in der antiken Welt und die 'Torheit' des 'Wortes vom Kreuz,'" in *Rechtfertigung: Festschrift für Ernst Käsemann zum 70. Geburtstag* (ed. Johannes Friedrich, Wolfgang Pöhlmann, and Peter Stuhlmacher; Tübingen: J. C. B. Mohr [Paul Siebeck]; Göttingen: Vandenhoeck & Ruprecht, 1976), 125–184.

11. Hengel, "Mors turpissima crucis," 153f.

12. On the divided people of God in the Lukan writings (Luke and Acts), cf. Hubert Frankemölle, *"laos,"* *EWNT,* 2 (1981): 837–848, esp. 843–845.

13. For evidence, cf. Peter Lampe, "Die Apokalyptiker — Ihre Situation und ihr Handeln," in *Eschatologie und Friedenshandeln* (ed. Luz et al.), 59–114.

14. Cf. Joachim Gnilka, *Das Evangelium nach Markus* (EKKNT; Zurich: Benziger; Neukirchen-Vluyn: Neukirchener Verlag, 1979), 2:153f.

15. N. Brox, "Zur christlichen Mission in der Spätantike," in *Mission*

im Neuen Testament (ed. Kurt Kertelge; Freiburg: Herder, 1982), 190–237.

16. Cf. Schottroff and Stegemann, *Jesus and the Hope of the Poor,* 54–88.

17. Cf. Gerhard Schneider, *Die Botschaft der Bergpredigt* (Aschaffenburg: Paul Pattloch Verlag, 1969), 61f.

18. Schottroff and Stegemann, *Jesus and the Hope of the Poor,* 63ff.; differently in Paul Hoffmann, *Studien zur Theologie der Logienquelle* (Münster: Aschendorffsche Verlagsbuchhandlung, 1972), 326ff.

19. Schottroff and Stegemann, *Jesus and the Hope of the Poor,* 89; cf. more detail below under point 7.

20. Matthew Black, "The Violent Word," *ExpTim* 81 (1969–1970): 115–118, esp. 116f.

21. H. W. Bartsch, "Jesu Schwertwort, Lk 22,35–38," *NTS* 20 (1973–1974): 190–203, 199ff., 202.

22. Cf. Theissen, *Sociology,* 194f., n. 75, with critical reference to Hoffmann, *Studien,* 74–78.

23. Cf. Peter Trummer, "Gewalt und Gewaltlosigkeit: Die Zeugnisse der Schrift und der Urkirche," *Wort und Wahrheit* 26 (1971): 504–517, esp. 512; more detailed, Adolf von Harnack, *Militia Christi: The Christian Religion and the Military in the First Three Centuries* (trans. and intro. David McInnes Gracie; Philadelphia: Fortress Press, 1981) [*Militia Christi: Die christliche Religion und der Soldatenstand in den ersten drei Jahrhunderten* (Tübingen: J. C. B. Mohr [Paul Siebeck], 1905)]; and John J. O'Rourke, "The Military in the New Testament," *CBQ* 32 (1970): 227–236.

24. Trummer, "Gewalt," 513, in a somewhat nonhistorical formulation, since he ignores the concrete speaking situations of the passages cited.

25. Joseph Blank, "Antworten des Neuen Testaments," in *Wer ist das eigentlich — Gott?* (ed. H. J. Schultz; Munich: Kösel-Verlag, 1969), 111–122, esp. 114.

26. Gustav Stählin, "The Wrath of Man and the Wrath of God in the NT," *TDNT,* 5:419–447, esp. 423–424 [*TWNT,* 5:419–448]; on the general biblical problem and specifically on Pauline theology, cf. Gerhart Herold, *Zorn und Gerechtigkeit Gottes bei Paulus: Eine Untersuchung zu Röm. 1,16–18* (Bern: Herbert Lang, 1973).

27. Cf. Trutz Rendtorff, *Gott — Ein Wort unserer Sprache?* (Munich: Chr. Kaiser Verlag, 1972), 20–24.

28. Franz J. Ortkemper, *Leben aus dem Glauben: Christliche Grundhaltungen nach Römer 12–13* (Münster: Aschendorffsche Verlagsbuchhandlung, 1980), 112–119 (Exkurs: Zorn Gottes und Gericht), which gives a good overview of the Pauline problem and of the significance of this theme for contemporary theology.

29. Cf. on this and on the overall praxis of Jesus, Hubert Frankemölle, *Jesus von Nazareth: Anspruch und Deutungen*[2] (Mainz: Matthias-Grünewald-Verlag, 1979), 58–91, 122–160.

30. Originally this involved cosmic preconceptions, which the author of Ephesians made historical; cf. Joachim Gnilka, *Der Epheserbrief* (Freiburg: Herder, 1971), 139f., 151f.; in general, cf. below, point 11.

31. For a good overview, cf. V. Hasler, *"eirene," EWNT,* 1 (1980): 957–964.

12

The Significance of the Biblical Witnesses for Church Peace Action

Ulrich Luz

Introductory Remark, prepared by Ulrich Luz for use with this article

This text, as also the text by Jürgen Kegler (pp. 69–109 above), had its origin within the framework of an interdisciplinary project, undertaken by the Forschungsstätte der Evangelischen Studiengemeinschaft in Heidelberg in the years 1976–1978. The project was oriented to the "Relationship of Eschatology and Peace." The fundamental question, which the old philologist Albrecht Dihle had raised, resounds: Was not Christianity with its world-denying eschatology and, with it, the absolute claims it made for itself in the contemporary stabilized world of *Pax Romana* a negative force for peace? This question was connected to the observation that again and again in the history of Christianity both peace-promoting and peace-hindering forces were set in motion. Christianity has been the root cause of both war and peace. That is easy to understand when one considers the tension and distance between the cross-carrying Knights and the Quakers, or some of the different historical consequences of the state-loyal Russian Orthodox, the aggressive (often harsh, anticommunist) ideology of fundamentalist groups, the revolution as the ultimate rationale for affirming liberation theology, the anti-racial programs of the World Council of Churches, or the Lutheran two-kingdom doctrine.

From these basic questions arose a very extensive research program that embraced: (*a*) contemporary areas of conflict among the churches, (*b*) the foundational biblical texts bearing on the topic, and (*c*) consideration of non-Christian worldviews and religions regarding a common

Translation of "Die Bedeutung der biblischen Zeugnisse für kirchliches Friedenshandeln," in *Eschatologie und Friedenshandeln* (ed. Luz et al., 1981), 195–214.

profile on these matters, that is, whether their expectations of the future and their peace potential are interrelated. To the first category belong investigations into the political posture of the WCC, liberation theology, the German Evangelicals, and the Kimbanguists. To the second category belongs research into the prophets, the apocalyptic literature, Judaism, Jesus, and Paul. Into the third category falls research on perspectives of the future held by the Club of Rome, the so-called American ideology of progress, Russian, Czech, and Chinese Marxism, Buddhism, and traditional cultures. The results of these studies have been published in three volumes by Gerhard Liedke under the title *Eschatologie und Frieden,* in the series Texten und Materialien der Forschungsstätte der Evangelischen Studiengemeinschaft, Series A, vols. 6–8 [Heidelberg, 1978]. A major part of the biblical studies of the second volume was published later under the title *Eschatologie und Friedenshandeln: Exegetische Beiträge zur Frage christlicher Friedensverantwortung,* SBS 101 (Stuttgart: Verlag Katholisches Bibelwerk, 1981).

The present text is the "Summation of Common Perspectives," which are the fruit of the exegetical studies of the second volume. Naturally such a summation without knowledge of the individual studies can be only conditionally understood. The individual studies put "flesh" on these perspectives. Here I can only give the exact title of each of the respective essays, to which I refer in the footnotes:

Paul Hoffmann. "Eschatologie und Friedenshandeln in der Jesus-überlieferung," in *Eschatologie und Friedenshandeln,* 115–152.

Jürgen Kegler. Essay in this volume, pp. 69–109.

Peter Lampe. "Die Apokalyptiker — Ihre Situation und ihr Handeln," in *Eschatologie und Friedenshandeln,* 59–114.

Pinchas Lapide. "Zukunftserwartung und Frieden im Judentum," in *Eschatologie und Frieden II,* TM.FEST, Series A, vol. 7, 127–178.

Ulrich Luz. "Eschatologie und Friedenshandeln bei Paulus," in *Eschatologie und Friedenshandeln,* 153–193.

Points in Common

Reviewing the exegetical papers as a whole, six points of commonality, contrasting to most non-Christian concepts of peace, stand out. Although these points may seem virtually self-evident, they should still be specified, because they play a role in the search to identify the unique contribution of the church and theology to peace.

1. All the biblical authors reckon with a *real acting of God in history,* for which no human action can serve as substitute. The human person appears as God's partner. Thereby God stands over against the person as the independent acting "subject." There is no biblical conception in which God acts merely through the

mediation of people, so that in the end God's action can be understood as a specific way of interpreting and treating a purely human action. God's action always supersedes the human, preceding, encompassing, completing, or terminating it. In all situations, the human person appears before God as the respondent, as the one reacting, as predetermined and limited. When God acts through a person, then the person becomes active together with the actual historical actor, God, in a "successive consubjectivity" (H. E. Tödt).

On this point we find the deepest gulf between the biblical early Christian perspective and the modern secular one.

2. Since the time of the apocalyptic writings, the biblical authors have assumed the view that *God will put an end to this history*.[1] The constitutive factors are, on the one hand, the universal dimensions of history as world history and, on the other hand, its boundaries and finitude. God will put an end to history and bring in a new age, a new world. Points of difference appear with regard to the relationship of the two ages to each other. The new world can be understood as the eternal continuation of the old world that has been transformed into good, or it can be understood as a totally new establishment replacing the old history. Continuity or discontinuity between the old and the new may predominate. Foundational for all of this, however, is the notion of a new world condition that supersedes all human capability, something that gives to past history the stamp of the terminal, the temporary, the incomplete, the ambiguous, or the negative.

In view of modern post-Christian and non-Christian conceptualizations, the question arises whether the finiteness of history, whose final fulfillment or completion is not to be achieved by humans, can ever be imagined without God, or again, whether it even needs to be imagined with reference to human peace action.

3. Closely connected to this point was a conclusion drawn in all of the studies, namely, of God's turning to the people, not only motivating them to action but also carrying them through in their entire action. This turning of God to the people need not be in the realm of eschatology, although that could be the case. Already in Deutero-Isaiah, but more particularly in apocalyptic, the promise of a new salvation in God's future is the deciding factor that allows oppressed believers to live in the oppressive present, to be steadfast and to undertake action. The Christian conceptualizations, which here *mutatis mutandis* must also take Jesus into account, transform Jewish apocalyptic hope in the future through the

knowledge that, in Jesus, God was eschatologically at work bringing life. Common to all the concepts is the sense that there is something that brings human identity, a reason for living, for acting, for hoping, which humans are not themselves responsible for and to which they can always return. It is possible for humans to attain in history a trust that is independent of the degree of minimization of poverty, oppression, and violence.

On this point modern secular concepts should be examined to see whether there are any analogies, that is, whereby they would function as additional confirmation of the same.

4. It is no accident that in all the essays of this book the so-called *"inner dimension"* played a notable role. All the participants found it necessary to add a fourth dimension to the three dimensions of peace identified at the outset of this study (poverty, violence, and oppression),[2] which they described variously as "minimization of fear," of "sin," with "comfort" or "gaining of identity."[3] In virtually all the studies it became clear that this inner dimension need not stand as a contrast to the outer dimensions of peace. Forgiveness of debt, the lifting of fear, experiencing comfort, and gaining of identity do not replace active expressions of peacemaking but rather enable them. It became evident that the "inner" and the "outer" are modern points of contrast, whereas in biblical anthropology they are integrated. It appears that the two dimensions are most threatened to polarize in Paul. But precisely in Paul's thought the homogeneity of "inner" and "outer" is retained most clearly, as in the conceptual relationship of the indicative and the imperative. With the modern individualism that withdraws into the private sphere or even becomes solipsist, this dimension obviously has nothing in common. That became particularly evident in the essay on apocalyptic, where the minimization of fear, insecurity, and inner wants remained for many as almost the only option left for action. But the communicative process initiated by the apocalyptists through their writings, the presence of apocalyptically oriented fellowships, and the call to repentance addressed to all Israel that constantly accompanied the apocalyptic sermons, all show that even here the concern for the minimization of fear and inner want was not purely a concern for the inner peace of the individual. All the essays point to the fact that the relationship between inner and outer freedom, the minimization of soul needs and material needs and violence cannot be seen in a nondialectical, linear fashion. Outer needs, such as persecution, threats to religious freedom, or hunger can lead to

a deeper experience of inner freedom. In the Pauline dialectic of cross and resurrection living, of suffering and of love, such thoughts have probably been most tightly formulated. Also for Paul, liberation through Christ is no substitute for earthly, civil slavery (1 Cor. 7:20–24), although it significantly relativizes the meaning of slavery.

Based on these observations, it seems to us that perhaps it is time to raise serious questions not only about modern secular concepts but also about modern theological concepts, insofar as they tend to evaluate a theological effort purely or mainly on the basis of its ability to produce peace action and emancipation, to minimize outer oppression, violence, and want. Is it not true that often from the side of Christianity, a specifically Christian contribution to the peace problem (even if not the only contribution) is too quickly relativized or even negatively evaluated in a one-sided manner? Should not theology insist that the concept of peace be expanded to include an "inner dimension" for the sake of our total experience of living as humans?[4]

5. Concerning the criteria and the perceived primary lines of action, it became evident that these were not directed toward an inner goal but *were oriented solely around the will of God.* The Jew is a peacemaker, not simply for the sake of world peace, and certainly not because peace is necessary for the preservation of the species, but because God desires shalom. In a very similar way, both Jesus and Paul allow their actions to be determined by the eschatological revelation of God. If the central issue here is love, it is not primarily because in the modern sense love has an eirenic quality but because God showed his love toward Jesus and revealed love to be a quality of his reign. Therefore a situation may develop in any part of the Bible in which an orientation toward the will of God is no longer peaceable. In the prophets the best example is probably Isaiah's announcement to Ahaz: "If you will not believe, surely you shall not be established" (Isa. 7:9), which Ahaz ignored for a good reason, namely, for the peace of the country. Similarly also Jesus' message can have an initially inhibiting impact on peace. One thinks first of the provocative nature of his challenge to forgo violence (Matt. 5:39ff.) and his other radical statements,[5] or one thinks of his own violent end, to some degree consciously provoked through the cleansing of the temple.

In Pauline texts there is also a thread of latent tension between the realization of the eschatological power of Christ's love in the congregation, in which Paul is deeply interested, and the relatively limited interest shown for the minimization of poverty, oppression, and violence in society generally. It is significant that Paul fails to speak about the blessing and perennial problem of the Pax Romana, about which all the world was talking and from which he, as a traveling missionary, also profited. This develops later into a full tension between the will of God and the striving for worldly peace under conditions of crisis, identified in intellectual history with the dualistic eschatology of the apocalypse. Given the conditions of the Maccabean wars, any kind of striving for peace had of necessity the appearance of a doubtful compromise. In this situation the will of God required resistance from all groups faithful to God.

We should not be too hasty in identifying individual abstention from violence with peacemaking in the modern sense. To flee, or indeed to allow oneself to be put to death on the Sabbath, is not a form of peace action; rather, it is one of protest and resistance. The point of concern was God and his coming; the commandment was to be faithful to God. This applies to John's Apocalypse in similar fashion. To be at peace with a state that one can now regard only as a beast from the abyss is unthinkable. The motto reads: endure, suffer, wait for God. In the worldly sense, such an attitude is called obstinacy and harmful to peace. That conflicts may thereby arise is shown in the early Christian statement originating from the church circles of the apocalyptists: "Do not think that I have come to bring peace on earth" (Matt. 10:34). The difference between this position and that of the pro-Maccabean and Zealot type of apocalyptists who resorted to military force in their resistance for the sake of God's will is only a relative one.

Common to all the texts is a certain divergence of interest from that of secular peace research. Since what was at stake was the will of God, the concern for world peace, in which others during New Testament times were indeed interested and which has become for us today a vital necessity for survival, was not of direct interest to the writers of these texts.

6. A final point to note is that all the essays drew attention to the *role of the individual.* Certainly we will need to acknowledge differences. For the prophets and Judaism, the individual is an integral part of the nation. What counts is that the individual remain within the relationship of God to God's people. In apocalyptic an increased individuation is evident. With Jesus and Paul this may be connected with the rise of a dualist eschatology. At the point where the challenge would arise to remain within God's relationship to God's people, a call also came to a complete conversion, to *metanoia.* Knowledge of the provisional nature of reality, of injustice, and of the power of evil in the world led to

the appeal to turn around and to reorder one's actions on the basis
of a new perspective, one that is shaped by a sense of God's future.
"The possessing of the individual person is the eye of the needle
through which the eschatological message must pass" (W. Liene-
mann). The category of the individual coheres with eschatology,
not merely in that alienation and isolation prepare the ground for
the Christian message but also, objectively speaking, in that God's
future gives the individual person a new identity and a new motivation for acting and leads the person into a new fellowship.

This biblical evidence brings us to the question of whether the
role of the individual is given adequate attention in modern proposals for church peace action. But since the category of the
individual is interconnected to a quite specific historical situation,
it should be introduced into the current debate on peace theology
and peace action only with due reservation and appropriate
reflection.

We have now briefly indicated the common points emerging out
of the exegetical studies, which need to be considered more carefully
as they come into confrontation with other proposals, especially
non-Christian ones. We take note immediately of one point of negation. A specific form of peace action was apparently not one of
the obvious unifying constants. Even though there are traditional
attempts to be cited, such as the command to love, which can be
traced throughout the Bible, still no comprehensive biblical clarity
emerged with reference to peace action. There is nothing which
could be compared reasonably closely to the parameters of minimization of oppression, poverty, and violence that is of importance to contemporary peace research. Rather, the spectrum of
possibilities for biblical action in this sphere turned out to be
expansive. To this we must now turn.

Points of Correlation

If peace action, taken as a whole, cannot be considered to be
a biblical constant, then we must still ask whether there might not
be solid ties and firm points of linkage that correlate individual
peace actions to other crucial emphases that have arisen in these
studies. Certain points of consideration do indeed permit one to
come closer to a summary thesis of the main question.

1. The first question to be considered is whether the fundamental
difference between the more limited and historically internal future
expectation in the prophets and the expectation of a future end
to history, which has shaped the thinking of both Judaism and

Christianity since the time of the apocalyptic, actually caused appropriate changes in how peace action was determined. In the main, the answer has to be negative. The frequently noted close connection between the ethic of Jesus and the prophetic ethic provides initial evidence for that. *Ethical content was apparently not determined by the question of whether or not future expectation envisioned the end of history.*

The enmity toward the world, and therefore also toward world peace, in the eschatology of the apocalyptic writings, has its basis, in my judgment, in the eschatological dimension itself. That is, it is not due to a comprehensive view of history which, in view of God's perspective, is seen as limited. At best, one could say that it is only through an end-of-history eschatology that a pessimistic and totally antiworld view of history could become possible. The overcoming of this antiworld attitude in rabbinic writings[6] and in Christianity, however, shows that an end-of-history eschatology need not be linked to an antiworld attitude. So it was with the revolutionary apocalyptists. It was not the eschatological expectation itself that turned them to violence and an antipeaceful orientation, but rather their perception of the Maccabees, that in their struggle they received decisive aid from God as a gift.

One achievement of apocalyptic that has indirect bearing on peace action is an eschatological dimension to future expectation; now for the first time it became possible to think of the future as fully predetermined and not to be questioned. Anyone who "knows" the course of the future can withdraw into that knowledge and need no longer be in communication with those who do not know. Here I can merely draw attention to the fact that this possibility had been reached in the Qumran group after it constituted itself as a closed sect. Accordingly, it had knowledge of the full heavenly plan for the world and one's role in it (cf. 1QS 3:13ff.). It adhered to strict separation from those outside and maintained a quite different conduct within the in-group from that shown toward the out-group (inside the group, love toward the sons of light resulting in the greatest minimization of need through the community of goods; to those outside, hatred toward the sons of darkness). Further in accordance with this, they had a hierarchical organization and a very detailed and extremely command-oriented form of action. The fact that Qumran followed a thoroughgoing predestinarianism, which the outsider Josephus described as deterministic, fits the picture. The philosophy of history that was required for the "closed" world and future vision of the Qumran sect was an apocalyptic eschatology.

The close correlation between a closed vision of the future — with its universalistic and end-of-history dimension, a hierarchical type of organization, a command structure for action, sectarian separatism — and a missionary impulse, all of which the Qumran community shows, serves as an interesting model of comparison to modern orthodox Marxism.[7]

But it would be wrong to treat the apocalyptic movement as a whole under the term "closed vision of the future," although its eschatology makes that possible in principle. The open stance of the apocalyptic groups toward Israel as a whole, the nonspeculative, comforting nature of their future statements, and the marks of a communicative structure within apocalyptic groups make this assumption unlikely for the apocalyptic groups, at least in times of crisis.

The universal historical and eschatological dimension, into which the future expectations had developed in the apocalyptic writings, allowed a faith in the God of the Old Testament to endure even in a changing and very threatening world situation. But it did not in any direct way open up new norms of action for peace.

2. The impact of dualism on ethics is especially noticeable in the realm of eschatology itself. Some clear correlations can be shown. When dualistic tendencies dominate the future expectation, that is, when the weight falls on the idea of a transcendent future, coming from beyond, and when discontinuity is the stronger element in the relationship of history to the eschaton, then the ethically oriented type of person emphasizes faithfulness and the endurance of the saints and shows a tendency to avoid active participation in world affairs, accenting rather the inner dimension of comfort and consolation. God is the sole actor in the eschaton. That describes the "quietistic" apocalyptic type.[8]

Monistic eschatological tendencies belong on the other side. Here there is an emphasis on locating the eschaton in this world, on the possibility of continuity between history and the eschaton and of a gradual transition toward the eschaton, together with the possibility of humanly reshaping the world in the light of the eschaton. It is characteristic of such a line of thought that it may include very many and diverse groupings and that the phrase "active shaping of the world" can cover a very large variety of possible modes of action.

Included in this group would be rabbinic Judaism, which sees a line of continuity between creation, history, and the eschaton, as well as those types which regard the eschaton as having already broken in upon the present. To the latter belongs Christianity, which sees the eschaton entering with Jesus and which acts in accord with his authorization. Also in this group are the pro-Maccabean apocalyptic writers and the Zealots, who see God decisively at work in the Maccabean wars and the Zealot uprisings. In both cases one must speak of an anticipation of the eschaton in the present. The mode of action therefore is determined not through the structure of the eschatology but through a concrete anticipation of the eschaton, that is, through the Maccabees (in war) or through Jesus (via love).

The following table shows the correlative tendencies:

Type of Eschatology	Transition to Eschaton	Relationship of History to Eschaton	Conduct
Transcendent	Often as rupture, sudden	Discontinuity (difference)	Inward, nonviolence avoidance of world endurance of faithful
This-worldly	Often over a period of time	Continuity (coincidence)	Active cooperation of humans in God's eschatological action

3. Within each eschatological type that is determined by a historical anticipation of the eschaton, that is, essentially within Christian eschatology,[9] there is a distinction evident between a stronger presentist accentuation and a more futurist accentuation, that is, the "not yet" of salvation emphasis. The latter type is more purely represented in the Johannine Apocalypse and, to a certain degree, also in Luke's Gospel, as shown in Paul Hoffmann's essay. An example of the former type would be the "enthusiasts" who appear only incidentally but against whom Paul and John's Revelation were struggling;[10] such a tendency appears also in John's Gospel.

Is it possible to identify points of correlation between the type of eschatology and the mode of action? A certain degree of correlation seems evident in the presentist eschatology, as seen in the following table:

Presentist Eschatology	Concentration of salvation on the congregation	Weak in external action
Resurrection has come Spirit, Cult	Internalization	Eventual focus on in-group dealings
Relinquishing those promises applying to the world		Fitting in and adapting to the world (religious society)

These points of correlation do not apply generally to each presentist eschatology; that is, one cannot attribute weaknesses in external action to each presentist eschatological type. The correlation applies mainly to early Christianity living under the special cultural and situational circumstances of the Hellenistic world and under the special, given presuppositions of presentist Christian eschatology. Its most important features — Spirit, resurrection of Jesus, miracles, Lord's Supper, and so forth — would lead it in those times when its futuristic aspect declined, as in a Hellenistic cultural context, into a tendency toward self-satisfaction, toward living exclusively for its own religious experiences, toward becoming a congregation constituted as a purely religious society, whose most vital interests lay elsewhere than in externally oriented practical peace actions.

For the more futuristic type, such a correlation becomes more difficult. Generally speaking, one can say that an interest in the world develops in accord with an expectation of its continuing future. This need not mean *eo ipso* a pro-worldly manner of action that transcends one's own group, as can be seen in the differences between the Apocalypse of John (tending toward world negation) and the more world-affirming theologies of Luke and rabbinic Judaism, for which what is constitutive for the world is all those still unfulfilled prophecies. These differences can be accounted for partly by the differing external and social situations, partly by the absence or presence of future expectation, and partly through differing eschatological types. The following correlations might apply:

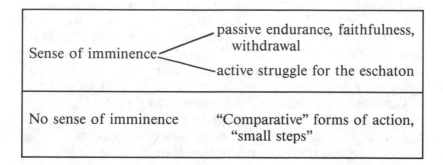

Sense of imminence	passive endurance, faithfulness, withdrawal
	active struggle for the eschaton
No sense of imminence	"Comparative" forms of action, "small steps"

Both Jesus and Paul, who combined "comparative" action with a sense of imminence, demonstrate the relativity of such a schematic diagram.

Basic Thesis

The considerations expressed above bring us in various ways to the basic thesis, which can be divided into a negative part and a positive part. Negatively speaking, we can join H. E. Tödt in saying that *eschatological statements, to the degree that they constitute statements about a future still to come, do not provide any concrete norms and criteria for human action.* Futuristic eschatological statements have much more of a motivating character. They formulate the hope that the present will not lead to nothing. They underline the urgency of alternative decisions. Indirectly they make possible certain modes of action. A person who reckons with God's coming for judgment will decide differently from the person for whom the world passes away when death comes. But the impending future never provides norms and criteria for determining the content of the action. That certainly holds for God's eschatological future, which must be distinguished from the future that humans can make for themselves. Only where the future is viewed as something of human making is future expectation able to offer direct criteria for action. Future expectation is a statement, in that case, of what is to be done or to be prevented.

Where, then, do the criteria for action come from? We must draw attention here to the complex interaction of tradition and situation. The tasks that are to be done are determined by the situation, in terms of their relative urgency and hence also their priority, in terms of the options for action, of the roles to play and of the framework for activity. Tradition provides the measuring stick and the norms. The precise nature of the reliance on tradition, the selecting from it and the value judgments applied, are largely determined by the situation. The scholar, the prophet, the king, and the peasant will each have a different orientation toward tradition. During a time of hardship other elements of tradition will come to the fore than those which emerge in a time of relative peace.

Our thesis is confirmed in the study of the prophets. The criteria and norms for action have been given by tradition. Future expectation can sharpen the action, encourage, or even imply that the possibility for action has been missed (Micah). The study of the apocalyptic also speaks to this point in its own way. The fact that there the political situation and the sociohistorical orientation of the actors determined the content of the action is due, in my opinion, to the fact that tradition, that is, the Old Testament ethic, was being threatened during the time of apocalyptic. For the first time in hundreds of years the orientation to tradition, that is, the possibility of living according to the law, had been called into question. The fact that it was precisely this situation of crisis that led to new proposals, with new group images and new advances, confirms once again the significance that the orientation to tradition had for Jewish life. It becomes understandable, at the same time, why the reference back to traditional patterns of action could not suffice in such an entirely new situation.

That brings us to the second and positive part of our thesis. *Eschatological expectation is capable of determining criteria and lines of action when the eschaton is linked in some way with present or past events.* While this was true for the Zealots, it is even more true and decisive for Christianity. In Jesus and his love the reign of God breaks in. His resurrection is the beginning of the coming new world. Based on Christian texts, our thesis might be restated: *Only to the degree that futurist eschatology is anticipated christologically do instructions and norms for action spring directly from eschatology.*

Jesus shows this point clearly: What is new about Jesus is that he, by his heralding the impending reign of God, determined in specific manner its content, namely, the unlimited goodness of God toward everyone, in particular to the poor, the sinners, and the outcasts. Such concrete occurring of the *basileia* ("kingdom") approximates ethics. The potency of the kingdom parables, intended to achieve a parabolic representation of the kingdom of God in the life of the hearer, relies on this hidden inbreaking of the kingdom of God in Jesus.

This generalization applies to Paul in a similar fashion in that the possibilities for action are introduced christologically and hence eschatologically. In living and suffering, the Christian conforms to the love and the cross of Christ and thus conforms also to the justice of God, or the kingdom of God, that is coming. In John's Apocalypse the christological point of reference achieves a restructuring of the challenge to suffer and to endure. The substance of peace action can be based in eschatology, because the future hope has become in part historically concrete in the present or the past. Historically this means that with the coming of Jesus a decisive new effort has begun, most evident in the prescribed relationship between eschatology and ethics. Theologically it means that it is in Christology, that is, in Jesus, that the possibility rests for the substance of human peace action to be in accord with the eschaton. *It is Christology that makes the traditional Jewish apocalyptic eschatology relevant for peace.* In view of contemporary peace research, however, the qualifier made earlier still applies. It is not world peace or some other secular worldly peace situation that is at the center of interest for the New Testament but rather the realization of the eschatological reality of Christ in the world.

The Central Point of the Biblical Witness

Important preliminary decisions for settling the final issue that must yet occupy us have thereby been made. The final issue is: Where do we find *the center of the biblical witness* for the relationship between eschatology and peace action? Here our thesis is: *Jesus marks this center.* Paul lays out *how* Jesus is the center, an approach that applies as well to other New Testament proposals. It is as the crucified and risen One that Jesus determines the life reality of Paul's congregations. Resurrection is the signal for the beginning of the eschaton, with the form of the crucified Jesus as sign and with the congregation as the primary locus for realizing this beginning. "Crucified" and "risen" are the two decidedly new catchwords that Paul contributes.

That Jesus is the center of the biblical statements on eschatology and peace action is naturally a Christian theological position which the Jew and the Muslim cannot support in that way. Nevertheless there are a series of secondary reasons, which, although not normative, still help to clarify the importance of Jesus for this issue. We can posit the following:

1. With Jesus, for the first time, a connection between eschatology and peace action becomes clear. It is exactly these characteristics, the "small steps" approach of Jesus and his "comparative" peace activity, which indirectly point above and beyond their own specific meaning to something superlative, namely, the kingdom of God. This marks the point where differences with the modern secular peace approach emerge.

2. Within the parameters of his time, Jesus shows the possibility of a holistic way of life that can absorb boundary type experiences without letting them split up into polarities.

a. Jesus takes seriously the experiences of alienation resulting from the antithetical relationship of the eschaton to history, but the antithesis between eschaton and history does not make it impossible for him to act in history. In his "small steps" manner of acting he stands close to the rabbinate, but unlike them he does not view the eschaton as a simple extension and completion of history in which God is already at work so that the qualitative differentness of the eschaton, over against history, would threaten to disappear. In Jesus, the eschaton stands in antithesis to oppression, poverty, religious discrimination, deeds of violence, and to a history marked by efforts of certain groups to claim God for themselves. But at the same time it permits, indeed demands, a new manner of action — love.

b. Jesus distinguishes himself from those proposals in which the inner dimension and the creating of a new identity completely dominate action (pacifist apocalyptic); at the same time, he does not thereby align himself more closely to those proposals in which the concern is purely in human action and where the notion of creating human identity completely recedes before deeds of human action. For Jesus, as well as for Paul, it is characteristic that the inner and the outer dimensions, God and one's neighbor, the gift of one's own identity and love of enemy, belong inseparably together; to be human is understood holistically in a most pre-eminent way.

c. Jesus represents an approach to the future that is neither closed in on itself, nontestable, nor so completely open as to tend toward agnosticism or skepticism. He believes that God is at work in the future and on that basis already at work in the present. But at the same time he rejects every form of speculative foreknowledge concerning God's future and stresses by means of the parables of contrast that there is no direct identity between the divine future and a human beginning of this future. In short, Jesus maintains a middle line between human control over the future and a completely indeterminate future. This middle line is a prerequisite for an open, responsive form of action that draws from the future.

The post-Easter theological proposals do not contradict this depiction. The dialectic between the reality of the cross and hope in the resurrection, which is fundamental for Paul, accords with Jesus' dialectic between the hidden reality of the kingdom of God in the present and the kingdom of God to be made manifest in the future. The potentially substantial difference between Jesus and the post-Easter conceptions consists in the fact that the latter distinguishes the church as a special sphere of action, which is distinct from the world. Without going into the complex question of the necessity of the formation of a church after Easter, and without going into the various nuanced designations of the relationship of the church to the world found in the post-Easter proposals in individual detail, let me merely draw attention once again to the importance that the church had for Paul as the principal sphere of action.[11] Because of the fact that where Christ reigns, a special sphere of action has appeared (Paul's idea of the body of Christ as reality and as task!), Paul is able to maintain that to be appointed by Christ signifies a definite material prescription for human action. Because the love that counts within the body of Christ is not based on the measure of worldly rationality and sense of proportion, Paul maintains that the church that is ordained by Christ to be a parable of the eschatological kingdom of God may not simply lose itself in the world. The church as the sphere of action is not, in my judgment, a designation for Christian action after Easter that is alien to Jesus. Rather, it is an attempt to hold fast to the fact that Christian action must be determined by the hidden reality of the kingdom of God which in Jesus has become historical. That is, Jesus remains central to the biblical witness to the relationship of eschatology and peace action. Paul has taken up the claim of Jesus that in his actions the coming kingdom of God is reflected in a unique way. He distinguishes the sphere of the church as ordained through Christ from that of the older sphere, the world that is passing away.

The Contribution of the Bible to
the Peace Actions of the Churches

The project within whose parameters these essays were developed was not concerned merely with history but was intended to serve the present.

Exegetical scholars are fully aware, and the essays make that sufficiently clear in particular ways, that there can be no direct, unmediated orientation to the Bible for us today. The questions that were addressed to the biblical materials were modern ones. Often the texts did not provide a direct answer. Above all, it was shown, that our framing of the questions, which proceeded within the three parameters of the minimization of oppression, violence, and poverty — namely, the questions of world peace — was alien to the texts, not only for reasons of contemporary history but also for theological ones. The historical differences between the time of the biblical texts and our own contemporary situation turned out to be major. Technical possibilities, the sphere of action, the area of responsibility, and global interdependence have changed fundamentally since biblical times. But above all, one must state clearly again and again that because of its heteronomous nature the Bible itself resists a direct programmatic application to contemporary Christian peace action. *A christologically determined mode of action that is fundamental, and that has love as its main line of orientation, excludes any form of orientation toward biblical imperatives that would suppress one's own situation, one's own freedom, and one's own new proposals.* In short, it was clear to the authors of these essays that there was no one single biblical proposition that could simply be made to serve as basis for a proposed peace praxis by the church. Perhaps it was not a bad idea that this study was conducted within the framework of an interdisciplinary project in which many nonexegetical scholars and nontheologians participated. That made it possible to carry on an open debate between the biblical texts and the present situation, in which the former were not automatically considered authoritative. Arising from the biblical studies, this debate surfaced the following impulses and perspectives that were considered important and worthy of consideration:[12]

—The reference to the *inner dimension* of peace, the minimization of fear, of sin and meaninglessness, the bringing of identity to persons and of faith. Understood thereby was not only the reference to the "religious" dimension of Christian faith but also the reference to the necessity of a *holistic peace concept.* That is, for an understanding of peace that takes the entire human being with all of his or her longings and hopes seriously, there must be an inner dimension to peace, not as a substitute for outward peace but as an additional dimension of depth.

—The reference to *the individual person as the subject of peace action.* Again, this does not stand in contrast to the active involvement of groups or churches but is a prerequisite to their involvement.

—The reference to the *church as a sphere of action. In that the church incorporates love, that is, truly is the church, it becomes a peace factor in the world.* Concretely this means a reformation of the church in its leadership and its membership, so that it truly represents the cross of Christ in the world. That would be the decisive contribution of the church to peace.

At the conclusion of this interdisciplinary project there were also some insoluble problems. The most substantial issue, which we were unable to resolve, was the drastic experiential difference between our contemporary struggle for peace and the New Testament peace witness. A common premise for us was that today the question of a world peace is one, if not simply the sole, fundamental issue on which the survival of humanity depends. This was not so in the Bible, not merely for reasons of contemporary history but just as much for theological ones. The actions of the New Testament witnesses, especially the practice of love, stood under the rubric of the kingdom of God, not of this world. One got the impression that in the apocalyptic tradition the question of the afterlife of humanity was indeed present; but obviously now, in view of Christology and in the light of the kingdom of God, this question no longer had existential urgency. This would conform to the fact that ultimately, for the biblical witnesses, all their hopes were pinned on the real acting of God in history, whereas for us, human actions seem to be sharply in the foreground. Here was a fundamental experiential difference between the Bible and the present time that could not be covered up and one that we should not relegate too hastily to the rubric of "belief—unbelief." For one's own experience can hardly be overridden and, from the perspective of the biblical witness, must not be allowed to be overridden. So we end this book with an open question.

Notes

EDITOR'S NOTE: In these notes Luz frequently refers to the four studies of Jürgen Kegler, Peter Lampe, Paul Hoffmann, and Ulrich Luz in the German volume, *Eschatologie und Friedenshandeln* (ed. Luz et al.). The pagination has been retained so the reader can check the original; since Kegler's article has been translated and is included in this volume, I have added the pagination of this volume in brackets.

1. The prophets anticipate these dimensions in part in various ways: Micah in that he offers no perspective for going beyond the coming judgment (Kegler, 23 [72ff.]); Isaiah through his universal historical perspective (Kegler, 27 [75ff.]); and Deutero-Isaiah through his expectation of a new salvation (Kegler, 41ff. [78ff.]).

2. See Luz's "Introduction" to *Eschatologie und Friedenshandeln*, 9f.

3. Kegler, 35 [82f.](Faith!), 46 [92f.], 58 [106f.]; Lampe, 70f., 74, 112; Hoffmann, 127f.; and Luz, 173ff.

4. The Hebrew concept of shalom includes this element.

5. Cf. Hoffmann, 130: "socially provocative rhetoric."

6. Cf. P. Lapide, "Zukunftserwartung und Frieden im Judentum," in *Eschatologie und Frieden* II (ed. Liedke), 127ff.

7. Cf. the study by V. Horsky, "Zukunftsvorstellungen und Frieden im Sowjetkommunismus und im Prager Reformkommunismus," in *Eschatologie und Frieden* III (ed. Liedke), 123–186.

8. Model examples are Daniel and John's Apocalypse, but compare also the Apocalypse of Weeks (Lampe, 78f.).

9. I am excluding here the revolutionary apocalyptists and the Zealots because it does make a difference whether one sees the beginning of the eschaton as an enduring happening (the struggle) or whether one sees in a specific event (the sending of Jesus) a onetime anticipation of the eschaton, which then continues in effect in a specific way. Attention needs to be drawn to the presentist elements in rabbinic Judaism, e.g., the anticipation of the eschaton in the Sabbath or in the Passover feast (cf. Hoffmann, 122).

10. Luz, 173; and Lampe, 107f.

11. Cf. Hoffmann, 146ff., plus 151f.; and Luz, esp. sec. 3.4, 191f.

12. I am basing this on the formulations in Liedke's evaluation of the study: "Zur Revision der Nullhypothese des Projektes 'Eschatologie und Frieden,'" in *Eschatologie und Frieden* III, ed. G. Liedke (Texten und Materialien der Forschungsstätte der Evangelischen Studiengemeinschaft, Series A, Vol. 8; Heidelberg: Forschungsstätte der Evangelischen Studiengemeinschaft, 1978), 381ff.

Introduction to
the Bibliography

Willard M. Swartley

The bibliography[1] that follows indicates that much of the scholarly work available has been done by German scholarship. Of the work done in the first third of the twentieth century, however, the British contribution of James Hastings stands as distinct and perhaps unique in its extensive coverage of the theme. It consists of eloquent sermonic essays based on the various parts of the New Testament where peace is a prominent emphasis. The work is not primarily exegetical but, in keeping with a more homiletical format, appropriates scripture to the issues of war and peace faced by the church in the aftermath of World War I and its sobering impact on theology. Hans Windisch's essay (1921), from this same period, makes a significant contribution even though it focuses primarily on one text, Matt. 5:9. It demonstrates how good scholarship can contribute to the church's reflection on and utilization of scripture's peace teachings. It shows also how the theme is inherently linked to other basic biblical emphases, such as gospel and discipleship/imitation.

Other contributions of this period focus on the study of peace in antiquity, giving attention to scriptural texts only in a comparative vein. Except for Willem Silvester van Leeuwen's study (in Dutch, 1940), little appears on the topic until a decade after World War II. This itself is a telling indictment. Then in the next period, between 1958 and 1973, the bulk of publications are from German scholarship. Heinz-Horst Schrey's summary and interpretive report on this literature (1981; pp. 152–157) are very helpful.

Schrey's analysis indicates that while numerous scholars (Stuhlmacher, Dinkler, Strobel, Hegermann, Brandenburger, Klemm, and
the FEST publications) used different methods for their study and
accented different parts of the New Testament canon, they unani-
mously agree that *eirene* is of central importance in the New Testament literature. But while Dinkler (for whom the primary focus
of *eirene* is christological, bonding believers to God and to one
another) and Klemm and Brandenburger (for whom the plurality
of New Testament emphases yields non-normative results) contend
that the peace understandings in the New Testament do not give
an adequate basis for peace praxis in the political arena today, both
Strobel (basing his work largely on Luke-Acts) and Hegermann
(appealing to the overall thrust of the unfolding peace declarations) argue for a significant, even direct, connection between the
biblical textual emphasis and our contemporary peace understandings and quests (Strobel on the basis of Luke's earthly sociopolitical
eirene vision and Hegermann on the basis of analogical intent).
Both Stuhlmacher and the summation of the FEST project by
Ulrich Luz (pp. 234–252 in this volume) focus on the church as
the sphere through which the New Testament *eirene* vision and
teaching are to be mediated to the contemporary sociopolitical
order, and that through repentance and suffering witness.

Other contributions that fall into this period are those of Bartsch,
Biser, Brandenburger, Comblin (French), Fischinger, Fitzer, Gnilka,
Hollenbach and Maier, Kostner, Leipoldt, Leroy (which comes
between this and the next era), Meurer, H. P. Schmidt, Stamm and
Bietenhard, and Stohr-Gollwitzer-Tietz. Many of these make helpful contributions to the understanding of peace in specific parts
of the canonical text, but most do not take up the issue of how
these biblical perspectives are to be appropriated by the contemporary church or enacted in public policy.

Later German contributions (Pesch, Blank, Korff, Kremer, Luz,
Frankemölle, and Haufe) often, but not always, give more attention to these questions. Luz and Haufe address the issues and accent
the role of the church in mediating the New Testament vision of
peace to the larger world; Korff demurs on the possibility of love
for neighbor and enemy working for politics and focuses on the
role of truth in conflict resolution. But in most of these contributions no sustained effort is given to developing a hermeneutical
appropriation of the New Testament peace teachings to the contemporary political arena. Luz's work, together with the other
essays in *Eschatologie und Friedenshandeln,* certainly makes the
most significant contribution in this regard. Frankemölle's work

represents the most comprehensive and adequate study of peace in the New Testament, prior to Mauser's work launching this SPS series. Wengst's *Pax Romana and the Peace of Jesus Christ* must be noted also for its comprehensive dimensions and for its distinctive approach of examining the peace of Jesus Christ as presented in the New Testament in contrast to the character of the Pax Romana. Hengel's writings are valuable in that they distinguish the Jesus movement and teaching from the revolutionary impulse (note also Cullmann's work here), but they do not provide a hermeneutical basis for appropriating Jesus' peace teaching for criticism of established governments in their use of violence. For Hengel, the church has at most only an indirect contribution to make: by being the "city on the hill" it may give out positive impulses to society and politics.[2]

Schottroff's, Trummer's, and Wengst's contributions move the discussion along new lines in that they utilize social world analyses as part of both their exegetical work and the appropriation of their findings to our contemporary setting. On the American side, Richard A. Horsley's extended study of Jesus' social and political world — with its depiction of a four-stage cycle of oppression, non-violent resistance, counteroppression, and revolution — and the placement of Jesus' efforts toward social transformation in that cycle, shifts the focus from study of peace in scripture (as do Hengel's and Cullmann's contributions also) to the endeavor to find an adequate hermeneutical grid for understanding Jesus' peace teachings. Wink also accents the sociopolitical context but reconstructs it differently from Horsley. Hence peace is correlated with differing strategies for action (see SPS 3, forthcoming).

Girard's and Schwager's work on the interconnection between violence and sacrifice opens up new vistas for grasping and analyzing the New Testament peace emphases, the dimensions of which have hardly yet been identified. Several essays in Semeia 33 (1985) suggest the import of these studies for New Testament peace theology,[3] but more intensive and comprehensive work might be undertaken.

The North American contributions are mostly post-1970, except for Henry Grady Ketchum's dissertation in 1933 (which, unpublished, has gone unnoticed). This also is a telling indictment of North American scholarship, in that it took the United States' Vietnam debacle to stimulate scholarly work.[4] Here the stream of work is very disparate in nature and until recently not very thorough in either depth or scope. Harris's work (1970) focuses primarily on shalom in the Old Testament and appears to dodge the task of appropriating the significance of these findings to the issues faced by the contemporary church and world politics. The United Church Press efforts (Hammer, Powers, Brueggemann) are helpful for both scope and hermeneutical appropriation to our contemporary sociopolitical setting, but they do not represent depth textual analysis. Brueggemann's work, however, is penetrating on specific texts and integrates the peace theme with biblical theological thought more broadly, but it does not represent a comprehensive study of biblical peace texts. William Klassen's essays contribute depth on selected topics (see Preface, n. 5). The most thorough contributions are those of Topel and McSorley, complemented by the earlier Macgregor and later Ferguson contributions from the British side. While Topel's work was done in clear support of liberation theology, the other three represent efforts to show biblical support for pacifism. Perry Yoder's book *Shalom* shows interest in both pacifism and liberation agenda; it also has the distinction of breaking new theological ground in integrating *shalom/eirene* exegesis into other basic strands of theological agenda: law, justice, atonement, and eschatology. Indeed, this study points a direction in showing how the study of peace in scripture can play an important role in the study of biblical theology more broadly. With Mauser's complete monograph on peace in the New Testament a long-standing deficiency in American scholarship has begun to be rectified.

But there is much yet to be done, especially for English and American scholarship, since so much of the scholarly work until now has been in German. My own essay on Luke, together with Strobel's work on Luke, needs further analysis and expansion in relation to Luke's overall theological emphasis. Reid's essay makes a helpful contribution to this task. Dinkler's point (p. 187) that Jesus nowhere links peace to the kingdom of God, the central aspect of his mission and message, needs reassessment. Do not Matt. 5:9 and Luke 10:6–9 have foundation, perhaps origin, in Jesus' own teaching and action? More work needs also to be done on Dinkler's disagreement with Brandenburger (see p. 205 n. 123) regarding the role of peace in Jewish messianism as a context for understanding Jesus' ministry. One point is clear: Dinkler's view that Luke depoliticized and then eschatologized *eirene* and Conzelmann's view that Luke deeschatologizes hardly fit together. Further, the analysis of Luke's *eirene* redaction must take account of how this fits into the overall structural design of Luke, and Acts as well, since the emphasis continues there (see Comblin's *ETL* article). Mauser's work, treating both Luke and Acts, contributes valid insights and focuses the topic for further investigation. Frankemölle's suggestion that Luke's peace understanding of Jesus responds to the moral ambiguity of historical reality by positively acknowledging in the "two swords" saying those Christians who participated in the Jewish revolt needs examination. One major task in the Gospels is to work for consistency between a given writer's use of *eirene* and the theological accent of that particular Gospel as a whole. Or at least good reason should be given why that is not so.

Numerous other scholarly tasks also need doing, of which I mention the following:

1. As noted above, further work is needed on the implications of René Girard's and Raymund Schwager's studies for the New Testament understanding of Christ's death-resurrection as the potential end to violence — and the consequence of this for peace to all humanity. This investigation will certainly have significant bearing also on our exegetical and theological understandings of atonement in the New Testament. Such analysis calls us to give more attention to evil and its endemic power in human experience.

2. The biblical-theological significance of the linkage between peace and mission (see Reid's essay) merits further study, especially in Lukan thought (and perhaps Matthean also, in view of Matthew's placement of 10:34 in the mission discourse). A study of Matthew 10 and Luke 10 in relation to peace and mission would be quite helpful.

3. Some reassessment of Paul's view of peace, in all its dimensions — humans with God, corporate societal, and socio-political — is called for in the light of the new interpretations of Paul's relation to the law and the meaning of *ek pisteōs Christou* which makes God's justification of humans rest upon the faith of Jesus Christ. What are the peace implications of this emphasis on Jesus' faithful trust in God as the basis of our justification?

4. The relationship between *shalom/eirene* and healing/health in the biblical text needs careful examination. Almost nothing has been done on this to date, although some recent significant study has sought to understand the biblical view of health in its social context (see especially the work of John Pilch[5]). Once this study is done, the essays in this volume will inadequately represent the scope of agenda to be considered in the biblical meaning of peace (this matter has been suggested by Luz above in calling for the recognition that scripture's use of peace includes an inner dimension).

5. In view of the recent flowering of social world and literary-narrative studies, we will also need to ask to what extent our fuller

understanding of the world and the text of the Bible will enable us to do better exegesis and then more adequately appropriate these findings to the current urgent need for peace with justice in our Christian communities and the contemporary world in the inner-personal, relational, and sociopolitical dimensions of human experience.

Notes

1. This introduction focuses on the New Testament entries; the more important Old Testament sources were introduced by Perry Yoder in his essay at the beginning of this volume.

2. See Hengel's articles in *Evangelische Kommentar:* "Das Ende aller Politik" (December 1981): 686–690, and "Die Stadt auf dem Berge" (January 1982): 19–22. For some discussion of Hengel's work, and the different emphasis between his anti-Zealot Jesus writings of the early 1970s and his early 1980 articles, when the peace movement was strong in Germany, see Willard M. Swartley, *Slavery, Sabbath, War and Women: Case Issues in Biblical Interpretation* (Scottdale, Pa.; Kitchener, Ont.: Herald Press, 1983), 148.

3. Both Raymund Schwager's article, "Christ's Death and the Prophetic Critique of Sacrifice" (pp. 109–123) and Burton Mack's essay, "The Innocent Transgressor: Jesus in Early Christian Myth and History" (pp. 135–165), identify specific ways in which Jesus' life and work demonstrate nonviolent response. In *René Girard and Biblical Studies* (Semeia 33; ed. Andrew J. McKenna; Decatur, Ga.: Scholars Press, 1985). The just now available full-scale study by James G. Williams, *The Bible, Violence, and the Sacred: Liberation from the Myth of Sanctioned Violence* (San Francisco: Harper & Row, 1991), responds significantly to this need, but the issue merits investigation from diverse points of view.

4. Some of the entries in the bibliography are pre-1970, but most of these are either a defense or an exposition of pacifist readings of the text (Hershberger, Edward Yoder, Rutenber). Indeed, these are important and do pay attention to New Testament peace teachings (hence they are included in the bibliography). For the most part, however, they are not scholarly studies that have functioned with any significance in the New Testament guild of scholarship.

5. John J. Pilch, "Understanding Biblical Healing: Selecting the Appropriate Model," *BTB* 18 (1988): 142–150; "Healing in Mark: A Social Science Analysis," *BTB* 15 (1985): 142–150; "Reading Matthew Anthropologically: Healing in Cultural Perspective," *Listening* 24 (1989): 278–289; "Sickness and Healing in Luke-Acts," in *The Social World of Luke-Acts: Models for Interpretation* (ed. Jerome H. Neyrey; Peabody, Mass.: Hendrickson Publishers, 1991), 181–209.

Bibliography:
Biblical Studies
on *Shalom* and *Eirene*

Perry B. Yoder
and Willard M. Swartley

The focus of this bibliography is on peace (*shalom* and *eirene*) studies within the biblical literature. Related topics such as war, love command, and reconciliation are included only if a connection is made to peace in the article or book. In regard to style, when an entry is from a collection of essays and that volume of essays is listed with its editor, the entry will cite only an abbreviated form of the title, the last name of the editor, and the page numbers. For an example, see under Geyer, the first entry below.

Bibliographical Works

Geyer, Klaus. "Theologie des Friedens: Literaturbericht zu Arbeiten aus dem Bereich der neutestamentlichen Wissenschaft." In *Frieden — Bibel — Kirche,* edited by Liedke. Pp. 187-199.
Huber, Wolfgang. "Theologie des Friedens: Literaturbericht zu Arbeiten aus dem Bereich der systematischen Theologie." In *Frieden — Bibel — Kirche,* edited by Liedke. Pp. 200-216.
Liedke, Gerhard. "Theologie des Friedens: Literaturbericht zu Arbeiten aus dem Bereich der alttestamentlichen Wissenschaft." In *Frieden — Bibel — Kirche,* edited by Liedke. Pp. 174-186.
Scharffenorth, Gerta, and Wolfgang Huber. *Bibliographie zur Friedensforschung: Studien zur Friedensforschung* 6. Stuttgart: Ernst Klett Verlag; Munich: Kösel-Verlag, 1970. Pp. 143-144.
——. *Neue Bibliographie zur Friedensforschung: Studien zur Friedensforschung* 12. Stuttgart: Ernst Klett Verlag; Munich: Kösel-Verlag, 1973. Pp. 266-270.
Schrey, Heinz-Horst. "Fünfzig Jahre Besinnung über Krieg und Frieden." *TRu* 46 (1981): 58-96, 149-180.

Swartley, Willard M., and C. J. Dyck. "The Bible, Peace, and War." In *Annotated Bibliography of Mennonite Writings on War and Peace: 1930–1980,* edited by Swartley and Dyck. Scottdale, Pa.; Kitchener, Ont.: Herald Press, 1987. Pp. 96–127.

Swinne, Axel Hilmar. *Bibliographia Irenica 1500–1970: Internationale Bibliographie zur Friedenswissenschaft.* Hildesheim: Gerstenberg Verlag, 1977.

Monographs and Articles

Albertz, Rainer. "Schalom und Versöhnung: Alttestamentliche Kriegs- und Friedens-Traditionen." *Teologia Practica* 18 (1983): 16–28.

Alt, Franz. *Peace Is Possible: The Politics of the Sermon on the Mount.* Translated by Joachim Neugroschel. New York: Schocken Books, 1985.

Bartsch, Hans Werner. "The Biblical Message of Peace: Summary." In *On Earth Peace: Discussion on War/Peace Issues, Between Friends, Mennonites, Brethren, and European Churches, 1935–75,* edited by Donald F. Durnbaugh. Elgin, Ill.: Brethren Press, 1978.

———. *Die evangelische Predigt vom Frieden.* Hamburg: Herbert Reich Evangelischer Verlag, 1958.

Bastian, Hans-Dieter. "'Krieg führen können': Über die friedensgefährdende Rede vom Frieden.—Ein Mittel der Erpressung—." In *Christen im Streit um den Frieden,* ed. Brinkel et al. Pp. 161–165.

Batto, Bernard F. "The Covenant of Peace: A Neglected Ancient Near Eastern Motif." *CBQ* 49 (1987): 187–211.

Bauernfeind, Otto. *Eid und Friede: Fragen zur Anwendung und zum Wesen des Eides.* Stuttgart: Verlag W. Kohlhammer, 1956.

Baumbach, Günther. "Das Verständnis von *eirene* im Neuen Testament." In *Theologische Versuche* 5, edited by J. Rogge and G. Schille. Berlin: Evangelische Verlagsanstalt, 1975. Pp. 33–44, 49–52.

Bea, Agostino. "L'idea della pace nel VT." *XXXV Congresso Eucaristico Internacional 1952, La Eucaristia y la Paz, Sessiones de Estudio,* I. Barcelona: n.p., 1952. Pp. 49–59.

Bergant, Dianne. "Peace in a Universe of Order." *Biblical . . . Reflections . . . Peace,* edited by Pawlikowski and Senior. Pp. 17–30.

Biser, Eugen. "Der Friede Gottes." In *Ist Friede Machbar?* Munich: Kösel-Verlag, 1969.

———. *Der Sinn des Friedens: Ein theologischer Entwurf.* Munich: Kösel-Verlag, 1960.

Blank, Joseph. "Die Entscheidung für den Frieden." In *Das Evangelium des Friedens,* edited by Eicher. Pp. 13–26. Portions appeared earlier as: "Gewaltlosigkeit—Krieg—Militärdienst," *Orientierung* 46 (1982): 157–163, and "Zieht die Waffenrüstung Gottes an . . . ," ibid., 213–216.

———. *Im Dienst der Versöhnung: Friedenspraxis aus christlicher Sicht.* Munich: Kösel-Verlag, 1984.

Bohn, Ernest J. *Christian Peace Teaching According to New Testament*

Peace Teaching Outside the Gospels. Peace Committee of the General Conference Mennonite Church, 1938.

Bolduc, Norman P. "The Biblical Vision of Peace in Our World." *Military Chaplains' Review* 16 (1988): 5–9.

Borg, Marcus J. *Jesus: A New Vision.* San Francisco: Harper & Row, 1987. Ch. 7.

Bosold, Iris. *Pazifismus und prophetische Provokation.* Stuttgart: Verlag Katholisches Bibelwerk, 1978.

Brandenburger, Egon. *Frieden im Neuen Testament: Grundlinien urchristlichen Friedensverständnisses.* Gütersloh: Gütersloher Verlagshaus Gerd Mohn, 1973.

———. "Grundlinien des Friedensverständnisses im NT." *WD* 11 (1971): 21–72.

———. "Perspektiven des Friedens im Neuen Testament." *BK* 37 (1982): 50–60.

Brinkel, Wolfgang; B. Scheffler; and M. Wächter, eds. *Christen im Streit um den Frieden.* Freiburg im Breisgau: Dreisam-Verlag, 1982.

Broer, I. "Frieden durch Gewaltverzicht? Vier Abhandlungen zu Friedensproblematik und Bergpredigt." Kleine Reihe zur Bibel 25. Stuttgart: Verlag Katholisches Bibelwerk, 1984.

Brueggemann, W. *Living Toward a Vision: Biblical Reflections on Shalom.* A Shalom Resource. Philadelphia: United Church Press, 1978.

Budde, Ludwig. *Ara Pacis Augustae: Der Friedensaltar des Augustus.* Hannover: Tauros-Presse, 1957.

Burkholder, J. Richard, and John Bender. *Children of Peace.* Elgin, Ill.: Brethren Press; Nappanee, Ind.: Evangel Press; Newton, Kans.: Faith and Life Press; Scottdale, Pa.: Mennonite Publishing House, 1982.

Canellas, G. "Paz (*Shalom*) en el Antiguo Testamento Profetas." *Olivo* 14 (1981): 49–78.

Carey, George L. "Biblical-Theological Perspectives on War and Peace." *EvQ* 57 (1985): 163–178.

Carmichael, Calum M. "A Time for War and a Time for Peace: The Influence of the Distinction Upon Some Legal and Literary Material." In *Studies in Jewish History in Honor of David Daube,* edited by B. S. Jackson. *JJS* 25 (1974): 50–63.

Caspari, Wilhelm. *Der biblische Friedensgedanke nach dem Alten Testament.* Berlin-Lichterfelde: E. Runge, 1916.

———. *Vorstellung und Wort "Friede" im Alten Testament.* BFCT 14,4. Gütersloh: C. Bertelsmann Verlag, 1910.

The Challenge of Peace: God's Promise and Our Response; A Pastoral Letter on War and Peace by the National Conference of Catholic Bishops. Washington, D.C.: United States Catholic Conference, 1983. Pp. 13–25.

Charles, Howard H. "The Quest for Peace." *Builder* 18 (June 1968): 18–19.

———. "Blessed Are the Peacemakers." *Builder* 31 (January 1981): 31–35.

Chase, Debra A. "A Note on an Inscription from Kuntillet 'Ajrud.'"
    BASOR 246 (1982): 63–67.
Cheli, Giovanni. "Sieg der Abrüstung – ein Sieg des Friedens." In *Das
    Evangelium des Friedens,* edited by Eicher. Pp. 189–206.
Clark, Robert E. D. *Does the Bible Teach Pacifism?* New Malden, Surrey,
    England: Fellowship of Reconciliation, 1976.
Cloete, W. T. W. "*Ntn yhwh shalom.*" Papers Read at the 24th Meeting
    of "Die Ou-Testamentiese Werkgemeenskap in Suider-Afrika," edited
    by F. E. Deist and J. A. Loader. *OTS* 24 (1982): 1–10.
Comblin, Joseph. "La Paix dans la théologie de saint Luc." *ETL* 32 (1956):
    439–460.
——. *Théologie de la paix: Principes (Encyclopédie universitaire).* Paris:
    Editions Universitaires, 1960.
——. *Theologie des Friedens: Biblische Grundlagen.* Graz: Verlag Styria,
    1963.
Corbato, Carlo. "La nascita di Eirene." In *Interrogativi dell'Umanesimo,*
    edited by G. Tarugi. Florence: Leo S. Olschki, 1976. Pp. 117–127.
Coste, Rene. "Paix." *Dictionnaire de spiritualité ascétique et mystique . . .*
    vol. 12 (1983), 40–55.
——. "Les fondements biblico-théologiques de la justice et de la paix."
    NRT 105 (1983): 179–217.
Couto, Filipe J. "Zur Kultur des Friedens." In *Das Evangelium des
    Friedens,* edited by Eicher. Pp. 147–164.
Cullmann, Oscar. *Jesus and the Revolutionaries.* New York: Harper &
    Row, 1970.
Delcor, Mathias. "La paix et le messie juif, nouveau Salomon, en Zach
    9, 10." *XXXV Congresso Eucaristico Internacional 1952, La Eucaristia
    y la Paz,* I. Barcelona: n.p., 1952. Pp. 331–334.
Delling, Gerhard. "Die Bezeichnung 'Gott des Friedens' und ähnliche
    Wendungen in den Paulusbriefen." In *Jesus und Paulus,* edited by E.
    E. Ellis and E. Grässer (FS G. Kümmel). Göttingen: Vandenhoeck &
    Ruprecht, 1975. Pp. 76–84.
Detweiler, Richard C. "Peace Is the Will of God." In *Peacemakers,* edited
    by Lapp. Pp. 67–74.
Dewey, Joanna. "Peace." *Harper's Bible Dictionary,* edited by Paul J.
    Achtemeier. San Francisco: Harper & Row, 1985. Pp. 766–767.
Dickey, F. L., Jr. "The Development of the Hebrew Idea of *Hesed* in the
    Biblical Literature." Diss., School of Theology at Claremont, 1976.
Dinkler, Erich. *Eirene: Der urchristliche Friedensgedanke.* Heidelberg:
    C. Winter Verlag, 1973. Sitzungsberichte der Heidelberger Akademie
    der Wissenschaften Phil. hist. Kl., Abh. 1. ET: pp. 164–212 in this
    volume.
Dinkler, Erich, and Erika Dinkler-von Schubert. "Frieden." *RAC* 8 (Stutt-
    gart: Anton Hiersemann, 1972), pp. 434–505.
Donahue, John R. "The Good News of Peace." *The Way* 22 (April 1982):
    88–89.

Douglass, James W. *The Non-violent Cross: A Theology of Revolution and Peace.* New York: Macmillan Co., 1968.

Duchrow, Ulrich, and Gerhard Liedke. *Shalom: Biblical Perspectives on Creation, Justice and Peace.* Geneva: World Council of Churches, 1989. [*Schalom: Der Schöpfung Befreiung, den Menschen Gerechtigkeit, den Völkern Frieden.* Stuttgart: Kreuz Verlag, 1987.]

Durham, John I. "Shalom and the Presence of God." In *Proclamation and Presence: Old Testament Essays in Honour of Gwynne Henton Davies,* edited by John I. Durham and J. R. Porter. Richmond, Va.: John Knox Press, 1970. Pp. 272–293.

Eicher, Peter, ed. *Das Evangelium des Friedens.* Munich: Kösel-Verlag, 1982.

———. "Er ist unser Friede." *Das Evangelium des Friedens,* edited by Eicher. Pp. 42–102.

Eichrodt, W. *Die Hoffnung des ewigen Friedens im alten Israel: Ein Beitrag zur Frage nach der israelitischen Eschatologie.* BFCT 25,3. Gütersloh: C. Bertelsmann Verlag, 1920.

Eisenbeis, Walter. *Die Wurzel שלם im Alten Testament.* BZAW 113. Berlin: Walter de Gruyter, 1969. Eng. orig.: "A Study of the Root Shalom in the Old Testament." Ph.D. diss., University of Chicago, 1966.

Eller, Vernard. *War and Peace from Genesis to Revelation: King Jesus' Manual of Arms for the Armless.* Scottdale, Pa.: Herald Press, 1981.

Elsbernd, Mary. *A Theology of Peacemaking: A Vision, A Road, A Task.* Lanham, New York, and London: University Press of America, 1989.

Engnell, Ivan. "Frid." In *Svensk Biblisk Uppslagsverk,* edited by Ivan Engnell. Stockholm, 1962. Vol. 1, 655ff.

Enz, Jacob J. *The Christian and Warfare: The Roots of Pacifism in the Old Testament.* Christian Peace Shelf Series 3. Scottdale, Pa.: Herald Press, 1972.

Epsztein, Léon. *Social Justice in the Ancient Near East and the People of the Bible.* Translated by John Bowden. London: SCM Press; Philadelphia: Fortress Press, 1986. [*La justice sociale dans le Proche-Orient ancien et le peuple de la Bible.* Paris: Editions du Cerf, 1983.]

Fast, Heinhold. *Beiträge zu einer Friedenstheologie: Eine Stimme aus den historischen Friedenskirchen.* Maxdorf: Agape Verlag, 1982.

———. "Christologie und Friedensethik: Eine Stimme aus den historischen Friedenskirchen." In *Der Friedensdienst der Christen,* edited by Werner Danielsmeyer. Gütersloh: Gütersloher Verlagshaus Gerd Mohn, 1970. Pp. 29–44.

Fast, Henry A. *Jesus and Human Conflict.* Scottdale, Pa.: Herald Press, 1959.

Ferguson, John. *The Politics of Love: The New Testament and Nonviolent Revolution.* Greenwood, S.C.: Attic Press, n.d.

Fischer, James A. "War and Peace: A Methodological Consideration." in *Blessed Are the Peacemakers,* edited by Tambasco. Pp. 17–39.

Fischinger, Dietrich. *Von der Volkskirche zur Friedensgemeinde unter den Volkern: Eine Einladung zum Dialog.* Hamburg: H. Reich, 1968.

Fitzer, G. "Friede." *BHH* (Göttingen, 1962), 1:500.

Foerster, W. *"Eirene."* *TDNT,* 2:406–420. [*TWNT,* 2:405–418.]

Ford, J. Massyngberde. *My Enemy Is My Guest: Jesus and Violence in Luke.* Maryknoll, N.Y.: Orbis Books, 1984.

———. "Shalom in the Johannine Corpus." *HBT* 6 (1984): 67–90.

Frankemölle, Hubert. *Friede und Schwert: Frieden Schaffen nach dem Neuen Testament.* Mainz: Matthias-Grünewald-Verlag, 1983. ET of ch. 2 in this volume, pp. 213–233.

"Frieden ist der 'Weg zum Frieden': Dienst der Versöhnung als Auftrag der christlichen Gemeinde." *PrTh* 18 (1983): 1–2.

"Frieden und Gewaltlosigkeit." *BK* 37, 2 (1982). Contributions by E. Brandenburger, I. Broer, N. Lohfink, and A. Schenker.

Fuchs, Harald. *Augustin und der antike Friedensgedanke.* 2nd ed. Berlin: Weidmannsche Verlagsbuchhandlung, 1965.

Furnish, V. P. "War and Peace in the New Testament." *Int* 38 (1984): 363–379.

Gabriel, Ingeborg. *Friede über Israel. Eine Untersuchung zur Friedenstheologie in Chronik I 10–II 36.* Klosterneuburg: Verlag Österreichisches Katholisches Bibelwerk, 1990.

Garcia Cordero, Maximiliano. "Shalom; hacie la paz mesianico." *Ciencia Tomista* 3 (1984): 211–228.

Gerleman, Gillis. *"šlm* genug haben," *THAT,* 2:919–935.

———. "Die Wurzel *šlm." ZAW* 85 (1973): 1–14.

Gesellschaft für evangelische Theologie: "Den Frieden ausbreiten." In *Christen im Streit,* edited by Brinkel et al. Pp. 107–110.

Gnilka, Joachim. "Christus unser Friede — Ein Friedens-Erlöserlied in Eph. 2:14–17. Erwägungen einer neutestamentlichen Friedenstheologie." In *Die Zeit Jesu,* edited by G. Bornkamm and K. Rahner (FS H. Schlier). Freiburg: Herder, 1970. Pp. 190–207.

Goetze, Albrecht. "Peace on Earth." *Bulletin of the American Schools of Oriental Research* 93 (February 1944): 17–20.

Good, E. M. "Peace in the OT." *IDB,* 3:704–706.

Goppelt, Leonhard. "Der Friede Jesu und der Friede des Augustus." *Wort und Wahrheit* 27 (1972): 243–251.

Gordon, Cyrus H. "War and Peace [Meaning for the Totaling of life]; The Theoretical Structure of Israelite Society." In *Fields of Offerings: Studies in Honor of Raphael Patai,* edited by Victor Sanua. Rutherford, N.J.: Fairleigh Dickinson University Press, 1983. Pp. 299–303.

Gowan, Donald, and Ulrich Mauser. "Shalom and Eirene." In *The Peacemaking Struggle,* edited by Ronald H. Stone and Dana W. Wilbanks. Lanham, New York, and London: University Press of America, 1985. Pp. 123–133.

Grimsrud, Ted. "Peace Theology and the Justice of God in the Book of Revelation." In *Essays on Peace Theology and Witness,* edited by Willard M. Swartley. Occasional Papers No. 12. Elkhart, Ind.: Institute of Mennonite Studies, 1988. Pp. 135–153.

Gross, Heinrich. "Friede." *Bibeltheologisches Wörterbuch,* edited by J. B. Bauer. Graz: Verlag Styria, 1967. Pp. 436ff.

——. *Die Idee des ewigen und allgemeinen Weltfriedens im Alten Orient und im Alten Testament.* Trier theologische Studien 7. 2nd ed. Trier: Paulinus Verlag, 1967.

Gwyn, Douglas; George Hunsberger; Eugene F. Roop; and John Howard Yoder. *A Declaration on Peace.* Scottdale, Pa.: Herald Press, 1991.

Haacker, Klaus. "Der Römerbrief als Friedensmemorandum." *NTS* 36 (1990): 25–41.

Hammer, P. L. *The Gift of Shalom: Bible Studies in Human Life and the Church* (A Shalom Resource). Philadelphia: United Church Press, 1977.

——. *Shalom in the New Testament.* Philadelphia: United Church Press, 1973.

Hanson, Paul D. "War and Peace in the Hebrew Bible." *Int* 38 (1984): 341–362.

Harris, Douglas J. *Shalom: The Biblical Concept of Peace.* Grand Rapids: Baker Book House, 1970.

Hasler, V. "*eirene.*" *EWNT,* 1:957–964.

Hastings, James. *The Christian Doctrine of Peace.* Edinburgh: T. & T. Clark, 1922.

Haufe, Guenther. "Eirene in the New Testament." *CV* 27 (1984): 7–17.

Hegermann, Harold. "Die Bedeutung des eschatologischen Friedens in Christus für den Weltfrieden heute nach dem Zeugnis des Neuen Testaments." In *Der Friedensdienst der Christen,* edited by Werner Danielsmeyer. Gütersloh: Gütersloher Verlagshaus Gerd Mohn, 1970. Pp. 117–139.

Hendrickx, Herman. *A Time for Peace: Reflections on the Meaning of Peace and Violence in the Bible.* London: SPCK, 1988. Available also as *Peace Anyone? Biblical Reflections on Peace and Violence.* Quezon City, Philippines: Claretian Publications, 1986.

Hengel, Martin. *Victory Over Violence: Jesus and the Revolutionists.* Translated by David E. Green. Philadelphia: Fortress Press, 1973.

——. *Was Jesus a Revolutionist?* Translated by William Klassen. Philadelphia: Fortress Press, 1971.

Hennig, Kurt. "Der Friede Gottes und der Friede der Welt — 18 biblische Thesen zum Frieden." In *Christen im Streit um den Frieden,* edited by Brinkel et al. Pp. 48–54.

Hermann, Johannes. "Friede." In *Calwer Bibellexikon.* Stuttgart: Calwer Verlag, 1959 ed., pp. 337–338 [1924 4th ed., p. 201].

Hershberger, Guy. *War, Peace and Nonresistance.* Scottdale, Pa.: Herald Press, 1953.

Hesselink, I. John. "John 14:23–29." *Int* 43 (1989): 174–177.

Hill, David. "The Background and Meaning of δικαιοσύνη and Cognate Words." In *Greek Words and Hebrew Meanings.* Cambridge: Cambridge University Press, 1967. Pp. 82–162.

Hoffmann, Paul. "Eschatologie und Friedenshandeln in der Jesusüberlieferung." In *Eschatologie und Friedenshandeln,* edited by Luz et al. Pp. 115–152.

———. "Tradition und Situation. Zur Verbindlichkeit des Gebots der Feindesliebe in der synoptischen Überlieferung und in der gegenwärtigen Friedensdiskussion." In *Ethik im Neuen Testament,* edited by K. Kertelge. *QD* 102. Freiburg: Herder, 1984. Pp. 50–118.

Hollenbach, Alexander, and Hans Maier, eds. *Christlicher Friede und Weltfriede: Geschichtliche Entwicklung und Gegenwartsprobleme.* Paderborn: Ferdinand Schöningh, 1971.

Hoppe, Leslie J. "Religion and Politics: Paradigms from Early Judaism." In *Biblical and Theological Reflections on Peace,* edited by Pawlikowski and Senior. Pp. 45–54.

Hopwood, Keith. "Peace in the Ancient World." In *World Encyclopedia of Peace,* edited by Linus Pauling, Vol. 2. New York: Pergamon Press, 1986. Pp. 197–208.

Horsley, Richard A. *Jesus and the Spiral of Violence.* San Francisco: Harper & Row, 1987.

Howe, Allan. "The Congregation as Peacemaker." *CovQ* 47 (August 1989): 27–35.

Howe, Günther, and Heinz Eduard Tödt. *Frieden im Wissenschaftlichtechnischen Zeitalter: Ökumenische Theologie und Zivilisation.* Stuttgart: Kreuz Verlag, 1966. Bib. sec.: 32–33.

Huber, Wolfgang. "Theologische Probleme der Friedensforschung." *EvT* 31 (1971): 559–575.

———. *See* Scharffenorth, Gerta, in "Bibliographical Works," above.

Humphrey, Hugh M. "Matthew 5:9: 'Blessed Are the Peacemakers for They Shall Be Called Sons of God.'" *Peacemakers,* edited by Tambasco. Pp. 62–78.

Janzen, Waldemar. "Christian Perspectives on War and Peace in the Old Testament." In *Still in the Image: Essays in Biblical Theology and Anthropology.* IMSS 6. Newton, Kans.: Faith and Life Press, 1982. Pp. 193–211.

Jegen, Carol Frances. *Jesus the Peacemaker.* Kansas City, Mo.: Sheed & Ward, 1986.

Jenni, Ernst. "Gehe hin in Frieden (*lšlwm/bšlwm*)!" *ZAH* 1 (1988): 40–46.

Jeremias, Jörg. "Quelques témoignages bibliques relatifs à la paix." *PosLuth* 30 (1982): 177–190.

Jeske, Richard L. "Expository Article: John 14:27 and 16:33." *Int* 38 (1984): 403–411.

Juárez, Miguel A. Martin. "La paz: potencial liberador. A Testamento." *ByF* 17 (1991): 5–28.

Jüngel, Eberhard. *Zum Wesen des Friedens: Frieden als Kategorie Theologischer Anthropologie. Traktate 74.* Munich: Chr. Kaiser Verlag, 1983.

Kegler, Jürgen, "Prophetisches Reden von Zukünftigem." In *Eschatologie und Friedenshandeln,* edited by Luz. Pp. 15–60. ET: pp. 69–109 in this volume.

Ketchum, Henry Grady. "EIPHNH in the New Testament." Diss., Southern Baptist Theological Seminary, 1933.

Kirchschlager, Walter. "Voraussetzungen und Wege des Friedens: Erwägungen und Imperative aus biblischer Sicht." *Bibel und Liturgie* 56 (1983): 24–27, 110–111.

Kitzberger, Ingrid R. "Paulinische Perspektiven zu Friede — Gerechtigkeit — Schöpfung." *BK* 44 (1989): 163–170.

Klassen, William. "A 'Child of Peace' (Luke 10:4) in First Century Context." *NTS* 27 (1981): 484–506.

———. "The God of Peace." In *Towards a Theology of Peace,* edited by Tunnicliffe. Pp. 121–131.

———. *Love of Enemies: The Way to Peace.* Philadelphia: Fortress Press, 1984. See also Klassen's numerous articles on "love of enemy," in bibliography of forthcoming vol. 3 in the SPS series.

———. "Peace." *Anchor Bible Dictionary.* (Forthcoming).

———. "Peace." *Illustrated Dictionary and Concordance of the Bible,* edited by G. Wigoder. New York: Macmillan Publishing Co. (1986), 767–769.

———. "Peace." *Illustrated Jerusalem Dictionary of the Bible.* Jerusalem: Macmillan, 1986.

———. *The Realism of Peace.* Sackville, New Brunswick: Mount Allison University, 1986.

———. "Religion and the Gift of Peace." In *Tantur Yearbook,* 1984–1985. Jerusalem, 1986. Also as Tantur Occasional Paper No. 1, 1986.

Klemm, Matthys. *EIPHNH im neutestamentlichen Sprachsystem: Eine Bestimmung von lexikalischen Bedeutungen durch Wortfeld-Funktionen und deren Darstellung mittels EDV.* Forum theologiae linguisticae 8; Bonn: Linguistica Biblica, 1977.

Klöne, Arno. "Zur Geschichte des 'anderen Katholizismus.'" In *Das Evangelium des Friedens,* edited by Eicher. Pp. 103–124.

Konferenz Bekennender Gemeinschaften in den Evangelischen Kirchen Deutschlands, "Gottes Friede in friedloser Welt." In *Christen im Streit um den Frieden,* edited by Brinkel et al. Pp. 111–118.

Korff, Wilhelm. "Der Christ und der Frieden: Grundsätze einer christlichen Friedensethik." In *Den Frieden sichern,* edited by W. Korff. Düsseldorf: Patmos Verlag, 1982. Pp. 120–143.

Kossen, Henk B. "Der Friedensbegriff in der Bibel." In *Christen im Streit um den Frieden,* edited by Brinkel et al. Pp. 36–47.

Kostner, Georg. "Eirene in den Briefen des hl. Apostels Paulus: Eine bibeltheologische Studie." Diss., Gregorian University, 1956.

Krämer, Werner. "Ethische Perspektiven der Friedenssicherung." In *Das Evangelium des Friedens,* edited by Eicher. Pp. 125–146.

Kreck, Walter. "Theologische Kriterien für politisches Handeln in der Friedensarbeit." In *Christen im Streit um den Frieden,* edited by Brinkel et al. Pp. 141–152.

Kremer, Jacob. "Der Frieden—Eine Gabe Gottes: Bibeltheologische Erwägungen." In *Stimmen der Zeit* 200 (1982): 161–173. ET: pp. 133–147 in this volume.

Kuzlivelil, Matthew V. "Reconciliation in the Old Testament." *Bible Bhashyam* 9 (1983): 168–178.

Lamadrid, Antonio G. "'Shalom' y 'tob' en relacion con 'berit.'" *EstBib* 28 (1969): 61–77.

Lampe, Peter. "Die Apokalyptiker—Ihre Situation und ihr Handeln." In *Eschatologie und Friedenshandeln,* edited by Luz. Pp. 59–114.

Lapide, P. "Zukunftserwartung und Frieden im Judentum." In *Eschatologie und Frieden* II, edited by Liedke, 1978.

Lapp, John A., ed. *Peacemakers in a Broken World.* Scottdale, Pa.: Herald Press, 1969.

Lasserre, Jean. *War and the Gospel.* Translated by Oliver Coburn. Scottdale, Pa.: Herald Press, 1962.

Lattke, Michael. "Salz der Freundschaft in Mk. 9:50c." *ZNW* 75 (1984): 44–59.

Leeuwen, Willem Silvester van. "Eirene in het Nieuwe Testament: Een Semasiologische, Exegetische Bijdrage op Grond van de Septuaginta en de Joodsche Literatuur." Diss., Leiden, 1940. Wageningen: H. Veenman, 1940.

Leipoldt, Johannes. "Herrscherkult und Friedensidee." In *Umwelt des Urchristentums.* Berlin: Evangelische Verlagsanstalt, 1965. Pp. 127–142.

Leroy, J. *Friede und Versöhnung nach dem NT.* Donauwörth: Verlag Ludwig Auer, 1976.

Levick, Barbara. "Concordia at Rome." In *Scripta Nummaria Romana: Essays Presented to Humphrey Sutherland.* London: Spink & Son, 1978. Pp. 217–233.

Liedke, Gerhard. "Das christliche Verständnis vom Frieden." In *Christen im Streit um den Frieden,* edited by Brinkel et al. Pp. 29–35.

———. "Die heutige Friedens-Problematik als Anfrage an die Bibel." *Wiss Prax Ki Ges* 59 (1970): 283–289.

———. "Israel als Segen für die Völker: Bemerkungen zu Lothar Perlitt, 'Israel und die Völker.'" In *Frieden—Bibel—Kirche,* edited by Liedke. Pp. 65–74.

———, ed. *Eschatologie und Frieden.* Vol. 2: *Eschatologie und Frieden in Biblischen Texten.* Heidelberg: Forschungsstätte der Evangelischen Studiengemeinschaft, 1978.

———, ed. *Frieden—Bibel—Kirche.* Studien zur Friedensforschung 9. Stuttgart: Ernst Klett Verlag; Munich: Kösel-Verlag, 1972.

Linskens, John. "A Pacifist Interpretation of Peace in the Sermon on the Mount?" In *Church and Peace* (Concilium 164), edited by Virgil Elizondo, Norbert Greinacher, and Marcus Lefebure. New York: Seabury Press, 1983. Pp. 16–25.

Lockwood, Gregory. "Eirene Reaffirmed." *Lutheran Theological Journal* 21 (1987): 123–132.

Loewen, Howard John. "Peace in the Mennonite Tradition: Toward a Theological Understanding of a Regulative Concept." In *Baptism, Peace and the State in the Reformed and Mennonite Traditions,* edited by Ross T. Bender and Alan P. F. Sell. Waterloo, Ont.: Wilfrid Laurier University Press, 1991. Pp. 87–121, esp. pp. 88–95.

Lohfink, Norbert. "'Der den Kriegen einen Sabbat bereitet.' Psalm 46 — Ein Beispiel alttestamentlicher Friedenslyrik." *BK* 44 (1989): 148–153.

———. "Der gewalttätige Gott des Alten Testaments und die Suche nach einer gewaltfreien Gesellschaft." *Jahrbuch für biblische Theologie* 2 (1987): 106–136.

———. "Die Schwerter zu Pflugscharen umschmieden: Weg zum Frieden im Alten Testament." *Entschluss* 38 (1983): 24–27.

———. "The Unmasking of Violence in Israel." *TDig* 27 (1979): 103–106.

———, ed. *Gewalt und Gewaltlosigkeit im Alten Testament. QD* 96. Freiburg: Herder, 1983.

Lohfink, Norbert, and Rudolf Pesch. *Weltgestaltung und Gewaltlosigkeit: Ethische Aspekte des AT und NT in ihrer Einheit und in ihrem Gegensatz.* Düsseldorf: Patmos Verlag, 1978.

Lux, R., ed. ". . . und Frieden auf Erden." *Beiträge zur Friedensverantwortung von Kirche und Israel.* VIKJ 18. FS Christoph Hinz. Berlin: Institut Kirche und Judentum, 1988.

Luz, Ulrich. "Die Bedeutung der biblischen Zeugnisse für kirchliches Friedenshandeln." In *Eschatologie und Friedenshandeln,* edited by Luz et al. Pp. 195–214. ET: pp. 234–252 in this volume.

———. "Eschatologie und Friedenshandeln bei Paulus." In *Eschatologie und Friedenshandeln,* edited by Luz et al. Pp. 153–193.

———. "Feindesliebe und Frieden." *ThEv* 16 (1983): 3–13.

———. "Jesu Gebot der Feindesliebe und die kirchliche Verantwortung für den Frieden." In *Christen im Streit um den Frieden,* edited by Brinkel et al. Pp. 21–28.

——— et al. *Eschatologie und Friedenshandeln: Exegetische Beiträge zur Frage christlicher Friedensverantwortung.* SBS 101. Stuttgart: Verlag Katholisches Bibelwerk, 1981.

McCarthy, Dennis. "Psalm 85 and the Measuring of Peace." *Way* 22 (1982): 3–9.

———. "*Ebla, horchia temnein, tb, slm:* Addenda to Treaty and Covenant (2 ed.)" *Bib* 60 (1979): 247–253.

Macgregor, George H. C. *The New Testament Basis of Pacifism.* Nyack, N.Y.: Fellowship Publications, 1954.

Maciel, Creuza Rosa. "Peace as the Fruit of Justice: Biblical Roots." In *Towards a Theology of Peace,* edited by Tunnicliffe. Pp. 147–151.

Macquarrie, John. *The Concept of Peace.* N.Y.: Harper & Row, 1973.

McSorley, Richard, S.J. *New Testament Basis of Peacemaking.* Scottdale, Pa.: Herald Press, 1985.

Martens, Elmer A. "God's Goal Is Shalom" and "The Lord Is a Warrior." In *The Power of the Lamb,* edited by Toews and Nickel. Pp. 25–44.

Mauser, Ulrich. *The Gospel of Peace.* SPS 1. Louisville: Westminster/ John Knox Press, 1992.

Mette, Norbert. "Zum Friedenshandeln erziehen." In *Das Evangelium des Friedens,* edited by Eicher. Pp. 165–188.

Metzler, James E. *From Saigon to Shalom.* Scottdale, Pa.: Herald Press, 1985. Part 2.

Meurer, Siegfried. *Das Recht im Dienst der Versöhnung und des Friedens.* Zurich: Theologischer Verlag, 1972.

Miller, Marlin E. "The Gospel of Peace." In *Mission and the Peace Witness,* edited by Robert L. Ramseyer. Scottdale, Pa.: Herald Press, 1979.

Mitton, C. Leslie. "Peace in the NT." *IDB,* 3:706.

Moreno, Antonio C. "Acerca de la paz y la violencia en el Antiguo Testamento." *Teologia y Vida* (Santiago, Chile) 25 (1984): 3–21.

Myers, Larry W. "Eirene in the Lukan and Pauline Literature." *Military Chaplains' Review* 16 (1988): 23–31.

Myhre, Klarb. "'Malidsofferet'; Det gamle testamente. En Undersohelse av offertypen delamim/zoebah selamim." *TTK* 52 (1981): 107–210.

Nestle, Wilhelm. *Der Friedensgedanke in der antiken Welt.* Supplement vol. to *Philologus* 31. Vol. 1. Leipzig: Dieterich'sche Verlagsbuchhandlung, 1938.

Nibel, J. *Der Friedensgedanke des Alten Testaments.* Leipzig: Dieterich'sche Verlagsbuchhandlung, 1914.

Nordheim, Echard von. "Die biblische Begründung des Friedens in der Friedensdenkschrift der EKD." In *Anwalt des Menschen,* edited by Friedrich Hahn. Schmalenberg: G. Giessen, 1983. Pp. 199–207.

———. "Das Reden vom Frieden im Alten Testament." *Deutsches Pfarrerblatt* 82 (1982): 354f.

O'Connor, Kathleen M. "Wisdom Literature, Women's Culture and Peace: A Hermeneutical Reflection." In *Blessed Are the Peacemakers,* edited by Tambasco. Pp. 40–61.

Olyan, Saul. "Hashalom: Some Literary Considerations of 2 Kings 9." *CBQ* 46 (1984): 652–668.

Pagán, Samuel. "And Peace Will Be Multiplied Unto Your Children: An Introductory Study on Shalom in the Old Testament." In *Conflict and Context: Hermeneutics in the Americas,* edited by Mark Lau Branson and C. René Padilla. Grand Rapids: Wm. B. Eerdmans Publishing Co., 1986. Pp. 178–184.

Pákozdy, Ladislaus M. "Der Begriff 'Frieden' im AT und sein Verhältnis zum Kampf." *CV* 14 (1971): 253–266.

Palmer, Earl. "The New Testament Concept of Peace." In *Perspectives on Peacemaking: Biblical Options in the Nuclear Age,* edited by John A. Bernbaum. Ventura, Calif.: Regal Books, 1984.

Pannenberg, Wolfhart. "Diskussionsbeitrag." *EvT* 44 (1984): 293–297. ET: pp. 127–132 in this volume.

Pawlikowski, John T., and Donald Senior, eds. *Biblical and Theological Reflections on Peace.* Wilmington, Del.: Michael Glazier, 1984.

Peace Is the Way. Netherlands: Doopsgezinde Vredesgroep, 1984.

Pedersen, Johannes. *Israel: Its Life and Culture,* vol. 1. Copenhagen: Branner og Korch, 1926. Pp. 263–335.

Perkins, Harvey. "Four Bible Studies on Development in the Asian Context." *SEAJT* 21 (Manila 1980): 78–110.

Perlitt, Lothar. "Israel und die Völker." In *Frieden — Bibel — Kirche,* edited by Liedke. Pp. 17–64.

Pesch, Rudolf. "Neues Testament — Die Überwindung der Gewalt." In *Weltgestaltung und Gewaltlosigkeit,* edited by Lohfink and Pesch. Pp. 62–80.

Petit, Paul. *Pax Romana.* Berkeley and Los Angeles: University of California, 1967.

Porteous, Norman. "SHALEM-SHALOM." *Glasgow University Oriental Society Transactions* 10 (1940): 1–7.

Powers, Edward A. *Signs of Shalom.* Philadelphia: United Church Press, 1973.

Preuss, Horst-Dietrich. "Das biblisch-theologische Zeugnis vom Frieden." In *Vom Frieden.* Hannover: Landeszentrale für politische Bildung, 1967. Pp. 209–232.

Prieb, Wesley J. "The Power of the Lamb." In *The Power of the Lamb,* edited by Toews and Nickel. Pp. 117–128.

von Rad, Gerhard. "Shalom in the Old Testament." *TDNT,* 2:402–406 [*TWNT,* 2:400–405].

Rakotondraibe, Richard. "Biblical Reflection on Peace." In *Towards a Theology of Peace,* edited by Tunnicliffe. Pp. 115–120.

Ravitsky, Aviezer. "Peace." *Contemporary Jewish Religious Thought,* edited by Arthur A. Cohen and Paul Mendes-Flohr. New York: Charles Scribner's Sons, 1987. Pp. 685–702.

Reid, David P. "Peace and Praise in Luke." In *Blessed Are the Peacemakers,* edited by Tambasco. Pp. 79–115.

René Girard and Biblical Studies. Semeia 33. Decatur, Ga.: Scholars Press, 1985. Contributions by Andrew J. McKenna, R. Girard, S. Goodhart, R. Hamerton-Kelly, Th. Weiser, E. Gans, R. Schwager, B. Levine, B. L. Mack.

Reventlow, Henning Graf. "Friedensverheissungen im Alten und im Neuen Testament." *Friede über Israel* 62 (1979): 99–109, 147–153.

Rinaldi, G. "Salom Gn 41.16." *BibOr* 23 (1981): 166.

Rost, Leonhard. "Erwägungen zum Begriff *šalom.*" In *Schalom: Studien zu Glaube und Geschichte Israels,* edited by Karl-Heinz Bernhardt (FS A. Jepsen). Arbeiten zur Theologie series 1, vol. 46. Stuttgart: Calwer Verlag, 1971. Pp. 41–44.

Roth, Wolfgang. "Language of Peace: Shalom and Eirene." *Explor: Journal of Theology* 3 (1977): 69–74.

Rutenber, Culbert G. *The Dagger and the Cross: An Examination of Pacifism.* Nyack, N.Y.: Fellowship Publications, 1958.

Sakenfeld, Katharine D. *The Meaning of Hesed in the Hebrew Bible.* Missoula, Mont.: Scholars Press (HSM 17), 1978.

Sauer, F. *Die Friedensbotschaft der Bibel.* Graz: J. A. Keinreich, 1954.

Scharbert, Joseph. "SLM im Alten Testament." *Lex tua veritas,* edited by H. Gross and F. Mussner (FS H. Junker). Trier: Paulinus Verlag, 1961. Pp. 209–229.

Scheibler, Ingeborg. "Götter des Friedens in Hellas und Rom." *Antike Welt* 15 (1984): 39–57.

Schlier, Heinrich. "Der Friede nach dem Apostel Paulus." *Geist und Leben* 44 (1971): 282–296.

Schmid, H. H. "Creation, Righteousness, and Salvation: 'Creation Theology' as the Broad Horizon of Biblical Theology." In *Creation in the Old Testament,* edited by Bernhard W. Anderson. Philadelphia: Fortress Press, 1984. Pp. 102–117. ["Schöpfung, Gerechtigkeit und Heil." *ZTK* 70 (1973): 1–19; and *Altorientalische Welt in der alttestamentlichen Theologie,* edited by H. H. Schmid. Zurich: Theologischer Verlag, 1974. Pp. 5–30].

———. *Frieden ohne Illusionen: Die Bedeutung des Begriffs schalom als Grundlage für eine Theologie des Friedens.* Zurich: Theologischer Verlag, 1971.

———. "Heiliger Krieg und Gottesfrieden im AT." In *Altorientalische Welt in der alttestamentlichen Theologie,* edited by H. H. Schmid. Zurich: Theologischer Verlag, 1974. Pp. 91–120.

———. *Šalom: "Frieden" im Alten Orient und im Alten Testament.* SBS 51. Stuttgart: Verlag Katholisches Bibelwerk, 1971.

Schmid, H. H.; W. Thiessen; and G. Delling. "Frieden" II–IV. *TRE* 11 (1983), 605–618.

Schmidt, H. P. *Frieden.* Themen der Theologie 3. Stuttgart: Kreuz, 1969.

———. "Schalom: Die hebräisch-christliche Provokation." In *Weltfrieden und Revolution,* edited by H. E. Bahr. Hamburg: Reinbek, 1968. Pp. 185–235.

Schmithals, Walter. "Theologische Überlegungen zum Problem des Friedens." In *Christen im Streit um den Frieden,* edited by Brinkel et al. Pp. 153–160.

Schottroff, Luise. "Der doppelte Begriff vom Frieden." In *Christen im Streit um den Frieden,* edited by Brinkel et al. Pp. 135–140. ET: pp. 156–163 in this volume.

———. "Die Friedensbotschaft des Neuen Testaments." In *Religion von gestern in der Welt von heute: Streitgespräche und Positionen,* edited by Peter Weidhaus. Gelnhausen: Burckhardthaus-Laetare Verlag, 1983. Pp. 36–41 (also pp. 41–52 for the Discussion–Response).

———. "Frieden und Friedenstifter in Neuen Testament." In *Orientierung: Berichte und Analysen aus der Arbeit der Evangelischen Akademie Nordelbien* 2 (1981): 33–42. Reprinted in condensed and full form in numerous other places: see no. 7 on p. 365 in Luise Schottroff, *Befreiungserfahrungen* (Munich: Chr. Kaiser Verlag, 1990).

———. *Der Sieg des Lebens: Biblische Traditionen einer Friedenspraxis.* Munich: Chr. Kaiser Verlag, 1982.

Schottroff, Luise, and Willy Schottroff. *"Die Parteilichkeit Gottes":* *Biblische Orientierungen auf der Suche nach Frieden und Gerechtig-* *keit.* KT 80. Munich: Chr. Kaiser Verlag, 1984.

Schrey, Heinz-Horst. "Frieden." *RGG* (3rd ed. 1958), 2:1133–1135.

———. "Krieg und Frieden im Neuen Testament." *Für Arbeit und Besin-* *nung* 5 (1951): 466–480.

Schwager, Raymund. *Must There Be Scapegoats? Violence and Redemp-* *tion in the Bible.* Translated by Maria L. Assad. San Francisco: Harper & Row, 1987. [*Brauchen wir einen Sündenbock? Gewalt und Erlösung* *in den biblischen Schriften.* Munich: Kösel-Verlag, 1978.]

———. "Offenlegung der Gewalt und christliche Offenbarung." In *Das* *Evangelium des Friedens,* edited by Eicher. Pp. 28–41.

Schwarzschild, Steven. "Shalom." Unpublished, Institute of Mennonite Studies File, 1980.

Senior, Donald. "Jesus' Most Scandalous Teaching." *Biblical and Theo-* *logical Reflections on Peace,* edited by Pawlikowski and Senior. Pp. 55–69.

Shetler, Sanford G. "God's Sons Are Peacemakers." In *Peacemakers,* edited by Lapp. Pp. 75–84.

Shults, Fount L. "*Sh-l-m* and *t-m-m* in Biblical Hebrew: An Analysis of the Semantic Field of Wholeness." Ph.D. diss., University of Texas at Austin, 1974.

Sider, Ronald J. *Christ and Violence.* Scottdale, Pa.: Herald Press, 1979.

Sisson, Jonathan. "Jeremiah and the Jerusalem Conception of Peace." *JBL* 105 (1986): 429–442.

Sklba, Richard J. "'A Covenant of Peace.'" *The Bible Today* 21 (1983): 149–155.

Soe, N. H. "Frieden." *EKL* 1 (1956): 1388–1390.

Sorg, Theo. "Die Bibel zum Thema Frieden." *TBei* 12 (1981): 254–267.

Spiegel, E. *Gewaltverzicht: Grundlagen einer biblischen Friedenstheo-* *logie.* Kassel: Weber, Zucht & Co., 1987.

Spiegel, Nathan. *War and Peace in Classical Greek Literature.* Jerusalem: Magnes Press, 1990.

Stahl, R. "Das Verhältnis von Frieden und Gerechtigkeit als theologisches Problem." *TLZ* 109 (1984): 161–172.

Stamm, J. J., and H. Bietenhard. *Der Weltfriede im Alten und Neuen* *Testament.* Zurich: Zwingli Verlag, 1959.

Stassen, Glen. "A Theological Rationale for Peacemaking." *RevExp* 79 (1982): 623–637.

Steck, Odil Hannes. *Friedensvorstellungen im alten Jerusalem: Psalmen,* *Jesaja, Deuterojesaja.* Zurich: Theologischer Verlag, 1972.

———. "Jerusalemer Vorstellungen vom Frieden und ihre Abwandlungen in der Prophetie des Alten Israel." In *Frieden — Bibel — Kirche,* edited by Liedke. Pp. 75–95. ET: pp. 49–68 in this volume.

———. "Prophetische Kritik der Gesellschaft." In *Christentum und Gesell-* *schaft,* edited by Wenzel Lohff and Bernhard Lohse. Göttingen: Van-denhoeck & Ruprecht, 1969. Pp. 46ff.

Stier, Hans Erich. "Augustusfriede und römische Klassik." In *ANRW* II.2. Berlin: Walter de Gruyter, 1975). Pp. 4–53.

Stierlin, Helm. *Die Christen in der Weltfamilie: Auserwählt zur Friedensstiftung? Ein Essay.* Maintal: Hochstadt-Verlag, 1982.

Stohr, Martin; D. Helmut Gollwitzer; and Reinhard Tietz. *Dimensionen des Friedens: Kirche-Gesellschaft-Staat.* Evangelische Zeitstimmen 4. Hamburg: Herbert Reich Evangelischer Verlag, 1961.

Story, Cullen I. K. "Bible Study on Peace: Ephesians 2:11–3:21." *PrincSB* n.s. 5, 1 (1984): 59–66. Also in *EvRTh* 9 (1985): 8–17.

Strecker, Georg. "Die biblische Friedensbotschaft." *KD* 30 (1984), 1331–1346.

Strobel, August. "Die Friedenshaltung Jesu im Zeugnis der Evangelien – Christliches Ideal oder christliches Kriterium?" *ZEE* 17 (1973): 97–106.

Stuhlmacher, Peter. "Aggression, Friede und Versöhnung." In *Das Wort und die Wörter,* edited by H. R. Balz and S. Schulz (FS G. Friedrich). Stuttgart: Verlag W. Kohlhammer, 1973. Pp. 211–220.

——. "Der Begriff des Friedens im Neuen Testament und seine Konsequenzen." In *Historische Beiträge zur Friedensforschung,* edited by Wolfgang Huber. Studien zur Friedensforschung 4. Stuttgart: Ernst Klett Verlag; Munich: Kösel-Verlag, 1970. Pp. 21–69.

——. "'He Is Our Peace' (Eph. 2:14): On the Exegesis and Significance of Eph. 2:14–18." In *Reconciliation, Law and Righteousness: Essays in Biblical Theology.* Philadelphia: Fortress Press, 1986. Pp. 180–200.

——. "'Er ist unser Friede' (Eph 2, 14): Zur Exegese und Bedeutung von Eph 2, 14–18." In *Versöhnung, Gesetz und Gerechtigkeit: Aufsätze zur biblischen Theologie,* 224–245. Göttingen: Vandenhoeck & Ruprecht, 1981.

Stuhlmacher, Peter, and Helmut Class. *Das Evangelium von der Versöhnung in Christus.* Stuttgart: Calwer Verlag, 1979.

Stuhlmueller, Carroll. "The Prophetic Combat for Peace." *Way* 22 (1982): 79–87.

——. "The Prophetic Price of Peace." In *Biblical and Theological Reflections on Peace,* edited by Pawlikowski and Senior. Pp. 31–44.

——, ed. *Peace and the Bible: The Bible Today* 21 (May 1983). Special issue: response to the Bishops' Letter.

Swaim, J. C. *War, Peace and the Bible.* Maryknoll: Orbis Books, 1982.

Swartley, Willard M. "The Bible and War." In *Slavery, Sabbath, War and Women: Case Issues in Biblical Interpretation.* Scottdale, Pa.; Kitchener, Ont.: Herald Press, 1983. Pp. 96–149.

——. "Peacemakers: The Salt of the Earth." In *Peacemakers,* edited by Lapp. Pp. 85–100.

——. "Politics and Peace (*Eirene*) in Luke's Gospel." In *Political Issues in Luke-Acts,* edited by Richard J. Cassidy and Philip J. Scharper. Maryknoll, N.Y.: Orbis Books, 1983. Pp. 18–37.

——. "War and Peace in the New Testament." In *ANRW* II.26.2, edited by H. Temporini and W. Haase. Berlin and New York: Walter de Gruyter, 1992. Forthcoming.

Tambasco, Anthony J. "Method and Content of Peace Studies." In *Blessed Are the Peacemakers,* edited by Tambasco. Pp. 1–16.

———. "Principalities, Powers and Peace." In *Blessed Are the Peacemakers,* edited by Tambasco. Pp. 116–133.

———, ed. *Blessed Are the Peacemakers.* New York and Mahwah: Paulist Press, 1989.

Tate, Marvin E. "War and Peacemaking in the Old Testament." *RevExp* 79 (1982): 587–596.

Thiel, W. "Aspekte des Frieden im Alten Testament." In *Nachfolge und Friedensdienst: Die Religionen in ihrem Engagement für die Rettung des Lebens,* edited by K.-W. Tröger. Berlin: Union Verlag, 1983.

Thyen, Hartweg. "Zur Problematik einer neutestamentlichen Ekklesiologie: Ein Beitrag zur Frage der Relation von Kirchenstrukturen und Weltfrieden." In *Frieden — Bibel — Kirche,* edited by Liedke. Pp. 96–173.

Toews, John E. "Love Your Enemy Into the Kingdom"; "Be Merciful as God Is Merciful"; and "Peacemakers from the Start." In *The Power of the Lamb,* edited by Toews and Nickel. Pp. 7–24, 45–56.

Toews, John E., and Gordon Nickel, eds. *The Power of the Lamb.* Winnipeg, Manitoba, and Hillsboro, Kans.: Kindred Press, 1986.

Topel, L. John. *The Way to Peace: Liberation Through the Bible.* Maryknoll, N.Y.: Orbis Books, 1979.

Towner, W. Sibley. "The Preacher in the Lion's Den." *Int* 12 (1981): 254–326.

———. "Tribulation and Peace: The Fate of Shalom in Jewish Apocalyptic." *HBT* 6 (1984): 1–26.

Trocmé, André. *Jesus and the Nonviolent Revolution.* Translated by Michael H. Shank and Marlin E. Miller. Scottdale, Pa.: Herald Press, 1973.

Trummer, Peter, et al. *Gedanken des Frieden.* Graz: Institut für Ökumenische Theologie und Patrologie an der Universität, 1982.

Tunnicliffe, Stephen. *Towards a Theology of Peace.* London: European Nuclear Disarmament, 1989.

Unnik, W. C. van. "Noch einmal 'Tiefer Friede,' Nachschrift zu dem Aufsatz von Herrn Dr. Beyschlag." *VC* 26 (1972): 24–28.

Valliere, Paul. *Holy War and Pentecostal Peace.* New York: Seabury Press, 1983.

Vellanickal, Matthew. "Reconciliation and Peace." *Bible Bhashyam* 9 (1983): 187–199.

Vögtle, Anton. *Was ist Frieden? Orientierungshilfen aus dem Neuen Testament.* Freiburg: Herder, 1983.

Voolstra, Sjouke. "The Search for a Biblical Peace Testimony." In *Mission and the Peace Witness,* edited by Robert L. Ramseyer. Scottdale, Pa.: Herald Press, 1979. Pp. 24–35.

Vos, Geerhardus. "Peace." In *Dictionary of the Apostolic Church,* vol. 2. Pp. 159–160.

Wansbrough, Henry. "Blessed Are the Peacemakers." *Way* 22 (1982): 10–17.

Weigel, Richard D., and Matthew Melko. *Peace in the Ancient World.*
Jefferson, N.C.: McFarland & Co., 1981.
Weinstein, Samuel. "Shalom in the Jewish Tradition." *Military Chaplains'
Review* 16 (1988): 17–21.
Weinstock, Stefan. "Pax and the 'Ara Pacis.'" *JRS* 50 (1960): 44–58.
Wenger, J. C. *Pacifism and Nonresistance.* Scottdale, Pa.: Herald Press,
1968.
Wengst, Klaus. *Humility: Solidarity of the Humiliated.* Translated by
John Bowden. Philadelphia: Fortress Press, 1988.
———. *Pax Romana and the Peace of Jesus Christ.* Translated by John
Bowden. Philadelphia: Fortress Press, 1987.
Westermann, Claus. "Der Frieden (*Shalom*) im AT." *Zeichen der Zeit*
24 (1970): 361–375.
———. "Der Frieden (*Shalom*) im Alten Testament." In *Studien zur
Friedensforschung* 1, edited by G. Picht and H. E. Tödt. Stuttgart:
Ernst Klett Verlag, 1969. Pp. 144–177. [ET: pp. 16–48 in this volume].
———. "Frieden, Altes Testament." In *Theologie, VI x 12 Hauptbegriffe,*
edited by Claus Westermann. Stuttgart: Kreuz Verlag, 1967. Pp. 58–63.
———. "Was ist Frieden – Eine Anfrage an die Bibel." In *Christen im Streit
um den Frieden,* edited by Brinkel et al. Pp. 21–28.
White, Hugh C. *Shalom in the Old Testament.* Philadelphia: United
Church Press, 1973.
Will, James E. *A Christology of Peace.* Louisville: Westminster/John
Knox Press, 1989.
Williamson, Lamar, Jr. "Jesus of the Gospels and the Christian Version
of Shalom." *HBT* 6 (1984): 49–66.
Willrich, Hans. "Eirene." In PW (Stuttgart: Metzler, 1905), 2128–2135.
Windisch, Hans. "Friedensbringer – Göttessohne: Eine religionsge-
schichtliche Interpretation der 7. Seligpreisung." *ZNW* 24 (1925):
240–260.
Wink, Walter. "The Third Way: Neither Passivity nor Violence." In *Society
of Biblical Literature 1988 Seminar Papers.* Atlanta: Scholars Press,
1988. Pp. 210–224. Also in SPS 3, forthcoming.
Winter, Paul. "Note on Salem-Jerusalem." *NovT* 2 (1957): 151–152.
Wiseman, D. J. "'Is It Peace?' Covenant and Diplomacy." *VT* 32 (1982):
311–326.
Wogaman, J. Philip. "Shalom: The Theological Vision of Peace and
Justice." *ChrSocAc* 2 (July–August 1989): 4–7.
Wolff, Hans Walter. "Swords Into Plowshares: Misuse of a Word of
Prophecy?" *CurTM* 12 (1985): 133–147. In this volume, pp. 110–126.
Woodruff, Archibald. "EIPHNH in the Pauline Corpus." Ph.D. diss.,
Pittsburgh University, 1976.
———. "Review of *The Biblical Concept of Peace: Shalom,* by Douglas J.
Harris." *Perspective* 12 (1971): 268–269.
Yoder, Edward, et al. *Must Christians Fight? A Scriptural Inquiry.* Akron,
Pa.: Mennonite Central Committee, 1943.

Yoder, John H. *He Came Preaching Peace.* Scottdale, Pa., and Kitchener, Ont.: Herald Press, 1985.

——. *The Original Revolution: Essays on Christian Pacifism.* Scottdale, Pa.: Herald Press, 1971.

——. *The Politics of Jesus.* Grand Rapids: Wm. B. Eerdmans Publishing Co., 1972.

——. "The Way of the Peacemaker." In *Peacemakers,* edited by Lapp. Pp. 111–125.

Yoder, Perry B. *Shalom: The Bible's Word for Salvation, Justice, and Peace.* Newton, Kans.: Faith and Life Press, 1986.

——. "Toward a Shalom Biblical Theology." *Conrad Grebel Review* 1 (1983): 39–49.

Yoder, Perry B., and Willard M. Swartley, eds. *The Meaning of Peace: Biblical Studies.* SPS 2. Louisville: Westminster/John Knox Press, 1992.

Zampaglione, Gerardo. *The Idea of Peace in Antiquity.* Notre Dame, Ind.: University of Notre Dame Press, 1973.

Index of Scripture
and Ancient Writings

279